Modern Africa

MODERN AFRICA

Edited, with Notes and Commentaries,
by Peter J. M. McEwan and Robert B. Sutcliffe

THOMAS Y. CROWELL COMPANY

NEW YORK   ESTABLISHED 1834

First published in Great Britain, 1965, under the title
The Study of Africa by Methuen & Co Ltd
First published in U.S.A., 1965, by
Thomas Y. Crowell Company, 201 Park Avenue South, New York
All Rights Reserved
Copyright © P. J. M. McEwan and R. B. Sutcliffe, 1965
Printed in Great Britain by The Camelot Press Ltd
London and Southampton, England
Library of Congress Catalog Card Number: 65-23747

Contents

Contents

Contents

Maps

vii

Maps

Acknowledgements

In the preparation of this book the authors have received kindness and co-operation from a very large number of sources, both public and private.

Although it is regrettably impossible to mention all these sources by name, our particular thanks are due to the authors and publishers who have kindly granted us permission to include their works, and to the many librarians whose help has been as necessary as it has always been forthcoming.

We would also like to thank Professor Aidan Southall, Dr Elliot Berg, Dr Ahmed Haffar, Mr Sam Bowles, Miss Janet Henshall and Mr Harry Langworthy for their comments and advice, Mr J. A. N. McEwan, O.B.E., for his assistance in a variety of ways, and our secretarial assistants, Madeleine Allen, Susan Bradeen and Pat Siekman, whose collective endurance has earned our sincere gratitude.

To all these kind people our most grateful thanks.

Preface

This volume is designed primarily to satisfy two needs. The first is to help university students and teachers who are concerned with the study of Africa, either from the disciplinary or the general point of view. An increasing number of courses now being offered at Universities and Colleges throughout the world, including the African continent itself, aim at a broad understanding of this vast area. Yet, as we have found from our own recent experience, there is no single volume which can be used satisfactorily as a general guide. Those that are available are either too specialized or too superficial. We have therefore endeavoured in the present book to present the writings of established authorities about those aspects of African civilization and contemporary life which have seemed to us the most critical. Where gaps remain, and in order to provide an understanding of how different aspects – social, political and economic – are closely interwoven, we have added our own commentary.

The second need we have tried to meet is for a greater understanding of some of the major issues facing this continent on the part of the intelligent layman who lacks the stimulus of examinations or the guidance of experts. There must be very many people, in Britain, in the United States, in Africa itself, and elsewhere, who would welcome a deeper insight into the causes and nature of contemporary events in Africa, but who do not have the time to embark on a detailed examination of specialist writings.

It is sometimes argued that the term Africa has little meaning except as the expression of a geographical fact, and that an accurate understanding of current developments can only be made country by country. We do not share this view. Although it is, of course, true that detailed knowledge can only be obtained by the study of details, and that each State has certain unique conditions and problems, there remains a large volume of general material that has to be grasped before the details can be properly understood and given their true perspective. In economics, for example, while the nature and size of specific problems will vary from one country to another, the transition from a traditional subsistence economy to a modern market economy (as in many eastern portions of the continent particularly) is a basic fact that has to be appreciated before the details of the transition in any one location can be fully appreciated. The same is true in other spheres of knowledge, in political and social development, in the transition from traditional to modern systems of value, in the field of education and of health.

In presenting these readings and our own commentaries, we have preferred to use a limited number of uncut selections rather than a larger number of abridged versions. By doing so we hope to have preserved a sense of continuity, and to have avoided the dangers of fragmentation.

The plan of the book falls into ten parts designed to follow as closely as possible the logical sequence of factors influencing the most significant contemporary events. In Africa the speed of change in almost every field of human endeavour is something that observers coming from long-established nations find difficulty in comprehending. It is this speed of change that persuades many people, including some educationalists, to believe that the present can be studied without reference to the past. No one with any first-hand knowledge, however, could nourish such a belief. We have therefore devoted four sections to an examination of the traditional, concentrating on value systems, social structures, systems of government and economic activity.

The remainder of the book is devoted to an examination of the contemporary scene; this being divided into the rise of nations, the increasing complexities of modern government, the progress of economic development, changes in the social order, and some of the more crucial social problems, particularly health and education.

Our choice of readings has been determined by a number of criteria, the most important of which have been the following: the general applicability of the argument or description; the overall importance of the material presented, whether to events in general or to a specific set of problems; the clarity of style; the date of authorship; the accepted authoritativeness and reliability of the author; and how closely the content fits the established pattern of the book. The one factor we agreed to disregard was expense; no reading has been included just because it was given free, nor has any reading been excluded because the conditions of permission seemed too expensive.

For the benefit of teachers and others who may find some of the bare facts useful as guiding lights, a number of appendices have been included containing some statistics not readily available together elsewhere.

Finally, a word about the authorship. We are together responsible for the selections and for all the editorial matter that has been added. For whatever merits this book may have, for all the opinions we have expressed, and for all the errors it may contain (which we trust are few), the two of us are equally and alone responsible.   P. J. M. MCEWAN

R. B. SUTCLIFFE

I: The Physical Environment

Introduction

Africa is becoming an increasingly significant part of the modern world. In many respects, however, it remains the most enigmatic and the most mysterious of all the continents. There are several reasons why this is so.

In the first place, our knowledge of its peoples, their history and social dynamics, is probably less extensive than for any other area of comparable size.

Second, although in some ways Africa forms one homogeneous unity, just sufficiently apparent perhaps to justify its existence as an area study, in most respects it contains widely divergent patterns of natural resources, human history and cultural behaviour. The twentieth century finds the continent being introduced for the first time to the facts both of its homogeneity and its differences, two concepts – one the mirror of the other – that are sometimes difficult to reconcile. We find, for example, emergent nationalism coinciding with a growing sense of pan-Africanism or continental unity.

Third, there are three stages in the development of peoples and cultures that should be distinguished: the extinct, the traditional and the new. The extinct refers to those ways of life, economic and social, that have now passed away, existing only as history, leaving an influence but no living example. The traditional is the old which nevertheless still survives. The new may be either the traditional, when freshly developing from within, new flowers off the same stem, or the innovation, introduced from without, a graft from a foreign plant.

To comprehend the contemporary requires an understanding of both the traditional and the new. For this reason we shall consider first, the traditional, then the new, and, finally, the reciprocated impact and its resultant effect, each upon the other. This, indeed, is the fourth reason for the extent of the challenge Africa provides the modern world. How are her people responding to the dramatic changes being involuntarily thrust upon them? How do people, used to growing food only in order to feed themselves, react to the introduction of a money economy which requires them to buy and sell rather than only to barter and exchange? How do remote rural villagers respond when they find themselves in an industrialized city? What is the impact of literacy on preliterate magic and superstition? What are the chances that out of Africa may come some unique answers to the problems that beset us all, problems of national economics, international politics and supranational conflict?

For a sound knowledge of the present and how current circumstances have been forged on the anvil of tradition, the student must first become acquainted with the geography of Africa.

One of the limitations placed upon what is possible in any country is the physical environment: the geology of the land, its topography and its climate. At the same time, to understand what is politically possible, especially in affairs between states, it is necessary to know the national boundaries and their relative position to one another.

The Size and Variation of Africa

The first requirement in the student is a sense of proportion. The continent of Africa stretches for 5,000 miles from near Bizerta, Tunisia, in the north, to the Cape of Good Hope in the south, and for 4,600 miles from Dakar, Senegal, in the west to Cape Guardafui, Somalia, in the east. Within its area of $11\frac{3}{4}$ million square miles, 9 million of which lie in the tropics, could be accommodated all the landmasses of the United States, India and western Europe.

Geologically, Africa has greater variety than is often supposed. An extensive, high plateau covers most of the continent. This is composed of a hard, crystalline basal complex that has remained virtually unchanged for millions of years. Changes in the plateau itself, however, have produced great strains leading to the corrugations that are a feature of large areas of the continent. In this way have been created some of Africa's most conspicuous physical features, the Great Rift Valley of East Africa, towered by Kilimanjaro, 19,565 feet above the sea, and the volcanic peak of Mount Cameroon, 13,353 feet high, in West Africa.

These massive thrusts of the surface of the earth have trapped, in the past, large volumes of water to form extensive inland seas which have in turn provided the source of long, meandering rivers. Although many of these inland seas have either disappeared or dwindled, some, such as Lake Chad and the lakes of East Africa, remain. Two of the largest of the inland basins are the Congo and the upper Niger. The former includes a large interior tropical forest area draining into the Congo river, 3,000 miles in length; the latter provides the source of the River Niger, wandering 2,600 miles to the sea through areas of divergent climate and vegetation. Other large basins of the interior include the Chad region in the central Sudan, the accumulated waters of which flow into Lake Chad, and the northern Kalahari basin whose waters form the great Zambesi river which eventually reaches the sea in Mozambique.

4

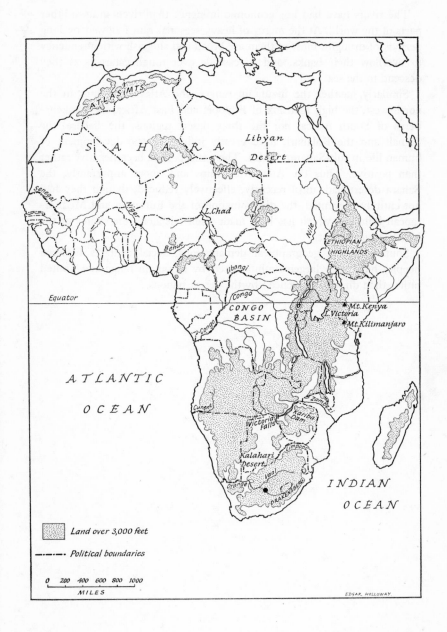

ATLAS MTS.

S A H A R A

Libyan
Desert

TIBESTI

Senegal

Niger

L.Chad

Benue

Ubangi

Congo

ETHIOPIAN
HIGHLANDS

Equator

Congo

CONGO
BASIN

Nile

▲ Mt.Kenya
L.Victoria
▲ Mt.Kilimanjaro

ATLANTIC

OCEAN

Cunene

Victoria
Falls

Zambezi

Kariba
Dam

Kalahari
Desert

Limpopo

Orange

Vaal

DRAKENSBERG

INDIAN

OCEAN

Land over 3,000 feet

----- Political boundaries

0   200 400 600 800 1000

MILES

EDGAR. HOLLOWAY.

5

The rivers have had less economic influence than rivers in most other parts of the world. At the mercy of heavy seasonal rain followed by long periods of drought, most of them are broad and sluggish with a tendency to overflow their banks, and to cascade over rough cataracts as they descend to the sea.

Similarly, neither the mountain ranges, the Atlas Mountains in the north-west, the high plateaux of Ethiopia and East Africa, the Drakensbergs of South Africa, nor the three desert regions, the Sahara, the Somali and the Kalahari, have greatly influenced the development of human life in sub-Saharan Africa. Their effects have been negative rather than positive. Thus the Atlas Mountains and, more importantly, the Sahara desert had, until recently, effectively reduced, though they had not entirely prevented, the dissemination of the European and Mediterranean influence which has long made itself felt along the shores of the North African coast.

South of these geographical demarcations, social contacts between peoples have been largely uninfluenced by mountain range and limited rather than directly influenced by the desert regions.

I

The Climate and Weather[1]

George Kimble

Tropical Africa has such a great range of altitudes and exposures that, its name notwithstanding, it is comparable in climatic diversity with any other region of equal size. Most of its climates, however, have two traits in common – sustained heat and marked seasonality of rainfall – traits in sharp contrast to those marking the climates to which the majority of Europeans and North Americans are accustomed. Many of the qualities and problems of human life, economic, social, and, perhaps, political, are related to these two facts. The high temperatures obviate the need for heated shelter and heavy clothes over most of the inhabited territory and provide an abundant source of energy for the year-round growth of crops. On the debit side, they create, especially when combined with high humidity, a physiologically uncomfortable situation for man, African, Asian and European alike; and, on that account, they put a premium on the cooler uplands. The unevenly spread rains tend to divide the year into times of plant activity and plant dormancy, abounding food and hunger, work and unemployment.

SOLAR RADIATION

The fierceness of the sun's rays is a favourite topic with both travellers and residents in the tropics. There is no denying that the rays can be fierce, especially during the middle hours of the day. At the same time, in most parts of tropical Africa so much of the incoming radiation is cut off, even in cloudless weather, by the atmospheric screen of dust and smoke (in the dry season) and invisible moisture particles (especially in the rainy season) that the danger from exposure to sun is seldom very great. At its greatest, the danger is probably no greater than it is in middle latitudes. The daily duration of sunlight is much less within the tropics than at mid-summer in middle and high latitudes as a consequence of the tilting of the earth's axis at an angle to the plane of its path around the sun. In contrast to the

[1] Reprinted from *Tropical Africa*, I, Twentieth Century Fund, 1961.

more than 15 hours of possible sunlight at New York and 16¾ hours at London at the summer solstice, places on the equator can never get more than 12 hours 7 minutes of sunlight a day, and even at the tropics (Cancer and Capricorn) the longest days can have no more than 13½ hours of sunshine.

In cloudy weather the amount of solar radiation is still further reduced, and over a large part of tropical Africa a high percentage of days are cloudy. The average daily amount of sunshine received by the coast of the Cameroons is less than four hours, making it one of the most sunless. Many inland places in the Congo basin receive less than 2,000 hours of sunshine a year, or less than any lowland area in the United States. Only the most cloudy, foggy margins of the far northern and southern oceans have less sunshine than equatorial Africa.

But this is not to belittle the *climatic* role of the tropical sun. Its two equinoctial crossings of the equator and its solstitial swings to the northern and southern tropics set both the pace and the range of all major seasonal changes of temperature, wind, storm and rainfall.

TEMPERATURES

Lowlands

The amount of solar radiation received is large enough to produce high mean annual temperatures in the lowlands everywhere, the year around. Within 10° of the equator, they run between 77° and 81° F., much on a par with the mean July temperatures along the eastern coastal plain of the United States south of Washington, D.C. Differences between the mean temperatures of the warmest and coldest months are small near the equator, amounting, as a rule, to between 2° and 6°.

This striking uniformity or, as many would prefer to call it, monotony of mean temperature can be attributed partly to the fact that the sun rises high in the heavens at all times of the year, and partly to the fact that the time of highest sun is, with few exceptions, the time of greatest cloudiness, the time when the atmospheric screen against the sun's rays is most effective. This screen is so effective that the season of greatest heat often occurs either well before or well after the sun reaches its vertical noonday position. When this happens, 'summer', using the word in its astronomical sense, is cooler than 'winter'.

The diurnal temperature range[1] over most of the lowlands is greater than the annual range, a state of affairs that gives more than a grain of

[1] i.e. the range of temperature over a twenty-four-hour period.

truth to the saying that 'the night is the winter of the tropics'. But it is the hot days, rather than the cool nights, that cause most of the climatic discomfort of the low tropics, and practically no part of them is altogether immune to it.

Highlands

Although the schoolboy's rule of thumb that temperature drops roughly 1° F. with every 300-foot rise in elevation is far from unexceptionable, it works well enough in the African tropics for us to be able to say that places located within 10° or so of the equator about 6,000 feet above sea level are likely to have a mean annual temperature of between 57° and 61°. In other words, such places are more temperate than equatorial.

RAINFALL

Nobody can be long in tropical Africa before coming to realize that it is rain, or its lack, that is the big conversation-opener. Heat and, where it applies, high humidity are taken for granted, but rain, practically never. Nor is it difficult to see why. While every day is hot, not every day is rainy, not even in the rainiest regions. Again, while there is unlikely to be more than a fractional difference between the mean temperature of a given day, month or season and the next, the order of magnitude of rainfall differences between two consecutive days, months or seasons may be 50, 500, even 5,000 per cent. Then, too, while the thermometer seldom springs a surprise, the rain gauge frequently does. Days that promise to be very rainy do not always live up to their promise. Months that should be wet turn out to be dry. A run of abnormally rainy seasons can be followed by a run of subnormal rainy seasons, to the undoing of many a farming community. And conversely.

The most striking features of tropical African rains are, in fact, the sharpness of their average seasonal differences, their uncertainty, and their range of intensity and amount.

The significance of this phenomenon of seasonality is fundamental. It governs, as will be seen, the responses of plants and animals and it confronts almost every man, woman and child with problems of food and water supply, problems which are not made any easier by the frequent failure of the seasons to observe the practice of seasonality!

Nor is it only the duration and timing of the wet and dry seasons that vary. The amount of rainfall is subject to very considerable seasonal variation, and here again the magnitude of the variation tends to increase with the length of the dry season, which compounds still further the difficulties of those people who, in the absence of wells, rivers and storage waters, must live off the rainfall.

Even when rainy seasons arrive and depart on schedule and their yield is up to par, they are still capable of posing a problem or two. For tropical rains often come in the form of short concentrated showers and thunderstorms. And the concentration can be ferocious. It is not uncommon for three to four inches of rain to fall in a single shower, or for a month's rainfall of 10 to 15 inches to fall in half a dozen showers on as many different days. Such falls cannot easily be accommodated by the African earth. All too often more rain is lost in run-off than is saved in seepage. And the run-off is frequently the cause of other losses, such as removal of precious topsoil from unprotected surfaces, siltation and flooding of low-lying areas, which in turn is likely to ruin standing crops even as it is likely to redeem the life of every stagnant-water-loving insect. . . .

I I: The Traditional Background

IIa: Traditional Social Structure

In this section, as a necessary preliminary to understanding the human scene, our attention is directed toward a general review of the kinds of peoples and social organizations that are to be found in Africa.

In societies, such as those of traditional sub-Saharan Africa, which have a *comparatively* simple socio-economic structure, the various sectors of human life which are organized and from which stem a measure of established authority are more closely interwoven than in more complex societies. Each area of life is more sensitive to change and to influences emanating from every other part. Human life is simpler, because its needs are fewer and the methods of satisfying them are more restricted and more sharply defined. The room for personal initiative may be less but social participation and an implicit sense of social purpose, of belongingness, are more clearly developed and uniform. With the spread of modern, complex, industrialized social organization, Africans find their former affiliations weakening and the old modes of life becoming incompatible with the demands of an expanding present. To appreciate the nature of these processes, and to provide them with a context in which their significance can be understood, it is necessary to know something of how the old is organized. Before we examine the parts of the various social machines we must first learn something of the machines themselves. That is why the first reading in this section reviews the many peoples and cultures, so that an insight may be gained into the range and manner of their diversity as well as of the extent of certain underlying similarities.

This broad outline has an additional relevance which should not pass unnoticed. When all the details of tribal life have been forsaken by the modern African as he steps into the second half of the twentieth century, and even when he assumes nationalistic pride and political ardour in place of the narrower allegiance of the tribe or village, he nevertheless remains, in a very real sense, the child of his early environment. Differences of tribal environment will continue to be reflected in adulthood for the individual just as the past influences of tribal government colour problems

13

of national government for the State. Thus in the Congo, for example, the Tutsi remains not only very different from the Hutu, but both are very conscious of the difference, a fact which social pressures and economic manipulations help sustain.

With this in mind, the serious student of African affairs would be well advised to study in greater detail than is possible within these pages a number of African traditional societies broadly representative of the great diversity that is to be found within this vast continent.

2

Peoples and Cultures in sub-Saharan Africa[1]

Melville J. Herskovits

The importance of this paper is twofold. In the first place it examines the distribution of racial types and basic cultural orientations throughout the continent, south of the Sahara. Secondly, it demonstrates how, even within these broad categories, it is possible and useful to explain certain basic differences which stem from this distribution.

The reader is advised to study these facts in conjunction with the map provided.

The population of Africa south of the Sahara cannot be given with any degree of accuracy, but an approximation of 150 million seems acceptable to most authorities. This, for native Africans, is to be contrasted to some 3 million Europeans, 750,000 Indians, and a sprinkling of Syrians, Lebanese, and others. The numerical difference is emphasized when we find that some two-thirds of the Europeans and about half of the Indians live in South Africa. Elsewhere, as in French West Africa, we find ratios of 17 million Africans to 63,000 non-indigenous residents, or in the Congo 11 million Congolese to 60,000[2] from outside, or even in Kenya, with what is for Africa a large non-African population, over 5 million Africans in contrast to some 30,000 Europeans and about 120,000 Indians, Arabs, and Goanese. This disparity gives a special character to the impact of the outside world on Africa, and renders it imperative that any evaluation of the present situation on the continent and particularly any planning for the future regard the indigenous African and his traditional ways of life and thought as a major factor in determining the facts and assessing the probable results of change.

PHYSICAL TYPES

It is not likely that, as between Africans, differences in physical type have

---

[1] Reprinted from *Annals of American Academy of Political and Social Science*, 298, March 1955.

[2] Although no exact revision is possible, this figure is now much reduced—Eds.

been of any great significance in influencing relations between the indigenous peoples of sub-Saharan Africa. In the technical sense of the term 'race' as a major division of mankind, the racial factor over all this region is a constant, for all the Africans belong to the Negro race, despite variations in stature, in body build, in hair form and facial characteristics, even pigmentation. The Africans of the Guinea Coast are classical Negroids, dark in colour, longheaded, broad-nosed, with everted lips, small, finely formed ears, and in the main short of stature, having slender legs and powerfully developed torso. North of them lives the Sudanese type, marginal to the 'true Negro' and the Caucasoids who inhabit the Mediterranean littoral of the continent. In East Africa the so-called 'Hamitic' form finds its most extreme expression in the peoples of the Upper Nile, Kenya and Ruanda-Burundi, a type with bodily proportions that accentuate the vertical axis, slender in build, with long, narrow face and nose, smaller lips, and numbering among them the tallest peoples of the world. They are very heavily pigmented, however, and their hair is of the wiry, curled Negroid type, standing off the head instead of matting close to it as in the western part of the continent.

Inhabiting most of the vast region of the central and southern parts of Africa are the forms that, for want of a better term, are called 'Bantu-speaking peoples'. Migrations in Africa have been generally west across the northerly half of the continent, south-west from the region of the lakes toward the Atlantic, and south along the eastern portion. This has resulted in continuous mixture in central and eastern Africa and has produced the many Negroid groupings, from the Cameroons and French Equatorial Africa south to Angola and south-eastward to Mozambique and the Republic, that exhibit the heterogeneity resulting from continuous ancestral crossing. In the Congo, too, are enclaves of Negroid pygmies, while at the extreme south of the continent, the pygmoid Bushman and the larger Hottentot, both highly specialized, lighter-coloured forms, have survived a harsh environment only to face extinction under contact with European peoples.

The reason why these differences of physical type have not significantly influenced contacts between African peoples is not far to seek. For one thing, the principal sub-divisions encompass great areas, so that contacts between them in significant number have, on balance, been slight. Though instances are to be found, some striking – as in Ruanda-Burundi, where conquest by the Watutsi of the indigenous peoples, the Bahutu and Batwa, of markedly different physical characteristics, resulted in the imposition of a hierarchical social system correlated with these differences – such instances are not numerous. It was only with outside contacts and, indeed,

16

only in relatively recent times that the racial problem, as such, became important in Africa.

The importance of the racial problem obviously derives from the fact that Africans and Europeans differ sharply in skin colour, that human physical trait which marks off groups of men most readily and is the first to be noted on initial contact. This trait provides a ready frame for drawing racial lines, and for distinguishing groupings to which all kinds of differences of a nonbiological order, actual or assumed, can be assigned. To it are attributed positive as well as negative influences, as where African preference for Mohammedanism as against Christianity is held to result from the fact that no element of colour difference enters, with Negro Mohammedans converting Negroes, and no colour line drawn in any mosque. That propositions of this sort overlook the existing tensions in the relations between Africans and Indians in eastern Africa, in which colour differences are not important, does not lessen the significance of the overriding fact that, in contemporary Africa, the presence of physical differences between Africans and non-Africans is critical in shaping present-day alignments in all aspects of African life.

LANGUAGES

The linguistic picture is dominated by the great sweep of a language family called Niger-Congo, which encompasses the whole of the Guinea Coast deep into the interior, including languages previously termed Sudanic and the Bantu forms of speech as well. The Hamitic family disappears. One part, termed Afro-Asiatic, encompasses Ethiopia, moving north-eastward into Asia Minor and north and west through Egypt and the northern part of Africa. The remainder is differentiated into a number of smaller units, while Bushmen and Hottentot are grouped as an independent 'Click' family, taking its name from the phonetic device that, among the languages of mankind, almost uniquely distinguishes them.

The fact that African languages were unwritten poses many questions. In what languages, for example, should Africans be taught to read and write? There seems general agreement that secondary and higher education should employ languages of world-wide distribution, so that students may have direct access to the world's knowledge. Yet what of primary education? Or one may consider the fundamental query as to the relation between language and thought, which has been posed by Africans who reason that to rely for the acquisition of knowledge on a foreign tongue imposes an unreasonable handicap to comprehension, to expression, and particularly to creativity.

BASIC CULTURAL ORIENTATIONS

As with languages, the similarities and differences among African cultures are to be balanced against each other, to give perspective against which current happenings are to be projected.

On the broadest level, the similarities include those elements in African cultures which are continental in their distribution and mark off these ways of life from those of other major world regions. Next comes the conventions that, while spread less widely, are none the less found in areas of broad compass and distinguish the major culture types of the continent. As we move to the tribal or local group level, the special characteristics that mark each off from its neighbours come to the fore. These characteristics, described in intensive studies of specific societies, are from the comparative point of view to be regarded as variations on the broader cultural themes of wider areal or continental distribution.

The accompanying map, which delimits the culture areas of Africa projected against present political boundaries, indicates an important potential source of tension arising out of the disregard of ethnic lines in partitioning the continent. The areas are given according to their spread at a time which may roughly be designated as the beginning of intensive European expansion in Africa. That changes in these cultures have occurred since that time is obvious, though with a few exceptions the basic patterns that dictate the differentiation of these areas are still operative despite the way in which colonial boundaries are at variance with them.

The most dramatic of the changes that have resulted from contact is found in the Khoisan area, where the fate of Bushman and Hottentot cultures has paralleled that of the peoples themselves. The Bushmen, whose ways of life are among the simplest known to man, have been reduced to a few surviving bands in south-west Africa and Angola. Never having developed herding or agriculture, and possessing a sparse technology, they were always hard put to it to survive the rigours of their desert environment. Contact first with cattle-owning Bantu and later with the migrating Boer settlers, whose herds they raided as they would any herd of wild animals, made them fair game. The Hottentots, themselves a herding people who, unlike other cattle-keeping Africans to the east and north, regarded their herds as consumption rather than prestige goods, became servants and farm workers of the incoming whites, and later wage labourers. They were gradually absorbed into the Coloured population of South Africa, whence their culture has, except among a few small groupings, almost disappeared.

18

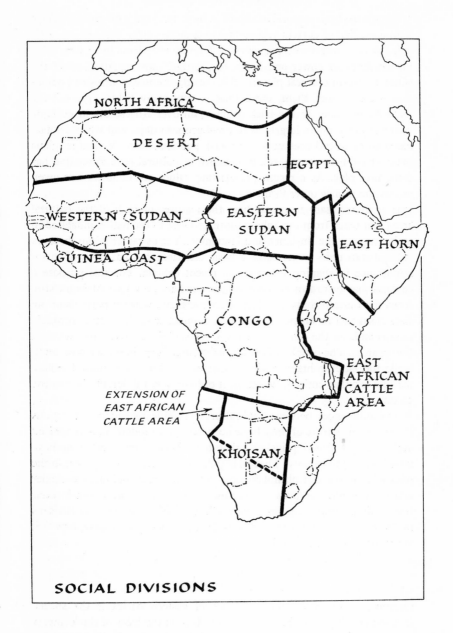

NORTH AFRICA

DESERT

EGYPT

WESTERN SUDAN

EASTERN SUDAN

EAST HORN

GUINEA COAST

CONGO

EAST AFRICAN CATTLE AREA

EXTENSION OF EAST AFRICAN CATTLE AREA

KHOISAN

SOCIAL DIVISIONS

head. Political structures, as might be expected over so vast a region, show great variation. Yet the importance of segmentary kinship sections, the role of groupings based on age, technically termed age grades, and the emphasis on local autonomy all tend to distinguish this part of the continent.[1] Art forms are, in the main, those of the household – basketry, which is of high order, beadwork, and designs incised on calabashes. This again brings us to the slight degree of specialization here, in contrast to that which is present where the better-known African art products in wood, metal, and cloth are executed.

AGRICULTURALLY BASED SOCIETIES

The contrasts between the cultures of eastern Africa and those of the western part of the continent are most striking in the elements that have been noted in the preceding paragraphs. In explaining these differences, the ecological factor cannot be neglected. The high, dry plains invite herding, just as they pose many difficulties for the agriculturist, as those who would introduce new farming techniques are discovering. On the other hand, the lower-lying forested area that comprises so much of the Congo Basin and western Africa inhibits pastoralism and makes the emphasis on agriculture that marks the cultures in it a logical adaptation to environmental demands. With agriculture as the sole economic base, the division between subsistence and prestige systems is absent; with a more productive ecological setting and concentration on agriculture, denser populations can be supported, an appreciable economic surplus is produced, and the cultures manifest a degree of specialization of labour that ranks high in the non-industrialized world.

This specialization of labour takes on two forms. In west-central Africa, especially in the basin of the Congo, it is tribal; along the Guinea Coast and to the north, it is by craft. The tradition of specialization explains why this area has developed the great variety of textiles and the many kinds of pottery found there. This tradition, too, has been responsible for the development of metal working, which not only provides implements of all kinds for daily use, but has produced such recognized art forms as the Ife and Benin bronzes, the Agni-Ashanti gold weights, the Dahomean and Cameroons brass figures, and the intricately designed Congo throwing-knives. It has made possible the embellishment of houses and temples with carvings and paintings of a high order, and the development of

---

[1] For a series of descriptions of the social structures of a number of societies of British Africa, see A. R. Radcliffe-Brown and Daryll Forde (Eds.), *African Systems of Kinship and Marriage* (London, 1950).

sculpture that from Guinea and Sierra Leone to the Congo has given the world the masks, statuettes, and other carved figures that today have world-wide renown.

Specialization has made for trade, and trade for markets and the development of pecuniary units of value. These, in turn, have encouraged commercial and, concomitantly, cultural contacts which, though restricted in the case of any given people, have resulted in an interlocking series of relationships that have facilitated the diffusion of the basic patterns which mark off the region. As concerns other aspects of the social structure, the phenomenon of specialization has caused the development of stratification and a class structure. This is the region of stable kingdoms, of established priesthoods and explicit theological systems maintained by those specialists in government and in the manipulation of the supernatural that only economies capable of producing substantial surpluses over subsistence needs can carry in the highly developed forms found in this region.

The empires of the Western Sudan – Melle, Fulah, Ghana, Bornu, Songhai and Hausa – the kingdoms of Ashanti-Dahomey, Yoruba, Benin along the Guinea Coast, and those of Kongo, Lunda, Bushongo in the Congo are among the best known; but there are many others, down to the smaller principalities that, with simpler but comparable political forms, were interspersed among these more powerful, more numerous, and more widely spread entities. And with the ability to support a larger population has come urban living, especially in the Guinea Coast and the Western Sudan, where the writings of the earliest explorers attest to the existence of popular centres since before the time of initial contact with the literate world.

BASIC PATTERNS AND CULTURAL ADJUSTMENTS

It is evident that the differences between these two great cultural provinces – the pastoral east and the agricultural west – have been significant in the adjustments of their peoples to European contact and control. One need but consider the differential adaptation that had to be made in the policies of indirect rule in British East and West Africa to see one manifestation of this. The relative ease with which Africans in the western part of the continent and the Congo took over the growing of cash crops may, again, be contrasted with the difficulty experienced in inducing the cattle-keeping peoples of the eastern portion to accede to the commercial utilization of their herds, or to adopt methods of improving the quality of their beasts. The very fact that the world economic order has a pecuniary base made adjustment in this sphere less of a break with earlier tradition for the

23

agriculturalists than for the pastoralists. This factor is also operative in some of the concomitant features of modern commercial enterprise, such as selling for profit or the institution of credit. One need but contrast the degree of business success of the Indians in the eastern part of Africa, for example, with the experience of Near Eastern traders in such a Nigerian city as Onitsha, where the Ibo market women and shopkeepers hold a virtual monopoly of trade because of their skill in trading.

Underlying regional and areal differences are broader unities. Such elements of culture as unilateral descent systems, the religious importance of the ancestor – which is great even where ancestral worship does not predominate – and the consequent respect for age as evidenced in the rule of senior members of any given grouping, are found everywhere. This stress on age differences underlies the institution of age grades and the educational device of the puberty school, which has set a tradition that predisposes the African to formal training in literacy. Everywhere, also, we find an aboriginal tradition of land tenure that has as constants the concept that ownership of land vests in the community, that control over it by an individual persists only during its occupancy and use, and that the sanctions of tenure, in the final analysis, are supernatural. A pluralistic world view, with controlling but manipulatable forces near at hand, has made for a receptivity of Christianity and Islam, and goes far to explain the relation between separatist cults and nationalist movements. The actual, as against the institutional, position of women is everywhere similar, whereby women play a decisive role, often unrecognized by outsiders, in determining attitudes and reactions and in shaping tribal policy. Nor can the African technique or social control through satire in song and narrative sequence, or the role of magic which as elsewhere in the Old World continues with functional significance, even where industrialization is most advanced, be overlooked when the major unities of sub-Saharan Africa are considered.

The retention of old ways under new conditions can be richly documented by comparing the accounts of early travellers with those of contemporary observers of present day modes of behaviour.

On the other hand, we must also recognize the receptivity of the African to innovations, as is apparent from the instance of this noted during the early days of penetration of the Congo by Torday and Joyce among the Bushongo, whose traditions tell how one of their rulers, Shamba Bolongongo, had many years before travelled widely, bringing to them from the Bapende the techniques of weaving raffia fibre, the embroidery of raffia cloth from the Bakalai, and the planting of tobacco and the game of *mancala*; how he reformed the hierarchy of the court by naming representatives of the various trades to office; how he instituted military reforms by abolishing arrows and throwing knives as weapons and restricting arms to the sword; and how he added the police function to the duties of his soldiers.

If to traditions of this sort we add the historical implications of the migrations, conquests, and subsequent mingling of peoples throughout sub-Saharan Africa down the years, we come to understand how the present situation, as regards cultural change, is nothing essentially new to the African, and that his techniques of adapting to innovation go deep into his past. Yet at the same time we cannot forget the local and regional differences in aboriginal culture, with the evidence they yield that despite contact and the resultant borrowing, African peoples have known how to maintain old ways as well as to accept new ones. Granting the primacy of the African in the African scene, the considered treatment of any given situation in the light of these two mechanisms is thus seen to be essential to adequate comprehension and skilful resolution.

3

Social Groupings[1]

Simon and Phoebe Ottenberg

In the following, concisely written paper, the Ottenbergs discuss the principles that govern the association between people in traditional African society. In spite of all that is said of the extent of change, it remains true that a large majority of the inhabitants of Africa are still attached to the old ways of life.

It is important to remember that the groupings with which this article is concerned take place within a wider context of political authority. This authority may vary in size and complexity from the twenty or so who may comprise a Bushman society in south-west Africa to the hundreds of thousands who once comprised the Kingdom of Ashanti in West Africa. Generally speaking, the size of the society will largely depend on economic viability, as shown in the previous reading.

In African societies, as in others, the division and grouping of people may be considered under three broad principles: kinship; association, or non-kinship groupings; and residence, or locality. A particularly useful concept in the study of these principles and their operation in social systems is that of the *corporate group*, introduced in studies of social structure by British social anthropologists. The term is used in much the same way as *corporation* in the dictionary sense, that is, a group of persons having an identity, rights, and obligations distinct from those of the individuals who make up the group. A group may be spoken of as corporate if it possesses one or more of the following characteristics: its members (or adult members) come together from time to time to carry out some corporate action; it has a chief or council with the authority to represent the group as a whole; it owns or controls property as a group. The type of corporate group most common in African societies is the descent group, usually in the form of lineages and clans.

Corporate groups play an essential and prominent part in the organization of African societies. Not only is kinship the core of the social structure of most African peoples, but associations such as age classes and grades

[1] Reprinted from *Cultures and Societies of Africa*, Random House, 1961.

26

or groups based on common interests are often corporately organized. It is important to remember that the body of theory that has grown up around the concept of the corporate group in the study of African society is not a purely abstract formulation by the social scientist but that Africans themselves conceive of social relations in terms of group membership, with its duties and privileges and symbols of identity. The role in Nuer marriage of cattle owned by the lineage is an example of this.

KINSHIP

The three basic kin relationships are those of descent, filiation, and marriage. The first two, which are closely related, are commonly referred to by the term consanguinity, or 'blood' ties. As used in anthropology, descent refers to the relationship of a group of persons to a common ancestor or ancestors through a number of generations; filiation denotes the relation between parent and child. Thus, filiation is the fundamental process upon which descent is based: successive links of filiation make up lines of descent. The third type of kin relationship, by marriage, often referred to as affinity, is that between a husband and wife and between a person and his spouse's family – the so-called in-law relationship.

Filiation and descent may be thought of as giving a society continuity through the birth of new members, and affinity as the way of arranging for this. Marriage assures an ordered means of providing parents for potential members of the descent groups. Actually, a fourth type of relationship, fictional kinship ties, such as by adoption or by belief in a common descent from an animal or plant totem, fill in the gaps in descent systems, so to speak, providing heirs or ancestors to replace any missing in the actual kinship system.

In African kinship systems filiation and descent refer to the social relationship between kinsmen rather than the physical relationship in the strict sense. The two are usually identical, but they may not be in cases of adoption, adulterine birth, or proxy parenthood on behalf of a sterile husband or wife. Generally, the man who has paid bride wealth for a child's mother is its legal and social father, regardless of who its genitor may be.

Many forms of descent and affinity are found in African societies. In most societies, descent is unilineal, or reckoned on one side only. Unilineal systems consist of three fundamental types: patrilineal, in which descent is reckoned through males on the father's side; matrilineal, in which it is reckoned through females on the mother's side; and double unilineal descent (also called double descent or dual descent), in which a person traces descent both patrilineally and matrilineally, belonging simultaneously to patrilineal and matrilineal corporate descent groups. This is not to say that in a matrilineal descent system a person is related only to his mother, and not to his father, or vice versa, as has sometimes been thought; two lines of filiation, between mother and child and between father and child, occur simultaneously. In a patrilineal or a matrilineal system, however, the so-called line of descent – that is, the line of filiation in which descent is reckoned – is said to be ascendant and the other line is said to be complementary. In such a descent system a person's relations with both his father's and mother's kin are structured and meaningful, but they differ in nature and content. In double unilineal descent, on the other hand, both lines of filiation can be said to be complementary; that is, they are more or less equally balanced and neither dominates the other.

A system also found in some African societies is that of bilateral descent, in which a person traces descent from *both sides* of his father's and mother's families, as in our own society. This is to be distinguished from double descent, which is traced on the father's and mother's sides, but uni-lineally on each, that is, it is dominantly matrilineal on the mother's side and patrilineal on the father's.

Patrilineal descent is widely found throughout Africa. Matrilineal descent is found in scattered groups in West Africa and in a wide band – sometimes called the 'matrilineal belt' – across central and southern Africa from Angola through the southern Congo and the Rhodesias to Mozambique. Double descent is relatively unusual, found in scattered groups in the Guinea Coast, the Sudan, and in south-western Africa. Bilateral descent is also unusual for Africa as a whole, occurring in south-west Africa and in some central African groups.

The basic unilineal descent groups are the lineage and the clan. As defined by social anthropologists, a lineage is a unilineal descent group whose members can trace descent to a known ancestor; a clan is a unilineal descent group whose members claim common descent from an original ancestor but are not able to trace all the generational steps between the living members and the founder. The founder may be either human or mythical – sometimes in the form of a totem that is a symbol of the group. A clan is usually larger than a lineage and may or may not be made up of a number of component lineages. Although the size of these descent groups varies greatly in different societies, the membership of lineages usually numbers in the dozens or hundreds, while that of clans may number in the thousands.

Lineages are often spoken of as being of two to seven generations (and occasionally more) in depth from the founding ancestor to the young adult generation, while clans may be ten or more generations in depth, with the actual knowledge of descent ties lost in the earlier generations. What sometimes happens in lineage organization is that there is 'telescoping' of the generational links in the system, some of the earlier ancestors being simply dropped out in the memory of the lineage members. In some societies the 'creation of man', that is, the birth of the first known lineage ancestor of a tribal group, remains the same number of generations behind the present at any given time, moving forward continually to keep the age of mankind constant rather than having it increase within an absolute context as in our conception.

An important characteristic of African lineages and clans is that their membership includes not only the living but the dead, for death signifies not the end of existence, but rather a change from the corporeal to the non-corporeal. As in the Chinese family, the ancestors are served through the ministrations of the ancestral cult and in many respects maintain a position of authority over the living.

Another characteristic of African descent systems is subdivision of lineages and clans with the passage of time. In lineage segmentation, lineages (and sometimes clans) subdivide according to the model of relationships within the primary or elementary family – a man, wife, and their children – or the polygynous family – a man, two or more wives, and their children. For example, in a matrilineal system the first, second, and third sons of the lineage founder and his wife may become the founders of three lineage segments. Or, if the founder of the lineage is polygynous, the eldest son of each of his wives may become the founder of a segment. In a matrilineal system the founders of lineage segments would be daughters of a single mother. (While they might conceivably have different fathers if the mother had remarried, this fact would be irrelevant in terms of matrilineal descent.)

Within a clan or lineage, segmentation is a continuing process. At any one time there may be as many as four or five levels of segmentation within a unilineal descent group, with subdivisions on each level associated with particular activities and interests. As smaller segments grow with the birth of new members, they in turn divide into new segments. Socially, the activities, functions, and prerogatives of the larger and smaller groups are divided in terms of broader and narrower corporate interests. For instance, sections of farmland might be owned and used individually by lineages of a clan, but blood revenge would be the concern of the clan as a whole.

A related process is the fission of the unilineal descent group, by which lineage or clan segments break off to form new descent groups, often also changing residence. The process of fission prevents a lineage or clan from growing beyond a size consistent with ecological and social feasibility for a given society.

There are two basic types of clan organization. In the first, and most common in Africa, the clan is internally segmented into lineages, whose interrelationships are not always clear but who claim common descent from the clan founder. In the second type the clan is not internally differentiated. Some clans are not corporate in nature, and they may be dispersed and very limited in function.

Thus in African societies there may be either matrilineal or patrilineal lineages and clans; there may be lineages but no clan organization; or there may be clans but no lineages. In many cases, lineages or clans are associated with recognized territories, but in others their membership is dispersed. Dispersal, however, does not necessarily mean the weakening of group functions, for strong ties may be maintained despite the geographic separation of the members.

As a corporate group, a clan or lineage may own the farm and grazing land its members use or the herds they keep. The dwellings and other buildings used by the members may be group property. Religious shrines owned by the group serve the members, are maintained by them, and are a focus for ritual activities. This is true particularly in the case of the ancestral cult. Leadership of the lineage or clan is usually in the hands of the eldest male members. In many African societies individual discipline, and by extension community order, is the responsibility of the leaders of descent groups, who are often also the political leaders. In other words, lineages and clans are groups that have jural, or legal, rights over their members and in relation to one another.

An important characteristic of the corporate nature of lineages and clans is that to an outsider one member represents the entire group. This may be seen clearly in the case of clan revenge for the murder of a member of one clan by a member of another. It is common for a murder to be avenged by the death – or the adoption into the victim's clan – of a member of the killer's clan, without concern for the identity or fate of the actual killer, the matter being interpreted as between clans rather than between individuals.

Most clans and lineages are exogamous, and any sexual relations between members are considered incestuous. Again, however, this varies in different societies and in different descent groups in the same society.

The members of a unilineal descent group have strong feelings of solidarity and group identity. Members often greet one another by use of the lineage or clan name, and if two members who do not know each other are introduced, as may happen in a large clan, they greet each other with the warmth and enthusiasm of compatriots meeting in a foreign land.

Membership in a unilineal descent group is expressed in family organization as well as in the interests and activities of the group as a whole. In addition to belonging to an elementary family, most individuals belong also to an extended family – a grouping of component elementary families according to the system of descent and marriage residence of a given society. In a patrilineal society in which residence is patrilocal (that is, a man remains in his father's place of residence after marriage and brings his wife to live with him), an extended family might include a grandfather, his sons and grandsons, and all their wives and unmarried children. It might, of course, be much smaller, consisting of a father and sons, or of two or more brothers, and their wives and children. Whatever the composition of the extended family it is a widely found type of domestic grouping having certain common basic characteristics: it is usually a residence group, sharing the same compound or homestead and led by the senior male member in the dominant line of descent. Further, it is the group within which a great many of the face-to-face relations of daily life take place.

In societies having unilineal descent, the group of parent and children – or even the children alone – in the dominant line of descent may form a minimal segment of a lineage. Thus, within a family, a father and his children, or two children of the same father, may be a minimal patrilineal segment, or a mother and children a matrilineal segment, and so on. One of the effects of the unilineal basis of the extended family is the drawing of a sharp line between the interests and activities of the sexes, for in most unilineal societies members who have married into the family remain to some extent always outsiders with little or no part in the affairs of their spouses' lineage. The extent to which this is so depends on the degree of ritual and social incorporation of the in-marrying spouse into the lineage or clan, a highly variable factor in African societies.

Concerning the third type of kinship, affinity by marriage, varying forms exist in Africa. What constitutes a marriage is defined in different ways in different societies. In some, a man and woman are considered husband and wife if they have had sexual relations, whether or not the relationship has been sanctioned by the couple's kinsmen or a marriage payment made. In others, bride wealth must be paid in full before establishing the conjugal relationship, and a marriage is not considered completed, or confirmed, until one or more children of the union have been

31

weaned. These examples represent perhaps the extreme types of African marriage, but there are, of course, many other forms.

Monogamy is found in all African societies, but polygyny, or the marriage of one man and two or more women, is found in most. In the Lele of the Kasai district of the Belgian Congo a specialized form of polyandry, or the marriage of one woman to two or more men, sometimes occurs concurrently with the predominating polygynous marriage, and this may also be true of other societies.

Although polygyny is a distinctive characteristic of African marriage, as far as is known there is no striking inequality in the sex ratio. However, the age of first marriage differs markedly for men and women: women usually marry soon after puberty but men often not until their late twenties or early thirties. Thus, though many men may have several wives at one time, many women are widowed early in life and remarry. There are several possible explanations for the difference in marriage age. In many societies men traditionally devoted their young adulthood to warfare and defence; for example, in parts of East Africa a man could not marry until after he and others of his age class had served an allotted period in a military regiment. In most African societies that require the payment of bride wealth before marriage, the acquisition of the necessary wealth often takes a number of years. But probably the most significant explanation of this age differential is that the combination of polygyny and the early marriage of women affords the maximum exploitation of women's fecundity, a factor that must have been of great importance in terms of group survival in societies having high infant mortality, limited economic surplus, and, often, a tradition of warfare.

The polygynous family is found in societies having all the different types of descent. Marriage residence often follows the dominant line of descent, being patrilocal in patrilineal societies and matrilocal in matrilineal ones. Here again there is much variation. In several matrilineal societies marriage is initially matrilocal while the husband performs obligatory services for his wife's parents, but later he sets up his own household, often in a place of his choosing, and takes his wife with him. In some societies a wife remains with her own family until after she has borne her first child, and then goes to live with her husband and his lineage. In others the place of marriage residence is optional.

One factor seems constant in polygynous marriage: regardless of the location of the household, each co-wife of a husband has her own quarters, either separate houses or rooms within a larger building, in which she and her young children live. The resources and property of co-wives are also usually kept separate. The relations between co-wives are structured in some societies by a set system of ranking in order of marriage, with a position of honour and prestige accorded the first wife; other societies have a strict convention of equality of co-wives. Similarly, the relations between children of co-wives are patterned by their mothers' relative positions in the family. Although jealousy and hostility between co-wives are more marked in some societies than in others, co-wife relations seem to be regarded as a stress point in the social structure of all polygynous societies.

In most African societies there are so-called preferred forms of marriage, that is, one is expected to marry a person standing in a designated kin relationship to him, such as his cross-cousin – the child of his father's sister or of his mother's brother. Other forms of preferred marriage are the sororate, in which if a wife dies or is barren her family supplies her husband with her sister (or cousin) as a wife, and widow inheritance, in which a widow is 'inherited' as a wife by her dead husband's brother (this institution is known as the levirate), or by a son of her husband other than her own son. Both the sororate and widow inheritance are based on the idea that the marriage contract is not broken by the death – or by the failure to reproduce – of one of the spouses, and the marital obligation continues throughout the lifetime (or at least the reproductive period) of each. For example, in some patrilineal societies a woman is married not only to her husband, but also in a sense to his lineage; that is, her reproductive powers are permanently transferred to her husband's patrilineal descent group, and if he dies it is still her duty to bear children for the lineage by his brother or son. In matrilineal systems, in which children belong to their mother's, rather than their father's, lineage or clan, this is not true, for the wife's obligation to bear children is to her own descent group rather than to her husband's.

Such arrangements accord with the view universally held in African societies that the goal of marriage is reproduction. The institutions described above also clearly reveal the concept of social relationships in terms of group membership, with the interests of the lineage, for example, being paramount over those of the individual if there should be a conflict between the two. It should not be assumed, however, that a kinship group is, in effect, a strait jacket into which the individual may be forced for the sake of the group, for in almost any situation there are alternative forms of behaviour. Young people will not usually be forced to marry cross-cousins if a match is distasteful to them. A widow who does not wish to be 'inherited' may in some societies enter into a relationship of so-called widow concubinage with a stranger, any children of the union belonging to the lineage of her late husband and being considered his children. Her obligation to the lineage is thus carried out by a fictional kinship bond, and the interests of the group are served without undue hardship to the individual.

There is wide variation in the stability of marriage in African societies. Since marriage is seen as an alliance between the kin groups of husband and wife as well as a union between individuals, the problem of stability must be considered on two levels: the jural, or legal, aspect, and the conjugal aspect seen in terms of relations between spouses within the psychological-social context. In societies that forbid divorce or make it difficult – as when it is necessary for a wife's kinsmen to return a substantial number of cattle to her husband before she can be freed of her marital ties – a marriage may be spoken of as jurally stable simply because a divorce has not taken place, despite the fact that the husband and wife may no longer be living together.

Traditionally, African marriage seems to have been more stable jurally, and perhaps conjugally, in patrilineal societies than in matrilineal ones. In matrilineal systems there is a basic inconsistency between a man's role as a father, with only limited authority over his children, and as maternal uncle and guardian of his sister's children, with distinct power and influence. In the event of divorce he loses custody of his own children, who are members of their mother's descent group. It is thus much more difficult for a husband to maintain controls over his wife than it is in a patrilineal system, in which he would retain custody over his children if his marriage were dissolved.

Aside from type of descent, other factors seem important in marital stability, both jural and conjugal. One is the degree of social absorption of the in-marrying spouse in the local groupings and activities of the other spouse's community, that is, whether he or she is granted full membership in the group or is considered an outsider. Another is whether a means exists for proxy parenthood on behalf of a sterile husband or wife. This is effected in some societies by a man's calling upon a 'seed-raiser' to impregnate his wife, or a woman's paying bride wealth for a co-wife, whose child by their common husband she will consider her own. In societies that have no such arrangements, childlessness is often a recognized ground for divorce.

ASSOCIATION

The second principle of social grouping, association, is of particular importance in the social structure of some African societies, though it has been less thoroughly studied than kinship and some of its basic classifications are still being worked out. It is paradoxical that in a part of the world where kinship is of such great importance in social organization, non-kinship groupings should also figure importantly in many aspects of people's lives, cutting across kin groups, and uniting members of different families, lineages, and clans in common interests and activities. Membership in associations may be either voluntary or prescribed, and many forms of associations are found.

The type of association of probably the greatest overall importance for Africa is age groupings. These are primarily men's associations. Women's age groupings are also present in some societies, but they tend to be simpler in organization and more limited in function. Although age groupings are widely found, they are of greatest importance in east and south-east Africa.

Associations based on age are of two types, which have been referred to in past writings by an inconsistent set of terms. In recent attempts to unify the terminology, groups of the first type are called age sets, or sometimes age classes, and those of the second type, age grades. An age set may be called a 'vertical' group. It is formed of persons born in the same year or within a designated time and has the same personnel and group identity, signified by a distinctive name, throughout its existence. An age set endures from formation, usually in adolescence, until its members have died. An age grade may be characterized as a 'horizontal' category. It consists of an age set, or group of sets, performing specific functions and occupying a particular status during a given period. For instance, we may compare an age set to a group of persons who go through school together. The academic statuses through which they pass – elementary school, secondary school, university – may be compared to age grades, with the group of persons also referred to as an age grade while occupying one of these categories. As in a school, new sets are formed as older ones move upward in the system. Thus an age set may be said to be *in* the warrior grade – or to *be* the warrior grade – at a particular time in its career. An age set has a recognized leader or leaders throughout its existence; leadership in an age grade is usually determined by that in the set or sets occupying the grade at any one time. Within a given society the existence of one type of age association does not necessarily imply the presence of the other, though societies having age grades usually have age sets as well.

Though membership in an age set is associated in some societies with puberty initiations, there is no connection between them in others. In some areas, particularly East Africa, boys acquire membership in an age set at initiation early in adolescence. In others there is no formal initiation, or initiation is into a secret society rather than into an age grouping.

35

In such cases age sets may be organized informally during adolescence or early adulthood, and a set's identity may be officially recognized by the older age sets in a ceremonial which is sometimes referred to as the 'initiation' of the set as a whole. In an age grade system, not only is the initiation of a new set ceremonially recognized, but the periodic moving up of sets within the hierarchy is ritually observed.

The prescribed functions of age grades are related to qualifications of age, training, and experience, and to the particular needs of the social system. A common pattern for East African societies is that of the following broad categories: initiates, youths who have recently been initiated; a warrior's grade of young men in their physical prime, responsible for the defence of the community; one or more grades of mature men who take an important part in government; and old men, the elders. These may be subdivided, and conventions vary concerning the social status of the warrior group, the age of those responsible for government, the relative responsibility and prestige of the men in their declining years, and so on.

In addition to the integrative and regulatory functions of systems of age groupings for a society as a whole – such as social training, defence, and government – they also have internal functions for their members irrespective of their relation to outside groups. Between age mates, members of the same age set, there is usually a strong bond, and age sets serve in some respects as mutual aid societies for their members. They support one another in ceremonials such as marriage and other personal rituals, acting in some ways like kin groups. They are corporate groups but differ from descent groups in several ways: they do not usually own property, they are non-perpetuating – they cease to exist with the death of the last member – and they usually lack the religious shrines or cults often associated with descent groups.

The secret society is a type of association of great importance in West Africa and the Congo. Usually a men's group resembling somewhat in organization and ritual the fraternal orders of Western society, it often involves complicated initiation procedures and constitutes a major force in training for adulthood. It may help to maintain social order within a community by enforcing the rules of correct behaviour among the population as a whole, and it is often backed by strong religious sanctions. Secret societies are often characterized by the following features: they may own a section of sacred bush associated with initiation, but they do not usually own productive property, they may have guardian or other spirits, there may be a system of ranking and positions of prestige within the society. Though less common than men's, women's secret societies are found in some areas, particularly in Liberia and Sierra Leone. Among the Mende and related peoples of these countries, the role of secret societies is extremely pervasive and includes the canalizing of supernatural power, the structuring of social training and standards of conduct, and even the supervision of various political and economic activities.

Associations for the purpose of co-operative labour and craft work have already been mentioned in the context of economics. Though some such groups are based on kinship, most are based on the association principle. Membership in some work groups, such as those organized for farm work or for building, is usually voluntary – a group of friends and sometimes relatives joining in a common task; and it is often limited in time – for a season or simply for the duration of a project. However, the chain of obligations built up by certain individuals' working for others tends to lead to the later formation of similar groups.

The patterning of craft and professional organizations is more formal than that of co-operative work groups. Craft guilds are similar to those of medieval Europe, with the classifications of apprentice, journeyman, and master, and with a similar type of contract, period of training, and economic and quasi-parental responsibility for the apprentice on the part of the master. Professional organizations found in Africa include societies of medical and religious specialists and of artists, such as drummers or praise singers. These protect the interests of the specialists and help to maintain the standards of the profession as defined by the society. In some cases, particularly those of religious functionaries, they enforce the moral standards of the community and guard against the encroachment of undesirable change, whether from foreign innovations inconsistent with traditional cultural values or from improperly qualified persons, for example, 'quacks' seeking personal gain at the expense of the community.

RESIDENCE OR LOCALITY

The third principle of social grouping, residence or locality, though perhaps not as pervasive in Africa as kinship, is nevertheless an important aspect of the structure of a society and may have a great influence on its basic organization. A number of considerations are involved. First, residence is related to habitat, though it is not necessarily determined by it. The natural surroundings of a people are often more favourable to one method of earning a living than to another, and this in turn is often reflected in patterns of residence. In addition to natural resources, seasonal differences may determine patterns of population movements in response to the needs of people and their domestic animals – as in the case of the transhumance, or seasonal movements, of herding peoples.

Another factor related to residence is the level and type of technology of a people. This constitutes a screen through which they perceive their natural environment, seeing its potentialities or limitations in terms of the techniques they have devised for coping with it. Examples of this may be brought to mind by the mention of the words irrigation, fertilization, or well-digging – techniques whose presence or absence may make very fundamental differences in the residential patterns of a society.

In addition to natural environment and technology, the relations between societies may be an important factor in residence. In a continent with long traditions of population expansion and warfare, defence considerations have influenced the size of social groupings and their choice of locations to settle; and these, of course, have been further influenced by the factors already mentioned. Parts of Africa are inhabited jointly by tribal groups with different types of technology, such as agricultural and hunting, or agricultural and herding, peoples. When certain peoples move in and out of territory inhabited more or less permanently by others, the ownership or control of the land used by both must be agreed upon so as not to encroach upon the rights of either, and such a situation often affects residence, particularly that of the migratory groups. Here also, the factor of warfare was sometimes involved in pre-European times.

Social factors internal to the organization of a society may also be important in determining its type of residence. Although kinship is very often the basis of local groupings – a common pattern being an extended family living together in a homestead or compound, or a lineage forming the basis of a village segment – the principle of association may also strongly influence residence. This seems to be particularly true in parts of East Africa, where a warrior age grade traditionally had to be a mobile unit of defence for a people and their cattle. A South Central African people, the Nyakyusa of south-western Tanganyika, have quite an unusual system of age villages, the local unit being a group of age mates, their wives, and young children. An age village begins when a group of young herd boys of approximately the same age build huts outside their fathers' village. They sleep in them and spend their spare time there, and gradually, as new boys join, the group of huts assumes the proportions of a village, to which the boys later bring their wives. The village 'dies' with the death of the last age-mate founder. The Nyakyusa stress the ideal of good fellowship among age mates, and this concern is backed by supernatural sanctions associating tendencies toward social isolation with witchcraft. Also, they feel strongly that the sex activities of parents and children should be kept separate – thus there is an avoidance taboo that forbids familiarity between a man and his son's wife. Residence

38

in age village facilitates this avoidance pattern as residence in a patrilineal lineage with patrilocal marriage, for instance, could not.

To illustrate the variation in residence found in Africa, it may be helpful to imagine a continuum from a small, truly nomadic band living on the simplest level of technology to a large, compact sedentary grouping possessing the industrial and scientific techniques of the Western world. Although the latter is present in Africa only as a result of European contact, many positions on the continuum are represented by traditional African societies, as a few examples will indicate.

The Bushmen of the Kalahari Desert, as previously mentioned, are a nomadic hunting and gathering people, each band living in its own recognized territory. Their residential pattern is to congregate during the dry season around a permanent water hole, where both water and game are most likely to be available, and to disperse over the band's territory in search of food during the wetter part of the year.

The various Pygmy hunting groups of the Congo region are nomadic peoples who move about from place to place in search of game and other forest products. They differ from nomadic groups such as the Bushmen, however, since their so-called symbiotic relationship with the sedentary Negro farmers within whose territories they move about makes them part of a system of limited social interdependence and economic exchange unlike the marked self-sufficiency of the Bushmen. Because the rainfall of the forest region in which the Pygmies live is fairly evenly distributed throughout the year, they do not have the pattern of congregation and dispersal in response to seasonal demands, but rather migrate in a body when the supply of game in the band's temporary camp becomes exhausted. Here the factor of technology is important also, for the Pygmies hunt and gather in an area where their Negro neighbours farm successfully. This distinction is, in fact, said to be the basis of the Negroes' feeling of superiority towards the Pygmies, who, they think, have an inferior and backward way of life.

The Pastoral Fulani are a cattle-herding people of the Western Sudan, who derive their subsistence from cattle, sometimes supplemented by a few camels, sheep, or goats. They move about from place to place, living on dairy products and exchanging surpluses for grain in the markets of agricultural peoples of the area. The direction of Pastoral Fulani transhumance is southward in the dry season in search of water and pasture, and northward in the wet season to avoid the attacks of the tsetse fly and of wild animals such as the hyena. The people congregate during the wet season and disperse in the dry season, when the amount of water and pasture in any one location is most limited. Unlike many of the cattle-herding peoples of East Africa, the Fulani do not have permanent places of residence or own the land upon which they keep their herds. Rather, they must obtain water and grazing rights from the acknowledged owners of the land, the sedentary agricultural peoples of the region. Thus their seasonal movements vary from local area to area and from year to year, depending on such factors as the length of the wet and dry seasons, the number of cattle in the area in relation to the resources necessary for their maintenance, and the arrangements with local agricultural peoples, including the availability of markets for the exchange of farm and dairy products.

Among the East African herding peoples, the Masai, who live in the grassland area of Kenya and Tanganyika that is transected from north to south by the Rift Valley, practice a limited form of transhumance. They settle near permanent water supplies such as springs, water holes, and wells in the dry season, and in the wet season they move out to temporary waters that form, leaving the pastures near the permanent waters to re-establish themselves. In both seasons they live in kraals (settlements of cattle-herding peoples, including houses and cattle enclosures) of two basic types: that of the elders, including married men, their wives, and children; and that of the warriors, inhabited by the members of the warriors' age grades for the district and their mothers, younger sisters, and sweethearts. The elders' kraal approximates a village in its organization, while the warriors' kraal was in pre-European times the unit of defence. At present the people of both kraals keep cattle, each moving as a group between the wet- and dry-season settlements. The Masai own the land on which they live and graze their herds, but, holding the practice of farming in disdain, must trade with neighbouring agricultural peoples for the vegetable products with which they supplement the foods provided by their cattle. For the Masai, the residential division into elders' and warriors' kraals fitted their former status as feared warriors among other tribal groups in the area. The members of the elders' kraal maintained the herds, while the warriors fought and raided neighbouring tribes for cattle, thus expanding the holdings of the Masai and increasing their territory. As for ecological factors, the presence of enough water and pasture for their cattle free the Masai of the need for frequent migration, population dispersal, or marked dependence on neighbouring peoples, and social factors perhaps play as large a part in determining their residence pattern as ecological considerations.

The Nuer of the Eastern Sudan are a cattle-herding and farming people living in marshes and savannas along the Nile. Although cattle provide their chief means of subsistence, shortage of pasture during the dry season and the presence of such cattle diseases as rinderpest make it necessary for them to supplement their food supply with grain and vegetable crops from their gardens. These needs determine the ecological cycle of Nuer life, their village sites, and the relationships between the various tribal segments into which they are divided. Many of the villages are located on elevated grounds high enough to be free of the wet-season floods; as the rains increase, cattle graze higher and higher on the slopes leading to the villages. Within a village the homesteads are strung out along a ridge, with garden land at the back and grazing land in the front; thus the size of a village depends on the amount of high ground suitable for cultivation. With the coming of the dry season, the youths and girls take the cattle temporarily to small early cattle camps where water is more plentiful, while the older people remain in the villages to harvest millet. After the harvest the cattle are brought back and fed on the millet stalks. As the pastures become exhausted toward the height of the dry season, all the people of the villages leave with cattle for the later dry-season camps along the banks of rivers or on the edges of permanent swamps. There is a short period of wandering between the two periods of stable residence. As pastures become scarcer in the different Nuer villages, the population of the cattle camps increases. With the beginning of the rains the older people return to the villages for sowing, and the rest follow with the cattle a month or so later. The size of the later dry-season camps varies according to the amount of available water and pasture, but on the whole their population tends to be larger than that of the villages. Neighbouring villages usually share the same cattle camp, co-operating in the tasks of caring for their cattle that are usually performed separately by the members of each homestead in the village. Thus the transhumance patterns demanded by the environment of Nuerland create an interdependence between the people of different villages that makes impossible the self-sufficient isolation in smaller village units that is found among some neighbouring peoples who place greater emphasis on cultivation.

A group whose exceptional type of residence has an important effect on its social organization is the Lozi (Barotse) of Northern Rhodesia. Practising a mixed economy of gardening, fishing, and cattle herding, most of them live in villages on mounds in the flood plain of the Upper Zambezi. The number of persons who can live on one mound is limited by its size, and during the flood season the Lozi must move from the mounds to settlements on the margin of the plain. They go to stay with kinsmen in other communities, but there is no consistent pattern of migration, so that throughout the year the same people are not in any territorial unit. This pattern is reflected in their bilateral descent system in which there are no lineages or clans and in which specific kinship groups are not associated with particular territories.

Many sedentary peoples are agriculturalists, but some combine farming and herding. They require pasture and water sufficient to avoid the necessity of mass seasonal movements of people and cattle and also land fertile enough to permit successful cultivation. The Nandi of Kenya, to the north of the Masai and with a similar culture in many respects, inhabit an area of abundant water and grassland. They live in homesteads scattered across the countryside, near which they keep their herds of cattle, sheep, and goats and cultivate grain and vegetable crops. The economic unit is the family, made relatively self-sufficient by the presence of sufficient resources to free it of dependence on others for its basic subsistence needs.

Agricultural peoples also have variations in patterns of residence, with implications for their social structure as a whole. As has been mentioned, a group may practise shifting cultivation, moving from one location to another every few years, or they may be truly sedentary, using techniques such as fertilization, crop rotation, or bush fallowing in order to maintain soil fertility. Sedentary agricultural peoples may live in small homesteads, dispersed across the countryside, in villages with outlying farmland belonging to the community, or even in cities.

In Northern Rhodesia, the Bemba, an agricultural people of Congo origin, live in villages located as much as sixteen to twenty miles apart. Since the area is one of generally poor soils, they practise shifting cultivation, the villages moving to new farming sites every few years. Land is selected that has a growth of trees suitable for pollarding – cutting off the top branches – and burning the lopped branches to form an ash bed in which seeds are sown. The village develops as a kinship unit when a man with a sufficient following of relatives applies to the chief for, and is granted, permission to set up his own community. The personnel of Bemba villages tends to be variable, with young men moving to their wives' villages at marriage and later taking them away after their obligatory services to their in-laws have been fulfilled, established men setting up new villages, and so on. The practice of moving villages every few years as a part of the agricultural system seems to give impetus to the internal changes in village composition. The Lele of the Belgian Congo also live in villages and practise shifting cultivation. Here also the personnel is changeable, but the villages are compact and coherent social units.

Another sedentary agricultural people is the Ibo of south-eastern Nigeria, who practise a system of bush fallowing in which plots of land are cultivated for a year or two and then left unused for several years, after which the bush that has grown up is cut down and burned in preparation for another period of cultivation. Residence among various sub-groups of the Ibo is of two types. The great majority live in homesteads dispersed across the countryside, with farmland and bush lying between them. The basis of the homestead is the patrilineal extended family, with a group of neighbouring homesteads forming the basis of a patrilineage. A larger population group, the village, consists of several contiguous lineages plus the women from other lineages who have married into it. Here the village is not a compact, visible unit, however, for it extends from a central meeting place into the bush, sometimes for a distance of several miles. In contrast, the villages along the eastern periphery of Ibo country are compact in organization, with a central meeting place, which is sometimes also the market. They are divided into wards or quarters and further subdivided into compounds, each having one or more patrilineages as its basis. The farmland of each village extends sometimes for several miles from its borders and is divided into sections which are alternately farmed and lain fallow. For both types of Ibo residence the kinship basis of village organization and the system of bush fallowing are similar in principle, though spatial relationships differ.

Although the Yoruba of western Nigeria are an agricultural people, more than a third of them are city dwellers. The city is a traditional form of residential grouping, early European travellers having estimated populations of close to a hundred thousand for some Yoruba cities over a century ago. Unlike the cities of Western countries and African urban centres that have arisen through European culture contact and industrialization, Yoruba cities were and are culturally homogeneous entities. Their principle of organization is similar to that of the villages in which a considerable proportion of the tribal population lives. The different segments are based on patrilineal lineages; in the cities they are organized politically into wards, which are subdivided into precincts, while in small villages the population may consist of a few lineages, or sometimes only one. In both village and city, the individual's orientation is first in terms of his lineage, and after that in terms of the larger grouping. The basis of the Yoruba economy is farming, supplemented by craft production and trade. Belts of farmland surround the cities, extending outward for as much as fifteen miles. Although some persons with farms in the more outlying districts maintain temporary shelters where they may stay for a few days at a time during the height of the agricultural season, they have permanent dwellings in the city and consider it their home.

In parts of Africa, particularly the Western Sudan, trading cities have existed for a thousand years and more. These are characterized by heterogeneous populations that are more unstable in composition than those of the Yoruba, for example. Timbuctoo, on the Niger Bend in French

43

West Africa, was the meeting place of trans-Sahara caravan routes and the river trade to the south. Developing from the eleventh century as a trade centre, Timbuctoo grew into a city with a large number of crafts and professions practised by persons of different ethnic backgrounds, predominantly Arabs from North Africa, Tuareg from nomadic Caucasoid groups in the Sahara, and Songhai, who were Negroid inhabitants of the Niger Bend area. The present-day city is divided into a number of quarters and outlying districts, each identified with certain ethnic groups and their economic activities, such as Arab caravaneers, wholesalers, and retailers, Songhai craftsmen, butchers, barbers, and so on. Unlike the Yoruba agricultural cities, some of which are much larger, Timbuctoo influences, and depends on, quite distant peoples, having a commercial hinterland extending for hundreds of miles in several directions.

Modern commercial, administrative, and industrial cities have developed in many parts of Africa as the result of European contact, particularly along the coast and in areas of rich mineral resources. These are essentially European in their organization and activities, though distinctive patterns of African urban life which represent a blend of European and African cultures are gradually emerging.

In summary, two generalizations may be made concerning the relationship between the principles of kinship, association, and residence. First, many functions can be performed for a society as a whole by either kin or association groups. For example, among the Konkomba of Northern Togoland, whose social structure is strongly dominated by the principle of patrilineal descent, government is in the hands of patrilineal clans, while in other societies having the same type of descent government may be in the hands of senior age grades. Similarly, certain aspects of child training may in some societies be the function of the family but in others be the prerogative of a secret society.

Second, kinship and association are by definition mutually exclusive: a kinship group cannot be an association, and vice versa. However, the third principle, residence, plays a significant role in the organization of both. In many social systems it may be secondary to kinship in importance, but it still is vital in shaping interpersonal relations within the kin group. In associations, by contrast, the factor of residence may be primary in determining the membership of a particular group – for example, an age set or secret society will draw its members from the persons living in a particular location. Different African societies may, in fact, be characterized by their relative emphasis upon kinship and association and the particular manner in which residence affects their total organization.

4

The Modern Family in Social-Anthropological Perspective[1]

M. G. Marwick

The basic social unit is the family. This being so, to understand a society it is immediately necessary to learn the sanctions and customs of marriage. Furthermore, any changes in the structure or pattern of family life, whether occasioned from within by, for example, changes in belief, or whether influenced externally by the necessities of economics or, more subtly, by the pressures of urban life, these must have the most profound impact and repercussions on society generally.

In traditional society, the relationship of the family structure to economic life and government – to mention only two sectors of corporate activity – are indivisibly inter-linked, each helping to sustain the others in an intricate web of sanction, obligation and right so as to produce the maximum social harmony. With the arrival of external forces, however, the traditional ways of living, the old systems and values relating to the association between husband, wife, kinsmen, village and tribe, no longer meaningfully or harmoniously relate. Pressures between rival demands multiply and man, with his bearings shattered or lost, finds himself in danger of becoming morally and spiritually marooned, leading a life shorn of meaning and bereft of the ancient inner tranquillity that is the gift of unquestioned, undeviating tradition.

When the reader who has never visited Africa reads the following section he should bear in mind that, in Africa, the traditional way of life is intensely personal. The family extends to the village so that all one's fellow villagers may be regarded as cousins or even, quite commonly, brothers and sisters; one eats and drinks and talks and works and plays and hunts and perhaps fights, alongside the same set of people. This constant succession of face-to-face relationships covering all the activities of living gives to tribal life a special quality and makes the rules governing the formal relationship between people particularly important. Nowhere is this more true than in the case of marriage. Hence, as marriage affects economic and sometimes even political life in a much more direct and personal way than in more modern societies, its variations are many. It is also unusual for a man or woman, especially the latter, not to be married so that, throughout the continent, marriage rates are among the highest in the world.

To understand better not only the traditional as it still exists but also to appreciate more fully something of the pressures and forces that are involved

[1] Reprinted from *African Studies*, Vol. 17, 3, 1958.

when the old meets the new, we now examine the family as a social phenomenon in detail, and with especial reference to its relationship with other
aspects of culture.

Since we are to view our family against the corresponding social units
found in non-literate societies, we should be clear regarding what we mean
by 'family'. In English as in certain other languages this term or its
equivalent has a wide area of meaning. For instance, I may say that my
family is in Johannesburg; for that is where my wife and children live; or
in Pietermaritzburg; for that is where my mother and sister are; or I
may say that my family is scattered over South Africa, especially Natal;
and by this I mean relatives on both sides, i.e. reckoned through both my
mother and my father, or I may mean only those of my paternal relatives
who share my surname. To clarify the chaotic situation that this example
illustrates, social scientists now make a number of distinctions. Firstly
they distinguish between the small group of husband, wife and children,
and the more composite group in which this narrower one is included with
a wider circle of kin. They call the former the biological, conjugal, immediate, elementary or nuclear family; and they call the latter, i.e. the wider
group, the extended family, or, where it shares one roof or one commissariat (as in India and China) the joint family. More often than not an extended family has as its nucleus a group of consanguineal or blood relatives
known as a lineage, which, in turn, in many societies is a segment of a clan.

Even when we have distinguished the elementary from the extended
family there is still the problem of designating clearly the two elementary
families to which every married adult belongs, or has belonged, the one
into which he was born or adopted and the one that he has set up on
marriage. The first, since it has given him his outlook on life, is termed
his family of orientation; and the second, since it sets the stage for his part
in human reproduction, is termed his family of procreation.

Societies differ (with regard to marriage) in a number of respects, such
as the mode of reckoning descent, the location of authority, emphasis on
consanguineal as against conjugal ties, the number of spouses allowed on
either side of marriage, the place of residence on marriage – and so on.

As to descent, some societies, like the Zulu, reckon it through males,
i.e., through fathers and sons (I am now disregarding the complexities
brought about by the ranking of wives in polygynous marriages); others,
like the Cewa of East Central Africa, reckon it through mothers and sisters;
some, like the Herero of south-west Africa, through males and females;
and others, again, like our own society, have a tendency to trace it through
either males or females according to the advantage or the whim of the
moment. Thus we may describe descent as *unilineal* if it follows one line

46

consistently. There are two unilineal types, the *patrilineal* and the *matrilineal* (according to whether descent is through the father's or the mother's line).

Some societies, e.g. the Herero, reckon descent through both lines. What generally happens in these double-descent systems is that patrilineage is recognized for one type of function and the matrilineage is recognized for another. Thus among the Herero the patrilineage is the basis for the division of society into groups through which social control is effected; and the matrilineage brings together in friendly co-operation and in marriage persons separated by patrilineal reckoning. Among the Yakö of south-eastern Nigeria, the patrilineage controls the use of land and houses and provides co-operative labour; while the matrilineage is concerned with the transfer and inheritance of wealth. Thus the Yakö say that a man eats in his patrilineage and inherits in his matrilineage.

The second of the characteristics in respect of which societies differ is the location of authority. In this connection we may note that patterns of domestic and sometimes even political authority are often concordant with modes of reckoning descent, i.e. that domestic and political authority are often vested in descent groups represented by authorities such as headmen. Thus in societies reckoning descent through males, i.e. patrilineally, authority is usually vested in the father and the senior male members of his descent group or agnatic lineage; in those reckoning descent through females, i.e. matrilineally, it is vested, as I hinted when I referred earlier to the myth of matriarchy, not in the mother but in the mother's male matrikin, such as her brother or her mother's brother. In our society the optional, multilineal character of the kinship system is reflected in the fact that the influence of the husband's or of the wife's blood relatives is of almost random incidence; and, as we shall see later, in the fact that, especially since the industrial revolution, there has developed within the family an uneasy, and sometimes highly dynamic, compromise between male and female authority.

Turning to the third mode of variation, the emphasis on consanguineal or on conjugal organization, we find that in unilineal societies, i.e. those that emphasize *either* the male *or* the female line to the virtual exclusion of the other, there is a tendency for the descent group or lineage, consisting of *either* patrilineal *or* matrilineal blood relatives, to eclipse the family as we know it in Western society. Thus, in any society with well developed lineages, the functional kinship group is, to follow Linton's well-known passage,[1] a nucleus of blood relatives surrounded by a fringe of spouses; whereas in a society such as our own, the functional kinship group is a

[1] Ralph Linton, *The Study of Man*, p. 159 (New York, 1936).

nucleus of spouses and their children surrounded – often at a distance – by a fringe of blood relatives.

As to the number of spouses allowed, it should be noted that in most human societies monogamy is the prevailing form of marriage, but that in many of these, for instance the South African Bantu, a plurality of wives (polygyny) is regarded as an ideal and brings high prestige to those, estimated at less than 30 per cent. of married males among the Swazi, for instance,[1] who manage to achieve it. In a few societies, especially those living under severe economic circumstances in which over-population is a constant threat, a plurality of husbands (polyandry) is resorted to. This institution is often associated with female infanticide which brings about the required sex ratio.

Polygamy, strictly speaking, means plurality of either husbands or wives and includes both polygyny and polyandry. It is often used in reference to polygyny because this is the commoner form.

Group marriage, i.e. plurality on both sides, has only been very rarely reported.

Finally, societies differ in the rules of marriage residence. Strongly patrilineal societies, e.g. the Zulu, usually require newlyweds to live at the husband's home settlement, in which case marriage is said to be *virilocal*, a term which, being more precise, is displacing the older term *patrilocal*.

Matrilineal societies sometimes follow the same rule and sometimes the opposite one. For instance marriage among the Trobriand Islanders is virilocal, i.e. the couples settle at the husband's village. In Northern Rhodesia, the matrilineal Cewa, usually, but not invariably, follow the rule that the couple should reside at the wife's home settlement, i.e. most of their marriages are *uxorilocal*. The term *uxorilocal* is displacing the less precise one, *matrilocal*. Working-class people in Western society have recently been found to show a slight preference for uxorilocal residence. There are other possibilities as well, of which I shall mention only the one prevailing in our (Western) society, where marriage may be said to be *neolocal*, i.e. we tend to be neither virilocal nor uxorilocal, but to set up a completely new *ménage* on marriage, and then, incidentally, to feel that we are at a sufficiently safe distance to make our mothers-in-law the butts of our more aggressive jokes.

In order to understand the nature of marriage in different societies let us return to Linton's distinction between conjugal and consanguineal organization. In Western society the effective social and domestic unit is a conjugal one, a nucleus of spouses and their children surrounded – but at a distance spatially and socially – by a relatively unimportant fringe of

[1] Hilda Kuper, *An African Aristocracy*, p. 37 (London, 1947).

blood relatives. Our kinship terminology gives a clear indication of the importance we attach to the nucleus and of our vagueness with regard to the fringe. As Parsons points out, there are seven terms, father, mother, brother, sister, spouse (i.e. husband or wife), son and daughter, which are reserved for members of what he calls the inner circle, i.e. the families of orientation and procreation.[1] Moving to the outer circle, we become less discriminating and use terms like 'uncle' and 'aunt' for persons between whom other societies, e.g. the South African and Central African Bantu, would be careful to distinguish. Beyond the outer fringe is the vague fringe of more distant blood relatives, most of whom we classify as 'cousin', qualifying this term with 'first', 'second', 'once removed', etc., only when called upon to be more precise.

When we turn to societies in which unilineal descent is followed more consistently (than in the West), we find the basis of kinship organization – and in most small-scale societies this means general social organization as well – reversed. Take the patrilineal Zulu and my tribe of adoption, the matrilineal Cewa of the country where Nyasaland, Northern Rhodesia and Mozambique meet. These two societies are similar in that the unilineal descent group, the patrilineage of the Zulu and the matrilineage of the Cewa, forms a corporate group. It does this in a number of ways. It forms the nucleus of the residential unit, the Zulu homestead and the Cewa village-section; it acts as a politico-jural unit, protecting and being responsible for its members in their relationships, including marriage, with the members of other lineages; and it is a religious corporation by virtue of its sharing descent from, or kinship with, a group of spirits, both lineal ancestors and collaterals, who are believed to censure its 'members' misconduct and watch over their welfare. Again kinship terminology gives a scale of importance. Both these tribes use terms like 'father', 'mother' and 'brother' not only within the inner circle but outside it as well. Thus, among the Zulu, 'father' as a term of both reference and address includes paternal uncle; among the Cewa, 'mother' includes maternal aunt; and in both tribes the equivalent of our 'brother' includes all male lineage members of Ego's generation, even first and more distant cousins.

These two societies, in contrast to our own, fit Linton's conception of consanguineal organization in that in each case the effective social unit consists of a nucleus of blood relatives, surrounded by a fringe of comparatively unimportant spouses. The Cewa fit the definition more closely than the Zulu; for in their case the position of the spouses is more heavily overshadowed by the consanguineal nucleus. The Cewa do not tack on the

[1] Talcott Parsons, 'The Social Structure of the Family' in *The Family: Its Function and Destiny*, ed. R. N. Anschen, p. 176 (New York, 1949).

fringe of spouses very securely. Their divorce rate is probably about three times that of the Americans and five or six times that of South African whites.

Many students of Western society look upon a high divorce rate as a symptom of social disorganization. Among the Cewa it does not seem to be; in fact it appears to be an essential condition for effective social organization. The solidarity of the matrilineage is so marked that, if a person – man or woman – is the victim of conflicting loyalties towards his spouse and his matrilineage, he usually resolves the conflict by getting rid of his spouse; and the interests of the matrilineage, the important social group, are thereby maintained. If you are puzzled why the high divorce rate among the Cewa is not a threat, but rather a support, to the matrilineage, remember that in a matrilineal society the children born of every marriage automatically belong to their mother's, not their father's descent group. They acquire membership of a corporate matrilineage, i.e. their mother's, regardless of who their fathers are or of how many husbands their mother may have buried or divorced.

No one, to my knowledge, has estimated this type of divorce rate among the South African Bantu, but ethnographers are unanimous in reporting that divorce, while possible, is extremely rare. This brings us to the main difference between the Cewa and the Zulu. Among the Zulu the nucleus of the effective kinship unit is again a group of blood-relatives; but the fringe of spouses is by no means unimportant. The Zulu seems to have succeeded in far greater measure than the Cewa in firmly tacking it on. How and why have they done this? They have done it through the institution of bride-price or *lobolo*, which the Cewa do not observe, and this institution exists as a convenient solution to one of the problems confronting any markedly patrilineal society. Jeffreys has effectively shown that the primary function of *lobolo* is to establish the rights of the person or group giving it to the children born to the woman in respect of whom it is given.[1] He rightly insists that, if we must refer to it as a price at all, we should call it child-price rather than bride-price. This institution has the effect of getting round the difficulty that women born into a given patrilineage cannot, as in a matrilineal system, legitimately produce children for their own group; and for this purpose women must be brought in from other patrilineages, their reproductive powers being secured for a consideration. Among some patrilineal tribes, such as the Amba of Western Uganda, patrilineages exchange women without using the ceremonial currency of cattle. The South African Bantu use cattle as a means of

[1] M. D. W. Jeffreys, 'Lobolo is child-price', *African Studies*, 10, Vol. pp. 145–84, 1951.

balancing the asymmetrical movement of bride to bridegroom's group and of ensuring that the children born of the union so effected will be members of their father's group. This elaborate procedure appears to produce a degree of marital stability as a by-product; for divorce involves the return of the cattle. Among the Cewa there is no transfer of goods or cattle to balance the asymmetrical movement of the groom to the bride's matrilineage, and correspondingly a lesser degree of marital stability; but, as I have shown, this does not affect the situation in a matrilineal society where the prevailing principle of descent operates no matter how weak the marriage link happens to be.

Africans are still in the grip of a kinship system that imposes on them a clannishness quite out of keeping with urban living. And even when in response to modern urban-industrial conditions large-scale patrilineal grouping breaks down – as, for instance, when a marriage is contracted without *lobolo* – the domestic group that emerges is not similar to the Western one, but is still based on the consanguineal rather than the conjugal principle. The father of the child born to an un*lobola*'d woman can secure no rights to it; it belongs to its mother's descent group. There is even a suggestion that the father's attempts to legitimize his offspring by *lobola*'ing their mother are resisted by her parents, who see in their daughter's illegitimate children a source of security in their rootless urban old age.

At present the unmarried mother's descent group is usually patrilineally defined; but with a few more generations of urban living we may expect the emergence of what Smith in reference to the Negro family in the New World has called a 'matri-focal', rather than a matrilineal system.[1] In this development, the mother-child relationship, of fundamental importance in any society, is thrown into high relief by the fact that the husband-father's role becomes peripheral to the functioning of the domestic group.

There is fairly general agreement that as a minimum the modern family produces children and co-operates with other agencies like schools in preparing them for social living; and that it provides a stable anchorage for the personal ties of its adult members. If we seek these functions of procreation, socialization and stabilization in non-literate societies, we often find that some of them are performed not by the elementary family alone but by it in association with the wider kin-group. It is true that, with the exception of the extreme matrilineal organization of the Nayars and the occasional occurrence of illegitimacy in nearly all societies, the

[1] Raymond T. Smith, *The Negro Family in British Guiana*, pp. 142–3, 221, 226–8 (London, 1956).

procreation of children the world over is the concern of the elementary family. But, turning to socialization, we find that this function is performed by the elementary family in association with the lineage, especially when the latter, or a segment of it, forms the core of the residential group. Similarly, the emotional stability of adults is promoted, not only by their membership of the elementary family, but also, and in some instances, primarily, by their membership of the lineage, which is the source of much of their general security and the object of their proud identification.

II b: Value Systems

The choice, Aldous Huxley somewhere wrote, is never between having or not having a philosophy, but between having a good philosophy or having a bad one. In other words, every man has a set of precepts which helps explicitly to determine the quality of his behaviour and which, implictly, is reflected by that behaviour. This is true not only for individuals acting within the sphere of inter-personal relations, but is equally true when applied to social values and to the principles underlying government. Whenever choice presents itself, the question of priorities arises, and for priorities to be determined a set of principles are required.

Closely associated with the precepts themselves is the manner of thinking. In the west, the logic of science with its chains of reaction between cause and effect, the randomness of chance, and a Christian faith which, although sometimes confused with scientific thinking, belongs to a different order of belief, these have all so permeated thought in the Western world that they are taken for granted. Other possible ways of thinking, other kinds of explanation for things that appear to happen, are not considered. The student of Africa who is not himself an African has to recognize not only with his understanding but also, if he can, with real empathy, that other modes of thought are both possible and meaningful.

The manner in which values influence the quality and the functions of government, of society and of individual lives is nowhere more clearly seen than in African tribal life. The student should study these things not only for the great insight that can be obtained, but also for the relation they have with contemporary developments and problems.

What, for example, are the inconsistencies between the logic of witch-craft and the logic of western science, on which all industrial civilizations have hitherto been based? These inconsistencies may not worry the man who seeks to live with both, indeed he may not even be conscious that any inconsistency exists. Nevertheless, incompatibles such as these have a way of making their presence felt. The witch-doctor represents the old way of life, he is the embodiment of its approach to the problems of living, and, therefore, although much of his knowledge may contain real wisdom, his presence is an influence and a symbol that runs contrary to the direction of events. There comes a time, often after higher education, when a man, and the society in which he lives, has to chose between these competing conceptions of how the world operates.

We have therefore to understand these traditional modes and contents of thinking themselves and then, having done this, to relate what has been learned to the problems of a transitional state, when man changes his habits and affiliations from the rigid old to the uncertain new.

Finally, we may hope to detect from the customs of tradition how new values may evolve. It is possible, for example, that the impinging of industrial economics and democratic government on subsistence economics and tribal government may produce unique ideologies and fresh insights into many of the problems which perplex and divide the modern world. To those who are concerned with the quality of human life this is perhaps the most exciting thing about Africa today.

5

Values in African Tribal Life[1]

Meyer Fortes and E. E. Evans-Pritchard

This reading, taken from the Introduction to what has become the classic comparative study of traditional African political systems, explains the great importance of symbolism, what symbols signify and the functions they serve.

The urge for an explanation of all things may be regarded as one of the basic needs of any society. In modern societies there is the spiritual order of explanation on the one hand, and a scientific answer in the realm of material things on the other, and beside each of these there is the world of fortuitous chance. In Africa, however, these three worlds of knowledge intermingle and one of the greatest difficulties during the period of transition is the vacuum left when the old myths, dogmas and ritual beliefs become questioned and then discarded.

An African ruler is not to his people merely a person who can enforce his will on them. He is the axis of their political relations, the symbol of their unity and exclusiveness, and the embodiment of their essential values. He is more than a secular ruler; in *that* capacity the European government can to a great extent replace him. His credentials are mystical and are derived from antiquity. Where there are no chiefs, the balanced segments which compose the political structure are vouched for by tradition and myth and their interrelations are guided by values expressed in mystical symbols. Into these sacred precincts the European rulers can never enter. They have no mythical or ritual warranty for their authority.

What is the meaning of this aspect of African political organization? African societies are not models of continuous internal harmony. Acts of violence, oppression, revolt, civil war, and so forth, chequer the history of every African state. In societies like the Logoli, Tallensi, and Nuer the segmentary nature of the social structure is often most strikingly brought to light by armed conflict between the segments. But if the social system has reached a sufficient degree of stability, these internal convulsions do not necessarily wreck it. In fact, they may be the means of reinforcing it, as we have seen, against the abuses and infringements of rulers actuated by

---

[1] Reprinted from *African Political Systems*, International African Institute, 1958.

their private interests. In the segmentary societies, war is not a matter of one segment enforcing its will on another, but is the way in which segments protect their particular interests within a field of common interests and values.

There are, in every African society, innumerable ties which counteract the tendencies towards political fission arising out of the tensions and cleavages in the social structure. An administrative organisation backed by coercive sanctions, clanship, lineage and age-set ties, the fine-spun web of kinship – all these unite people who have different or even opposed sectional and private interests. Often also there are common material interests such as the need to share pastures or to trade in a common market-place, or complementary economic pursuits binding different sections to one another. Always there are common ritual values, the ideological super-structure of political organization.

Members of an African society feel their unity and perceive their common interests in symbols, and it is their attachment to these symbols which more than anything else gives their society cohesion and persistence. In the form of myths, fictions, dogmas, ritual, sacred places and persons, these symbols represent the unity and exclusiveness of the groups which respect them. They are regarded, however, not as mere symbols, but as final values in themselves.

To explain these symbols sociologically, they have to be translated into terms of social function and of the social structure which they serve to maintain. Africans have no objective knowledge of the forces determining their social organization and actuating their social behaviour. Yet they would be unable to carry on their collective life if they could not think and feel about the interests which actuate them, the institutions by means of which they organize collective action, and the structure of the groups into which they are organized. Myths, dogmas, ritual beliefs and activities make his social system intellectually tangible and coherent to an African and enable him to think and feel about it. Furthermore, these sacred symbols, which reflect the social system, endow it with mystical values which evoke acceptance of the social order that goes far beyond the obedience exacted by the secular sanction of force. The social system is, as it were, removed to a mystical plane, where it figures as a system of sacred values beyond criticism or revision. Hence people will overthrow a bad king, but the kingship is never questioned; hence the wars or feuds between segments of a society like the Nuer or the Tallensi are kept within bounds by mystical sanctions. These values are common to the whole society, to rulers and ruled alike and to all the sections and segments of society.

56

Values in African Tribal Life

The African does not see beyond the symbols; it might well be held that if he understood their objective meaning, they would lose the power they have won over him. This power lies in their symbolic content, and in their association with the nodal institutions of the social structure, such as the kingship. Not every form of ritual nor any sort of mystical ideas can express the values that hold a society together and focus the loyalty and devotion of its members on their rulers. (In some societies[1] the mystical values bound up with the kingship may, for example, refer to fertility, health, prosperity, peace, justice to anything, in short, which gives life and happiness to a people.) The African sees these ritual observances as the supreme safeguard of the basic needs of his existence and of the basic relations that make up his social order – land, cattle, rain, bodily health, the family, the clan, the state. The mystical values reflect the general import of the basic elements of existence: the land as the source of the whole people's livelihood, physical health as something universally desired, the family as the fundamental procreative unit, and so forth. These are the common interests of the whole society, as the native sees them. These are the themes of taboos, observances and ceremonies in which, in societies of the kind we have just mentioned, the whole people share through its representatives . . . since they are matters of equal moment to all.

---

[1] Those which have centralized authority, administrative machinery, and judicial institutions, e.g. the Zulu, the Bemba, the Ngwato.

6

African Modes of Thinking[1]

Daryll Forde

In this reading the same theme is developed as it affects the ultimate explanation, in other words, religion.

Just as all the paraphernalia of everyday living are much more personal in the tribal environment, so are natural events and objects imbued with a personification that finds its closest parallel in the West in superstition. Thus a storm may be interpreted as the wrath of God, or individuality ascribed to a stone transcending its mere material qualities.

The reader should clarify at this point the important distinction between magic and religion. The essence of magic is that physical events, usually but not necessarily of a favourable kind, may be brought about by propitiating the spiritual forces that are responsible. Magic is therefore a practical affair, concerned with changing or directing the course of events. These events, of course, may be within the human body as when it is afflicted with disease, or quite outside it as when a harvest is threatened by drought. Religion is what a man believes about the ultimate power(s) in the world.

When these studies (of different African societies) are considered together one is impressed, not only by the great diversity of ritual forms and expression of belief, but also by substantial underlying similarities in religious outlook and moral injunction. In the first place in myth, ritual and social code there is always a strong sense of direct dependence on local resources: on, for example, the rains and the harvest that they should bring forth or the grass to maintain the herds. There is often, too, an equally vivid expression of concern lest pestilence overtake men and crops and livestock. Primitive techniques in the production of food supplies, the small and localized scale of that production, and severe limitations on the accumulation, transport, and storage of surplus, combine to render hazardous the very basis of subsistence for household and community. The practical measures that can be taken to combat disease and sickness whether individual or epidemic are equally limited. Where the natural processes involved in good fortune and in bad remain largely unknown and

[1] Reprinted from *African Worlds*, Oxford University Press, under the auspices of the International African Institute, 1954.

uncontrollable by practical means, men have at all times rationalized their fate by postulating mysterious forces and beings in nature, and mysterious powers among their fellows.

To all this Africans have been no exception. Gods, spirits, and magical forces beyond the community, together with witches and sorcerers within it, are postulated in explanation of the workings of the universe, of the incidence of benefits and misfortunes, and of the strains of life in society. Means are employed according to the situation and the diagnosis to enlist or avert the anticipated action of such beings and powers. Africans, in the same way as Europeans, have appreciated and successfully based their routines of living on principles of causation linking events, on the logical implications of ideas, and on an understanding of mechanical and organic process. Their techniques of farming, fishing, and stock-raising, their procedures in training the young, their judgements of men and of social situations all reveal this at every turn. Where they have differed from the Europeans who have recently come among them has been in the depth and range of their collective knowledge of natural process and in the degree of control and security that they could thereby command.

Under primitive conditions of life and in the absence of a coherent body of scientific theory so much more lies beyond the reach of natural-istic explanation, so much more elicits interpretation and action in terms of the mysterious agents called into being in response to hopes and needs. Beliefs of this order are not capable of verification but neither do they require it. In such spheres the peoples of Africa, like those of the West and, indeed, all mankind save the tiny minority which is able to suspend belief, have adopted theories that project on to a plane of supernatural action the desires and aspirations that they know in the realm of human action. Passion and will, virtue and malevolence, compassion and indignation as they are known among men are attributed to unseen powers. The physical limitations on human action that are accepted in everyday life are thought no longer to restrict men who can command supernatural forces. Limita-tions of knowledge, and the absence of a tradition of critical inquiry and philosophic doubt, combine with the greater frequency of unforeseen distress to accentuate the universal dichotomy between explanations, common sense or scientific, of processes directly involved in the occurrence of events and the desire to know why a particular chain of events should occur to particular people at a particular time.

Some educated Europeans in some situations are able to apply western knowledge concerning the complexity of causation, to maintain the distinction between *post hoc* and *propter hoc*. But there is a deeper propen-sity which tends to supervene outside fields of special training or knowledge – the tendency to seek the cause of any event which touches men closely in some antecedent and emotionally charged situation affecting themselves or other persons. The crops are known to wither from lack of rain, the cattle are known to flourish because the rains came early and in abundance; it is recognized that a man fell from a tree and died because he climbed out on a dead branch, that another is prosperous and has many children because he and his wives are healthy and able. But when the metereological processes involved in fluctuations of rainfall are unknown, when the notion of chance is not applied to the occurrence of a dead branch, when the conditions of human well-being and ability can be so little analysed, what is to be the answer to the further questions: why should the rains fail or be abundant *now* for *us*? Why should *my* kinsman and not another have fallen from the tree? Why should one man and his wives enjoys prosperity while neighbours sicken and lose their children? All these questions remain open to explanation in terms of attendant emotions and the moral ideas of virtue and guilt associated with them. In other words, success and prosperity, so long as they are socially approved, may be seen as the rewards of virtue and dependent on its continuance; misery and catastrophe are linked through anxiety and anger to notions of wrongdoing or envy in oneself or others and thence to the punishment or elimination of these faults.

So it is that in misfortune, not merely attendant circumstances, but explanations in moral terms are sought and the consequences of human or supernatural action divined. Where does the guilt or anger lie and how may it be requited or expiated? And explanations in these terms take different directions according to the actual or assumed locus of the emotions and desires in question and the moral status of the persons concerned. Thus, for example, where guilt is ascribed to the sufferer of misfortune the misfortune tends to be attributed to supernatural beings – to gods and ancestral or other spirits, symbolic guardians of the moral order, whose anger has inflicted punishment. But where the context of misfortune does not elicit guilt on the part of the sufferer, then the injurious desires of others, of evil spirits and malevolent human beings, tend to be invoked. Where malevolence from other persons is feared, magical instrumentalities – powers of witchcraft or sorcery – can be attributed without contradiction from experience or in logic. Needless to say, the particular situations in which persons consider themselves, or are considered, to be guilty and those which arouse apprehensions of the evil intentions of others are so judged neither abstractly nor capriciously, but in terms of accepted cultural values and approved social conduct. Thus, as so many studies have shown, the reaction to misfortune and apprehension is to take stock of the past conduct and social relations both of those concerned and of others towards them. And, since there is always wrongdoing to be observed, recalled, or feared, there is always opportunity for the release of tensions by accusation and expiation or punishment, whether through sacrifice to the supernatural custodians of moral values and social obligations, or through denunciation of and vengeance on persons believed to be malevolent practitioners of witchcraft or sorcery.

Similarly, since there are always needs to be satisfied and doubts as to the outcome of any venture, there is always anxiety to be stilled and assurance to be gained, whether by invoking the aid of supernatural guardians of security and success, and thereby submitting to their authority and accepting the code of conduct they enforce, or by seeking magical means to harness supernatural forces that are supposed to aid men to gain their ends. Thus the desire for protection and success where technical competence is lacking or in doubt reinforces the postulation and propitiation of more powerful supernatural agents or the manipulation of hidden forces.

But while beliefs in supernatural action and in human ability to control it through prayer and sacrifice, rite, and spell have their foundations in universal features of human psychology, the forms they take, the contexts in which they are invoked, are related to the rest of the cultural pattern and to the social system. For the individual, for groups with important common interests, and for the community as a whole they are responses to the tensions and emergencies of life. Accordingly, when analysed in this sense they reveal these tensions and emergencies together with the material situations and the frustrations or conflicts of values from which they arise. Furthermore, although they may not be rational and may lack empirical foundation, they must, to persist, be mutually adjusted or apportioned to different contexts of need and activity so that they do not explicitly contradict one another. Thus, collectively, they express both the general framework of ideas concerning the relations of men to one another and to the world they know and the articulation of different spheres of action and their degree of integration. Again, the extent to which cosmological ideas and social values are integrated in an explicit system affords insight into the degree of coherences of a cultural pattern and the stability of a social system, and correspondingly into the range of the repercussions and the disintegrations that are likely to follow from sudden change in any one field of social life. That there can be inconsistencies between dogma, ethic, and action in different fields will be as apparent in these studies as is the fact that cultural totalities and social systems do not automatically maintain equilibrium. The capacity for overall adjustment may well be exceeded by the impact of new forces, and it is to be expected that changes affecting techniques or the organization of society will be reflected in the spheres of cosmology and ethics.

7

African Ideas of God[1]

E. W. Smith

This paper provides a general account of how the African ideas of God vary and how the notion of a Supreme Being has evolved from spiritism and pantheism.

For people who live in an environment where spirits are thought to be controlling most objects and events, it is not surprising that a belief in a personal God, or Gods, should be widespread.

'The high-god is sometimes identified with, or personified in, the sky or the sun, and thus has similarities with a nature god, whereas in certain regions, notably in East and South Africa, where ancestor worship is predominant, he stands in relation to the first forbear of the group. But his nature is elusive. In West Africa he is sometimes hardly distinguishable from the personal genius of man, so that each person has his own God; on the other hand the boundary-line between the Supreme Being and the impersonal power pervading the Universe is fluctuating.'[2]

Speaking in general terms, African religion is 'communal', an affair of the family, the clan, the tribe rather than of the individual.

Sociologically speaking, African religion is one element of African culture. No one element in the cultural complex can be exhaustively studied and understood in isolation from the rest. Religion permeates African life and therefore any full explication of it involves complete exploration of social and political organization, material culture, law and custom, as well as the physical environment. To dissect out one phase of religion, such as theism, may easily lead to erroneous conclusions.

Physical environment does not predetermine a man's beliefs concerning God, but it certainly colours them. The religion of the Hebrews, as delineated in the Old Testament, would have been different in some respects had it developed in a flat, arid desert rather than in a land of mountains. In Africa we may naturally expect that belief and practice

---

[1] Reprinted from *African Ideas of God*, ed. Edwin W. Smith, Edinburgh House Press, London, 1961.

[2] D. Westermann, *The African Today and Tomorrow*, pp. 91–92 (Oxford University Press, 1949 (third edition)).

assume divergent shapes in the wide open spaces and in the dense equatorial forest. Where rains are uncertain and are accompanied by terrific thunderstorms it seems natural that the people's theology should be affected thereby. The Ngombe, described by J. Davidson, are born, they live and they die in the forest; they have never seen any kind of country but forest. The dense foliage, the short field of vision, the dark recesses, the eeriness, all encourage faith in a vast number of impish spirits.

Similarly, we may expect that social organization will be reflected in religious belief and practice. Where the kingship is strong, and the king is hedged about with divinity and only to be approached through a graded hierarchy of underlings, it is natural that the Lord of the universe should be thought of as a remote chief with whom communication is possible only through intermediaries. Where the governing functions are to some degree delegated, the atmosphere is favourable to the growth of departmental gods, one having to do with war, another with fertility, and so on. Where society is matricentral, the mother having paramount influence, it is easier for the godhead to be pictured as 'mother' rather than 'father'.

In addition to considering the sociological and ecological milieu, we have tried to relate the African's theism (such as it is) to other phases of his religion.

There are, we believe, three such phases, strands, levels or categories, which may conveniently be summed up in the words: theism, spiritism and dynamism. It would be quite a mistake to suppose that Africans place on the same plane of sanctity the High God, the ancestral and other spirits, and the amulets and talismans which figure so largely in their daily life.

From the point of view of the European, and of reflective Africans, the lowest level is dynamism, which we define as the belief in, and the practices associated with the belief in, impersonal, pervasive power or energy, something akin to the Polynesian *mana*, which is likened to an electrical fluid that could charge persons and thing, and be diverted from one to another. . . .

The African acts as if he believed in elemental powers resident in, working through, persons, things, words, even thoughts and desires.

This phase has been commonly labelled 'magic' in contradistinction to religion; and when it proves impossible to draw a clear line between the two, the adjective 'magico-religious' has been brought into use. We might follow Dr Marett in confining the term 'magic' to 'the black or anti-social branch of occultism'.[1] If we retain it as synonymous with dynamism or to denote the operating 'force', we must recognize that there is good magic

[1] R. R. Marett, *Faith, Hope and Charity in Primitive Religion*, p. 146 (Clarendon Press, 1932).

and bad magic—it may be productive as well as destructive. For the elemental forces are neither good nor bad in themselves; like electricity, radium, atomic energy, they can be used for beneficent or harmful purposes according to the intention of the user. They can be drawn upon by the malice of sorcerers to work harm to their fellows. In warlocks and witches they are often believed to have a physical basis, as Dr Parsons reports of the Kono and W. T. Harris of the Mende, in a substance or organ within the operator's body which can be revealed by post-mortem examination. On the other hand, 'magic' may be protective or productive, and therefore socially approved. The trustful attitude of Africans towards their amulets and talismans, vehicles of the mysterious powers, takes on a religious flavour.

It is this 'magical' element that hinders people from recognizing dynamism as essentially religious. They revolt against the idea of associating witchcraft with religion. We have always to remember the truth, insisted upon by Professor Whitehead, that religion is not necessarily good. 'The uncritical association of religion with goodness is directly negatived by plain facts.' He reminds us of the horrors which can attend religion: human sacrifice, cannibalism, sensual orgies, abject superstition, degrading customs.[1] There is a terribly dark and repulsive side of African religion – human sacrifice associated with spiritism, witchcraft associated with dynamism. The theism is remarkably free from these horrors.

To understand a people we must understand their philosophy. The best educated people can do is to try to construct their philosophy out of what they are observed to do and to say, always seeking to overcome the obstacle of translating their thoughts into our vocabulary. . . .

While European philosophy is based upon the concept of 'being' Bantu philosophy is based upon the concept of 'force' – it is dynamic, not static. The central principle he defines as *force vitale*.[2] I hardly know how to render the French words in English; at best we can only hope to reach an approximation of the meaning an African would give the words. Shall we say vital force or essential energy? In some respects this may remind us of Bergson's conception of life as one great force, one vast vital impulse, struggling to break a way through matter. Some of us who long ago recognized the place that a mystic energy occupies in African practice and thought, and therefore wrote of their dynamism, were inclined to interpret that energy as one continuum, all-pervasive, in things and in men. Father Tempels will not allow that the Bantu can be called

[1] A. N. Whitehead, *Religion in the Making*, p. 6 (Cambridge University Press, 1926).
[2] Defined by Father Tempels.

65

'dynamists' or 'energetists' as if their world were animated by one universal force: they draw an essential distinction between various forces; they recognize individual forces. I am not convinced that he is right on this point. Beings – Father Tempels continues – are divided by Bantu logic into kinds and classes according to their potency. *Nuntu*, 'person', signifies the vital force endowed with intelligence and will; *bintu* are what we call things – in Bantu philosophy, forces not endowed with reason. Above all forces is God, who gives existence and increase to all others. After Him comes the first fathers, founders of the various clans, who form links in the chain binding God and man. These occupy a rank so high that they are no longer considered human. Next to them come the so-called 'dead' of the tribe who are other links in the chain – or, say, channels through which the vital force influences the living generation. The 'living' in their turn form a hierarchy according to their vital power. The eldest of a group or clan is the link between the ancestors and their descendants. The chief, duly appointed and installed according to traditional rules, reinforces the life of his people and all inferior forces, animal, vegetable and organic. The Ruanda people say: 'The King is the Bull that fecundates the realm.' Inferior to the human forces are those resident in animals, plants and minerals.

The Bantu would say that this philosophy rests upon internal and external evidence. They have experimental knowledge of plants as drugs: 'This plant,' they say, 'possesses such and such force,' and that force can be released, excited, directed by men and women who have special powers. The soothsayer and the doctor are persons of pre-eminent position in a tribe, by virtue of those powers. The sorcerer and the witch can evoke and direct the forces inherent in themselves or in objects to the detriment and death of their fellows. The injurious influence flowing from the destructive will of certain persons is what the Bantu call *bulozhi* (or kindred terms), 'witchcraft' – one of the three or four inexpiable crimes in their estimation. The negative aspect of this belief in vital force is what we call tabu. Certain things may not be done, certain words may not be spoken, certain thoughts may not be harboured, because they release hidden forces and their reaction is automatic: it is like touching a live wire. Father Tempels seeks to show that the Bantu ethic is based on their philosophy. Every act, attitude and custom which strikes at the vital force, or at the growth and hierarchy of the *muntu*, is bad. What is ontologically and morally good and juridically just is, on the contrary, that which maintains and increases the vital gift received from God. . . .[1]

It finds some illustration or confirmation outside the Bantu area. From

[1] Placide Tempels, *Bantu Philosophy* (Présence Africaine, 1959).

numerous 'magical' practices of the Bambara of the Mali Republic, C. Monteil was led to conclude that they believed in a kind of universal energy, diffused through nature, invisible, imponderable, active, that no obstacle could stay and that can be captured and put to use.[1] There is also the concept of *nyama* revealed by the researches of M. Griaule and Madame Germaine Dieterlen among the Dogon people who inhabit part of the Mali Republic in the bend of the Niger. These people name the Supreme Being Amman, and believe that he created the world and all things in it, and endowed men and animals with individual souls (*kikinu*); he also endowed men, animals and some inanimate things with an imperishable force, *nyama*, which the French savants translate by the same term that Father Tempels employs, *force vitale*. They define *nyama* as 'an energy *en instance*, impersonal, unconscious, distributed in all animals, vegetables, in supernatural beings, in things of nature'. After death the *kikinu* joins the ancestral spirits; the *nyama* is, on the other hand, perpetually in the world of men; in this sense it is immortal, for it is being passed on from one generation to another.[2]

What Father Tempels says of the Bantu in general may be said also of the Dogon. 'Bantu psychology cannot conceive a man as an individual existing by himself, unrelated to the animate and inanimate forces surrounding him. It is not sufficient to say he is a social being; he feels himself a vital force in actual intimate and permanent *rapport* with other forces – a vital force both influenced by and influencing them.'[3]

It is pertinent to inquire as to the relation between the African's dynamism and his theology; in other words, what connexion is there between his belief in this essential energy and his belief in God?

Some Africans – reported, as we have seen, by Father Tempels and Madame Dieterlen – hold that the energies of the universe were created by God; and some would say that he is the fount from which they flow, and that they are under his control. There is a tradition in West Africa that when God deserted the earth he left behind as his representative something called *mkissi-nsi* or *bunsi* – the energy in things. In the pharmacopœia of the Luba the most powerful 'medicine' is named *Bwanga bua Mulopo*, 'God's medicine': both for protection and for bringing good fortune there is none like it. The doctor believes that it is God himself who reveals the secret to him and instructs him how to prepare it; and he invokes God's help in its administration, saying: 'O Mulopo, I go to help

[1] C. Monteil, *Djénné*, p. 135 (Société d'Editions Géographiques, Maritimes et Coloniales, Paris, 1932).

[2] G. Dieterlen, *Les Ames des Dogons*, pp. 73 ff., 246 ff. (L'Institut d'Ethnologie: Paris, 1941).

[3] Placide Tempels, op. cit.

a man in his sickness; give strength to my medicine so that the man's sickness may depart.' While the doctor prepares a charm for the protection of a client's garden, he prays thus: 'O Mulopo, let us have success with this *bwanga*; come thyself into our *bwanga* [*ubwele mu bwanga bwetu*]; drive off the evil-doer.'[1]

J. H. Driberg declared that he had no hesitation in affirming that the religious beliefs and philosophy of the African are fixed primarily on the concept of a universal Power or Energy, which informs and is the cause of all life. 'This spiritual force consists of an abstract Power or natural potency, all-pervasive and definitely never regarded anthropomorphically.' He complained that the tribal term used to designate this Power has often been translated 'God' and that 'God' in contrast with lesser deifications and with ancestors has been arrogated to the position of a 'High God', a supreme Creator and organizer of the world, comparable to the Hebraic or Christian conception; and he roundly asserted: 'In point of fact the "High God" idea does not exist in Africa.'[2] It may be granted that the godhead is generally conceived in terms of power. The praise-titles, or epithets, testify that God is believed to be all-powerful, omnipresent, eternal – attributes which might be ascribed to Cosmic Mana. It may be, though this cannot be proved, that Africans have personalized an original concept of an abstract Power or natural potency. . . .[3]

The criteria[4] of a High God as distinct from Cosmic Mana we take to include the following:

1. He has personality, is in sharp distinction from everyone and everything else. He has a personal name.

2. He has a life and consciousness analogous to that of man. In the tales that are told of him he speaks and acts like a man. In the myths he is often given a wife and children. Although no images are made of him, he is anthropomorphic.

3. He is a Being who is not human, and never in the recollection of

[1] R. Van Caeneghem, 'Gebeden der Baluba', *Aequatoria*, No. 1. 1947.

[2] J. H. Driberg, 'The secular aspect of ancestor worship in Africa', *Supplement to the Journal of the Royal African Society*, vol. xxxv. No. 138, January 1936.

[3] The development of the idea of God in Africa may have followed the same course as that of the Aryans. According to H. J. Rose, in the oldest evidence Jupiter was not more than sky-mana: a numen, pure and simple, i.e. a manifestation of mana, no object of adoration or appeal, but a factor in magical ceremonials. In the later literature Zeus is a mighty lord of the heavens, of most definite personality, an upholder of righteousness. The many statements that Zeus thunders, sends rain and so forth, do not invalidate this. ('The Wiro Sun-God', *Essays Presented to R. R. Marett*.)

[4] I may be allowed to say that these criteria were outlined in the course of discussion with Mr Driberg and he agreed with them.

men was human. This rules out such divinities as the Nilotic Nyikang.

4. He is Creator, or Fashioner or Constructor, if not directly of all things, at least of some.

5. He is the ultimate power and authority behind the world and all life.

6. He is worshipped, i.e. men offer prayers and sacrifices to him, rarely though this may be.

7. He is regarded as Judge, or at least as being in an ethical relationship with mankind.

On the other hand, the High God may be regarded as tribal or national; and may not be alone, but have co-equals or subordinates: that is to say, he may not be the God of a strict monotheism.

These criteria, as readers may apply them to the deities described in following chapters, lead me to the judgement that we have to do with a High God and not with 'an abstract Power or natural potency', Cosmic Mana.

It would seem that in general Africans are not conscious of any direct relation between their theism and the ethic of dynamism – all that we mean by tabu. An oath may be taken in the name of the High God. 'If I have done this of which I am accused may God himself fall and kill me by lightning!' a Lamba will say. This might be interpreted, 'Let Mana fall in the thunderbolt or electrical discharge!' but the oaths are taken in the name of Syakapanga, a personal epithet of the Supreme Being. God, say the Lamba, is angered when people sin deeply and he punishes by sending leprosy and smallpox.[1] It is a Personality who acts thus. But in other matters the hidden forces often seem to act independently of him. Heinous crimes like kin-murder are beyond human vengeance, but the criminal does not escape. It is not the chief who pronounces judgement on him; the ancestral spirits do not punish him. There is Something else, anyonymous, relentless, inescapable, that dooms him to certain and terrible death – a curse (the Ila call it *chikuto*) is upon him: he will go mad, or be driven to suicide, or be drowned, or be slain by a wild beast. . . .

By spiritism I mean the belief in, and the practices associated with the belief in, beings who are either (*a*) free nature spirits who never were human, or (*b*) discarnate human spirits.

The nature spirits are perhaps for the most part personifications of natural phenomena. Side by side with the High God, whose dwelling is the sky, many Africans place Mother Earth, a goddess who personifies, or symbolizes, the fertility of the soil. Others imagine trees and rivers,

[1] C. M. Doke, *The Lambas of Northern Rhodesia*, p. 228 (Harrap, 1931).

69

mountains and lakes, to be the resort or abode of spirits. On a lower level are hobgoblins like the *Sasabonsam* of the Ashanti; and the bogies that frighten children into good behaviour. In their cosmology the Bantu appear to give a lesser place than the Sudanic Negroes to these nature spirits. The spirits of the Bantu are mostly those of human beings who continue to live in the unseen world. These may take abode in trees or mountains or waterfalls or rivers; they may assume the form of snakes or other animals; some of them may be elevated to the status of demi-gods, as in the instance of Kibuka and Mukasa, the war-leaders (mentioned by H. B. Thomas in his chapter on Uganda). It may even be that fuller research would prove that here or there some ancient hero had been elevated to the status of a High God. As in the case of nature spirits it is extremely difficult to draw a hard and fast line between discarnate spirits and gods, between spiritism and polytheism.

The extremely important part that these discarnate human spirits play in African life is based upon a belief that the human personality survives the death and decay of the body. It is not so much a 'soul' that lives on – I would avoid use of the phrase 'immortality of the soul' – as the person. One who leaves his body in the grave and lives in invisible form is called by the Ila a *musangushi*, 'a changed, transformed, human'; changed, not so much in character as in status and in power. It is an essential element in African belief that 'living' and dead' live in symbiosis, interdependent, capable of communicating one with the other. No iron curtain separates them. There are recognized methods of ascertaining the will of denizens of the unseen world, of securing their help, of appeasing them when, as often happens, they are provoked to anger. Where the belief in reincarnation prevails, there is thought to be a constant going and coming between the two worlds; and where there is no such belief there is recognition that 'living' and 'dead' are linked in an indissoluble network by their *force vitale, nyama* or what not.

The *mizimu*, spirits of the departed, Rosemary Guillebaud writes in her chapter, 'have no power except over their own families, and this power when exercised is always for evil'. She goes on to tell of prayers in which the grandfather is besought to give peace and happiness in the home, in the herds and in the fields, thus demonstrating that, in the belief of the Urundi people, the *mizimu* are at least potentially beneficent. This may be said of Africans in general. There is one class of disembodied spirits which is an exception to this rule – the *revenants*, those whose death and burial were abnormal, who go into the other world, disgruntled, resentful and carrying their malice with them. They are commonly not named *mizimu*, but have a name of their own which inspires unmitigated fear. So Africans believe, as Archbishop William Temple[1] did, in evil spirits, and attribute much of human ill to their agency. But, on the other hand, their well-being is to no small degree dependent upon the good-will and activity of the good invisible members of the community – the *mizimu* – who, more-over, are the guardians of traditional morality.

Europeans have noted an apparent lack of reverence in ritual approach to the *mizimu*. Allowance has to be made for what W. C. Willoughby calls 'peculiarities of Bantu dialectics'.[2] Africans do not consider it unseemly to scold even their quasi-divine chiefs who have powers of life and death over them. The Matebele warriors, for example, on returning from a foray were wont to address Lobengula, who might with a nod condemn them to instant death, in these terms: 'Are we not your dogs who fight for you? And now you starve us! Give us beef, you niggard, that we may eat and be strong!'[3] The chief took such a scolding from his well-fed braves as the highest of compliments. . . .

Dr H. A. Junod quotes this example in a prayer offered by an uncle on behalf of his nephew: 'You are useless, you gods! You only give us trouble! For although we give you offerings you do not listen to us! You so-and-so are full of hatred! You do not enrich us! . . .' All this goes to show that the *mizimu* are human.

The term 'ancestor-worship' applied to this cult, as Cullen Young says in dealing with the people of Nyasaland, is 'a highly misleading term'. J. H. Driberg is of the same opinion. 'What we have mistaken for a religious attitude is nothing more than a projection of [the African's] social be-haviour.' The attitude is a purely secular one. The application of words such as 'worship', 'sacrifice', 'prayer', which have a highly specialized significance in English, to the Africans' ancestral system, 'is both a linguistic and a cultural offence'.

For no African prays to his dead grandfather any more than he 'prays' to his living father. In both cases the words employed are the same: he asks as of right, or he beseeches, or he expostulates with, or he reprimands, or (as the Eastern Ewe word *epode* puts it) he gives an address to, his ancestors,

[1] William Temple, *Nature, Man and God*, p. 503 (Macmillan, 1935). 'Shelve the responsibility for human evil on to Satan if you will; personally I believe he exists and that a large share of that responsibility belongs to him and to subordinate evil spirits.'
[2] W. C. Willoughby, *The Soul of the Bantu*, p. 84 (S.C.M., 1928). 'To rate the seemingly irreverent expressions of Bantu ancestor-worshippers at their true worth. the peculiarities of Bantu dialectics must be taken into account, and then it will be manifest that a worshipper addresses a discarnate spirit in much the same terms that he would use if he were speaking to the same person in the flesh.'
[3] J. P. R. Wallis (Ed.), *The Northern Goldfields, Diaries of Thomas Baines*, vol. ii, p. 332 (Chatto & Windus, 1946).

as he would do to the elders sitting in conclave: but he never uses in this context the words for 'prayer' and 'worship' which are strictly reserved for his religious dealings with the Absolute Power and the divinities. The Latin word *pietas* probably best describes the attitude of Africans to their dead ancestors, as to their living elders.[1] . . .

To many people this ancestral cult appears to be gross superstition. That imperfect men should be elevated to a position only inferior to that of the Supreme Being, that (in some cases) a man should actually, for all practical purposes, take the place of God in the minds of his descendants, what is this but idolatry, a dis-enthronement of the Almighty? Yet we must recognize that the cult answers to what lies deep in human nature – the desire for survival, the refusal to acknowledge that death ends all. . . .

If I interpret African thought aright – a very difficult thing to do – this twofold truth is latent in it. At times the impression is gained that God appears to the African as the complete Other, the absolute sovereign, external to his own creation, so far remote in his solitary glory as to be unapproachable save through intermediaries; but at other times he is thought to be immanent in man. His immanence is expressed symbolically in stories such as those of the Balozi about how Nyambe, while he still was living among men on earth, married several wives and by them begat children who became the nations which differ in appearance, language and custom. It is their belief that the pure Balozi descend from one wife and all the royal family from another.[2] In his book *The Akan Doctrine of God*, Dr Danquah is interpreting aright not only their conceptions but those of many other Africans when he says:

> Akan knowledge of God [Nyame] teaches that He is the Great Ancestor. He is a true high God and manlike ancestor of the first man. As such ancestor He deserves to be worshipped, and is worshipped in the visible ancestral head, the good chief of the community. . . . All ancestors who are honoured as such are in the line of the Great Ancestor. . . . Life, human life, is one continuous blood, from the originating blood of the Great Source of that blood.[3]

In our search for the African idea of God we may proceed by way of elimination.

The African's fundamental needs are not merely physical. His body craves for food, for sexual satisfaction; but he also has what Dr Linton calls 'psychic needs'.[4] He wants an emotional response from his fellows.

[1] J. H. Driberg, op. cit.

[2] Compare this with Luke iii. 38: '. . . the son of Seth, the son of Adam, the son of God.'

[3] J. B. Danquah, op. cit., p. 27.

[4] Ralph Linton, *The Cultural Background of Personality*, p. 4 (Routledge and Kegan Paul, 1947).

He wants to feel safe in this uncertain and hostile world. His desire is to be invulnerable. He lives in an organized community – a society which is a significant unit in the struggle for survival. He cannot outlive the hazards of infancy or satisfy the needs of maturity without collaboration with others, the visible and invisible members of his group. Society can survive only as individuals reproduce themselves in new members who shall carry on its traditions – that culture which is its way of life. To meet all these clamant needs, physical and psychical, he seeks power.

> This craving for power [as Dr Westermann says] is the driving force in the life of African religion. It has its origin, not in logical reflection, but in a feeling of incapacity and in an obstinate desire to overcome it; it is a search for help and comfort, a means of maintaining and strengthening life in the midst of a thousand dangers, and a way of conquering the fear which shoots its arrows from every hidden ambush. Man is weak, and what he needs is increased strength. . . . The absorbing question for him is how to acquire some of this power so that it may serve for his own salvation or that of the group for which he is responsible.[1]

Many of his individual needs are, the African believes, to some degree satisfied by his dynamism and spiritism. Amulets and talismans, vehicles of metaphysical energy, provide protection and good fortune in many directions and produce confidence in times of crisis. His confidence can never, however, be complete, for he never knows whether some malicious person will not get possession of more potent 'medicines' than his. When he joins in communal activities – such as hunting, fighting, iron-smelting – dynamism plays, he believes, an indispensable role in securing skill, courage and a happy issue. There is individual as well as communal approach to the revered ancestors, particularly to those of two previous generations and the more remote progenitor, and this communion lends sanctity to tribal custom, and is at once an assertion and a stimulant of that unity in which there is strength. The acid test of religion, says Robert H. Lowie, 'is man's behaviour in a crisis. What he does when stirred to the depths of his being, when he is racked with pain, when his crops fail . . . that constitutes his religion.'[2] In face of such contingencies, the African finds help in his faith in the hidden forces and in personal ancestral spirits. . . .

That is where God comes in. He is the ultimate Controller of natural forces and of human destiny. 'The destiny Onyame has assigned to you cannot be avoided,' say the Akan. 'God has snapped off his pumpkin' is the Ila homely way of describing death. He reigns in the cosmical sphere.

[1] D. Westermann, *Africa and Christianity*, p. 84 (Oxford University Press, 1937).
[2] R. H. Lowie, *An Introduction to Cultural Anthropology*, p. 304 (London: Harrap, 1934; New York: Rinehart and Company, Inc.).

Value Systems

Europeans commonly speak of certain functionaries as 'rain-makers';
and these play their part in the ritual, but not the most famous of them
would claim to make rain: it is God who sends or withholds this most
essential element. A childless woman will try the doctor's 'medicines';
if they fail she will pray for offspring to her family divinities; and if they
fail she will ask God to give her the desire of her heart. In short, God is the
last resort when all other helpers fail.

8

The Notion of Fate in West Africa[1]

Meyer Fortes

This is an interesting excerpt from Meyer Fortes' account of how the concept of fortune can find a place, beside its complement justice, in the African conceptual scheme. Here again it will be noticed that even luck itself has to be explained, nothing 'just happens' – for once this came to be accepted, the inner wall of security might crumble before the threatening external environment of aboriginal life.

The notion of Fate or Destiny as an innate, though not necessarily impersonal determinant of an individual's life-history, and its complementary, the notion of Justice as the actions of a personified and deified agency responding to the individual's moral conduct and to his moral relationships with supernatural powers, can and do occur in a single religious system. Both seem to be present in some form in the theistic Western and Oriental religions. It is the more interesting and instructive to find that both occur in the non-scriptural religious systems of many West African peoples. Indeed one of the characteristic marks of West African religions, as compared with other African religions (i.e. East and South African Bantu religions) in which ancestor-worship also plays a part, is the occurrence of the notion of Fate in them. What I wish to explore, with our paradigms to guide the inquiry, is how the two ideas are related in a West African religious system known to me at first hand.

But first let us take a few descriptive examples from other parts of West Africa. The Yoruba of Nigeria, Dr Bascom tells us, associate a person's 'luck' with his 'destiny'. Luck is connected with the head and derives from one's 'creator' or spirit guardian. One man may work hard yet remain poor. This is because his luck is bad. Another man may work little yet get rich because his luck is good. Bad luck affects not only its owner but also those with whom he associates. As to Destiny, it is best to quote Dr Bascom's own words:

[1] Reprinted from *Oedipus and Job in West Africa*, Cambridge University Press, 1959.

75

A person's luck and his success in economic and other affairs is also a matter of destiny (*ayanmope, ananmo*) or fate (*iwa*) which is also known as 'to kneel and choose' (*akunleyan*). Before a child is born its soul is said to kneel before the deity (*Olodumare*) and choose ('*yan*) its fate on earth. Those who humbly make reasonable requests for food, money or children receive what they ask during their life on earth. However, those who make their requests as if they had the right to expect whatever they wanted, do not receive them. . . . A person whose destiny on earth is poverty may be able to acquire some money by working hard, but he will never have very much. Diviners of various kinds . . . are consulted to find out what is in store for the future and what can be done to avert evil or ensure a favourable outcome . . . but while the diviners may be able to recommend sacrifices (*ebo*) which will influence events in the immediate future, they cannot alter the course of one's life or change his destiny.

Similar beliefs are held by the closely related people of Benin. We learn that before he is born a person tells the Creator what he plans to do with his life and asks for the means to accomplish this. If he is unsuccessful he is said to be 'fighting against the fate which he has determined for himself'. Luck is associated with the head, so that a person is said to have 'a good head' or a 'bad head' according as he has been fortunate or not in his life, and he makes offerings to his head when he has a piece of good fortune.

These notions also form the core of the rich and complex cosmology and religious system of the Dahomeans, portrayed by Professor Herskovits. Dahomean religion comprises three major categories of beliefs, mythology and associated cults; the worship of the ancestors, the worship of the great public deities, and the cult of personal gods and forces. These three categories are linked together by a 'complex and highly specialized system of divination' which is constantly resorted to for fatidical guidance and ritual advice. This system of divination is under the aegis of the cult of Fa, 'the destiny of the Universe as willed by the gods', as Professor Herskovits interprets it. But Fa is also a personal Destiny whose worship, as might be expected in a society with so highly developed a patrilineal descent organization, is restricted to men. What is significant is that a man does not acquire his full Destiny until he is mature. As a boy, his father, after consulting a diviner, endows him with his partial Destiny symbolized in some palm-kernels which form the nucleus of a small shrine, and in specific food, clothing and other avoidances ascertained by the diviner. The incentive for a man to acquire his full Destiny is a series of misfortunes such as illness, the death of children or the barrenness of a wife. Women have only a partial Fa, as they are deemed to share the destiny of their fathers or husbands, since they are dependent on them in the same way as children are.

'What is in store for a man', says Professor Herskovits, 'is foreordained.' Yet there is a way out through the 'divine trickster' Legba, the 'personification of Accident'. Legba is the messenger and spokesman of the gods and if he is properly propitiated he can divert predestined misfortunes. 'In this world ruled by Destiny', Professor Herskovits explains, 'man lives secure in the conviction that between the inexorable fate laid down for an individual and the execution of that fate lies the possibility of the way out. . . .' There is also a 'way out' through the doctrine of the four souls. A man who reaches maturity achieves fulfilment of his life through his wives and children, his slaves and his entire household. His Destiny includes theirs, and this collective Destiny is watched over by his fourth soul. This is conceived as a kind of heavenly counterpart guarding an array of containers in which are stored good things like riches, health and children, and bad things like poverty, illness and death. The setting up of a man's full Destiny as a cult object is a ceremony for persuading this soul to select the good things of life for the individual.

To cap it all there is the notion of Da, or luck, symbolized for the individual in the umbilicus and in cosmological terms by the snake and the rainbow. Da lies behind the vagaries of chance seen in particular incidents of good and ill luck. He pursues only men who have power and authority, such as heads of households or villages or kingdoms; and he manifests himself to them in the form of unexpected misfortunes which happen just when things are going particularly well. Hence he is regarded with apprehension. If he is neglected he becomes resentful and dangerous. A man learns through dreams or through a diviner that his Da desires to be established. If he is wise he establishes the Da in his house and worships it. This strengthens his luck and protects him against attacks from the Da of other men.

Brief as is this summary of Dahomean beliefs concerning Fate and Destiny, it can be seen that they bear comparison with those of the Greeks. The Dahomeans also have an elaborate Pantheon of sky and earth gods headed by a creator divinity which is both male and female and a complex ancestral cult correlated with descent groups, local communities and political units. The ancestors of a descent group are collectively enshrined and worshipped in a room specially set aside for this purpose. They are, as Professor Herskovits notes, the focal point of the descent-group organization. Appeal is made to them through sacrifice and prayer to watch over the health and safety of any member of the group who is in hazard, and great ceremonial celebrations are held at set times, such as the harvest, to honour them. In very broad terms, therefore, their supernatural powers are called upon to safeguard the numbers and well-being of the descent group, whereas Destiny is involved in the play of chance in the individual's life history.

The Yoruba, Bini and Dahomeans are closely related in culture. All have a complex system of ancestor-worship and a cult of gods or deified beings, together with the notion of Destiny. I have dwelt on their beliefs because they are characteristic of West Africa and the ethnographic data are so good. Similar patterns of cult and belief occur among other West African peoples, including some with no obvious linguistic or cultural links with the Yoruba. The Tallensi, whose social and religious institutions I have studied in the field, are typical of one such non-Yoruba cluster. I turn to them with a particular aim in mind. Generalized ethnographic descriptions have one serious defect. They do not enable us to see how ritual or belief is actually used by men and women to regulate their lives. A Tale friend once remarked to me, as he was going home from the funeral of a clan brother, 'Now that we have done the proper ritual our grief is soothed.' Another pointed out to me that when you consult a diviner you have the immediate relief of knowing what supernatural agency is causing your troubles and what ritual steps to take. It is only by considering it, in Malinowski's words, as 'a mode of action as well as a system of belief, a sociological phenomenon as well as a personal experience' that the living meaning of ritual and belief becomes apparent. For this we must see religious ideas and rites in the context of the situation, the context of personal history and the context of social relationships.

9

The Logic of Witchcraft[1]

Max Gluckman

'The belief in a latent, non-moral potency resident in men, gods and nature is the strongest, most general and most influential postulate which the old Africa applies to the business of daily living. It is also one of the last, if not the very last, to be discarded.'[2]

Magic takes various forms. There is homeopathic magic, thus termed because it is based on the principle that like produces like; contagious magic, whereby attributes may be passed on merely by contact; and personal and public magic.

Certain forms of magic are evil rather than good, the so-called 'black' magic, and there are two kinds of people who are concerned with its practice. One is the sorcerer, whose evildoing is conscious, and who performs his rites either to harm his enemies or to harm the enemies of others who pay him for the service. They are believed, especially in East and Southern Africa, to be able to use other men as their agents, and may even raise the dead for their evil purposes.[3] The other form of purveyor of black magic is the witch. 'They have no palpable apparatus of their trade, and their activities may properly be described as spiritual. They are secret agents and are not consulted by men anxious to harm their enemies as sorcerers are consulted.'[4]

Of these forms the witches are more greatly feared because they are thought to inherit their wickedness; they are also unconscious in their 'sinning' and usually operate secretly, stealthily and at night. To counteract their evil propensities is the function of the witch doctor.

In the year 1831 Nathaniel Isaacs, a young member of the first party of English traders to settle among the Zulu of Natal, made the following entry in his diary: 'A body of people in the neighbourhood came to us with pensive looks and complaining in a pitiful strain that sickness had invaded their families. They seemed to think it singular that they alone should be sick while all the people around them were enjoying good health.

[1] Reprinted from *Custom and Conflict in Africa*, Blackwell, 1955.

[2] G. Kimble, *Tropical Africa*, II, p. 25.

[3] The interested reader is advised to consult E. G. Parrinder, *African Traditional Religion*, Hutchinson's Univ. Library, 1954.

[4] Parrinder, op. cit., p. 123,

They had been to the inyanger or doctor, who told them there was an Umturgatie (or witch) who occasioned their sickness, and that the doctor wanted a cow before he would point him out.' Isaacs went on to say: 'I could perceive their sickness had arisen from eating green corn, but told them I had no objection to give the cow, provided it would discover the object which caused such superstitious notions to affect them, or if it would recover the sick. They assured me it would, and I was induced to promise them a cow.'

Thus it was early observed that the belief in witchcraft involved the idea that Africans thought it 'singular that they alone should be sick while all the people around them were enjoying good health'. In this observation lay an important clue to understanding the system of beliefs in witchcraft and magic. Another clue was the observation, made by many administrators and missionaries, that men accused their personal enemies of bewitching them: wherefore, said these observers, the charges of witchcraft were obviously fraudulent. This alleged fraudulence is exhibited in the standard picture of the witch-doctor, the old woman Gagool in Rider Haggard's novel, *King Solomon's Mines*.

Indeed, it wasn't until a hundred years after Isaac's diary was published that these separate clues were brought together by Professor Evans-Pritchard to explain the logic, the intellectual coherence, of witchcraft beliefs in their relation to natural events and to society. He did this in his analysis of Witchcraft, Magic and Oracles among the Azande of the Anglo-Egyptian Sudan. Subsequent research in other African tribes has confirmed this analysis entirely.

Clearly from Isaac's words, the belief in witchcraft explains not how a misfortune occurred, but why a particular person suffered that misfortune. It is said to be due to the powers of witchcraft possessed by someone who wished him harm – that is, a personal enemy. Bad feeling sets the power of witchcraft to work. But bad feeling does so in only certain kinds of relationship, and not in all relationships. Indeed, custom may exclude accusations of witchcraft from those relationships where difficulties and friction are greatest, as between a father and his son. For it is not believed that a father's feelings against a disobedient son set witchcraft to work. Evans-Pritchard laid the foundations for our understanding of the logic of witchcraft, and he pioneered our analysis of the more complex problem of why accusations of witchcraft arise in each tribe in some types of social relationships, and not in others.

I shall attempt to pursue these complex problems of who accuses whom of witchcraft in several tribes. Witchcraft fears and accusations breed quarrels between people: I want to explain how far they disrupt relationships between those people, and how far they lead to readjustments in social ties within a wider social order.

Young Nathaniel Isaacs noted that the Zulu 'seemed to think it singular that they alone should be sick while all the people around them were enjoying good health' – hence they thought a witch was at work. And if he had argued with them, as he noted in his diary, that their sickness was due to eating green corn, they would probably have replied: 'But these other people have also eaten green corn, and look, they are not sick.' Witchcraft as a theory of causation does not deny that men fall ill from eating certain foods, but it explains why some of them fall ill at some times and not at other times. What it is that belief in witchcraft explains emerges more clearly from what we call an accident. I knew a Zulu whose son was bitten by a snake and died. He said that his son had been killed by witchcraft. This did not mean that he didn't see that his son had been bitten by a snake, or that he didn't know that some snakes are poisonous while others are not, and that the bite of a poisonous snake may be fatal. When he said that his son was killed by witchcraft, he meant that a witch caused the snake to bite his son so that the son died.

For every misfortune, like every piece of good fortune, involves two questions: the first is 'how' did it occur, and the second is 'why' it occurred at all. The 'how' is answered by common sense empirical observation: the son died because he was bitten by a poisonous snake. But this does not explain why that son was bitten by that snake and at that time and place, and not by another snake at another time and place; or indeed why that man was bitten and not some other man altogether. Beliefs in witchcraft explain why particular persons at particular times and places suffer particular misfortunes – accident, disease, and so forth. Witchcraft as a theory of causation is concerned with the singularity of misfortune.

Other cultures give different kinds of answers to this metaphysical problem, why certain events happen to certain people at certain times and places. There are the will of God or of gods, Kismet, Karma, Fate, Providence, the action of ancestral spirits. African tribes also employ some of these other answers to varying degrees. The agnostic scientist may call it 'chance', the intersection of two chains of events in space-time: a boy taking the cattle to water, trod on a snake sunning itself in the path.

Hence the belief in witchcraft does not of itself exclude a considerable amount of what we can rightly call empirical observation and reasoning about 'how' events occur. Indeed, the beliefs clearly involve this kind of reasoning. Because a witch cannot just harm people: he (or often she) harms them by using disease and crop-blight, by making elephants charge them or lions eat them or snakes bite them, by causing them when climbing a tree after a beehive to stand on branches which are rotten at their heart. No people could survive without an extensive technical knowledge. Their witchcraft beliefs operate inside this technical knowledge. To some extent, it is even possible for scientific understanding of the 'how' of a misfortune to increase, without disposing of the 'why' of the misfortune – that it was caused by witchcraft.

Thus witchcraft as a theory of causation does not explain the whole of any misfortune. Every misfortune has its empirical side. And certain unfortunate events are clearly due to a man's own weaknesses. Thus if a man fails to exhibit proper technical skill in hunting, agriculture, or pot-making, he cannot expect his fellows to agree with him if he blames on witchcraft the startled game, a poor crop, or a pot cracked in firing. Similarly, if he lapses morally he cannot say that witchcraft made him sin. For witchcraft does not make a man lie, or steal, or commit adultery. A man must accept responsibility for his wrongdoings. Hence if a Zande murdered a fellow-tribesman with his spear he was tried in court by his chief and was convicted by evidence. He could not plead in defence that witchcraft made him commit murder. The situation was quite different when a man was killed by an enemy of a foreign tribe in battle. The enemy lived outside the control of the tribe, and he could not be arrested and tried. But by the Zande code the dead warrior's kin had to take vengeance for his death, and this was blamed on witchcraft within the tribe; witchcraft caused one man and not another man to be slain by a particular enemy in this battle. The witch was the internal murderer, from whom compensation could be demanded.

I have been describing how the belief in witchcraft as a theory of causation works, without mentioning the nature of the witch. For this is how the belief works in practice. Men suffer misfortunes and then believe that they have been attacked by a witch. In theory, of course, the witch has set his evil power to work and this has caused the misfortune. The Azande believe that witchcraft is a substance in the stomach whose soul goes out at night and harms others. Anyone may have this substance in his stomach, but not everyone sets it to work. If a man is upright – of sound principle, charitable, even-tempered, tolerant, generous – he will not set witchcraft to work even if he has it in his stomach. The Azande say it remains 'cool'. But if a man is quarrelsome, spiteful, bad-tempered, greedy, over-ambitious, his witchcraft will get 'hot' and go out at night to harm those against whom he bears grudges. Thus witchcraft as a theory of causation embraces a theory of morals, for it says that witches are wicked people. It is their wicked feelings which cause their witchcraft to do harm. Azande say: 'Jealousy comes first and witchcraft follows after'. The ethics of witchcraft thus disapprove of the common anti-social vices and approve of the virtues of many societies.

That the use of witchcraft is immoral is shown in the whole set of beliefs. Generally, African doctrine is not always altogether clear how far a witch is aware of what he is doing: ideas here vary from tribe to tribe. Mostly, the answer is that a person does not know what he is about when he begins killing; but after several crimes he realizes what is happening. But the doctrine is clear that unless a man has vicious feelings his witchcraft powers will do no harm. It is the use of witchcraft, and not its mere possession, which is immoral. The ethical wrongdoing involved is clearly exhibited by the sorcerers whom Evans-Pritchard contrasts with witches. A sorcerer is a man who has not witchcraft in his stomach, so that to harm others he has deliberately to take the wicked decision to use magical substances, rites, and spells against a fellow. Thus Zulus say that if you put a certain substance in a porcupine quill and stab an enemy's footprints you will afflict him with illness. It is important that among the Zulu, as in many other tribes, it is believed that men make this deliberate choice to do evil in these ways, while women are believed to be witches, who are possessed of innate evil power.

Any misfortune may be ascribed to this ill will of a witch, but if the trouble is slight Azande merely dismiss it as 'witchcraft', much as we might say 'bad luck'. The actual witch who is responsible is sought only if he has to be induced to remove a disease he is causing, or if he has caused a death – or rather, he used to be sought after a death, because this kind of witch-hunt has been banned by European governments. Few methods of seeking witches involve direct naming of the guilty person. More usually the sufferer puts the names of his personal enemies to the diviner or apparatus, in order to select from among them that enemy who has the power of witchcraft and who has used this power to cause the misfortune under investigation. The most important Zande technique consists in giving a substance, prepared with special taboos, to chickens while asking questions. Each question is framed to allow of a 'yes' or 'no' answer to the problem, thus: 'if X is the witch who is making my son ill, poison-oracle, kill the chicken; if X is not the witch, poison-oracle, spare the chicken.' The substance is a strychnine poison so that the chicken will either be killed or will vomit it; and its operation cannot be controlled by the amount which is given to the chicken. Eventually the oracle is likely to say 'yes' to some enemy's name. Other techniques of divination work similarly.

It is clearly absurd to say that the detection of personal enemies as

83

witches is fraudulent, because obviously it is reasonable that the witch who harms a man should be at odds with him. This is contained in the beliefs about witches themselves. The consultant in fact believes that all the persons whose names he submits to the oracle want to harm him: he wants to know which of them is working maleficently against him at the moment. In short, Evans-Pritchard clarified for us that the belief in witchcraft explains the 'why' of misfortune, and, through techniques of divination, he related this 'why' to personal animosities which cause men to wish others harm.

If the consultation is about an illness, the guilty witch has to be approached in certain customary ways to withdraw his witchcraft, and this he does with equal formality. If he reacts to the charge with anger, it is proof of his guilt and of his continued ill will. But if the witch is sought because he caused a death, the chief's oracle must confirm the verdict before he can be punished or required to pay compensation. In Central and South Africa he was required at the chief's orders to drink the oracle-poison himself. If he vomited it, he was declared innocent; if it stupefied him, he was guilty and might be killed. This ordeal had at least the merit that it was not death which proved innocence.

It is reasonable that the man who harms you should be your enemy. Or at least you should feel that he is your enemy. For clearly the selection of a witch is guided by a man's own view of his personal relations, by his own grudges, ambitions, and similar sentiments. But his accusations also have to appear reasonable before a general public, which may well debate the situation in advance. For Africans themselves appreciate what is implied in the processes by which witchcraft accusations are made. A Barotse king declared that they were 'lies fostered by hate and envy'. I heard one of his councillors reprimand villagers who had accused an aged female relative of killing them. He said: 'You are ungrateful. She cared for you when she was young; now she is old and you have to look after her, you hate her. Let me hear no more of this.' Again, in Zululand I lived with an important and wealthy governor of a district. Cheek by jowl with his homestead was the homestead of a cousin, descended from the same grandfather. One of the cousin's wives died after a long and painful illness. After brooding on it for a while, the widower burst out with an accusation that the governor, who, he said, had always hated him, had killed her by sorcery. The whole district was upset by the quarrel. I discussed the case with an old diviner, who himself hunted sorcerers and witches. Yet fully aware of what the psychologists call projection, he concluded: 'Obviously the accusation is absurd. Why should the governor hate his cousin? The governor possesses political power and has inherited the main family herd. The cousin thinks the govenor hates him, because he hates the governor.' So that Africans know that often a man accuses not someone who hates him or who is envious of him, but someone whom he hates or envies. They may stress this when they themselves are accused or, if for any reason they side with another alleged witch; but they forget it when they make an accusation. In this partiality they are not unique among mankind.

Anthropologists working in Southern and Central Africa have explored more fully the problem of why persons related in some ways to the sufferer are accused, while persons related to him in other ways are not accused.

To answer these problems, we have to look at accusations of witchcraft in several different ways. First, the belief in witchcraft as the cause of some misfortune is part of the African answer to the general problem of why misfortune and evil exist in the world. The belief states that if men feel immoral sentiments against others they may cause harm to these others. Natural events and the morality of social relations are, so to speak, involved in one another. For the argument is that bad feeling between some sort of people affects wild animals, the growth of crops, human health, and so forth. Society and its members and its natural environment form a single system of relations which are morally interdependent. Nothing happens by chance. Good fortune is due to harmony in particular social relationships; and disharmony in those social relationships leads to misfortune. A Yao hated his relative when he should have loved him. The relative went travelling and was sleeping against a wall with two men lying beside him; a lion stepped over the outside two and took his victim from against the wall. Hatred where it should not have existed led to death, for clearly witchcraft was at work. We do not, openly at least, believe in this involvement of social relations with natural events. The contrast between our views and those of Africans emerges graphically if we consider legal responsibility. In our society, you can sue a man for injury only if he has harmed you in some overt and observable manner; in a society which believes in witchcraft, every misfortune potentially founds a case against another for harming you.

Witchcraft beliefs are not unique in affirming this close relationship between the moral interaction of people, and what happens in the way of good and ill fortune. Ancestral cults embody similar ideas; but here the ancestral spirits punish people for not making due offerings to the spirits themselves, or for not observing their obligations to their kinsfolk. Witchcraft attacks the virtuous, ancestors attack the wicked. To be prosperous men must make sacrifices to their spirits, and they can only do this when they are in friendship with other members of the congregation. Otherwise the offering is spoilt. Sacrifices are the appropriate occasions for venting grievances: men must cleanse their hearts. An Anglican anthem similarly demands: 'See that ye love one another fervently.' But beliefs in the malice of witchcraft and in the wrath of ancestral spirits do more than ask this as an act of grace; they affirm that if you do not love one another fervently misfortune will come. Bad feeling is charged with mystical danger; virtue in itself produces order throughout the universe. Though a charge of witchcraft for causing a misfortune may exaggerate and exacerbate a quarrel, the belief emphasizes the threat to the wider social order which is contained in immoral sentiments. Hence the beliefs exert some pressure on men and women to observe the social virtues, and to feel the right sentiments, lest they be suspected of being witches. The beliefs act as a sanction against anti-social behaviour by supporting the social virtues. Thus the beliefs support the moral order of the community, over and above particular quarrels. Anger and hate are not only bad and sinful, as among ourselves, but they carry in them the mystical threat of disaster to others or to oneself. In religious beliefs virtues and values are clearly lifted out of this workaday world and placed on a spiritual plane where they are beyond question. Witchcraft beliefs by contrast invest wicked feelings with threats which they themselves do not contain, but which are charged with additional power.

African economic and political systems are limited so that ambitious men cannot create new enterprises nor seek for prestige in several different spheres. As a man grows up he comes into competition with his fellows for political position, and above all into competition with his own kinsmen for position and property. Hence it is not surprising to find that headmen of villages and men who gained political power are believed by many to do so by witchcraft. When a Yao headman in Nyasaland is installed his taste for human meat is tested in the installation ceremony: because Yao witches eat the corpses of those they kill.

I am trying to emphasize a general situation which contrasts strongly with the kind of society which we know, which developed after the industrial revolution and which itself saw the official end to witchcraft charges. Since then we have lived in our families and had relations of a sentimental kind with our kin and friends, but we have not been dependent on them for most of our needs. Economic, religious, educational, political, recreational activities, all these associate with us persons who are not our relatives and with whom we may have little other contact. We are affected throughout each day by the operation of large-scale institutional organization, and not by the same few relatives and neighbours. We can move away from unpleasant situations in our natal families or at work, to

86

establish ourselves elsewhere. If we, nevertheless, blame disturbances in the working of these complicated institutional arrangements on the moral defects of particular people, it is not surprising that Africans, living so intensively in their small groups, see that moral relations in these groups are closely involved in all happenings.

A sociological understanding of charges of witchcraft has first to be sought in this general situation. There are straightforward occasions of competition to which particular misfortunes can be ascribed. A very common one throughout Africa is the charge that may be made between two wives of one man, for they are competing for his sexual and other favours, and for the interests of their children. Men with equal claims to the headmanship of a village strive against one another, and the victor is suspected of triumphing through witchcraft. But the working out of other charges, and of certain specific forms of beliefs in different tribes, involves deeper analysis of the personal difficulties and struggles which at a particular moment may lie behind accusing someone of witchcraft. Increasingly we are finding that the charge of witchcraft may in effect be produced by the working out through time of two contradictory social processes within the group. These focus on a particular person, and the charge of witchcraft enables the rupture of the disturbed relationship to be effected with social approval.

Among the Zulu, domestic and kinship life centres on the linking together of men related to one another through males. There are strong animosities among these men, arising from living together itself, and from competition for the property and the positions of the group. Yet charges of witchcraft are still not often made by these men against one another. Much more frequently, they blame their misfortunes upon the women who have married into the group, on daughters-in-law and on sisters-in-law. Or their mothers bring charges against their wives. These are the strangers in the group who can be held responsible, through their ill-nature, for the ills of the group without destroying the loyalty of the group. But as outsiders we can say that these wives are socially responsible for many of the conflicts between the closely related men; for it is through their wives, and the children to whom these wives give birth, that men want to become independent of their fathers and brothers. This is as true of Zululand as it is of England; and in Hindu India wives were blamed for the break-up of large joint families of related men. A wife gives a man sons who strengthen his group and build up its power; but they are also independent persons who will force their father into competition with his brothers, and in turn will compete among themselves. Hence the growth in numbers of the group through the women who bear its children both strengthens the group and introduces dissension into it; and the wives are the focus of two conflicting social processes. They are seen as centres of mystical evil arising from their very ill-nature, which attracts to itself sexual familiars who begin to demand the lives of their relatives. If Zulu men wish to harm others, they have deliberately to enter on the arts of sorcery.

This Zulu example shows that even when we are dealing with the apparently straightforward sexual competition between the two wives of one man, we may have to seek below the surface. Here, too, conflicts arise between the pulls of different social allegiances, which are not ultimately reconcilable. The two wives have two sets of children who compete for limited power and property, and who cannot set out on their own to build up a livelihood. Children are desired by a Zulu kinship-group because they strengthen it: in the end this increase in numbers leads to the group's breaking up. The Zulu appear partly to conceal this funda-mental conflict from themselves by the argument that it is not competition between men which leads to rupture of relations, but wickedness on the part of the wives – who, in sociological fact, have bred the conflict, by producing the destructive children who are so desired. To protect their wives from these charges the men leave the group, but not of their own free will – apparently. The values of enduring loyalty to their fellow agnates, and of their own determination to live together, are not disobeyed. They go away because of their stranger-wives. And once they are in separate villages the situations producing the witchcraft charges become fewer in number and less acute: the different villages re-establish relations of a similar kind but at greater distance.

Witchcraft beliefs are the source of many disharmonies and quarrels; no anthropologist would deny this. But accusations of witchcraft also sometimes solve quarrels which arise between men from the conflict between allegiances to different and contradictory social principles. Thus the accusations allow new relationships to be set up, and new types of friendship to be established. In some respects, at least, the operation of the beliefs validates my general thesis. Custom creates conflicts, in certain ranges of social relations; it also resolves them when the wider social order is examined. If people had no wickedness in them, theoretically all social alterations could be carried out peaceably, or no alterations would be necessary.

African life nowadays is changing rapidly, and witchcraft accusations now involve circumstances arising from Africa's absorption in Western economy and polity. Conflicts between old and new social principles produce new animosities, which are not controlled by custom, and these open the way to new forms of accusation. Charges, previously excluded,

88

The Logic of Witchcraft

as by a Zulu against his father, are now made. The system of witchcraft beliefs, originally tied to certain social relations, can be adapted to new situations of conflict – to competition for jobs in towns, to the rising standard of living, made possible by new goods, which breaches the previous egalitarianism, and so forth. In response to this situation there have arisen in Africa movements designed to cleanse the country of witches, held responsible for social disintegration, for falling yields on over-cultivated lands, for new diseases. The philosophy of these movements against witchcraft is that if Africans would cease to hate one another and would love each other, misfortune would pass. These movements are short-lived, and they tend to be replaced by religious movements involving messianic elements.

We see that indigenous witchcraft beliefs are incompatible with our highly productive economy, and its emphasis on individual achievement and on raising one's own standard of living. They also seem to me to be incompatible with the emergence of the family of parents and children as the important group at the expense of the former extended kinship groupings. This process accompanies industrialization. The members of the family cease to be linked for important purposes with other kin, but become involved with unrelated persons in the specialized relationships within a large-scale impersonal set of institutions. During the years when the industrial system is becoming established in Africa, the increase of conflicts in personal relationships and in the organizing principles of social life has led to an increase in fears and charges of witchcraft, as happened at the beginning of our own industrial revolution. Nor are these fears and charges controlled by old sanctions.

The difficulty of destroying beliefs in witchcraft is that they form a system which can absorb and explain many failures and apparently contradictory evidence. Evans-Pritchard shows that the theory involved is a complete whole, in which every part buttresses every other part. Illness proves that a witch is at work, he is discovered by divination, he is persuaded to withdraw his witchcraft – the patient recovers, as most patients do recover. Or counter-magic used against the witch appears to be successful.

Nor are men required to look at the system as a whole at any one moment. They see it situationally. When you accuse your enemy of bewitching you, the system seems reasonable; when he accuses you, and you consider you are innocent, you can use other beliefs to explain away the charge as ridiculous. You can say he did not really consult an oracle, or that the true witch influenced the operation of the oracle, or that a taboo in the working of the oracle was broken and it just killed chickens.

89

Value Systems

This sort of system of belief is characterized by what Evans-Pritchard has called 'secondary elaboration of belief'. In most cases magic does not attempt the impossible: rain-magicians do not make rain in the dry season, and magic against thieves is made against unknown persons, not named persons. Hence there will be many successes, which are remembered. The failures can be interpreted within the system by invoking other beliefs. Every year before the Trade Winds bring their rains, Zulu call in special magicians to treat their villages against lightning. Most villages are not struck, but if a man's village *is* struck, he will say the magician was bad, his medicines were poor, a taboo was broken, a witch wielded the lightning, or Heaven itself was powerfully determined to strike the village. We reason similarly. If your house, which you have protected with lightning conductors, is nevertheless struck, you may say that the workman was bad, the wires poor, a rule of craft in installation was broken, the charge was too strong. You do not rush to the Royal Society to deny the validity of scientific theory. The total system of beliefs thus allows for a good deal of failure. It also allows for the existence of scepticism. But generally it is scepticism about particular charges of witchcraft, particular lots of oracle-poison, particular magical substances, and particular magicians or witch-doctors. Evans-Pritchard gives one example which drives this point hard home. In Africa witches are believed to cause illness by shooting objects into their victim; the doctor should extract these objects to effect a cure. Of course, doctors produce these objects by sleight of hand in poultices or by concealing them in their mouths. But not even the doctor doubts the belief as such. He regrets only that he does not possess the magic – which the doctor in the next district may have – to enable him really to extract the noxious object. Meantime, he has to pretend to do this extraction for that peace of mind of the patient which is necessary for recovery.

Practically all societies have stereotyped ideas about different categories of people. Experience is carefully sifted, by selection of incidents which support the stereotypes, to maintain the system as a whole. And if experience contradicts the system, there is always the individual exception. When Christians use the phrase 'he is a decent Jew' they confirm their stereotype that most Jews are not decent, since they know only a few Jews. And Jews may reason similarly about Christians, Whites about Blacks, and Black about Whites, employers and employees about one another.

To break into the closed circle is immensely difficult. I remember finding on a friend's bookshelf before the war a collection of anti-Hitler cartoons from all over the world. I turned to the title-page and saw the imprint 'Leipzig: collected by Ernst Hanfstaengel', who was personal aide-de-camp to Hitler. Those cartoons, which portrayed Hitler as a fool, a beast, a mountebank, and so on, were re-published in Germany by the Nazis to prove to Germans that Germany was encircled, and that other lands were ruled by Communistic Capitalistic Jews who encouraged these vilifications of the Führer. The moral for propaganda is clear: direct assault on a closed system of ideas is not easy, since the system absorbs the attacks and converts them to strengthen itself. That lice carry typhus is easily absorbed into the belief in witchcraft. Only developed science has outside criteria of truth and falsehood.

IIc: Tribal Government

The ways in which African peoples govern themselves, and the areas of activity falling within the authority of government, form the material of this section.

It has to be remembered that not one of the present independent States of Africa has any social or ethnographic homogeneity. Each is composed of different, and sometimes historically hostile, tribal elements. The forms of traditional government are important influences shaping the political development of modern States. In some areas there have been monarchs, Uganda for example has within her boundaries four hereditary kingdoms, while in others, a more representative form of government has operated. When reviewing the progress of the new States it is important to consider the variations of tribal government that form part of their political heritage.

African political systems are characterized by the close relationship of three groups of factors. The first of these is lineage, the importance of marriage and ancestral ties for government. The second is the personal quality with which political leadership is invariably imbued; there is widespread importance attached to the political leader as an individual to whom allegiance is fiercely given. This may be spontaneous, or it may be 'arranged' contractually or by conquest, and generally takes the form of personal attachment to the chosen or hereditary leader, or chief. The third common basis of political structure concerns the land. In Africa a unit of government is almost always based within broadly defined territorial boundaries of political power. Government has a territory with which it identifies and is identified.

As will be observed from the Readings which follow, the authority of government is wielded over a broader span of activity than is customary in the west, and most of the principles governing the relationship between the governed and the governors, however varied they may be, are clearly set down and strictly followed.

10

Government and Politics in Africa[1]

T.O. Elias

With the present reading we enter the realm of government. Some variations of tribal authority found in Africa are described in detail.

The most important modern study of the contemporary African political institutions has classified them into two main groups. The first group consists of those societies with a centralized authority, well-defined administrative machinery and established judicial institutions – the three major organs of a truly political community in the modern sense. The second group of African societies consists of those in which authority is dispersed through a number of counterbalancing segments, instead of being concentrated in a single central authority. Examples of the first group are those societies with chiefly systems such as the Barotse, the Baganda and the Bechuanas, while the Talle-nsi, the Kikuyu, and some of the other peoples of Central and East Africa are the principal examples of the second group. A major characteristic of societies with a kingly or chiefly system is that it tends to comprise homogeneous or relatively homogeneous ethnic groups within its fold while that of the chiefless society is that the units composing it may or may not be homogeneous and is probably often heterogeneous.

The first generally displays a large measure of cultural and ethnic identity, whereas the second does not generally have the same degree of cohesion and cultural identity. Also, in the chiefly society, it is possible for the communities to be either graded hierarchically on the pattern of paramount chief helped by a council of head chiefs who are sectional heads of the chiefdom and who are in turn assisted in the work of government by a council made up of heads of villages who are themselves again assisted by the local heads of families; or not graded in any way but merely composed of one unit of administration under a single head, but this is exceptional. On the other hand, the chiefless society normally consists of a council of elders chosen in virtue of their being the titular heads of

[1] Reprinted from *Government and Politics in Africa*, published for University of Delhi by Asia Publishing House, 1961.

local families, each such arrangement being in co-ordinate authority with neighbouring ones, but without any of the co-ordinate segments being regarded as having any supra-ordinate power over its equals. It is true, of course, that among the councillors, a definite degree of seniority is recognized, and that it is the most senior head among certain local families who are traditional religious officiants who act as a kind of superintendent or chairman of council.

In the chiefly society, there is usually a high degree of cultural and even material sophistication among the people, but in the chiefless society there is not quite the same level of cultural and social sophistication. Again, it is a marked feature of a chiefly society that tribal and sub-tribal affiliations are far less strong than in chiefless society in which the basis of social and political aggregation is normally the kinship group; in a chiefless society, the kin is supreme, and the society is normally knit together by blood relationships like a well articulated sheet of chain mail. This arrangement of a chiefless society also implies that certain rules must operate to prevent sexual promiscuity and incest, and so some of these societies are exogamous, i.e. that the members of a village or congerie of villages do not intermarry, although somewhat paradoxically some of these societies are endogamous, i.e. village members only marry among themselves.

The broad classification of African societies into two main groups must be taken as subject to a number of qualifications and reservations. Among the chiefly ones, for example, one notices a clear difference between purely indigenous political institutions like those of the Ashanti or the Yoruba or the Baganda, and those that have been fashioned and modified by Islamic influence such as the Northern Nigeria emirates, or the French Sudan, or even of the Yao.

It has sometimes been said that such theocratic states tend to be oligarchic in their exercise of political power and that they are even autocratic in their method of administration. But the history of the development of African societies, as of societies elsewhere, shows that the indigenous organization no less than the Christian ones have at various periods thrown up a Napoleon, a Bismarck, a Metternich, a Garibaldi, a Shaka Zulu, or a Cetewayo. It is therefore inaccurate to suggest that Islamic influences on indigenous African societies have always and everywhere turned them into dictatorships or oligarchies. It is at least doubtful whether African societies have produced on the whole anything to rival the reported acitivities of dynasties of the Ancient East. In this connexion we must record Lord Hailey's recent pronouncement on African societies:

African sentiment attaches special importance to the due observance of the procedure by which all members of the community concerned are able

94

to have some voice in determining issues which are of major interest to it. It is rare to find in British Colonial Africa any instance in which the indigenous form of rule previously in force could be described as autocratic, and there are not many cases in which it could be described as authoritarian. It was a prevailing characteristic of the indigenous system of rule that whether power was vested in the hands of individual chiefs or of a ruling class, these had (unlike the absolutist régimes of a certain stage in European history) no machinery by the use of which they could enforce obedience to their orders.

It is necessary now to describe briefly the composition and functions of the various types of traditional councils of government. The system described for the Akans of modern Ghana in Caseley-Harford's *Gold Coast Native Institutions* is very similar to that described for the Yorubas of Nigeria in Dr Samuel Johnson's *History of the Yorubas,* and both are in their turn not unlike the much smaller political arrangements of the Jukun, described in C. K. Meek's *Tribal Studies in Northern Nigeria* and of the Baganda described in J. Roscoe's *The Baganda.* All these are kingly or chiefly systems. In each case, the King or Paramount Ruler was assisted by a Council of State drawn from the head chiefs of provinces, where each head chief was himself assisted by district or subordinate chiefs making up his own council and so on down the line to the village level. This hierarchy of authority implies that the king, like the subordinate chiefs in descending order of importance must govern only with and through his council and not alone. Thus the margin for any arbitrary arrogation of power by a chief over his subjects is in practice made narrow. A tyrannical chief, when one did turn up in the past, might occasionally maintain himself in power by some subterfuge, but was ultimately brought to book by well-established indigenous methods of direct and indirect control. The indigenous polity looked upon the chief as only a *primus inter pares* so far as the other eligible candidates from the territorial ruling houses and from the numerous traditional Secret Societies were concerned. In some centralized societies, the office of Chief was elective, while in others it was hereditary. Where, as in Ashanti or in Yorubaland or among the Barotse of Northern Rhodesia, the office of Chief was and is elective, there was and is usually a body of kingmakers responsible for the choice of a successor to a deceased chief. Normally, the choice would be made from among those eligible candidates put forward by the local Ruling Houses. Sometimes the electors were a kind of political and quasi-judicial college of cardinals, like the secret societies which formerly could depose a tyrannical king or chief after a number of secret trials and warnings. Where the election was hereditary, however, the chief was not so subject to the organ of kingmakers, but such was the traditional system of checks and balances

95

that the chief could only defy his council at his own peril. The council could often tell him of the desires of the people and, where necessary, depose him or ask him to go into voluntary exile.

Another important characteristic of the traditional system of government is that the tributary or provincial or district chiefs must be specifically mandated by their own area councils before they could in any way commit their peoples to any major decisions of policy that might be arrived at in their deliberations in the Paramount Chief's council at the capital of the Chiefdom. If any matter affecting any of the territorial units came up for decision either at a specially convened congress or at one of the regular consultative assemblies, their delegates must, unless so previously authorized, be allowed to refer the particular matter to the local council and people so that they might signify their approval or disapproval. The only exceptions to this general principle were in respect of state policy decisions like the king's or paramount chief's order for war or defence of the state as a whole or in respect of fiscal matters of administrative necessity. In such cases, the local units had no choice.

Chiefless societies operated on more or less similar lines, since the local council of elders must take specific mandates from their families before committing them at council meetings over matters as to which the security and well-being of the republic were not in danger. The council of elders was not such an undifferentiated body of functionaries as is sometimes suggested. Within its framework were often to be found a number of committees, sometimes overlapping, sometimes uninstitutionalized, but almost always functioning as bodies of experts on a specific subject such as land tenure, or the markets, of defence, or war, or administration of justice. To a foreign observer the councillors appear to be an unchanging body of people who discharge the same functions in and out of season. In reality, however, there is this unostentatious division of labour among the ranks.

But whether the African society was monarchal, i.e. chiefly, or whether it was republican, i.e., chiefless, two important concepts of government are common to them. As Martin White put it in the *Gold Coast Legislative Council*: the African indigenous political arrangement shares with the imported British system of the Legislative Council the characteristics of (*a*) being government by discussion and (*b*) embodying the representative principle; both systems involve, in other words, the parliamentary principle of decisions arrived at by a majority after the fullest debate and discussion of different points of view expressed by duly accredited representatives of the people. Both the African and the British systems should, therefore, be able to accommodate each other in the emergent parliaments of post-war British Africa. There are no *a priori* reasons of political expediency why

Africans should not be able to operate the modern institutions of constitutional government, given the will to succeed.

It may be of interest briefly to consider the African ideas and concepts of government, in order to see whether the prospects for democracy in the emerging states of contemporary Africa are good or otherwise. Like the other racial groups, the African has also spun his own theories about the origin of human society. Africans have not been as articulate as European theorists. They have not had the benefit of the invention of writing by the Sumerians and the Assyrians of old Mesopotamia, who gave the art of writing to the European and Asian worlds. The absence of writing has therefore deprived the Africans of the opportunities for recording their thought and actions in the same systematic and continuous way as have men of other continents. It is, however, unsafe to conclude that the African has not indulged any intellectual effort or systematic theorizing about the problems of existence and of government. Among African societies there have existed various theories about the origin of human political organizations. Some have put forward the theory of the Original Ancestor, according to which all the members of a State originally belonged to one ancestor so that the subsequent inhabitants must be deemed to be the descendants of this founding father who must have immigrated from other parts to the present site. Others have not adopted this myth of the Original Ancestor but have put forward the theory that the first founder of the race or nation had sprung up from the earth and had later managed to people his kingdom through supernatural power of the gods and goddesses of the nation; hence the kingship was often regarded as divine, and therefore as dedicated to the promotion of the peoples' welfare. Yet other societies have evolved the theory that several founders had seceded from a previously existing State somewhere and had then journeyed together to the present site, either with their wives and children, or, though without these to begin with, they had taken as wives women from neighbouring or conquered peoples; and that these bands of founders later became the ruling houses of the community.

But whatever is the particular theory of a given society, there is a general consensus of opinion that the ruler was not above the law, that he was subject to the ultimate sovereignty of the people, and that he must surrender his authority when he has lost the confidence of a great majority of his subjects.

If, therefore, the African concept of government is not essentially dissimilar from the European, it is hardly to be wondered at that the emergence of African States in contemporary world politics is proving so successful and exciting.

II

The Activities of Tribal Governments[1]

Isaac Schapera

Although Professor Schapera is mainly describing the Bantu-speaking peoples of Southern Africa, his description of the multiple functions of political authority offers a sound general idea of how tribal government is organized and carried on.

It will be noted that the distinction between the legislative and juridical functions of government is non-existent, the two being merged around the person of the chief, who is the personification of the unity and identity of his people and the living symbol of their strength.

The Bantu chief in his official capacity has many duties, which if faithfully performed may take up much of his time and energy. He is commonly said to be the 'father' or 'herdsman' of his people. As such, he should care for them, watch over their interests, and seek to promote their welfare and security; indeed, the Zulu term Umbuso, 'mode of dealing with or governing the people', means also 'making life happy for them'.[2] In working to this end, the chief relies mainly upon his confidential advisers and executive assistants, but whenever necessary he also summons and presides over meetings of the tribal council and the general assembly. With them he arranges communal enterprises, takes appropriate action in case of war, famine, etc., and decides other questions of public policy. He also attends habitually at his council-place, a large circular enclosure or similar forum close to his residence, where he listens to news, petitions, and complaints from all over the tribe, and gives orders for whatever action is required. Nothing of public importance may be done without his knowledge and consent.

His recognized duties include certain specific types of activity, which despite many variations in detail are fundamentally the same everywhere. As representative and spokesman of the tribe, he deals with its external relations. He communicates with other chiefs on matters of mutual concern, and receives and entertains them or their messengers should they

[1] Reprinted from *Government and Politics in Tribal Africa*, Watts, 1958.
[2] Bryant (1905), p. 60.

98

come to see him. All other strangers visiting the tribe should be reported to him or to the nearest local ruler, and they may not settle or trade in his country without his consent. As among Tswana, too, none of his own people may go abroad without his permission.

The chief must also protect the right of his subjects, provide justice for the injured and oppressed, and punish wrongdoers. He should see that local segments are satisfactorily governed by their rulers, and to ensure this should intervene to end gross abuse or incompetence. Both he and the heads of all local segments have their own courts, with power to enforce decisions and to compel the attendance of litigants and witnesses. But his is the highest court, to which appeal lies from the verdicts of all others, and normally it alone can punish such offences as sorcery and homicide. He himself is usually the judge, but in larger tribes senior princes or special indunas may act on his behalf, verdicts in the more serious cases being then referred to him for confirmation.

The law enforced in the courts consists very largely of rules handed down from one generation to another. But in all tribes the chief, with the approval of his people, may also make laws of his own; after consulting his private advisers he usually submits his proposals to the full council, and among Tswana to the popular assembly as well. In modern times, owing to the new conditions created by contact with Europeans, legislation has become fairly common, especially among Tswana and Southern Sotho; some chiefs have even compiled written collections of the laws so introduced.[1] But although Bantu everywhere say that legislation has always been a recognized function of the chief, relatively few examples are known from the early days. It may be that others have been forgotten; more probably, however, there was seldom need in those days for changes in the existing system.

In his executive capacity the chief performs certain routine tasks of great public importance. Some affect the status of persons. For example, he periodically creates a new age-regiment (except among Cape Nguni and Southern Sotho) and thus formally admits youths into the social category of adults; and among Zulu and Swazi but apparently nowhere else, men may not marry until he gives permission to their age-group as a whole (which at one time, among Zulu, might not be before they were about forty years old).

Everywhere he also controls the distribution and use of land. This he does mainly through his sub-chiefs and headmen, all of whom manage the land within the areas they govern. They must see that every married man receives, free of special charge, private holdings for residence and

---

[1] cf. Schapera (*c.* 1943); Ashton (1952), p. 249 ff.

cultivation, and that the common pastures are sufficient for all. Should no more land be available locally for such purposes, the chief provides it either by re-arranging area boundaries or by moving some of the people to parts less densely settled. All land not specifically allotted to local rulers remains under his immediate control, and he uses it both to satisfy new internal demands and to accommodate groups of immigrants. He or his subordinates likewise decide where people may build their homes, and which tracts are to be used for cultivation and grazing respectively.

Very often he also regulates the calendar of agricultural and certain other activities. In most groups people may not plant or reap their crops until he has given the word, so ensuring that such work is done when conditions are considered most suitable, nor may they anywhere eat the first products of their fields until he has ceremonially inaugurated the new season of plenty. Among Twana and some Northern Sotho he every year imposes, and in due course lifts, seasonal taboos on such activities as clearing new land for cultivation, killing or castrating bulls, and making pots. Violation of the taboos is held to injure the growing crops, but is also a penal offence. In some groups, notably Tsonga and Venda, he similarly enforces 'days of rest' after new moon, a person's death, a violent wind-storm, etc.

From time to time, the chief everywhere organizes large collective hunts, which serve incidentally to provide the people with meat. As among Tswana, he may also summon age-regiments to destroy beasts of prey, or to round up stray cattle at the end of the dry season. In all groups he mobilizes tribal labour for the cultivation of his public fields, and for building or repairing his huts, council-place, and cattle-kraals. In these and various other ways he secures large-scale co-operation in tasks that often benefit the tribe as a whole.

He also mobilizes his people for defence against invading enemies or for aggression against weaker neighbours. Although, as among Cape Nguni, sub-chiefs occasionally embark on raids of their own, the tribal army is everywhere controlled by him alone, and only he can send it out on foreign expeditions. As a rule it is led on such occasions by one of his sons or brothers, or by a special induna noted for military capacity, but in some groups he himself may take command, especially against an invader.

The chief also has ritual functions. This aspect of his duties is more highly developed among Swazi, Venda and North-Eastern Sotho, than in most other groups, notably Cape Nguni and Southern Sotho, but some features seem to be universal. Everywhere, for example, he organizes religious ceremonies upon the due performance of which his tribe's security and prosperity are held to depend. His dead ancestors, so it is believed, provide supernatural protection and help to the people they had once ruled, and therefore he visits their graves to pray and sacrifice to them on behalf of the tribe. This he does not only regularly on such occasions as the start of the cultivating season and the eating of the first-fruits, but also in times of war, drought, pestilence, or whenever else the diviners decide that his ancestors need to be appeased. Only he, as chief, can officiate at these ceremonies and, as we shall see, that is one of the main sanctions for his authority.

Everywhere the chief is further expected to ensure that the rainfall is adequate, and his achievement in this respect may well affect his popularity. Among Tswana, Northern Sotho and Swazi, he organizes annual rainmaking ceremonies; elsewhere he usually resorts to them only in times of drought, and at the direct request of his people. Some of them are public, and may involve the participation of special categories of persons such as immature boys and girls, hunters, or recently bereaved widows and widowers; others are performed in secret either by him or by the specialists whom he employs. He himself is often versed in the art of making rain, which is a form of magic considered highly suitable for him to know and practise. The chiefs of the Lobedu and Swazi are indeed famous throughout South Africa for their skill, and the former, especially, received many pleas for help from rulers of more arid lands; and Sotho and Venda tribal histories show that in disputes about the succession preference was sometimes given to a son who had been taught the rainmaking magic or had acquired possession of the associated apparatus.

Most of the tasks mentioned above are performed by the chief with the aid of his advisers and officers, and although he alone can do some, his indunas, local subordinates and magicians, are his agents in others. One important duty only he personally can fulfil. He receives various forms of tribute from his people in both labour and kind. In consequence he is always the wealthiest man in his tribe. But he does not use his wealth merely for domestic purposes. Apart from specially rewarding his officers and other assistants, he entertains people, who come to visit him, and on great public occasions slaughters cattle and provides beer and porridge for all who gather at his village. He places cattle on loan with many of his subjects, supports destitute widows and orphans, sometimes sends food to sick people and newly-confined mothers, and in times of famine distributes corn from his granaries or, if the need is great, sends men to purchase supplies from his neighbours. 'The chief is the wife of the tribe' say the Tswana, i.e. he looks after the needs of his subjects, and Zulu refer to him as 'the breast of the nation', i.e. the source from which all draw sustenance; in the same context, he is often greeted as 'mother of the people', or 'mother of orphans'. One quality always expected of him is generosity, and should he fail in this respect he soon becomes unpopular.

Bantu local rulers have many duties similar to those of their chief. These duties are essentially the same for all grades, but sub-chiefs have wider jurisdiction and greater powers than headmen. In general, all headmen in a district are responsible to the local sub-chief, who in turn, is responsible to the chief; in each case the higher authority hears appeals from the court decisions of his inferiors, tries cases that they cannot settle, and has overriding authority in all other matters.

With the air of his own advisers and other assistants, every local ruler regulates the occupation and use of land in his area, and nobody may settle there or move away without his consent. His home is the administrative headquarters of the area. He judges cases involving any of his people as defendants or accused, and investigates serious crimes before referring them to his superior. He summons and presides over popular assemblies to discuss matters of general concern, organizes public labour, collective hunts, and other group enterprises, and among Southern and some Northern, Sotho arranges periodical initiation ceremonies for boys and girls. Among Cape Nguni and Southern Sotho he commands all the able-bodied men of his area as a single division or sub-division of the tribal army; elsewhere, as among Tswana, he is leader of his own age-mates only, his other subjects being similarly commanded by his brothers and sons in their respective regiments. He prays to his ancestors on behalf of his subjects, and performs various other ceremonies to ensure good harvests, keep off misfortunes, etc. He is also expected to reward all his assistants, entertain his people generously, and care for them in time of need.

Relations between a local ruler and his subjects tend to be more intimate than those between the chief and the tribe as a whole. In small groups, especially, he knows all his people individually and is usually related to many or even most of them; he helps them in their personal troubles and mediates between them and higher authorities, is notified of all births, weddings, and deaths and invited to beer-drinks and other feasts, and is often consulted on such matters of private concern as transactions about cattle or the employment of doctors.

Within his own area he is also the chief's local representative. He carries out the chief's general policy and special instructions, collects the tributes due to him, and is responsible for maintaining peace, order, and good government. He himself should visit the capital from time to time, not only to take part in council meetings, but also to report upon local conditions. Such visits are considered essential for it is largely through them that the chief keeps informed of what is happening in the tribe.

Among Western Tswana, some Northern Sotho, and Venda, there is another type of liaison between central and local authorities. Each outlying group, especially of foreigners, has a hereditary 'overseer' (termed 'mother' by North-Eastern Sotho), who lives in the capital. This man, a trusted noble or commoner, is the recognized intermediary between those people and the chief. He looks after them whenever they come to the capital, sponsors and assists them at court, may be sent to deal with local difficulties and disturbances, and among Tswana visits them periodically to collect the tribute they owe to the chief.

With the exceptions just noted, communications between the chief and the inhabitants of any outlying area normally pass through the recognized regional hierarchy. As will have been gathered, moreover, within his own group every local ruler has authority in many different fields: judicial, executive, economic, ritual, and maybe military. This wide range of activities helps to explain the facility with which groups can secede; from the smallest upwards, each is largely autonomous and can if need be exist by itself. During the many wars of the past, for example, tribes often broke apart; but owing to the all-round experience of even the most junior local authorities, it was almost always possible for the fragments to carry on with the traditional pattern of government.

As we have seen, one major duty in all Bantu tribes is the administration of justice. Since this illustrates clearly the hierarchy of authorities, and also the powers of the various grades, it merits fuller description. All Bantu have a well-developed system of legal procedure. Self-help is permitted if an offender is caught in the act, sorcerers are often 'smelt out' by diviners at special seances, the chief sometimes punishes rebels without formal trial, and, as among Tswana and Swazi, breaches of regimental discipline or privilege may be dealt with internally. With these exceptions, wrongdoers are normally tried in the regular courts, the general rule being that they appear first before their own local ruler.

In practice, though not in formula, Bantu distinguish between 'civil' and 'criminal' offences. The former violate private rights connected with personal status, property, and contract, and are dealt with by compelling restitution or compensation. This applies, for example, to breach of marital or filial obligations, seduction, adultery, unpaid debts, trespass, theft, and defamation. Action in regard to such wrongs lies with the person aggrieved. Unless he chooses to ignore the matter altogether, he should first try to reach a settlement by negotiation; many civil disputes are in fact resolved by direct discussion between the people concerned, usually at a special meeting attended by their close relatives and presided over by the offender's senior agnate. If this does not succeed, the injured person lodges a formal complaint with the offender's headman, who fixes a day for hearing the case; in some groups, such as Cape Nguni and Venda, a goat or sheep is paid as fee to 'open the court'. At the trial the plaintiff states what reparation he wants, and if he wins may be awarded the whole or only part of his claim, according to the merits of his case. Sometimes the judge simultaneously also punishes an offender who is held to have behaved very badly.

In South Africa the constitutional functions of chiefs and their assistants vary greatly from one people to another. This suggests that we can no more speak of 'primitive government' generally than we can of 'primitive law' or 'primitive religion' generally, except perhaps by contrast with some major characteristics of more advanced systems. Such a contrast has been attempted by MacIver. In his 'conspectus of the forms of government', he distinguishes *inter alia* what he calls 'primitive' or 'tribal' government. Its main features he defines as follows: 'The functions of government are minimal. There are few, if any, administrative officials. The duties of the chief may be casual, or vaguely defined. There may be no judicial apparatus whatever. Custom serves to regulate many things, that in a less primitive system are determined by law or decree.'[1]

Undoubtedly even Bantu government differs very greatly from that of a modern Western state. But the differences are perhaps more marked in form than in function. It seems to be widely agreed that the primary functions of government in any modern state are to maintain law and order, administer justice, organize defence against external enemies, and conduct formal relations with other communities. Everywhere in South Africa the chief also attends to foreign policy, and if need be mobilizes his people for defence or aggression, himself often taking command. But it is only among Bantu and Hottentots that he has legislative powers and maintains regular courts for punishing criminals and settling civil disputes. Among Bergdama and Bushmen legislation is unknown, and courts do not exist; public offenders are sometimes dealt with by collective attack, but for private wrongs, however serious, the only accepted remedy is personal retaliation. Bantu and Hottentot rulers thus perform all the primary functions of modern governments. But if we agree with MacIver and other writers that the administration of justice is a function that 'all governments always fulfil', then neither Bergdama nor Bushmen can be said to have government. Even among Bantu and Hottentots legislation is a far less conspicuous feature of governmental activity than in the modern state; in pre-European days, especially, chiefs usually pursued the same ends as their predecessors and performed tasks stereotyped by tradition, and

[1] R. M. MacIver, *The Web of Government* (1947), p. 156.

104

marked changes of policy such as often accompany a change of government in Western societies seem to have been uncommon, though not altogether unknown.

Modern governments have many other functions than those mentioned above. In varying degrees, for example, they also control the production and distribution of commodities; conserve unappropriated natural resources; manage public utilities such as transport, communications, fuel and water; and provide such other services and education, medical aid, poor relief, insurance, scientific research, and recreation. As Salmond says, 'the state has come also to organize constructively for the well-being of its members. We have moved away from the nineteenth-century idea of the police state, negative and repressive, to a new conception of the social-service state, and there is no sign that we have yet reached the end of the development.'

But although 'public service' may be a relatively new function of governments in Western societies, comparable tasks are also performed in South African societies, even if the situations to which they apply and the details with which they are concerned are far fewer than among ourselves. Everywhere, for example, the chief organizes and directs such collective enterprises as migrations and hunting, regulates the pursuit of certain subsistence activities and conserves natural resources, if only by prohibiting their use at certain times or in certain places. Among Bantu and to a lesser extent Hottentots he assists needy people and in various other ways uses his wealth for the public benefit. This function, which may be likened to the poor relief and social insurance of modern states, he does not perform among Bergdama and Bushmen, where indeed he is no wealthier than the rest of his subjects; he does see, however, that game killed by the hunters is distributed among all members of the band. Among Bantu, but nowhere else, he also controls the occupation and use of lands by members of the tribe, and provides people with private holdings for residence and cultivation. Except among Hottentots and some Bantu he likewise organizes initiation ceremonies, when youths are collectively admitted into the social status of adult and sometimes also receive formal instruction in rules of conduct.

In addition, among Bantu and Bergdama the chief either personally conducts or organizes many religious and magical ceremonies for the benefit of his people; he is thus in effect their high priest and leading magician. This intimate connection between rulers and ritual life is not usually a feature of modern governments, except perhaps where an established state church is maintained, and even then political authorities seldom act officially as clergymen. The chief also has ritual functions in some though not all groups of Bushmen, but among Hottentots his only comparable duty is to organize the annual rainmaking ceremony.

This rapid survey has shown that all chiefs in South Africa have some of the functions performed by more advanced governments; they conduct foreign relations and arrange defence against aggression, organize and direct collective enterprises, and provide certain social services. Many of them are also the ritual officers of their community, a duty not usually associated with government in Western States. On the other hand, among neither Bergdama nor Bushmen do they perform what is commonly held to be an essential task of all governments, the establishment and maintenance of law and order through legislation and the formal administration of justice. Bantu and Hottentot chiefs, although having many functions in common, also differ in certain respects. They make laws, administer justice, organize communal activities such as as warfare and hunting, and assist needy subjects; but the Hottentot chief, unlike his Bantu counterpart, has virtually no ritual functions and relatively little control of land and other economic resources.

12

African Chiefs Today[1]

Lucy Mair

With regard to the gradual transition from tribal authority to national government, it is important to know something of the methods employed by the colonial powers in facilitating the change.

In British Africa, a system of administration was established which came to be known as 'Indirect Rule', whereby the central government exerted its authority through the medium of the local chiefs.

The position of the chiefs in newly independent States is always difficult; they are naturally conservative and it is around their office that much local opposition rallies in an attempt to preserve long-cherished prerogatives and old methods of social control. Where there happen to be local economic interests, which it is felt the State does not sufficiently recognize, these also may seek to use the chief as a mouthpiece and political 'front'.

The manner of the removal of any significant power function from the chiefs' domain is determined by several factors, not least of which is the part they have had to play under colonial rule. It is this fact which lends importance to the subject examined here by Dr Mair.

It is a familiar fact that European rule in Africa has set in motion a radical change in African society. In some fields this has not been the result of any deliberate intention. In that of economic development, interest has generally been centred in the immediate problems of production, and the effects upon African institutions of the solutions that have been found for these have been neither planned nor even foreseen. But in the field of politics, European governments have been obliged to define their intentions towards the authorities whom they found already in existence, and here, in theory, there was a clear-cut choice from the start. Either the holders of power in the indigenous societies should be recognized, and utilized as part of an administrative structure of large scale, or they should be disregarded – their authority be perhaps deliberately destroyed – and replaced by what M. Albert Sarraut once called 'new and rectilinear architectures'. The British chose the first course, and this policy has now become inseparably associated with the name of Lugard.

[1] Reprinted from *Africa*, Vol. 28, 3, July 1958.

I believe that the forthcoming work by Miss Margery Perham will show that what has been called 'Lugardism' in the derogatory sense—the insistence on maintaining traditional authority almost for its own sake—was not Lugard's philosophy, but that of the successors who were in command during the period when he was away from Nigeria.[1]

The system of administration of African areas that is known popularly as 'Indirect Rule', and more precisely as the Native Authority system, was eventually extended to almost all the British dependencies. The term implies something more than a philosophy of respect for tradition, or a general principle that indigenous authorities should be given administrative responsibilities. The model which was generally copied was the Tanganyika Native Authority Ordinance, a development of Lugard's theme by Sir Donald Cameron. This included specific provisions which make the Native Authority system something very different from the relationship with indigenous rulers that is commonly associated with a protectorate. Under a protectorate the ruler surrenders his external independence but is left more or less free to manage the international affairs of his territory. Under Lugard and Cameron's system, traditional chiefs or other leaders are recognized as local agents of government and given the title of Native Authority. But their right to exercise authority depends upon this recognition, and recognition may be withdrawn; there is no question of their retaining power because it is inherent in their traditional position. A Native Authority need not be a single individual; in appropriate cases a council of elders may be recognized collectively, or a group of chiefs of areas which are too small to be considered viable by themselves.

The functions of a Native Authority are threefold, and in cases where African chiefs are recognized but do not perform these functions, it may be permissible to speak of Indirect Rule, but it is not correct to speak of the Native Authority system. A Native Authority has judicial, rule-making and financial powers, and in the exercise of all these powers it is subject to external supervision. The grant of financial powers is what made it possible to lay the foundations of local government, in the sense of the allocation of revenues raised in a locality to the provision of services for the direct benefit of those who pay the taxes; and European officials weigh the merit of African chiefs by the interest that they take in such services. The enlightened ruler, in their eyes, is he who introduces the type of local improvement that the government wishes to spread; or, one could put it with less appearance of cynicism, who is interested in the development in his country of institutions appropriate to the twentieth century. Not very many of those rulers who have retained a large degree of independence

[1] See M. Perham, *Lord Lugard* (Collins, 1960).

have spontaneously shown this kind of interest. When this was realized, two alternatives were possible; either all African rulers could be brought under the strict control implied in the Native Authority system, or some other instrument of local government could be developed. In fact, both these courses of action have been tried, sometimes one after the other in the same territory. At the present moment we can see in different British dependencies examples of every stage of the process.

The South African High Commission Territories provide one. The position of the chiefs in Swaziland, Bechuanaland, and Basutoland was defined by treaties made in the nineteenth century, which left them a considerable degree of autonomy. When complaints were made, in the period before the last war, that the development of these territories had been neglected, one step that was taken was to increase control over local administration by limiting this autonomy on the pattern of the Native Authority system. The chiefs resisted this change as long as they could, and by the time it had been made effective the climate of opinion had changed again, and the Native Authority system itself was under fire. Politicians in Europe and Africa were demanding that hereditary rule should be abolished altogether, and replaced by representative local government. When the Ngwato tribe were divided over the marriage of Seretse Khama, the British Government thought the opportune moment had come to do this and so put an end to rivalry between factions; but though there is still no recognized chief of the Ngwato, the people have not been persuaded to elect a council. In Ghana, however, a similar story had a different end. Here too the British Government tried for a long time to induce the chiefs of the coastal area to submit to control in the interests of efficient administration. They refused right up to 1945, and only agreed when they saw that their position was threatened by discontent among their own people. But for them reform was too late to save them from the radical policies introduced by Kwame Nkrumah. In Northern Nigeria, and in East and Central Africa, we are still trying to democratize the government of chiefs without destroying it.

We see today, then, the same opposition within British Africa that used to be regarded as typical of the contrast between the British and the French; the opposition between those who seek to improve what they find and those who prefer to make all new. The forces of African nationalism are on the side of the latter, and where African nationalism has won its first victories, in Ghana and in the Western Region of Nigeria,[1] the status of chiefs has been conspicuously reduced. Yet in these very territories we

[1] This was written in 1958. It would now be more accurate (in 1965) to speak in this respect of the state of Nigeria. (Eds.)

see that the chiefs are still a power to be reckoned with, and perhaps all the more so because their place in the formal organization of government has been so drastically diminished. And we sometimes see the same people extolling the traditional political system who at other times are most insistent that chiefs must be subordinated to a popularly elected government.

I do not intend to spend time discussing, in the light of hindsight, whether it was or was not wise to extend the Native Authority system through Africa. One could point to the most successful examples of it as an effective way of providing local services at a time when they could have been provided in no other way. On the other hand, one might ask whether, if Native Authorities had not been recognized in the British territories, political energies there might now be directed to problems of greater ultimate importance than the struggle for power between chiefs and representative leaders. Will a struggle of this kind be unnecessary in the French territories, where the status accorded to chiefs in the colonial system has been so much lower?

The interpretation of history that is popular with some young Africans sees the Native Authority system as a colossal mistake for which they are paying today. I have never heard one of them explain what he considers would have been the wiser policy, but I suspect that they dream of an alternative version of the past in which representative institutions would have been introduced much earlier and in consequence the goal of self-government would also have been reached much sooner.

I would suggest that the assumptions which they make are false in essentially the same way that some of the assumptions made by the architects of the Native Authority system were false. In both cases it is assumed that a political system can be modified by external action in just the direction which is desired. Of the two views, the African is the more naïve – the idea that an authority which is widely accepted can be not only destroyed – which is easy – but immediately replaced by something built on quite different principles: the 'new and rectilinear architectures' of which M. Sarraut spoke were not, in fact, raised in very many places. Behind the Native Authority system was a belief which to in some sense the converse of the African one: the belief, not that everything could be changed, but that nothing would change except under the direction of the European rulers. They, it was held, would guide the chiefs in the way of enlightenment, would remove abuses from the organizations that they found, control the infliction of cruel punishments, limit the demands that chiefs could make on their subjects. Then, having cleaned and polished their instruments, they would turn them to constructive use.

This vision did not take account of the dynamic nature of social relations. It did not recognize that the traditional relationship of chiefs with their subjects had been the result of a continuous interaction, in which some sort of balance was struck between the claims of the ruler and the expectations of the ruled. There have been a few cases, like that of the Fulani empires, where conquerors had military power strong enough to enforce the submission of conquered peoples. But more often the subjects acquiesced in a rule which they considered to be worth something to them, and the ruler had to approach their ideal of what a chief should be. Certainly this did not prevent him maintaining control over his immediate followers by means of ruthless punishments. Indeed I am not seeking to idealize African tradition, still less to argue that African rulers were in fact democratic, as became fashionable at the time when the Native Authority system was first under fire, and sometimes appears to be so again in Ghana. And when I speak of balance, I do not mean to convey the picture of some delicately poised construction which must not be touched lest its equilibrium be disturbed. I simply mean that authority was accepted as long as obedience was considered to be worth while, but that when this point was passed there were ways of refusing obedience; individuals could transfer their allegiance, larger groups could secede. Less commonly a ruler could be removed by force and a rival installed in his place. The Akan-speaking peoples of Ghana even had a formal procedure for the removal of chiefs; it is not clear how much force was involved in putting this into action in the days when it was still possible to resort to force. But nobody disputed the principle that people should be ruled by a chief, and that he should come from one particular line of descent.

Within this system, as within all social systems, rulers and subjects, nobles and commoners, pursued their own interests to the best of their ability. As long as the traditional African polities were largely self-contained, the principal way in which a commoner could do this was by pleasing some political superior, and the value of this patronage was one of the most important sources of political power. The populace at large might do no more than acquiesce in the system of rule, or they might regard it as part of a divinely sanctioned order. But the immediate followers of chiefs and their subordinate officials had a clear interest in the maintenance of their powers.

The establishment of alien rule had effects upon this system both direct and indirect. Directly, it tilted the balance of power in favour of authority. Certainly governments were greatly concerned to see that chiefs did not exploit their subjects, and that the revenues they collected were devoted to the public welfare, and not merely to their own enrichment. But they also made those chiefs whom they supported almost immune from any effect of popular dissatisfaction. There have indeed been revolts against chiefs under colonial rule, but if they have succeeded it has been indirectly, by calling the attention of the superior government to malpractices. The dual position of the chiefs, between the European government with its specific expectations, and their subjects with quite other expectations, has been discussed by various writers with reference especially to East Africa, notably in a perceptive work by Dr Lloyd Fallers. The officials of the superior government also had a dual role, as the supporters of chiefly authority and the defenders of its subjects against the abuse of authority. They too were not always able to play both roles with success.

In the long run, the indirect effects of colonial rule on the position of the chiefs have been the most extensive. The explanation that chiefs who had government support became indifferent to popular opinion, even in so far as it is true, is too simple to account by itself for the hostility which popular leaders have often shown towards them. We must look not only to the direct relationship of ruler to subjects, but to all the consequences of the fact that the drama of Africa is now being played on a wider stage. This one relationship is no longer of supreme importance. The chief has ceased to be the ultimate source of protection to the humble, aid to the needy, and advancement to the ambitious. It is not simply that the superior government has taken its place, but that the new world offers opportunities which depend on the creation of relationships right outside the traditional system. People can attain success in commerce, or eminence in the professions, without being beholden in any way to their political superiors, and in these fields the chiefs often could not compete with them. In these circumstances, resentment against the rule of chiefs is something more than a protest against injustice, even though it may express itself in that form. It is part of a wider demand: the demand for full participation in the institutions which control the destinies of Africans.

In this situation the chief can be looked at in two ways. He is an individual doing his best to retain the advantages which his status used to bring him, and sometimes coming into conflict with the new leaders in the process, but he is also a symbol, a rallying point for like-minded persons. At different times the chiefs have been found to symbolize different aspects of the complex modern situation. This is the reason why the same chiefs may be objects of hostility at one moment and of vociferous loyalty at the next, and also why the same persons may appear to be successively, or even simultaneously, opponents and supporters of the recognition of hereditary authority.

To some of their subjects, chiefs are the symbol of alien rule simply because they have been entrusted with some responsibilities of government. And when nationalism is militant, they are indeed in a difficult position, since they are part of the machinery for the maintenance of public order, and they have everything to lose if they align themselves with their subjects. It is not surprising that chiefs are usually 'loyal', as it is commonly called; yet it is worth noting that in Nyasaland[1] a few years ago a number of chiefs resigned their office so that they could stand with their people in opposition to the inclusion of their country in a federation with the Rhodesias.

Of course it is an absurd exaggeration to argue as if European supremacy could not have been maintained without the support of the chiefs, and it is also an absurd distortion to identify them with those policies against which the attack on 'colonialism' is commonly directed. These are economic policies, which are implemented through the relations between central governments and the enterprises operating under their protection, outside any field in which the chiefs can act. The only serious criticism that has ever been made of the type of small-scale developments that chiefs have been expected to further is that there has been too little of it.

Another way in which the chiefs are made symbols of resentment against foreign rule is in the interpretation that is put on the decisions made by governments when there is a disputed claim to recognition. Since no man advances a claim unless he has some following, some section of the public is bound to be disappointed whoever is recognized; and, as nationalism develops, it comes to be asserted that the official choice is always contrary to the popular will. Sometimes, even in cases where an individual's claim is not challenged, his critics or his enemies may assert that he has been forced upon them by an alien government; but let the government take action against the ruler, however unpopular, and all his subjects will instantly rally to his support.

This phenomenon, which continues to surprise those in authority, can be readily explained. Every hereditary ruler is the supreme symbol of the unity of his people, and therefore, also, of their opposition to outsiders: so an attack on him means much more than the invasion of his personal authority. To the sophisticated among his subjects, whatever their attitude may be towards the person, such an attack is an offence against national sentiment which cannot be tolerated. To the great majority who have little interest in, or comprehension of, the political conflicts of today, their ruler is a part of the fixed order of the universe, and his removal a disaster comparable to the reversal of the seasons. When the British Government

[1] Malawi

withdrew recognition from the Kabaka of Buganda, for one Muganda who had some idea of the matter in dispute there were a thousand who simply felt that they had suffered an appalling injury.

Where there is no external pressure, the politically sophisticated are free to criticize the individual actions of rulers and the hereditary principle itself. But they always have to reckon with the attitude of their simpler fellows and that is just what I have described in speaking of Buganda.

It is characteristic of African chiefs in all the territories that we are discussing that the political unit which each one symbolizes is only a small division of the political unit which is now recognized, or about to be recognized, as a self-governing State. This fact has created a number of different problems, which depend to some extent on the size of the unit headed by a chief. Ashanti constituted a major division of the Gold Coast under colonial rule. But if it had been merely a British creation, would it have demanded the autonomy of a State in a federated Ghana? Because they were subjects of the Asantehene, the Ashanti formed a collectivity that was more than a geographical expression, and it is because he is aware of this fact that Dr Nkrumah has decreed that Ashanti is to consist in future of eight autonomous divisions subject to no common head. This action, it might be noted, exactly parallels that of the British government some sixty years ago.

It is time now to consider the symbolic significance of the chiefs from another point of view. If they stand for the past, for people who are proud of that past, they stand for it also in the eyes of people who are impatient to move away from the past into a very different future. This desire is shared today by nationalist politicians and by the people in London who formulate policy for the territories that are still dependent; and to persons in both these categories the authority of the chiefs, if not their person, is the symbol of everything that must be left behind when Africa is modernized. Some journalists too, who, no doubt rightly, see history as a one-way street, describe the attempts of chiefs to assert their position as a 'last stand of reaction'. But some of the conflicts that we see in West Africa today arise from the fact that in the eyes of the same persons the chiefs may be symbolic of reaction, symbols of group unity, and symbols of pride in national history. That is why there has been no move to eliminate them from the political system altogether. If the new leaders do not take this step, I think it is not entirely because they are afraid of the strength of the support that the chiefs command. It is also because they themselves see the chiefs – in some aspects – as symbols of national pride; they cannot at the same time repudiate them altogether and assert the value of their own historic tradition. Thus we see in Ghana that when the possibility of establishing a republican form of government is being discussed, it can be asserted that the traditional system in its pristine form was essentially republican.

A place has been found for the chiefs in the new constitutions of Ghana and of the Western Region of Nigeria. In both these countries chiefs are the ceremonial presidents of the elected councils which have replaced the Native Authorities, and up to now they have been allowed to nominate a proportion of the members of these councils, though Dr Nkrumah has said that each local council is to include only one representative of the chief of the area. In the Western Region, in addition, the legislature is bicameral, and the chamber with powers of revision is a House of Chiefs.

The Eastern Region has always been thought of as the classic case where fully representative government could be introduced without any need for modification to meet the sentiments of traditionalists, because, it was held, there were no chiefs. Indeed it has been regarded as the home of African democracy, where everyone had a voice in all decisions, so that it should be a mere step from the direct to the representative form.

But what do we see in fact in the Eastern Region? A demand for the recognition of chiefs, or at any rate of some kind of traditional leader. It would be easy to explain this away as mere imitation; to say that the Ibo and their neighbours want to claim an institution that appears to be a matter of prestige in other territories. But this is not the whole story. We find now, what an anthropologist might have expected, that the democratic Eastern Region was never democratic as we conceive the Greek City State, in the sense that all the voices of all citizens were equal. It was the units of social structure – the small descent groups, each living in its own quarter in town or village – which were equal. No collective decision was taken unless the senior man of each of these groups consented in the name of its members. Sometimes a group might leave the meeting and thus dissociate itself from the decision. This procedure seems to have been carried over into the new parliamentary institutions, where it is less effective, since in this case absentees are bound by decisions taken in their absence.

When modern representative assemblies are being set up, it is clearly extremely difficult to find a place for the spokesmen of every group of this kind, even at the level of local government. Indeed this was tried long ago. In the first days of the introduction of the Native Authority system under Cameron, the principle was followed that the traditional political structure must be utilized *whatever it was*; and for some time assemblies of a hundred or more members were formally responsible for the conduct of business such as the allocation of revenues to local services. But very soon it was found necessary both to reduce the number of councillors and to amalgamate neighbouring units, so as to create economically viable authorities with councils of manageable size. Once this had been done, there was no link with tradition apart from the fact that the council members were reverend elders, and the opinion soon grew up among the officials responsible for the supervision of the councils that the business of a local authority should be in more competent hands. This led them to study the local councils of Kenya, which from their inception have been based on nomination or election and not on any traditional structure, and, taking Kenya as the example, they substituted wholly elected councils for the Native Authorities. The process was set in motion before a representative African Minister took over responsibility for local government. However, the law which authorized it had been examined in advance by a committee of Africans. At that time there does not seem to have been any general feeling that the dignity of traditional authorities must be respected. Evidently they were not thought of as a serious political force, as were those in the Western Region and in Ghana. In these two countries the respect felt for chiefs appears to be in part derived from religious veneration. Their chiefs used to perform ceremonies on what may be called a national scale; some of them perhaps still do. The head of a kin group, in contrast, is the intermediary only between his own kinsmen and their ancestors. Outside this field he earns the respect generally accorded to age, but no more. It appears, in fine, that the educated persons who were consulted on the original Local Government law did not consider that any account need be taken of traditional leadership.

Yet we now see a reaction. Mr G. I. Jones, who was invited to investigate the question of the due recognition of traditional authorities, refers in his report to 'a general feeling that the principle of representation by election has been carried too far', and this appears to be closely connected with a feeling that the new local council areas do not correspond with social units conscious of common interests. Again we seem to be seeing the importance of the recognized head as the symbol of unity, and the determination of the group whose unity has its roots in the past not to be submerged in new organizations artificially created.

This situation represents a serious problem for the organization of local government, not only in the Eastern Region but also in Ghana and in other territories. Over and over again we find that some section refuses to be included in a wider council, or insists on breaking away from one, on the ground that they are an autonomous political unit headed by their own chief. Now it is not only anthropologists who have remarked on their importance on community sentiment as a stimulus to the activity of local councils, and of community pride as a factor in willingness to contribute to the cost of common services. But if these feelings unite only populations too small to afford any common services, and are strong enough to divide councils representing larger aggregates, they can only hamper the development of effective local government. In time, no doubt, as communications improve, locality by itself will be a basis for community feeling. Meanwhile we must hope that if community pride is appeased by the appointment to councils of persons clothed with traditional authority, this may lead the general public to take more interest in local developments.

The Republic of South Africa, to which I now turn, sometimes appears to outsiders like a looking-glass land in which all the trends which are dominant, and seem to be irresistible, farther north are reversed. The attitude reflected in the Bantu Authorities Act is a case in point. To liberal South Africans of yesterday, no less than to progressive journalists today, Bantu chiefs have symbolized reaction, and South Africans have prided themselves on the elected local councils which had been set up in the native areas of the Cape before the end of the last century. At the same time the Native Affairs Department has found it convenient to rely on the traditional chiefs as agents of police power and as channels for the communication of official policy. Also, it was found here, as it has been found since in so many other places, that certain chiefs commanded so much respect that it was not practicable to exclude them from the representative councils which were set up among their people. Thus in Pondoland the Paramount Chiefs of the two major divisions of the country had to be given seats on the councils of the districts in which they lived, and they were also authorized to nominate a proportion of the members of all councils.

But with the advent of the Nationalist Party to power, and the adoption of the policy of apartheid, the rule of the chiefs over their people has come to acquire a new significance. Now they are symbols of difference; they embody the theory that Bantu culture is the expression of the specific nature of a people who are destined to be for ever separate from South Africans of European descent. Their responsibilities in the field of local government are to be increased, and they are to exercise these along with councils constituted according to tribal tradition. In this case the ruling group have deliberately chosen to recognize only the divisive forces in African social structure and only the rural populations which still cherish their distinctive traditions, and to disregard the great number, probably now the majority, of Africans who live outside their tribal territory, and for whom it is quite meaningless to say, as was said in the debate on the Bantu Authorities Act, that 'the tribe, the headman and the chief are the basis of their social and political structure'.

What is meant by the return to tradition appears from a speech that the

Secretary for Native Affairs made to a meeting of Zulu chiefs soon after the Act was passed. He claimed to be 'adding to the duties of the tribal authorities the all important one of moving with the times and thereby retaining leadership of the community as a whole', and told them 'to deal with community life in all its ramifications just as in the tribal life of old but on a higher level'. Alas, these exhortations ignore the essential factor in the present situation, that the times have changed, and modern community life is not the tribal life of old. The chief can move with the times only up to a point; to go beyond that point would make his own position meaningless. The support which chiefs retain today, and which, I repeat, is strong enough to make them a significant force in politics, comes from the people who do not want to move with the times.

I have spoken of the chiefs as symbols. In every case they are symbols of the differentiation of sectional groups in a complex society, but only in the last of a differentiation which is forced upon one section against its will. The kind of group loyalty which takes a chief as its symbol is often called 'tribalism'. Outside South Africa this word has a derogatory meaning; inside South Africa it is rather ambiguous; officially it means something which is different without being inferior, and which ought to be perpetuated. But some self-appointed members of the new African States condemn 'tribalism' and urge Africans to develop a sense of nationhood. In taking this line they forget that every society has, and must have, its internal divisions. Only two features are peculiar in the African political scene at the moment that the groups which seek to assert their autonomy are unduly small in the context of modern government, and that their unity is symbolized by the recognition of hereditary rulers.

Something must also be said of the chiefs as persons, who are seeking, like everyone else, to do the best for themselves in a fluid situation. I am not attempting to deny that the wide popular support which they command sometimes enables them to pursue their own interests rather than the benefit of society at large, even to the point of refusing to obey the law of the land. I am thinking particularly of the situation in Ghana, where the Akan chiefs in the past have derived considerable revenues from their position as the ultimate authorities over unoccupied land. Of course the mystical identification of a chief with the land of his subjects is not peculiar to the Akan-speaking peoples; it is probably universal. But in Ghana the opportunities of turning this position to account have been unusually great, since the country has a highly profitable cash crop, cocoa, and also valuable mineral and timber resources. The cocoa is produced by peasant farmers, many of whom are 'strangers', to use the West African word, in the chiefdoms where they have taken up farms. There is a steady migration of farmers to the better cocoa lands. For cultivation rights they usually pay something to the chief as well as to the rightholder whom they approach directly. Timber and mineral concessions have been granted directly by the chiefs and not by the central government, since the Gold Coast government never claimed any right to dispose of African lands. All these revenues should have been brought to account in the Native Administration treasuries which were set up in Ashanti in 1936 and in the coastal areas in 1945. But when the decision was taken to replace the Native Authorities by elected local councils, it appeared that it was not a simple matter to order the transfer of Native Administration assets to the new bodies. In the eyes of those who still revered their chiefs, their position as land authorities was sacred, and to take from them the revenues which were paid in recognition of this position would have been an outrage. A compromise in legal terms was found in the provision that stool lands, as they are called in Ghana, are the property of the traditional entities, the States ruled by the chiefs, but are to be administered on their behalf by the elected councils. This saves the prestige of the chiefs, but it does not alter the fact that the local councils and the chiefs have very different ideas on the question of the allocation of revenues. The councils want to build dispensaries and water storage tanks; the chiefs want to keep up their traditional state, maintain their courtiers and renew the elaborate paraphernalia with which they appear on ceremonial occasions. Their subjects probably want both the water supplies and the paraphernalia: I recall a case in which one of the smaller chiefs near Cape Coast complained to the council that he could not provide the necessary ritual objects for the appropriate yearly ceremony and his people were blaming him for the bad season. Thus there is room for a good deal of friction between hereditary and elected authorities. It has been common form for elected local councils in their first flush of power to cut down what might be called the chief's civil list. In Ghana repeated instructions have had to be given to councils regarding their duty to maintain chiefs, but it is not likely that there will ever be agreement about the proper cash value of maintenance. Already the central government has had to guarantee a payment to chiefs from its own revenues; this too the chiefs have criticised as inadequate.

This is what happens when the chiefs have handed over their revenues, or where the revenues are in any case not large. Where there is more at stake, the conflict arises earlier. The chiefs do not disclose their sources of revenue, or fail to agree with the council on the proportion which they should be allowed to retain; or they try to get in ahead of the council's servants and go on collecting the dues which were formerly paid to them.

It is quite easy to predict that the chiefs will eventually disappear from the scene, whether or not the governments of independent Ghana and Nigeria take forcible steps to bring this about. Although, as I hope I have shown, their position differs in many respects from that of a landed aristocracy in Europe, it is equally vulnerable to the forces of modern economic development. Even supposing that representative government does not flourish in the new States, it is unlikely that leadership will revert to the chiefs; it must remain in the hands of people who can organize their following over wider areas than those to which the chiefs are confined by the nature of their position. It may be that sociologists would regard them as constituting a class in modern African society, but they have not shown much ability to combine in defence of their own interests.

However, it is too simple to say that because they cannot last for ever, they are negligible now. It has been remarked that anthropologists, who study African societies intensively over short periods, exaggerate temporary conflicts. Historians tell us that with their long view they can see how these conflicts will be resolved; so, it seems to follow, the conflicts themselves do not really matter very much. I am reminded of Lord Keynes's remark that 'in the long run we are all dead'. The conflicts that people are living through are the only ones that matter *to them*, and it is a fact that the position of the chiefs is a subject of acute conflict in Ghana, and a live issue in the Eastern Region of Nigeria, and nobody has ventured to prophesy what may happen in a self-governing Northern Nigeria, where at present there is no power comparable with that of the great Emirs. We may think we see what the end of the story must be, but that does not enable the actors in the drama to sleep through it and wake up just in time for the denouement. They have to live through the period of conflict, and it is for them to decide whether the end will be reached through a series of compromises or forced in a violent struggle.

13

Traditional Authority & Social Action in Former British West Africa[1]

W. St. Clair Drake

The reader will find it instructive to compare the conditions and problems brought about by the exchange of political power in West Africa, with those described by Dr Mair in Reading 12.

The new *élite* has inherited a skein of knotty problems from the colonial régimes. Not the least important of these problems is that of how to secure effective collective action on the part of a bewildering diversity of ethnic groups at varied levels of economic development and social complexity, and with differential degrees of exposure to, and acceptance of, Western values. No colonial régime ever tried to solve this problem through the instrumentality of representative government. The new *élite*, however, is trying to do so. The presence of a 'traditional order' presents problems as well as opportunities.

THE STRUCTURE OF TRADITIONAL AUTHORITY

In each of these States, western-type executive, judicial, and legislative institutions exist side by side with 'traditional' institutions – familial, religious, economic, and political. A process of adjustment and fusion of these two types of political and social institutions is evident everywhere, a process which began in the days of colonial rule and which still remains. This process is inexorable and irreversible.

While local and regional variations exist throughout West Africa, it is possible to construct an ideal-type formulation of the major characteristics of 'traditional authority' as it existed prior to colonial contact:

1. The controls of kinship groups were basic. Within kinship groups (family, extended family, or clan), although lineage or clan leaders had extensive executive and judicial authority, there was a wide measure of discussion and consultation by adults of both sexes when crucial decisions

[1] Reprinted from *Human Organisation*, published by the Society for Applied Anthropology, 19, Fall, 1960.

were involved. *Legislation was not a primary issue. The rules of life were largely set by custom.* Discussion centred around the expediency of concrete actions within the framework of customary rules; rules were reinforced by sacred sanctions.

2. At the village or town level, even though 'chiefs' or other wielders of power might come from designated families or clans, the commoners often had some say about the selection of individuals, or where they did not, they frequently had the power to oust them. Where this power was not directly given to the populace, it was often invested in representatives of kin or 'ward' groups, elders, or other types of councils. Decisions – executive, judicial, and legislative – when taken by chiefs were normally decisions by 'chiefs-in-council', not their lone dictatorial decisions. Chiefs had ritual power as well as political power.

3. In the more complexly organized societies, covering wider geographical areas, there were tiers of political power. Sometimes a paramount chief existed as a ritual and political head, over subordinate groups of chiefs who formed his council, and these, in turn, were the representatives of groups of villages and clans whose interests they were inclined to protect, and which they sometimes represented as delegates.

4. Among some West African peoples, corporate groups existed which served as checks upon the abuse of power by chiefs. Cases in point would be the *asafo* groups or *mmerante* among the Akan peoples; or some of the so-called 'secret societies' in various places, one of the best known of which was the Poro Society among some of the Sierra Leonian and Liberian tribes. Where the political power of cults and societies was not direct, such institutions always influenced political decision-making indirectly.

Autocrats occasionally subverted this primitive democracy, and there were, of course, undemocratic elements in traditional African societies. Nearly all West African societies were characterized by a heavy male bias even when they were matrilineal, and many of them placed limitations upon the rights of 'strangers' or had depressed strata as an integral part of their structure. The prevailing ethos put the accent upon *age* as a primary attribute of power holders, and, therefore, limited the full utilization of intellectual talent or the verve of youth.

The prevalence of animistic beliefs and of a mystical attitude toward nature inhibited social innovation as well as technical inventions, while the widespread belief in witchcraft (*juju*) introduced an element of tension into group life that is not present in interpersonal relations in those cultures where the source of evil is located in a devil who exists outside the boundaries of the social group, or where one's destiny is attributed to Providence, Fate, the planets, or 'accident'.

Finally, no elements were present in these societies leading towards self-generated change in the direction of individualism and equalitarianism, as was the case in the capitalistic and rationalistic societies of Europe and America. African societies had to wait for the introduction of such elements from without. Traditional authority operated to buttress all of these conservative tendencies, for the merging of ritual and secular power (whether it resided in lineage elders or in chiefs and kings) stabilized the society by inhibiting social change.

However, there are some observers and leaders who feel that, at the rural local level, the still viable *communal ethos* of African cultures brings powerful reinforcement to the carrying out of contemporary development plans, and that the existence of extended family obligations obviates the necessity for devising elaborate social security systems. They would strive to retain these features, which are sometimes referred to as aspects of 'African Socialism'.

The old pattern of mandated authority and of frequent consultations between leaders and the led is also frequently cited as a feature worth preserving; but the new imperatives of budget making or the provision of sanitary services and village planning, require a degree of speed and efficiency of administration with which prolonged deliberation and a system of 'going back' for consultation before taking action is inconsistent. Few defenders of African traditional societies would contend that they can cope with the totality of demands imposed by the goals of democratization and modernization.

TRADITIONAL AUTHORITY AND COLONIAL RULE

Colonial rule in West Africa began less than 200 years ago despite over 500 years of trade relations with Europe and America, and of contact with missionaries among coastal peoples. Native rulers, even along the coast, preserved their hegemony throughout most of this period and a process of state-building, similar to that which occurred in post-neolithic Mesopotamia, began throughout the whole area bounded on the north and east by the Niger River. A pattern of 'traditional authority' had become stabilized in this entire area by 1840, involving three 'tiers' of political structure:

(*a*) A few 'royal families' and their retainers exercising sovereignty over relatively large areas which included the ancestral homeland of the specific ethnic group from which the ruler came and the territory of tributary ethnic groups (e.g. the Asantahene in Ashanti-land or the King of Dahomey, ruler of the Fon people);

(*b*) A larger number of 'kings' of city states and their immediate hinter-lands (e.g. the Obas of the Western Region of Nigeria);

(*c*) 'Paramount Chiefs' over smaller ethnic or regional areas often owing allegiance to rulers of types (*a*) and (*b*);

(*d*) Thousands of local chiefs at the village level;

(*e*) Chiefs and headmen exercising authority over enclaves of 'strangers' residing within towns or villages.

Throughout West Africa, traditional authority has survived the impact of colonial rule. 'Chiefs', the traditional rulers in West Africa, continue to settle cases of dispute according to customary law and to control the allocation of land in their role of custodians of the people's patrimony. They also have religious duties to perform; they have sacred as well as secular roles. Their right to tax and to dispose of tax monies was jealously guarded in the days of colonial rule and is still conceded. Their position, quite understandably, still gives them great prestige in the eyes of the illiterate people who are the bulk of their subjects. . . .

The fate of traditional authority will be finally settled primarily in terms of the extent to which traditional rulers can be rendered innocuous as a power threat to the new governments or can be turned into a positive asset; and to the extent to which traditional authority and political prac-tices can be fitted into a situation which demands the quick release of productive energies, and efficient, expeditious decision-making on econo-mic and political questions.

IId: Traditional Economic Activity

INTRODUCTION

A knowledge of the traditional features of the economy of Africa is essential for the understanding of contemporary economic problems; for it is in the economic field especially that Africa is still traditional in character. Most inhabitants of tropical Africa are predominantly occupied in growing crops and perhaps rearing some animals or hunting for their own 'subsistence'. Away from the large cities 'subsistence' production continues largely as it has for centuries. Some changes have occurred: the number of crops has expanded with the addition of such things as maize; some people are now permanent urban dwellers and many others go as immigrant workers to industrial locations and to plantations. Work habits in the rural areas have consequently undergone changes; and consumer goods have come to the villager through immigrants or the extension of rural retailing. But in spite of this and some schemes of rural development most areas of Africa today would be quite recognizable to the traveller of fifty or one hundred years ago. Fewer than 10 per cent. of Africa's potential labour force currently earn wages. Yet in hardly any part of Africa (with the exception of some areas of the Congo) has nothing at all changed. Nearly all its inhabitants have been in some way or other influenced by the impact of the money economy even if it is only through hearing tales of the city.

The economic changes most significant in disrupting traditional patterns in Africa's economic history were, first, the slave trade, which ceased in the nineteenth century, and, later, the exploitation for export of its mineral and agricultural resources – for instance, the diamonds and gold of South Africa, the copper of Northern Rhodesia and the south-east Congo (Katanga), and the cocoa and nuts and vegetable oils as well as minerals of West Africa.

As far as their place in the world economy is concerned African countries remain mainly 'primary-producing' countries and Africa exports very few manufactured products; the proportion of exports to total production in the money economy is comparatively high. In other words, in their patterns of production and trade they remain 'colonial' economies; and indeed many of them still trade principally with the former metropolitan country (especially in the case of former French territories). Trade between African countries is very small indeed. Since these economic features are partly the heritage of the colonial era, we must here digress briefly to assess the overall economic impact of colonialism which is so often criticized by Africans.

The economic legacy of colonialism is a curiously ambiguous one. On the one hand it has provided roads, schools, power, modern cities and the means to eradicate many diseases. In addition it has provided, more directly than could otherwise have been the case, an incentive to Africans to attain a higher material standard of life, and the economic development which brings it. How long, one wonders, would it have taken for this new ethic to flourish in African minds, had it not been for the direct contact with the colonial power? And relatively how much poorer, materially, would Africa be today? Colonialism brought also the national state, arbitrary as this often was, which is the framework within which so much of modern economic development must take place.

The other profile of colonialism is, however, less flattering. The pattern of primary production to serve the needs of the colonial (primarily manufacturing) powers in mines or plantations has often led to islands of development, the impact of which has been enormous in limited locations but has seldom dispersed its benefits very widely. It would, of course, be absurd to suggest that for this reason such development should not have taken place; any country is well-advised to specialize in producing those things in which it is economically most efficient. It may none the less have been the case that colonial governments and investors have been less than energetic in attempting to diversify the economies once these primary sectors had been established. Colonial governments and entrepreneurs have often been too 'export-minded' and have neglected the possibility of setting up local industry, which might have been opposed by manufacturers in the metropolitan country. And metropolitan banks have been conservative in their unwillingness to provide credit to indigenous entrepreneurs. Thus we find now that most African economies rely for their incomes on the export of a very few primary products. As demand for these products in the developed countries fluctuates so does the income of the exporting countries. Besides which, the demand for most of these products is not expanding very swiftly in the developed countries partly because of the development of synthetic substitutes for many raw materials.

We believe, therefore, that prospects of an economic advance sufficient to satisfy the 'revolution of rising expectations' by continued specialization in primary product exports is slim. To produce such an advance, therefore, it will be necessary to diversify African economies. Some diversification may be possible through the exploitation of further primary products. But the one answer to this need, consistently embraced by Africans themselves, is industrialization on the basis of a domestic market. This problem will be discussed in section IIIc, Economic Change and Development.

14

Agriculture in the African Tropics: the Observations of a Geographer[1]

Pierre Gourou

If African countries are to develop fast enough to meet their growing needs production within their economies will have to be diversified. While this is generally taken to indicate the desirability of industrialization, some countries with more fertile soil may be able to make rapid progress on the basis of agricultural diversification – Malawi, for instance. In either case, however, agriculture will have a further task to perform – to provide food to maintain, and if possible to increase, the consumption levels of a growing population of wage-earners who do not produce food for their own subsistence. Agricultural failure could prove the Achilles' heel of African development plans. Will traditional systems of production be able to meet this challenge? This reading closely analyses the position and concludes that they will not. It shows us the measure of the challenge with which African agriculture is faced before it can meet the demand upon it.

Our subject matter is the agriculture which occupies the labour of the greater part of all the inhabitants of Black Africa; that is to say, the 150 million people who live in the 6 million square miles south of the Sahara, and north of South West Africa, Rhodesia, and Natal. Our area includes Nyasaland, Angola, Madagascar, the Sudan south of latitude 15°, and Ethiopia. Urban population in this area totals only about 10 per cent. of the whole. This paper is presented from the point of view of a geographer; the facts of agriculture are taken as one element in determining the landscape; but at the same time agriculture is considered as only one among several means by which a population may adapt itself to its environment.

WEAKNESS OF AFRICAN AGRICULTURE

Even in performing its primary task, the feeding of the rural population, African agriculture shows deficiencies, in the first place, in the quantity of food – such shortages occur particularly at the end of the dry season, before the rains begin – and also in its quality, particularly a lack of animal

[1] First presented as a paper to the Institute of Agricultural Economics, Oxford University. Printed here for the first time.

protein, leading to the disease kwashiorkor; and also deficiencies of minerals and vitamins.

African agriculture, as it is now organized, is often also incapable of feeding the urban population, small though their relative numbers may be. There are many areas of Africa in which food supplies for the towns from local sources are unreliable. These shortages have to be met by importing flour, rice, etc., which should not be necessary with a climate so favourable to agriculture, and with a population density of only 25 persons per square mile. The cities of Pointe-Noire, Leopoldville, Libreville, Abidjan, Dakar, and several others are generally dependent on imported foodstuffs; the plains of Manitoba and Dakota, if not of France, have to provide part of the food supply for the city dwellers of West Africa.

Another way in which urban needs are met is for the town dwellers to produce some of their own food; in cities such as Libreville (Gabon), and many others, the women of the poorer families set out each day to work in gardens at some distance from the town; each evening they return carrying home on their backs roots of manioc, plantains, bunches of groundnuts, and green salad leaves to provide a meal. It is in this manner that the poorer families of Libreville are able to live on cash incomes which appear, at first sight, hopelessly insufficient; these families really would die of hunger if they had to pay cash for all that they eat.

Agricultural production in Africa also has to provide for exports, which are absolutely essential for Africa's economy, but which nevertheless only represent a modest fraction of total agricultural production. Statistical comparisons show how low is the volume of export of agricultural products, whether measured per unit of total area, per unit of cultivated land, or per head of the rural population. Congo (formerly Belgian), for example, exported in 1958 at the rate of 2s. per acre of the whole country, or £7 per acre of the cultivated land (8·7 m. acres) or £5½ per head of the 11 million rural population. These figures of course include exports from plantations established by Europeans.

The conclusions are clear. African agriculture provides insufficient food, both in quantity and quality, for the rural population; provides inadequately for the urban population; and provides inadequate exports.

This calls for explanation. Is it the natural conditions (climate and soil) in high-rainfall tropical Africa which are responsible for this situation?

NUTRITIONAL DEFICIENCIES

We will deal first with the qualitative nutritional deficiencies among Africans. Doctors and biochemists have diagnosed and analysed them.

The geographer cannot explain them in terms of inadequate natural resources. The nutrition of rural populations in Africa lacks adequate animal protein (meat, milk, eggs and fish); but it is inadequate too in vegetable protein – biochemists agree that a very small quantity of animal protein will suffice if the diet includes abundant supplies of vegetable protein. Signs of protein deficiency are frequently found.

It is true that the high rainfall areas of tropical Africa show a deplorable abundance of animal diseases, which until recently proved quite uncontrollable. Everybody knows that trypanasomiasis (sleeping sickness) prevented the keeping of cattle, or at any rate of the more valuable breeds of cattle, in a large part of high-rainfall tropical Africa. But there is nothing to stop peasant families in Africa keeping poultry, and giving each member of the family two eggs for breakfast. Unfortunately, a large proportion of African men, and nearly all African women, refuse to eat eggs, thereby depriving themselves of the most accessible source of protein. The natural resources of Africa are not to be blamed for this state of affairs.

What is true of eggs is also true of poultry meat, which is rarely consumed. Few domestic ducks or pigeons are found. An interesting exception is however that of guinea geese; the breeding of these small geese is an important agricultural activity in the mountains of Madagascar. They make a valuable contribution to the feeding of the people, both in meat and in animal fat. But they are rare on the African mainland. Africans greatly enjoy venison; but there are many wild animals whose meat is eaten, even in the non-Moslem populations. The crops are often severely damaged by the millet-eating birds kuelea; but many Africans refuse to eat these birds, which are no worse (or better) to eat than the larks and other small birds which are consumed in France and Italy. The authorities, at great expense, dynamite the nesting grounds of the kuelea; it would be much more sensible to net these birds when they raid the fields; this would provide quite good food too. Pig breeding is habitually neglected, even among peoples who are under no religious prohibition on the eating of pork. Fish farming is also neglected; all the efforts which have been made during the last decade to promote it will not succeed until the people have grasped the idea that an abundant supply of fish depends upon an abundant supply of nutrient matter in the fish ponds. So far this idea had not taken root, but the same is true of all forms of African livestock culture: with few exceptions, Africans do not make sufficient effort to keep their animals fed.

Much the same can be said of the production of milk. Among many peoples, the cows are not milked at all; nor are the goats, found everywhere in Africa. At Jumna Pari in India, Maltese goats yield nearly three-quarters of a gallon of milk per day, if they are well fed. The Africans' neglect of milk is in no way a consequence of their physical surroundings. It is a feature of their civilization.

We come now to our first conclusion: an improvement in the supply of animal protein in the diet of the rural population does not depend upon the introduction of animals hitherto unknown, or of methods not yet understood, but simply on the removal of prejudices and harmful customs, in the fields of hygiene as much as of economics. These are things which the Africans must put right for themselves. But it is permissible to hope that, in a state of political independence, they will come to these conclusions more rapidly than they would have done if they had been still subject.

Much the same is also true of vegetable proteins: without having to do appreciably more work, African cultivators could produce fewer carbohydrates and more vegetable protein, by providing for a higher proportion of pulses and legumes in their cultivations. On the sandy tablelands of Kwango (Republic of Congo – Leopoldville) the legume voandzou, high in protein, while not neglected altogether, has never received the attention which it deserves. Here it would give better results than groundnut, because it is even more tolerant of poor soils and uncertain climates. The problem with which we really find ourselves confronted is that of rural education.

These shortages of protein are being made worse by the spread of the cultivation of manioc (also known sometimes as cassava, or tapioca) which is even poorer in protein than yam or millet. However, manioc has powerful attractions for the African cultivator, causing it to be ever more widely grown, in spite of the warnings of the medical authorities. It yields very high returns, whether measured per acre, or per day of labour; it can be grown on poor soils; it is little affected by irregularities of the climate, which would damage cereal crops; the roots can be stored in the soil until required (an important point for an African village with its lack of storage space); it is not damaged by grasshoppers or locusts; and, finally, its leaves make an excellent green vegetable. I regard it as a piece of gastronomic heroism on the part of a people such as the Yoruba in Nigeria to remain attached to the yam (dioscorea) which requires, for the same harvest, a great deal more labour, particularly when one takes into account the fact that provision for seed yams may use up a quarter of the harvest, whereas manioc is propagated by cuttings; and also yams are much more difficult to store. Africans could indeed enjoy all the economic advantages of growing root crops if they consumed in addition (and there is nothing in their natural surroundings to prevent them) larger quantities of animal protein.

QUANTITATIVE INADEQUACIES OF PRODUCTION

The quantitative inadequacies of African agricultural production are considerably harder to evaluate than the qualitative.

The first point to be emphasized is this: throughout the whole of high-rainfall tropical Africa the cultivator suffers from no lack of land. In the whole area, the amount cultivated each year is only about 125 million acres, or one-thirtieth of the available land (and we are dealing with high-rainfall Africa, not with the desert areas). The cultivator has plenty of choice, and in fact lacks neither extent nor quality of soils. It is true that many of the soils are poor and fragile; but there are many more soils besides those now used which are fully capable of cultivation. African methods of cultivation do not damage these low quality soils, so long as cultivation is shifted from time to time.

The climate of high-rainfall tropical Africa would seem to be one of the most favourable in the world for agriculture. One of the outstanding physical resources of Black Africa, frequently ignored, is its abundance of solar radiation. With very few exceptions, on the highest mountains, there is no part of Black Africa as we have defined it where there is any month whose average temperature falls below 65° F. All the year round crops can grow and ripen. To get a quantitative idea of this advantage we can use the rough but convenient device of 'day degrees', to measure the comparative advantages of different places. Omitting all months with an average temperature below 10° C. (50° F.) and then scoring a point for each degree centigrade of average temperature for each day of the warmer months (e.g. 10 days at 20° C. would add up to 200 points) we obtain the following result:

Eala (Congo–Leopoldville)	0° 3′ N.	9344
Lagos (Nigeria)	6° 27′ N.	9818
Dakar (Senegal)	15° N.	9344
Tangier (Morocco)	35° 47′ N.	6350
Peking (China)	39° 57′ N.	4300
Milan (Italy)	45° 28′ N.	4050
Paris (France)	48° 48′ N.	2600
Aberdeen (Great Britain)	57° 10′ N.	2034

If we take as our standard a plant such as the soya bean, which grows equally well on the equator, or as far as latitude 48° N., and which requires 2,600 or more of these 'day degree' units, we come to the conclusion that these tropical regions in African would be capable of ripening three separate harvests of soya bean in a single year. We still do not know enough about the comparative results of growing such plants in high latitude with longer summer days, or on the equator with days of uniform length; but we still conclude that the tropics ought to derive very considerable relative advantages from their abundant supply of warmth.

This advantage however is offset by deficiencies of rainfall. We have taken the 20 in. rainfall isohyet as the limit of our area, which we describe as high-rainfall tropical Africa, in which agriculture can be practised without irrigation. This may leave, however, a long dry season in which some of the energy which the sun supplies so generously is wasted, from the agricultural point of view. These dry seasons do not yield the benefits sometimes obtained elsewhere from fallow cultivation, but seem to represent a mere idling of the soil; and many soils bake so hard during the dry season that cultivation cannot be begun until after some rains have already fallen (thereby wasting some of the precious short wet season). It is the risk of drought which, in effect, determines the seasons in which agriculture is possible. In the regions which do not have a clearly defined dry season, that is to say those which have a truly equatorial climate of more or less continual rainfall (it must be remembered that these cover a very large area) it has been observed, for example at Yangambi (Congo–Leopoldville) that the yield of the harvest is affected unfavourably if the rainfall is interrupted for as short a period as ten continuous days.

Nevertheless, subject to all that has been said above, it is clear that the climate of Black Africa should conduce to abundant agricultural productivity, and that the causes of the inadequacies of production must be sought in techniques, not in natural disadvantages.

The greater part of the area effectively harvested in any year in Black Africa has been cultivated by the well known method of ladang, or shifting cultivation; the cutting of the vegetation (indigenous or regrowth) found on the site, burning, hoeing of the surface (which is probably unnecessary), subsequent hoeing of weeds, harvest. There are, however, many transitional stages between the most primitive and the most developed forms of this subsistence agriculture. The most primitive form is perhaps that observed among some of the Zanda in the south of the Sudan; here the savannah is neither cleared nor burned; the eleusine millet are sown in the earth among the large grass clumps as the first rain is falling, then the grass clumps are laboriously grubbed out to leave room for the millet to grow. In the more developed forms of shifting cultivation, the soil is cultivated for several years in succession, and the fallow period is reduced to about the same length as the cultivation period.

No purpose is served by attempting to classify these forms of cultiva-

133

tion, because the transition between them is so gradual. In any case, it is dangerous to attempt classifications depending on both shifting *residence* and shifting *cultivation*. If the dwellings are moved about within a specified area, namely the land over which the cultivators in question enjoy the rights of tribal ownership, then it often happens that the choice of dwelling sites depends on considerations other than agricultural. Some of the Ibo in Southern Nigeria seek out abandoned dwelling sites as land which is particularly worth cultivation, because of the accumulation of excreta. However, if a whole tribe migrates right away from its own region, we can be fairly sure that they are doing so from motives other than agricultural.

Let us come back to the essential point, the larger part of the crops in Africa are gathered from fields which are formed by burning, and which rapidly revert to fallow. In this type of agriculture, we find several limiting factors which prevent the cultivators enlarging their area. What are these limiting factors? The first is that if the field has to be hoed, which is generally the case, this work cannot be undertaken until after the first rains have fallen, particularly in the soils baked hard by drought, which is generally the case in the savannah country; but experience shows that the harvest is seriously diminished if the sowing is delayed too late after the first rains; the whole tribe therefore has to work at top speed to cultivate even a limited area. A second limiting factor is the weeding, or weedings; it serves no purpose to clear and sow a large area if there is a lack of labour at the time when weeding is required, one of the reasons for the lack of success in growing groundnuts at Mokwa was that the large areas, made available to cultivators by the use of tractors, could not be weeded.

The third limiting factor arises from the fact that, in many parts of Africa, the men leave all the heavy work to the women. For example, it has been observed that among the Bamenda in North Cameroons that each family lives on the average on an agricultural area of $1\frac{1}{2}$ acres, to which the head of the family devoted only 10 days' work per year, the wife and daughters 160 each. A fourth limiting factor is that all the work of cultivation has to be done by hand, without any aid from either draught animals or machines, the only mitigator of hard labour is fire, which at times helps a great deal.[1]

The labour of the men and women has not been alleviated by any form of capital equipment; not only do they lack draught animals and machines, but also carts, mills (all the grain has to be crushed by hand in mortars),

---

[1] Might it not be possible, however, while continuing hand cultivation, to improve the tools? Allard (*Bulletin Agricole du Congo Belge*, 1960, pp. 603–15) concluded that redesigned hoes for hand weeding could give a productivity 10–20 per cent. higher than traditional hoes.

soil improvements, irrigation, drainage, terracing, roads, scientific knowledge.

The technical limiting factors which restrict the amount of land which can be cultivated are therefore numerous, and we have not yet said anything about the economic limiting factors such as the bad organization of markets or the lack of means of communication.

As for the inadequate amount of work done by the men in agriculture, in many parts of Africa, this must be considered a social, not a technical limiting factor.

AGRICULTURAL POPULATION DENSITY

The consequence of all the factors discussed above is that the average density of population in Black Africa is only 25 per square mile of total area – but 750 people per square mile of cultivated land, of whom 90 per cent. are rural. It may be convenient to attempt to calculate the potential density permitted by the various types of shifting cultivation observed in Africa. This can be defined by the formula AC/B, where A equals the cultivable land expressed as a proportion of the whole, B equals the total length of rotation in years (period of cultivation plus period of fallow) and C equals the number of inhabitants per acre cleared annually.

As an example, we may take A at 0·8 (80 per cent.), B at 8 (say one year of harvest and seven fallow, or two years of harvest and six of fallow), C at four inhabitants per acre cleared each year (that is to say a quarter of an acre for each inhabitant); then if each clearing is cultivated for three years each inhabitant on the average consumes the produce of about three-quarters of an acre.

We are dealing with a rural population, that is to say the population which must live off the land, not only to the extent of feeding itself, but also to the extent of earning the cash income which it requires.

Then $AC/B = 0·8 \times 4 \div 8 = 0·4$ (overall potential density measured in inhabitants per acre, or 256 to the square mile).

If such a formula were applied to the whole of Black Africa it would make it appear that, even with agriculture still organized on the basis of shifting cultivation, the general density could be 250 rather than 25 persons per square mile. There is a very wide margin between the actual and potential density of agricultural population, which latter would take a hundred years to reach, at the present rate of population growth.

However, to apply this formula properly, we must have a precise knowledge of the percentage of cultivable land in relation to the whole. We must not flatter ourselves that we yet know this proportion for the whole of Black Africa, or even for any of the component regions. Knowledge of length of rotation, however, can be obtained by close study in the field, and of rate of clearing by sample inquiries. Our formula, therefore, cannot be easily applied. However, it remains valuable as a means of research, and as a standard for different situations.

If the cultivators take only one harvest, and then leave the land for prolonged fallowing, they will inevitably be clearing a much greater quantity of land each year than if they take several harvests and short fallowing. For instance, with a twenty-year rotation, going back to our formula: $AC/B = 0.8 \times 1.6 \div 20 = 0.064$ per acre or only 41 per square mile. It must be remembered that C represents the number of inhabitants per unit of area *cleared* each year.

On the other hand, if agriculture becomes permanent, and if there is no fallow, B becomes equal to 1, and C becomes the number of rural population who can live on each acre cultivated under these circumstances, say 2. With A still 0.8, the formula gives 1.6 per acre, or over 1,000 per square mile.

Under these circumstances, Black Africa could support a rural population of 6,000 million as against the 135 million of the present day.

EXTENSIVE AND INTENSIVE ORGANIZATIONS IN TRADITIONAL AFRICAN AGRICULTURE

The agriculture based on burning and fallowing is described as *extensive*; yields are low, whether measured per acre cultivable, or per acre cultivated. But the productivity per day of labour is improved by the labour-saving operation of burning (which may obviate the necessity of hoeing, when clearing exposes a soft forest soil, enriched by ashes).

Agricultural progress in Africa clearly should be in the direction of improved yields, to be obtained by a variety of methods, in the first place by manuring and by irrigation. This is true, and is likely to come about in the future. However, we must not forget that Africa in the past used to practise an *intensive* agriculture, obtaining high yields from permanent cultivations.

This form of agriculture, however, gave a low yield per unit of labour input, and the peasants who practised it were very pleased to abandon it in favour of extensive agriculture, as soon as circumstances permitted. Those who practised settled, intensive agriculture were usually in fact refugees, in mountains, islands or swamps of limited agricultural area, where they could only support themselves by methods of intensive cultivation. Under these circumstances, Africans can labour prodigiously. The best example is from the island of Ukara in Lake Victoria (Tanganyika); density of population here is 580 per square mile and, as a large part of the island consists of bare rock (inselbergs), agriculture has to be even more intensive than the figures indicate. Each field yields on an average two crops per year; they are abundantly manured, thanks to numerous cattle which are kept in sheds, and fed on specially grown fodder crops; this feeding calls for considerable hand labour. However, the inhabitants of Ukara, once they were again at peace with their neighbours, were very pleased to begin again clearing the vacant land on the shores of Lake Victoria, and to go back to the extensive cultivation of axe, fire and fallow.

Similar examples are found among the Nuba of Kordofan, the Kabre of Togo, the Dogon of the Plateau of Bandiagara (Mali), and the Diola of Lower Dasamance (Senegal), the mountain dwellers of Mandara (North Cameroons), and many others.

African peasants have quite a shrewd knowledge of which methods of cultivation yield the best return to labour, and they prefer methods of high productivity per unit of labour to those of low productivity. This is what we find in the extensive agricultural plantations developed by Africans on the river banks in Guinea. The cocoa plantations of the Yoruba in Nigeria and in Ghana, and the palm oil plantations yield low returns, but do not call for any large input of labour per input area.

All this serves to draw our attention to the conclusion that the African is quite well aware of the difference in yield per unit area, and has deliberately chosen the low yielding methods because they give a higher return per unit of labour. The traditional intensive African agriculture called for meticulous labour, almost as in gardening, and deprived the cultivator of the economic gains of the burning process.

In consequence, if African agriculture is to move towards higher yields per unit of area, as it is desirable that it should, it is necessary to improve productivity per unit of labour at the same time. It should be no longer the haunting memory of famines (which inspired the old style settled intensive agriculture of Africa) but a desire for greater cash return, which should animate the movement towards intensive agriculture in the future. Irrigation (which should guarantee security for crops over a large area of Black Africa), manuring, soil improvement, breeding of farm animals, should all help to ensure a higher return per unit of labour as well as per unit of area.

Let us conclude with an interesting comparison of three cases of high plateau lands in Mysore (India), Imerina (Madagascar) and Northern Rhodesia respectively; overall population densities are 400, 200 and 5 per square mile respectively. All the areas have much the same climates and soils; the same tropical climate mitigated by high altitude, the same complex of basic strata eroded down to level surfaces, chequered with small flat-bottomed valleys. The difference between the areas is in their methods of cultivation – in general terms, between their civilizations. In Mysore irrigated rice is grown, with large artificial ponds to assure a regular flow of water; in Imerina, rice is cultivated, but without reserves of water, and therefore subject to much greater risk of drought, in Northern Rhodesia, the small valleys (dambo) are completely neglected and agriculture is carried out only by the system known as 'chitimene', one of the 'least populating' systems known – some fifteen acres of forest are cut down and burned to yield 2½ acres fertilized by ashes, to be sown with millet; the fifteen acres then go fallow for twenty to twenty-five years.

But is the yield per unit of labour higher in Mysore than in Imerina, and in Imerina than among the Lala of Northern Rhodesia? It is possible, but it is by no means certain. As technical progress is made, the return per unit of labour must also be improved, if we want to see the African peasant go forward with any enthusiasm towards new methods of cultivation.

15

The Economic Life of the Gikuyu[1]

Jomo Kenyatta

No single reading could do justice to the diversity of Africa's traditional economic systems. We have thought it best, therefore, to present a reading which describes in some detail the life of a single tribe, the Gikuyu (or Kikuyu) of Kenya. In economics, as in other forms of activity, there is no such thing as a typical African tribe. The Gikuyu, however, are a very large tribe and many aspects of the type of production and organization described here are repeated in other parts of Africa. Of course, different tribes grow different crops and use different methods of cultivation; some are not agriculturalists at all but pastoralists; and the patterns of participation in the labour force, methods of marketing, types of land tenure, and so on, differ markedly from place to place. This reading, however, gives us, as no general survey could, a clear idea of the nature of traditional African economic life.

The reader is warned not to conclude from the readings in this section that traditional economic activity in Africa is only agricultural. As an earlier reading[2] has already made clear, various goods were manufactured long before the arrival of the first colonists.

DIVISION OF LABOUR

Land tenure is the most important factor, as we shall see presently, in our analysis of the economic life of the Gikuyu, for the supply of material needs depends entirely on the land.

The chief occupations among the Gikuyu are agriculture and the rearing of livestock, such as cattle, sheep and goats. Each family, i.e. a man, his wife or wives and their children, constitute an economic unit. This is controlled and strengthened by the system of division of labour according to sex. From the homestead to the fields and to the tending of the domestic animals, every sphere of activity is clearly and systematically defined. Each member of the family unit knows perfectly well what task he or she is required to perform, in their economic productivity and distribution of the family resources, so as to ensure the material prosperity of the group.

[1] Reprinted from *Facing Mount Kenya*, Random House, 1962.
[2] Reading 2.

The best point for starting our analysis of the division of labour is from the homestead and then moving gradually to the fields. In house-building the heavy work of cutting timbers and putting up the framework falls on men. Carrying and cutting of the grass for thatching and plastering the wall with clay or cow-dung is the work of women. Men build fences around the homestead or gardens and also cattle-pens. They are the night watchmen to protect the crops against the wild animals.

The entire housework naturally falls within the sphere of women's activities. They cook, bring water from the rivers, wash utensils and fetch firewood from the forests or bush. They also perform the task of carrying the loads on their backs. According to the tribal customs which govern the division of labour, no man would dare to indulge in any of these activities except in a case of emergency, or otherwise he would scandalize the women and it would be difficult for such a man to get any girl to marry him. He would be given a nickname, *kihongoyo* or *moburabureki*, something like 'Nosy Parker'. Women are afraid of a man of this character, for they say that if he could perform women's work, what is the use of getting married, for how can a wife and husband be doing the same thing at the same time?

In cultivating the fields men clear the bush and cut big trees, and also break the virgin soil with digging-sticks or hoes. Women come behind them and prepare the ground for sowing seeds. Planting is shared by both sexes. Men plant bananas, yams, sweet potato vines, sugar-canes, tobacco, and also provide poles for propping up bananas and yams. Women plant maize, various kinds of beans, millet and sweet potato vines.

Weeding is done collectively. Cutting drains or water-furrows and pruning of banana plants, as well as making roads and bridges, is the work of men. Harvesting is done chiefly by the women. Tending of cattle, sheep and goats, and also slaughtering and distributing the meat and preparing the skins, is entirely the men's duty. Dress-making, pottery and weaving of baskets are exclusively women's professions. Wood-carving, smith's work, bee-keeping and hunting are men's occupations. Women take responsibility for grinding corn and millet, for making gruel, and pounding grains in wooden mortars. They also pound sugar-canes for making beer.

The brewing of beer is done jointly by both men and women. Men cut the canes from the field and peel them, and the women carry the canes home. While the women are pounding, the men are busy mixing the substance of the sugar-canes with the water and squeezing or wringing the juice out of it, and also straining the juice into fermenting gourds. Trading is done by both sexes. Carrying and selling grains at the markets is chiefly done by women, while taking sheep and goats or cattle to the markets and selling them is the job of men.

AGRICULTURE

The land being the foundation rock on which the Gikuyu tribal economy stands, and the only effective mode of production that the people have, the result is that there is a great desire in the heart of every Gikuyu man to own a piece of land on which he can build his home, and from which he and his family can get the means of livelihood. A man or a woman who cannot say to his friends, come and eat, drink and enjoy the fruit of my labour, is not considered as a worthy member of the tribe.

A family group with land to cultivate is considered as a self-supporting economic unit. The group work harmoniously with a view to satisfying their immediate needs, and with the desire to accumulate wealth in the form of cattle, sheep and goats. These are acquired through effective tillage of the land, except in a very few cases nowadays where some people are able to get money in some other ways than selling their products.

CHILDREN IN ECONOMIC ACTIVITIES

Children begin their activities in production when they are young as a part of their training in agriculture and herding. When children are very young they are left at home minding small babies, or are taken by their parents to the field where they are allowed to play in a corner of the cultivated field. Soon the children get interested in the work and are ambitious to participate in gardening. As soon as they are able to handle a digging-stick they are given small allotments to practise on.

The children are very proud of their small gardens and take great interest in learning how to become good agriculturalists. Parents help them to plant seeds and teach them how to distinguish the crops from the wild plants or weeds. For sometimes children keep on rooting out growing crops together with weeds, until gradually their eyes get to recognize what are weeds and what are crops. The children are very enthusiastic in their work, and frequently like to take their playmates and proudly show them round the small gardens, saying: 'Look how our crops are growing nicely, surely we are going to have a good harvest, and then we can have a big feast as a result of our labour.'

As a child grows, its sphere of activities in gardening increases. Instead of small fields, a large one is provided according to the capability of the child. Of course, the work is done collectively. The crops thus cultivated are in the care of the mother, who is the managing director of food supply in the homestead.

The children co-operate with their parents in production and distribution of the family's resources and wealth until the time of marriage. When a girl marries, if her husband's homestead is near, she continues to cultivate her childhood gardens and takes the crops home for the use of herself and her husband. On the other hand, if she goes far away to live, she leaves the gardens to her mother. In the case of a boy, he takes full control of his gardens when he marries. For although he still co-operates with his parents in the general economy of the family group, he and his wife are now responsible for supplying and satisfying their own immediate material needs.

SEASONAL CALENDAR

In the Gikuyu country there are four seasons and two harvests in one year. These are divided as follows: (1) The season of big rain (*mbura ya njahe*) from March to July; (2) the season of big harvest (*magetha ma njahe*), between July and early October; (3) short rain season (*mbura ya mwere*), from October to January; (4) the season of harvesting millet (*magetha ma mwere*), from January to March. There are various names attached to these seasons, according to the activities pursued during each season, such as clearing virgin land (*matuguta*), protecting millet from the birds (*marira ma mwere*), etc., but the names mentioned above are the main divisions of the seasonal calendar.

PREPARING FIELDS FOR PLANTING

Where land is available the system of cultivating it in rotation is the most favoured, for it gives a farmer or peasant an opportunity of getting a new field every four or five seasons, and at the same time letting the old one rest fallow. In this way a peasant is able to get good crops without using manure, because most of the Gikuyu land is very fertile. In cases where land is not available, especially nowadays owing to the alienation of the Gikuyu lands, people depend entirely on turning their land over and over again to renew it.

During the hot season a family group gets together and prepares their fields ready for planting. Every member of the group has his or her own fields for various seasonal crops, such as maize, a variety of beans, sweet potatoes and European potatoes and other vegetables. All these are planted at once when the rain starts. They are the mainstay of the Gikuyu diet.

The Economic Life of the Gikuyu

Permanent crops such as yams, sugar-canes, bananas, can only flourish in particular soils in various localities. The planting of these is a matter for individuals and for the custom of different districts. These are not crops that everyone in the community can afford to grow on account of the suitable soil and water they require. In some districts, especially Fort Hall and Nyeri, these articles of food are plentiful, but in other districts they are looked on as somewhat of a luxury.

To avoid repetition of magical aspects we will proceed to analyse the work and crops in the fields. Apart from the crops mentioned above, there are three kinds of crops which are planted in rotation, namely, millet (*mwere*), tree peas (*njogo*) and *njahe*, a very nourishing kind of bean used mostly to feed women after child-birth. *Njogo* and *njahe* are planted during the big rain season, and *mwere* during the short rain season. The reason being that if *njahe* and *njogo* are planted during the short rain season, the result will be a failure, because they are very slow-growing crops and need plenty of water. The same with *mwere*; if it is planted during the big rain, it will grow taller and taller, and bear very little or no grain at all. From a scientific and economic point of view, obtained from years of trial and error, the planting of crops and weeding of the gardens are done according to the seasonal calendar.

CLEARING WEEDS

When crops are about four or five inches high the weeding of the ground is started. During this time people join in a collective weeding. Four or five persons or more form a group for team-work, they cultivate one man's field one day then next day another man's field, and so on until they clear weeds from all their fields. Another way of cultivating the fields is by inviting a group of friends, ten or more, and providing them with a feast of beer or gruel and other edibles. This is not looked upon as a reward for the work done, but as hospitality to one's guests.

After a man has informed his friends about the work he wants them to help in, a day is fixed, generally three days ahead. On the day appointed, the friends meet in the garden or field early in the morning and start to work enthusiastically, singing cultivation songs. Sometimes they will challenge cultivators in the next field and compete with them in work and songs. About midday, when the sun becomes hot, they have finished clearing a big field. At this juncture they retire and start feasting joyously for having completed the work of helping their friend.

If a stranger happens to pass by at this time of enjoyment after labour he will have no idea that these people who are now singing, dancing and laughing merrily, have completed their day's work. For after they have cleaned off the dust which they got from the fields, they look, in all respects, as though they have been enjoying themselves the whole day. This is why most of the Europeans have erred by making general remarks that 'the African is a lazy being and likes to bask in the sun, while his wife or wives work for him,' not realizing that the African in his own environment does not count hours or work by the movement of the clock, but works with good spirit and enthusiasm to complete the task before him. In this way an African is able to work better and quicker in his own field, where he is his own master, than when employed by the Europeans where he has to be bossed about.

To turn to our analysis of the work in the fields, the correct method of ensuring a good crop is, that while the crops are growing the fields are weeded over and over again until there are no more weeds growing there. Then comes a time of relaxation waiting for the harvest. This is a period of numerous dances and songs and performing various ceremonies, especially if a good harvest is expected. About this time one of the quick-growing kinds of bean (*mboco*) is ripe, and is used as a supplement to food prepared from the grains stored during the previous harvest.

MARKETING

At this time people have finished the heavy work of weeding and there is little to do in the fields except that the crops are in need of protection against the birds. This work is generally done in rotation, one member of the family group taking charge of the field one day and another the next day. This gives all the members of the group an opportunity of participating in dances and visiting the markets to sell or buy.

Marketing begins when crops are ripe and have not yet dried to be harvested. Various things are taken to markets, principally bananas, yams, a variety of beans, tree peas, maize, millet, potatoes and sugar-canes. In these markets one finds all kinds of ornaments, articles of clothing, from skins of animals to Lancashire cotton, and different types of agricultural implements, running from digging-sticks to hoes made in Birmingham or Japan. There are also sheep and goats, milk and butter-fat, etc.

There are two ways of exchanging goods, one by barter and the other by money. The former is predominant, for the majority of the people still adhere to the old form of exchanging one article for another. For instance, if one man has beans and he wants yams, he goes to the man who has yams and is in need of beans and tells him: 'I have my beans and I want your yams.' Then they argue as to how many yams to a basket of beans.

If they agree they exchange there and then; if not, each goes his own way, looking for someone else who will agree with him, for the exchange depends entirely on individual buyer and seller.

There are also fixed prices for certain goods dictated by the seasonal law of supply and demand. For instance, if a man wants a cultivating-knife he goes to a smith who has fixed a general price for each of his articles according to their sizes. For example, a small knife is exchanged for a small basket of millet or two small baskets of beans. Again, if a woman wants an ornament she goes to a man or a woman who has them and there exchanges two heaps of sweet potatoes or one heap of yams for a bracelet or an ear-ring.

In the markets things are bought and sold in small and big quantities by people who have too much of one thing and too little of the other. Take the case of a man who is about to stage a big ceremonial feast, and perhaps has not cultivated sufficient grain to enable him to display his generosity to his friends. He takes one of his sheep or goats to the market and exchanges it for three or four big baskets of millet or for any other commodity that he lacks. If a man has too many cows and fewer sheep and goats, he takes one of his cows, especially one that has no religious implications within the family group, and exchanges it for ten or more sheep and goats. Sometimes there are people who have been working for wages and have saved a few shillings after paying their poll or hut taxes. When one such returns to his home and wants to own a few of these valued animals, which are the recognized standard of wealth among the Gikuyu, he goes to the market and makes a good bargain with the people who have brought their sheep and goats to raise sufficient money for the Government taxes. In these markets one can buy almost any conceivable thing that is available in the tribe. It is considered a sign of industry to be selling grain in the markets, for it proves that one has not only cultivated sufficient for the family, but also a surplus for accumulation of wealth.

HARVESTING

In many cases the harvesting-time is the busiest period for the majority of women, for the simple reason that they are the managing directors of the food supply in their respective family groups. Therefore it is considered right and proper for the women to handle the grain and store it according to the immediate and future needs of the family. The work of harvesting is almost equally divided between men and women. For while the women do the actual harvesting and carrying the harvest home, the men cut or root out maize or millet stalks, burn them and spread the ashes in the field as a part of the manuring and to kill certain insects. Men also make new granaries or repair the old ones.

When the harvesting is completed, a woman's first thought is to store sufficient grain to last her family until the next harvest. After she has done so, and there is surplus grain left, she consults with her husband. Then, if there is something that the family needs, the surplus grain is sold immediately in the markets to satisfy the needs. If there are no immediate needs, the surplus grain is kept back and sold later when there is a scarcity of that particular grain in the markets.

The stored grain is dished out carefully by the wife, with the view neither to be wasteful nor starve the family. She prepares family menus with a variety of daily changes to balance the diets. For example, if she had prepared sweet potatoes and gruel for today's meal, tomorrow she will cook a mixture of beans, maize, greens and perhaps bananas. Although menus are changed almost daily, the wife takes great care not to exhaust the supply of one article of food. So when there is plenty of beans and maize, and less bananas and sweet potatoes, she cooks more of what is abundant and less of what is scarce.

A wife who manages efficiently the economic affairs as well as other duties in her family group, is highly respected not only by her group but by the entire community.

ECONOMIC VALUE OF SHEEP AND GOATS AND CATTLE

We have seen that in the Gikuyu society almost every man has a garden or gardens from which his immediate needs are supplied. We have also dealt with the economic aspects of the crops raised in these fields, and how they are bartered in the markets or sold for money. Little has been mentioned about the marketing of domestic animals, but up to this point we have not yet discussed the economic value of these animals. It is therefore necessary to give a short description of how the Gikuyu look upon their cattle, sheep and goats.

To a Gikuyu the cattle in the first place are merely a display of wealth, for a man to be called rich he must own a number of cattle. Because, while every family has a number of sheep and goats, say, from one to hundreds, only a small minority own cattle, and therefore to own a cow or two is the first sign of being a wealthy man.

Apart from being the display of wealth, cattle play a part in the economic life of the people. To start with, cow's milk is used for babies by those who can afford it. The milk is very little used in the Gikuyu diet except by those who own a number of cows. Hides are used for various purposes, for bedding, making sandals and straps for tying and carrying firewood and other loads. As a source of meat or butter supply, cattle play a very small part. Cows are never killed for food, except at a time of famine, but bulls and oxen are now and again slaughtered for occasional meat feasts (*kerugo*), and this is regarded as luxurious and only practised by well-to-do persons.

Cows give the owner a prestige in the community, but are never killed for any particular sacrificial or religious ceremonies, except in very rare cases or when a bull or ox is substituted for a male goat or a ram. As economic assets cattle play a part in the marriage ceremony, where a cow or more is given as marriage insurance (*roracio*), but there, too, cattle are given as a substitute for sheep or goats, each cow being valued at ten sheep or goats and a bull or an ox at five sheep or goats.

In former days cattle had very little economic value to the owners, apart from the fact that such owners were looked on as dignified, respected rich men. The milk was not sold, but used by the herdsmen and by visitors, especially warriors, who were the protectors of the villages against Masai or other raiders. The rich men, who naturally had more property to be protected, were responsible for feeding the warriors in the way of milk and providing oxen for meat feasts (*kerugo*) to keep the warriors in good healthy condition.

Sometimes the owner of cattle hardly had the pleasure of drinking his cows' milk, especially if they were far away from his homestead. In spite of this the owner of a large number of cattle was sentimentally satisfied by praise names conferred upon him by the community in their songs and dances. Nowadays some people, especially those who are near European towns, do sell their milk and derive a good income from it. This income could be improved by introducing a better breed instead of keeping a number of cows which give very little milk. From the economic point of view the present breed of cattle reared by the Gikuyu is very poor, and it would be a great advancement if the Government could help the people to secure a few good bulls for breeding, and gradually replace the inferior types of cattle with better ones. This method would automatically improve the problem of congestion in grazing areas which faces the country at present, for people would learn the value of keeping a few cows which would be useful economically, instead of keeping a large number of cattle for sentimental satisfaction.

SHEEP AND GOATS AS STANDARD CURRENCY

In the Gikuyu country, before the introduction of the European monetary system, sheep and goats were regarded as the standard currency of the

Gikuyu people. The price of almost everything was determined in terms of sheep and goats (*mbori*). This system still operates among the majority of the Gikuyu people who have not yet grasped the idea of a monetary system and its value.

These domestic animals play an important role in the economic, religious, and social life of the Gikuyu. A man with a number of sheep and goats feels no less than a man with a large bank balance. The people look upon these animals as a good investment which gives them a yearly income, for if a man has two or three good sheep or female goats within a year they increase to six or more, and people consider this a good profit. They would argue saying that money is not a good investment, for one shilling does not bear another shilling, whereas a sheep or goat does. This, of course, is due to the ignorance of money speculation, and so they say it is better to buy a sheep or a goat instead of keeping shillings which, if buried in the ground (the only form of saving money the majority of the people know), would rot and lose their value.

Sheep and goats, unlike cattle, are used for various religious sacrifices and purifications. They are the chief means of supplying the people with meat, while the skins are used as articles of clothing. Finally, without them a man cannot get a wife, for it is sheep and goats that are given as *roracio* (marriage insurance). If a man has cash money and he wants to get married he must, in the first place, buy cattle or sheep and goats, because the parents of the wife-to-be will not accept cash money as *roracio*. To them coins have very little meaning and have no religious or sentimental associations within the people's custom.

The real value of money is only realized when a man takes it and buys a cow or sheep and goats, or pays the Government taxes, otherwise money as such has little function inside the Gikuyu country. With all the disadvantages connected with the rearing of sheep and goats, they are still regarded generally as the only means of expression of wealth. By disadvantages we mean that in some cases young men have been ruined by spending years earning money to buy these highly valued animals and sometimes sickness invades a homestead and kills every one of them in a few days. This means a loss of ten or thirty pounds, which if it had been put in a savings bank, would have remained there and helped the young man to improve his standard of living. This is a question which is very difficult to settle, for some people would argue that the animals give better profit yearly, whereas shillings do not multiply quickly and do not give the same sentimental satisfaction. But let us hope that gradually people will be able to decide which one of the two systems is suitable for their advancement.

The Economic Life of the Gikuyu

We have given a description of how the Gikuyu exchange goods amongst themselves in the markets, and the types of articles sold and bought. Having done so, we will now enter into discussion of how the Gikuyu trade with their neighbours, i.e. the Masai and Wakamba. The articles of special value in trading with the Masai are spears, swords, tobacco, gourds and red ochre. The Masai, who are not agriculturalists, and who regard the cultivation of soil as a crime against their gods, depend almost entirely on the Gikuyu for the supply of the three last-mentioned articles. Although the Masai have their own blacksmiths, the spears made by the Gikuyu were and still are regarded as the best.

There are inter-tribal markets where these goods are exchanged, but, apart from these markets, sometimes a group of men organize into a trading guild and take their goods into the heart of the Masai country. In former days this kind of trade was conducted in the homestead of a friend who acted as the guide and protector of his friends and their goods.

The Gikuyu, after collecting their trading goods, would send for their friend or friends in Masailand, asking them to meet the traders at the frontier and conduct them into the country. Thus goods were taken to villages, and, after exchanging them for sheep, the Gikuyu would return escorted by their friends to the frontier to avoid any molestation by the hostile warriors who would only be too glad to have someone on whom to blood their spears. The same thing happened when the Masai wanted to enter into Gikuyuland for the purpose of trade.

Nowadays the trade between the two tribes is mostly restricted to trading centres. Only those who can afford to pay heavy licence fees to the British Government can open a trading store in these centres.

As regards trade with the Wakamba, there are no special articles as in the case of the Masai. In fact the Wakamba being agriculturists grow almost the same crops as the Gikuyu. The two tribes are racially and linguistically identical. It can be said that in the beginning of things the Gikuyu and Wakamba were brothers, but how and why they came to part is a matter requiring some investigation.

In former days there was very little hostility between the two tribes, and their trade depended on seasonal harvests. If there was a shortage of food in Gikuyuland and abundance in the Wakamba country, the Gikuyu went and bought grain from the Wakamba, the exchange being sheep and goats or cows and sometimes ivory. The same thing happened in the case of the Wakamba. Apart from these contacts, there were frequent and friendly visits from both sides for trading or other purposes.

III: The Contemporary Scene

IIIa: The Rise of Nations

In 1957 Ghana (formerly the Gold Coast) became the first of the colonial states of tropical Africa to gain its independence; by the end of 1964 the only colonies remaining in Africa were Portuguese Angola and Mozambique and the few small Portuguese and Spanish colonies of the West Coast, and also Southern Rhodesia. Thus the unscrambling of colonialism will have taken place in an even shorter time than the remarkably rapid scramble for Africa by the colonial powers in the late nineteenth century.

The rapid coming of independence has been the combined result of a universal development of politically powerful independence movements among the Africans and the lack of any will to resist, even in some cases a readiness to co-operate, on the part of the European colonial powers.

The reasons for the rapid and comparatively frictionless achievement of freedom by Africa must be sought, therefore, both in colony and in metropole as well as in a changing political atmosphere in the world in general.

A new world atmosphere emerged after the defeat of Germany and Austria-Hungary in Europe in 1918. Ideas of nationalism and self-determination prevailed in the peace settlement in Europe – ideas which were to have an impact later on nationalisms in other continents. At the same time the German colonies were distributed among the Allies as mandated territories. South-west Africa went to the Union of South Africa, Kamerun was divided between Britain and France, Tanganyika became a British mandate, Togo a French mandate and Belgium took over the rule of Rwanda and Burundi. These mandates were given on the assumption (vague though it was) that their trustees would eventually lead them to independence; these obligations were later reinforced and made more explicit after 1945 by the United Nations charter which called the countries concerned 'trusteeship territories.'

These international trusteeship obligations fostered similar thinking with regard to other colonies. Colonial powers were to submit regular reports on their 'non-self-governing' possessions to the United Nations Trustee-ship Council; it became harder for them to pursue a colonial policy un-affected by the pressures and attitudes of the rest of the world. In British imperial thought the concept of trusteeship of its colonies, leading to eventual independence, had long existed, even if independence was usually regarded as an eventuality beyond the foreseeable future. The French colonial tradition tended more to regard its overseas possessions as integral parts of a greater France for whom closer partnership, though seldom full independence, was envisaged. The fact that Belgium had inherited the Congo from King Leopold II (whose private empire it had been) was partly the reason that Belgian intentions in her colonies had always seemed more confused. Portugal regarded her African possessions as provinces of the metropolitan country – an argument she has constantly employed to prevent outside interference. But the changing world atmosphere (power-fully reinforced by the emergence of communist governments and, after 1947, by newly independent states in Asia upon the stage of world politics) turned Britain, France and Belgium in a more liberal direction and en-couraged policies based on the concept of trusteeship. At the same time public opinion in these countries became less chauvinistically imperialist and more sensitive to criticism. Moreover, the growing power of Socialist parties in the colonial countries without colonialist predilections gave further impetus to the independence movement. It was a Labour govern-ment in Britain which in 1947 gave independence to India, Burma and Ceylon.

It was at about this time that mass independence movements through-out colonial Africa began to emerge. They were led by a new generation of African politicians – highly educated in France, Britain and the United States, and deeply influenced by liberal and socialist political ideas in Europe, grafting these ideas on to a new peculiarly African political awakening; it was based upon a vigorous opposition to all forms of foreign rule, oppressive or paternalist, to racial discrimination, and upon an aggressive and enthusiastic belief in and assertion of African traditions, rights and abilities. The national boundaries of the time had not existed before the scramble for Africa by the colonial powers; nations had not been conquered but rather diverse peoples had been pinned within often arbitrary borders into colonial states. The revolution against colonialism, therefore, was performed not so much by Ghanaians, Senegalese or Nigerians against French and British as by Africans against Europeans. It is this fact which has made some writers shun the term nationalism and call the political awakening 'Africanism'.

While this is not mere sophistry, it is nevertheless in the form of the states carved by colonialism that Africa acquired its nationhood. There were a few exceptions to this: after a plebiscite, for example, the Northern Cameroons joined Nigeria, and the Southern Cameroons joined the formerly French Cameroons; and on independence British and Italian Somaliland combined to form the republic of Somalia; and in 1964 Tanganyika and Zanzibar formed the republic of Tanzania. British Africa gained its independence pragmatically, territory by territory. Nearly all the French possessions in tropical Africa became internally self-governing within the French Community in 1958 (except for Guinea which asked for full independence then and complete severance of the French connexion). In 1960 the French government realized the inadequacy of its policy of 1958 and allowed for full independence – an offer which its African possessions swiftly took up. Belgium succumbed rapidly to unrest in the Congo in 1959 and granted independence in 1960. These different policies of the colonial governments, however, all produced the same result of separate independence for each of the colonial political units. Several territories which under French colonial rule had been administered as partial federations drifted apart upon independence. A Mali Federation of Senegal and Mali was short lived (lasting from 1960 to 1961) and the union of Ghana and Guinea in 1958, joined in 1961 by Mali, lapsed in 1963. The result is that by the end of 1964 there were thirty-five independent states in Africa (a continent whose total population is 200 million). Whether these countries will further polarize into nation-states jealous of their own sovereignty or whether they will move towards closer integration is a question which we shall examine later in this book.

16

Nationalism in Tropical Africa[1]

James Coleman

The following survey was written three years before Ghana became the first state in tropical Africa to gain its freedom from colonial rule. The events of subsequent years, however, have done little to invalidate this analysis. Some new personalities have moved into the political limelight – Mr Julius Nyerere in Tanganyika, Dr Hastings Banda in Malawi, Mr Kenneth Kaunda in Zambia, and in Kenya Mr Jomo Kenyatta returned from a long prison sentence to join Mr Odinga Odinga and Mr Tom Mboya in leading the nationalist movement there. The other major substantive change in the pattern of African politics since 1954 has been the growing importance of often monolithic parties which have continued to crystallize out of the multitude of forces which combined to create the African nationalist movement. This trend is examined in section IIIb.

This survey points to the effect of the policy differences (political, social, economic, and educational) of the colonial powers upon the character of political movements in their respective territories. It shows also the multifarious causes (colonial, metropolitan, and world) of nationalist political activity, and the forms which this activity took.

Post-war uprisings and nationalist assertions in Tropical Africa – that part of the continent south of the Sahara and north of the Union – have directed increased attention towards the nature and implications of the awakening of the African to political consciousness. Among scholars this neglected area has long been the preserve of the scientific linguist or of the social anthropologist; only recently have American sociologists, economists, and political scientists developed an active interest in its problems.[2] As a consequence, apart from certain efforts by anthropologists to popularize their findings and insights we have been obliged to rely primarily upon the somewhat contradictory accounts of colonial governments seeking to explain imperial connexions, or of African nationalists determined to achieve

[1] Reprinted from the *American Political Science Review*, Vol. XLVIII, No. 2, June 1954.
[2] Two notable pre-war exceptions were Professor Raymond Leslie Buell and Dr Ralph J. Bunche.

self-government and the good life of which national self-determination has become the symbol.[1] Thus, we have been placed in the uncomfortable position of having to formulate opinions and policy and to render judgements without sufficient knowledge, or, what could be worse, on the basis of evaluations provided by participants in the nationalist struggle. There is, therefore, a very real need for independent and objective research regarding the character and probable course of African nationalist development.

WHAT IS AFRICAN NATIONALISM?

Not the least burdensome of our tasks is the problem of correlating or distinguishing between the generally accepted political concepts elaborated with specific reference to developments in the Western World (i.e. state, nation, nationality, nationalism) and the conceptual tools developed by the Africanists. The latter have tended to feel that the traditional concepts and methods of the political scientists are unserviceable in the study of the political structure and life of pre-literate societies.[2] Yet, notwithstanding the importance of the lineage, clan, or tribe; the role of the diviner, the chief, or the age-grade society; or the wide variations in the organization of power within such societies, the concept and the institution of the modern nation-state, towards the creation of which African nationalism tends to be directed, is distinctly Western in its form and content. It is as exotic to Africa as Professor Toynbee has suggested that it is to the rest of

[1] As an excellent example of the application of the insights of anthropology to the problems of political development in this area, see William R. Bascom, 'West and Central Africa', in *Most of the World*, ed. Ralph Linton, pp. 331–405 (New York, 1949). For a historian's appraisal, see Vernon McKay, 'Nationalism in British West Africa', *Foreign Policy Reports*, Vol. 24, pp. 2–11 (15 March 1948).

[2] *African Political Systems*, eds. M. Fortes and E. E. Evans-Pritchard, pp. 4 ff. (New York, 1940). In so far as *traditional* concepts and methods are concerned, ethnocentrism has been freely confessed by political scientists in recent self-criticism. See David Easton, *The Political System*, pp. 33 ff. (New York, 1953); also Report of the Inter-University Summer Seminar on Comparative Politics, Social Science Research Review, Vol. 47, pp. 641–57, at pp. 642–3 (September, 1953). Amongst the modernists in political science one finds the argument that the political scientist should not be rejected too readily since he has developed skills and acquired insights that might well shed new light on the political process and pattern of government of pre-literate societies after the anthropologist has exhausted his resources. Another argument, rather different, is that such societies might profitably be regarded as microcosms in which the political scientist can discern with greater clarity the essentials of government that might be obscured in the more complex Western systems. A final argument might be found in the recent psycho-cultural studies, especially in terms of their implications for policy formulation. See Ithiel de Sola Pool, 'Who Gets Power and Why', *World Politics*, Vol. 2, pp. 120–34 (October 1949).

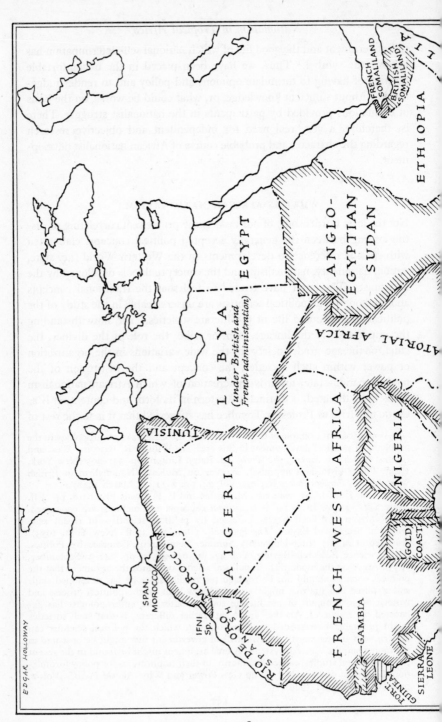

EDGAR HOLLOWAY

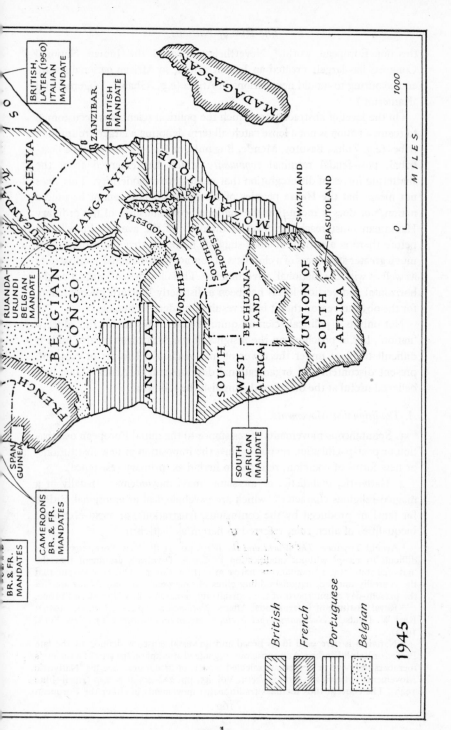

BR. & FR.
MANDATES

CAMEROONS
BR. & FR.
MANDATES

SPAN.
GUINEA

FRENCH

BELGIAN CONGO

RUANDA-
URUNDI
BELGIAN
MANDATE

ANGOLA

SOUTH
WEST
AFRICA

SOUTH AFRICAN
MANDATE

NORTHERN RHODESIA

SOUTHERN
RHODESIA

BECHUANA-
LAND

UNION OF
SOUTH
AFRICA

BASUTOLAND

SWAZILAND

NYASALAND

MOZAMBIQUE

TANGANYIKA

KENYA

UGANDA

SOMALILAND

ZANZIBAR
BRITISH
MANDATE

BRITISH,
LATER (1950)
ITALIAN
MANDATE

MADAGASCAR

1000

0   MILES

British

French

Portuguese

Belgian

1945

the non-European world.[1] Nevertheless, just as the Indian National Congress has largely created an Indian nation, so African nationalists are endeavouring to mould new nations in Africa (e.g. 'Ghana', 'Nigeria', and 'Kamerun').

On the level of abstraction at which the political scientist is accustomed to roam, a nation is not a loose catch-all term denoting a larger grouping of tribes (e.g. Zulus, Basutos, Mende, Buganda, or Hausa); rather it is a post-tribal, post-feudal terminal *community* which has emerged from the shattering forces of disintegration that characterize modernity. This does not mean that the Hausa peoples of Northern Nigeria cannot become a nation, nor does it mean that the 'national' consciousness of the ordinary Hausaman must reach the level of intensity of the average Frenchman before there is a nation. It does suggest, however, that there must be a much greater awareness of a closeness of contact with 'national' compatriots as well as with the 'national' government.[2] This closeness of contact on the horizontal and vertical levels has been a distinctly Western phenomenon, for the obvious reason that it is the result of modern technology.

Not only is a political scientist quite precise in his use of the concept 'nation', but in poaching on the insights of the Africanists he also finds it difficult to place under the cover of 'nationalism' all forms of past and present discontent and organizational development in Africa. Thus it is believed useful at the outset to distinguish the following:

A. Traditionalist Movements

1. Spontaneous movements of resistance to the initial European occupation or post-pacification revolts against the imposition of new institutions, or new forms of coercion, referred to herein as 'primary resistance'.

2. Nativistic, mahdistic, or messianic mass movements – usually of a magico-religious character – which are psychological or emotional outlets for tensions produced by the confusions, frustrations, or socio-economic inequalities of alien rule, referred to herein as 'nativism'.[3]

[1] Arnold Toynbee, *The World and the West*, pp. 71 ff. (New York, 1953). It is difficult to accept without qualification Professor Toynbee's argument that the 'national state' was a 'spontaneous native growth' in Europe. One could argue that the centrally-minded, nation-building élites of emergent Asia and Africa are but the present-day counterparts of the centralizing monarchs of early modern Europe.

[2] Royal Institute of International Affairs, *Nationalism*, pp. 1–7 (London, 1939); Karl W. Deutsch, *Nationalism and Social Communications*, pp. 1–14 (New York, 1953).

[3] Nativism is here used in its broad and universal sense, as defined by the late Professor Ralph Linton: 'Any conscious, organized attempt on the part of a society's members to revive or perpetuate selected aspects of its culture.' See his 'Nativistic Movements', *American Anthropologist*, Vol. 45, pp. 230–40, at p. 230 (April–June 1943). The concept thus includes traditionalist movements in either the European

B. Syncretistic Movements

A. Separatist religious groups, which have seceded and declared their independence from white European churches either because of the desire for religious independence or because the white clerics were intolerant regarding certain African customs; hereafter referred to as 'religious separatism'.[1]

2. Kinship associations, organized and led by the Western-educated and urbanized 'sons abroad' for the purposes of preserving a sense of identity with the kinfolk in the bush and 'brothers' in the impersonal urban centre, as well as of providing vehicles for pumping modernity – including the ideas and sentiment of nationalism – into the rural areas.[2]

3. Tribal associations, organized and led by Western-educated elements – usually in collaboration with some traditionalists – who desire to resurrect, or to create for the first time, a tribal sentiment ('tribalism'), for the purpose of establishing large-scale political units, the boundaries of which will be determined by tribal affiliation (i.e. those who accept the *assumption* of common blood and kinship) and the forms of government by a syncretism of tribal and Western institutions.[3]

C. Modernist Movements

1. Economic-interest groups (labour unions, co-operative societies, professional and middle-class associations) organized and led by Western-educated elements for the purpose of advancing the material welfare and improving the socio-economic status of the members of those groups.

or non-European world. This point is stressed because of the understandable sensitivity of many educated Africans to the root word 'native', which as a result of the colonial experience tends to carry with it the connotation of inferiority. See also A. LeGrip, 'Aspects Actuels de L'Islam en A.O.F.', *L'Afrique et l'Asie*, pp. 6–20 (No. 24, 1953); Katesa Schlosser, *Propheten in Afrika* (Albert Limbach Verlag, 1949).

[1] Daniel Thwaite, *The Seething African Pot*, pp. 1–70 (London, 1926); George Shepperson, 'Ethiopianism and African Nationalism', *Phylon*, Vol. 14, pp. 9–18 (1st Quarter, 1953); Hilda Kuper, 'The Swazi Reaction to Missions', *African Studies* Vol. 5, pp. 177–88 (September 1946); Jomo Kenyatta, *Facing Mount Kenya*, pp. 269–79 (London, 1953).

[2] James S. Coleman, 'The Role of Tribal Associations in Nigeria', Proceedings of the Second Annual Conference of the West African Institute of Social and Economic Research, Ibadan, Nigeria, April, 1952. See also *East Africa and Rhodesia*, p. 106 (5 October 1951), 'Nairobi is the happy hunting ground for the organizers of tribal associations, as there are to be found in the city representatives of practically every tribe in East and Central Africa.' Also K. A. Busia, *Report on a Social Survey of Takoradi–Sekondi* (Accra, Government Printer, 1950).

[3] Most advanced amongst the Yoruba, Ibo, Ibibio, Ewe, Buganda, and Kikuyu peoples.

2. Nationalist movements, organized and led by the Westernized *élite* which is activated by the Western ideas of democracy, progress, the welfare state, and national self-determination, and which aspires *either*: (*a*) to create modern independent African nation-states possessing an internal state apparatus and external sovereignty and all of the trappings of a recognized member state of international society (e.g. Sudan, Gold Coast, Nigeria, and possibly Sierra Leone); *or* (*b*) to achieve absolute social and political equality and local autonomy within a broader Euro-African grouping (e.g. French and Portuguese Africa) or within what is manifestly a plural society (e.g. except for Uganda, the territories of British East and Central Africa).[1]

3. Pan-African or trans-territorial movements, organized and led by the Westernized *élite*, frequently in association with or under the stimulus of American Negroes or West Indians abroad, for the purposes of creating a global *racial* consciousness and unity, or of agitating for the advancement and welfare of members of the *African* race wherever they may be, or of devising plans for future nationalist activity in specific regions.[2]

Once these very arbitrary analytical distinctions are drawn it should be stressed that none of the categories can be treated in isolation. Each of the movements is in one way or another a response to the challenge of alien rule, or of the intrusion of the disintegrating forces—and consequently the insecurity – of modernity. The recent so-called nationalism in Central Africa has been a mixture of 'primary resistance' by the chiefs and traditionalists of Northern Rhodesia and Nyasaland and the nationalist agitation

[1] The difference between the goal orientations of the two categories of movements is partly the result of the objectives of differing colonial policies (i.e., the British policy of self-government and differentiation versus the French, Portuguese, and in a qualified sense the Belgian policies of assimilation and identity) and in part the result of the presence or absence of a settled white population. Confronted with the overwhelming obstacles to the full realization of *African self-government*, African leaders in the second category tend towards the extreme either of accommodation (Union of South Africa) or of violence (Kenya). In the territories of the Central African Federation the leaders of the African Congress have tended not to define their ultimate objectives, preferring to act empirically. The strength and persistence of the autonomic drive is reflected, however, in their reported attraction to the original Gore-Brown partition plan adopted by the European Confederate party. See David Cole, 'How Strong is the African National Congress?' *New Commonwealth*, Vol. 27, pp. 5–10, at p. 9 (4 January 1954).

[2] For a variety of reasons these movements have thus far apparently accomplished little more than to dramatize their existence at infrequent *ad hoc* conferences. Until recently the initiative tended to be taken by Americans or West Indians of African descent (e.g., Marcus Garvey, W. E. B. DuBois, and George Padmore), although in the early 1920's there was a National Congress of British West Africa organized by the late Casely Hayrford of the Gold Coast. Also, M. Blaise Diagne, a Senegalese, was President of the first Pan-African Congress in Paris in 1919.

of the Westernized *élite*. Until the project of Federation became an active issue, African movements in this area were confined principally to religious separatist groups, tribal associations, or, in the case of Northern Rhodesia, labour unions.[1] On the West Coast, where nationalism is far more advanced, traditionalist and syncretistic movements have not been and are not absent. In some instances, kinship associations and separatist religious groups have been the antecedents of nationalist organization; in others they have provided the principal organizational bases of the latter (e.g. the National Council of Nigeria and the Cameroons was first inaugurated as a federation mainly of kinship associations, and the African National Congress of the Rhodesias and Nyasaland was the product of fusion of several African welfare societies). In certain cases unrest or protest of a nativistic flavour has been instigated by nationalists for their modernist ends; in others nationalists have claimed such uncoordinated uprisings, as well as purely economic protest movements, to be manifestations of 'nationalism', when in reality the participants were unaware of such implications.

One of the interesting differences between pre-war and post-war nationalism on the West Coast of Africa is that in the former period nationalism tended to be – as Lord Lugard insisted – the esoteric pastime of the tiny educated minorities of Lagos, Accra, Freetown, and Dakar; whereas in the latter period these minorities – greatly expanded and dispersed in new urban centres throughout the interior – have made positive efforts to popularize and energize the nationalist crusade in two ways.[2] The first has been to preach education, welfare, progress, and the ideal of self-government among the masses, largely through the nationalist press, independent African schools, and kinship and tribal associations. The aim here has been, in the words of one of their leading prophets, Dr Nnamdi Azikiwe of Nigeria, to bring about 'mental emancipation' from a service colonial mentality.[3] The second method has been to tap all existing nativistic and religious tensions and economic grievances among the tradition-bound masses, as well as the grievances and aspirations of the urbanized clerks and artisans, and channel the energies thus unleashed into support of the nationalist drive. The technique here has been (1) to make nationalism, and in particular its objective of self-government, an integrating symbol in which even the most disparate goals could find identification, and (2) to politicize – one would like to say nationalize – all existing thought

[1] See Ian Cunnison, 'The Watchtower Assembly in Central Africa', *International Review of Missions*, Vol. 40, pp. 456–69 (October 1951).

[2] Sir F. D. Lugard, *The Dual Mandate in British Tropical Africa*, pp. 83 ff. (London, 1923).

[3] *Renascent Africa* (Lagos, 1937).

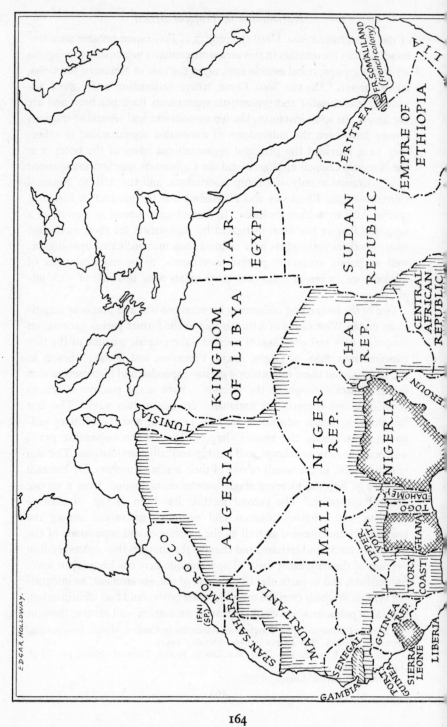

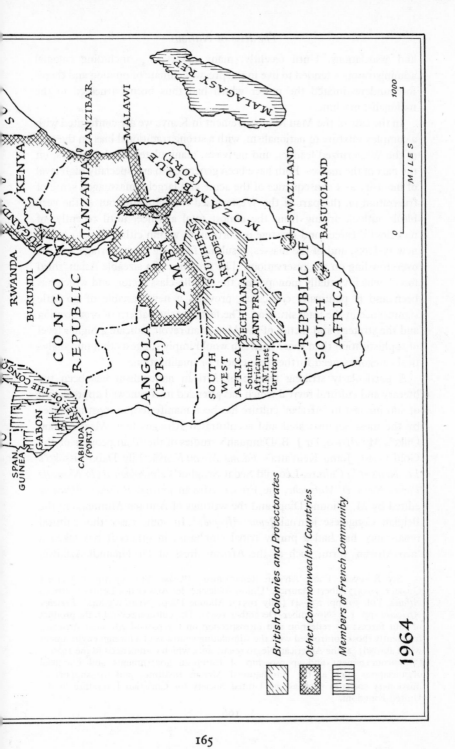

SPAN. GUINEA

GABON

REP. OF THE CONGO

CABINDA (PORT.)

RWANDA

BURUNDI

CONGO REPUBLIC

ANGOLA (PORT.)

ZAMBIA

SOUTHERN RHODESIA

BECHUANA- LAND PROT.

SOUTH WEST AFRICA

South African- U.N.Trust Territory

REPUBLIC OF SOUTH AFRICA

SWAZILAND

BASUTOLAND

MOZAMBIQUE (PORT.)

MALAWI

TANZANIA (ZANZIBAR)

KENYA

UGANDA

SO...

MALAGASY REP.

MILES

0

1000

1964

British Colonies and Protectorates

Other Commonwealth Countries

Members of French Community

and associations. Until recently, many observers – including colonial administrators – tended to live in the pre-war climate of opinion and therefore underestimated the power which had thus been harnessed to the nationalist machine.

In the case of the Mau Mau movement in Kenya we are confronted with a complex mixture of nationalism, with a strong traditional bias on the part of the Westernized leaders, and nativism, manipulated by the leaders, on the part of the masses. Both have been generated to an especially high level of intensity as a consequence of the acute and largely unassuaged sense of frustration on the part of the Westernized *élite*, growing out of the very bleak outlook arising from the almost total absence, until recently, of meaningful career and prestige opportunities within either the old or the new systems, and of the masses, resulting from the land shortage and the overcrowding on the reservations. The presence of a sizeable Asian 'third force', which virtually monopolizes the middle-class sector, and which has been and is politically conscious, provides a new variable of no little significance in the total situation. The fact that the pattern of organization and the strategy and tactics of the Mau Mau revolt indicate a higher level of sophistication than sheer nativism would imply suggests that our analytical categories need further refinement or qualification.

A particularly striking feature of African nationalism has been the literary and cultural revival which has attended it. A renewed appreciation of and interest in 'African' culture has been manifested, in most instances by the most sophisticated and acculturated Africans (e.g. Mazi Mbono Ojike's *My Africa*, Dr J. B. Danquah's studies of the Akan peoples of the Gold Coast, Jomo Kenyatta's *Facing Mount Kenya*, Fily-Dabo Sissoko's *Les Noirs et la Culture*, Léopold Sédar Senghor's *Anthologie de la Nouvelle Poésie Nègre et Malgache*, the French African journal *Présence Africaine* edited by M. Alioune Diop, and the writings of Antoine Munongo in the Belgian Congolese journal *Jeune Afrique*).[1] In some cases this cultural renaissance has had a purely tribal emphasis; in others it has taken a 'neo-African' form, such as the African dress of Dr Nnamdi Azikiwe,

[1] See Rosey E. Pool, 'African Renaissance', *Phylon*, Vol. 14, pp. 5–8 (First Quarter, 1953); Albert Maurice, 'Union Africaine des Arts et des Lettres', *African Affairs*, Vol. 50, pp. 233–41 (July 1951); Alioune Diop, 'Niam n'goura', *Présence Africaine*, pp. 1–3 (November–December 1947). The cultural revival is the product of four forces: (1) reflection and introspection on the part of educated Africans, frequently those confronted with the stimulating contrasts of a foreign environment while abroad; (2) the American Negro renaissance which commenced in the 1920's; (3) encouragement and sponsorship of European governments and unofficial organizations such as the International African Institute; and (4) support of missionary societies such as the United Society for Christian Literature in the United Kingdom.

nationalist leader in Nigeria. It has usually been accompanied by a quest for an African history which would in general reflect glory and dignity upon the African race and in particular instil self-confidence in the Western-educated African sensitive to the prejudiced charge that he has no history or culture. In short, there has emerged a new pride in being African. In French areas, the accent until recently has been upon French culture and literature, but there are increasing signs of a shift to African themes amongst the French African literati. The important point is that African nationalism has this cultural content, which renders more difficult any effort to separate rigidly the cultural nationalism of the urban politician from the nativism of the bush peasant.

Yet the differences are important to the student of African nationalism. Primary resistance and nativism tend to be negative and spontaneous revolts or assertions of the unacculturated masses against the disruptive and disorganizing stranger-invader. They are a reflection of a persistent desire of the masses to preserve or recreate the old by protesting against the new. Syncretism is different in that it contains an element of rationality – an urge to recapture those aspects of the old which are compatible with the new, which it recognizes as inevitable and in some respects desirable. Whereas all forms of protest are politically consequential – at least to colonial administrators – only nationalism is primarily political in that it is irrevocably committed to a positive and radical alteration of the power structure. In brief, nationalism is the terminal form of colonial protest.

Another reason for distinguishing between the various categories of assertion, which are basically differences in goal orientation, is not only to provide some basis for judging the nature of the popular support of a nationalist movement during its build-up, but also to have some means of predicting the stability and viability of the political order established by the nationalists once they achieve self-government. The governments of Pakistan, Burma, India, and Indonesia have each been plagued by internal tensions arising from what are fundamentally South Asian variants of traditionalism and tribalism. If a colonial nationalist movement comes to power atop a wave of mass protest which is primarily or even in part nativistic in character, this would have a direct bearing upon the capacity of the Westernized leaders of that movement, not only to maintain political unity and stability but also to carry out what is at the core of most of their programme – rapid modernization by a centralized bureaucratic machine. Any thorough study of the anatomy of a nationalist movement, therefore, must seek to determine the linkages and compatabilities between the goal orientations of the several forces from which that movement derives its *élan* and strength.

II. FACTORS CONTRIBUTING TO THE RISE OF NATIONALISM

It is far easier to define and describe nationalism than it is to generalize about the factors which have contributed to its manifestation. Put most briefly, it is the end product of the profound and complex transformation which has occurred in Africa since the European intrusion. It is a commonplace that the imposition of Western technology, socio-political institutions, and ideology upon African societies has been violently disruptive of the old familistic order in that they have created new values and symbols, new techniques for the acquisition of wealth, status, and prestige, and new groups for which the old system had no place. The crucial point here is not that nationalism as a matter of fact happened to appear at a certain point in time after the 'Western impact', but rather that the transformation the latter brought about has been an indispensable pre-condition for the rise of nationalism. Nationalism, as distinguished from primary resistance or nativism, requires considerable gestation. A few of the constituent elements have been:

A. Economic[1]

1. *Change from a subsistence to a money economy.* This change, consciously encouraged by colonial governments and European enterprise in order to increase the export of primary products, introduced the cash nexus and economic individualism, altered the patterns of land tenure and capital accumulation, and, in general, widened the area of both individual prosperity and insecurity.

2. *Growth of a wage-labour force.* This development has resulted in the proletarianization of substantial numbers of Africans, which has weakened communal or lineage responsibility and rendered those concerned vulnerable to economic exploitation and grievances.

3. *Rise of a new middle class.* *Laissez-faire* economics and African enterprise, coupled with opportunities for university and professional education, have been factors contributing to the growth of a middle class. This class is most advanced in Senegal, the Gold Coast, and Southern Nigeria, where it has developed despite successive displacement or frustration by the intrusion of Levantines and the monopolistic practices of European firms.

[1] L. P. Mair, 'The Growth of Economic Individualism in African Society', *Journal of the Royal African Society*, Vol. 33, pp. 261–73 (July 1934); Allan McPhee, *The Economic Revolution in British West Africa* (London, 1926); G. Wilson, *An Essay on the Economics of Detribalization in Northern Rhodesia*, Part I (Rhodes-Livingstone Institute, 1941). cf. Karl Polanyi, *Origins of Our Time* (London, 1946); P. C. Lloyd, 'New Economic Classes in Western Nigeria', *African Affairs*, Vol. 52, pp. 327–34 (October 1953).

B. Sociological[1]

1. *Urbanization.* The concentration of relatively large numbers of Africans in urban centres to meet the labour demands of European enterprise has loosened kinship ties, accelerated social communication between 'detribalized' ethnic groups, and, in general, contributed to 'national' integration.

2. *Social mobility.* The European-imposed *pax* coupled with the development of communications and transport has provided the framework for travel, the growth of an internal exchange economy, and socio-political reintegration.

3. *Western education.* This has provided certain of the inhabitants of a given territory with a common lingua franca; with the knowledge and tools to acquire status and prestige and to fulfil aspirations within the new social structure; and with some of the ideas and values by which alien rule and colonialism could be attacked. It has been through Western education that the African has encountered the scientific method and the idea of progress with their activistic implications, namely, an awareness of alternatives and the conviction that man can creatively master and shape his own destiny.

C. Religious and Psychological[2]

1. *Christian evangelization.* The conscious Europeanization pursued by Christian missionary societies has been a frontal assault upon traditional religious systems and moral sanctions. Moreover, the Christian doctrine of equality and human brotherhood challenged the ethical assumptions of imperialism.

2. *Neglect or frustration of Western-education elements.* Susceptibility to psychological grievance is most acute among the more acculturated Africans. Social and economic discrimination and the stigma of inferiority and backwardness have precipitated a passionate quest for equality and modernity, and latterly self-government. Rankling memories of crude, arrogant, or insulting treatment by a European have frequently been the major wellspring of racial bitterness and uncompromising nationalism.

D. Political

1. *Eclipse of traditional authorities.* Notwithstanding the British policy of

---

[1] J. D. Rheinallt Jones, 'The Effects of Urbanization in South and Central Africa', *African Affairs*, Vol. 52, pp. 37–44 (January 1953).

[2] William Bascom, 'African Culture and the Missionary', *Civilisations*, Vol. 3, pp. 491–501 (No. 4, 1953).

indirect rule, the European superstructure and forces of modernity have tended to weaken the traditional powers of indigenous authorities and thereby to render less meaningful pre-colonial socio-political units as objects of loyalty and attachment. There has been what Professor Daryll Forde calls a 'status reversal'; that is, as a result of the acquisition by youth of Western education and a command over Western techniques in all fields, there has been '. . . an increasing transfer of command over wealth and authority to younger and socially more independent men at the expense of traditional heads. . . .'[1]

2. *Forging of new 'national' symbols.* The 'territorialization' of Africa by the European powers has been a step in the creation of new nations, not only through the erection of boundaries within which the intensity of social communication and economic interchange has become greater than across territorial borders, but also as a consequence of the imposition of a common administrative superstructure, a common legal system, and in some instances common political institutions which have become symbols of territorial individuality.

These are a few of the principal factors in the European presence which have contributed to the rise of nationalism. As any casual observer of African developments is aware, however, there have been and are marked areal differences in the overt manifestation of nationalism. Such striking contrasts as the militant Convention People's party of the Gold Coast, the conservative Northern People's Congress of Nigeria, the pro-French orientation of the African editors of *Présence Africaine*, the cautious African editors of *La Voix du Congolais*, and the terroristic Mau Mau of Kenya are cases in point.

There are a number of explanations for these areal variations. One relates to the degree of acculturation in an area. This is a reflection of the duration and intensity of contact with European influences. The contrast between the advanced nationalism of the British West Coast and of Senegal and the nascent nationalism of British and French Central Africa is partly explicable on this basis.

A second explanation lies in the absence or presence of alien settlers. On this score the settler-free British West Coast is unique when contrasted to the rest of Africa. The possibility of a total fulfilment of nationalist objectives (i.e. *African* self-government) has been a powerful psychological factor which partly explains the confident and buoyant expectancy of West Coast nationalists. On the other hand, as previously noted, the

[1] Daryll Forde, 'The Conditions of Social Development in West Africa', *Civilisations*, Vol. 3, pp. 471–85 (No. 4, 1953).

tendencies toward accommodation or terrorism in the white-settler areas is a reflection of the absence of such moderating expectancy.

Certain African groups exposed to the same forces of acculturation and the same provocation have demonstrated radically different reactions. The Kikuyu versus the Masai peoples of Kenya, the Ibo versus the Hausa peoples of Nigeria, and the Creole and Mende of Sierra Leone are cases in point. It is suggested that the dynamism, militancy, and nationalist *élan* of the Ibo peoples of Nigeria are rooted partly in certain indigenous Ibo culture traits (general absence of chiefs, smallness in scale, and the demo-cratic character of indigenous political organization, emphasis upon achieved status, and individualism). Much the same might be said for the Kikuyu peoples of Kenya.

Differing colonial policies constitute another cause of these areal differ-ences. Nationalism is predominantly a phenomenon of British Africa, and to a lesser extent of French Africa. Apart from the influence of the foregoing historical, sociological, and cultural variables, this fact, in the case of British Africa, is explained by certain unique features of British colonial policy.

It was inevitable that Britain, one of the most liberal colonial powers in Africa, should have reaped the strongest nationalist reaction. A few of the principal features of British policy which have stimulated nationalism deserve mention:

1. *Self-government as the goal of policy.* Unlike the French and Portu-guese who embrace their African territories as indivisible units of the motherland, or the Belgians who until recently have been disinclined to specify the ultimate goals of policy, the British have remained indiscrim-inately loyal to the Durham formula.[1] In West Africa, this has enthroned the African nationalists; in Central and East Africa, the white settlers.

2. *Emphasis upon territorial individuality.* More than any other colonial power, the British have provided the institutional and conceptual frame-work for the emergence of nations. Decentralization of power, budgetary autonomy, the institution of territorial legislative councils and other

---

[1] Regarding Belgian policy, see Pierre Wigny, 'Methods of Government in the Belgian Congo', *African Affairs*, Vol. 50, pp. 310–17 (October 1951). Wigny re-marks (p. 311) that '. . . Belgians are reluctant to define their colonial policy. They are proud of their first realizations, and sure of the rightness of their intentions.' Since this was written, there have been some very dramatic changes in Belgian policy, especially regarding the educated *élite*, the potential nationalists. The great debate in Belgian colonial circles on 'le statut des Congolais civilisés' was terminated by four decrees of 17 May 1952 according to which educated Congolese are assimilated to Europeans in civil law. Regarding Portuguese policy, see Marcedo Caetano, *Colonizing Traditions, Principles and Methods of the Portuguese* (Lisbon, 1951). The keynote of the policy is the 'spiritual assimilation' of the Africans to a 'Portuguese nation dwelling in European, African, Asiatic and Indonesian Pro-vinces'. The African *civilisado* is thus a citizen of Portugal.

'national' symbols – all have facilitated the conceptualization of a 'nation'.[1]

3. *Policy on missionaries and education.* The comparative freedom granted missionaries and the *laissez-faire* attitude toward education, and particularly post-primary education, has distinguished and continues to distinguish British policy sharply from non-British Africa.

4. *Negelect, frustration, and antagonism of educated* élite. Not only have more British Africans been exposed to higher education, but the British government until recently remained relatively indifferent to the claims and aspirations of this class, which forms the core of the nationalist movements.

5. *Freedom of nationalist activity.* The *comparative* freedom of activity (speech, association, press, and travel abroad) which British Africans have enjoyed – within clearly defined limits and varying according to the presence of white settlers – has been of decisive importance. It is doubtful whether such militant nationalists as Wallace-Johnson of Sierra Leone, Prime Minister Kwame Nkrumah of Ghana, Dr Nnamdi Azikiwe of Nigeria, Jomo Kenyatta of Kenya, and Dauti Yamba of the Central African Federation, could have found the same continuous freedom of movement and activity in Belgian, Portuguese, and French Africa as has been their lot in British Africa.

All of this suggests that African nationalism is not merely a peasant revolt. In fact, as already noted, nationalism where it is most advanced has been sparked and led by the so-called detribalized, Western-educated, middle-class intellectuals and professional Africans; by those who in terms of improved status and material standards of living have benefited most from colonialism; in short, by those who have come closest to the Western World but have been denied entry on full terms of equality. From this comparatively affluent – but psychologically aggrieved – group have come the organizers of tribal associations, labour unions, co-operative groups, farmers' organizations, and – more recently – nationalist movements. They are the Africans whom British policy has done most to create and least to satiate.[2]

[1] Partly in response to nationalist pressures, the French Government has recently initiated certain measures of financial devolution to French West Africa. See G. Gayet, 'Autonomies financières Française', *Civilisations*, Vol. 3, pp. 343–7 (No. 3, 1953). These measures may enhance the powers of the territorial assemblies to the point that the latter might ultimately become the foci for territorial nationalisms.

[2] The thesis here is that there are at least four ingredients in the psychology of colonial nationalism, and that British policy in Africa has come closest towards inculcating or providing them: (*a*) an awareness of the existence or possibility of alternatives to the *status quo*, a state of mind produced by Western education and particularly by study and travel abroad; (*b*) an intense desire to change the *status quo*; (*c*) a system within which the major alternative to the *status quo* – self-government – has the status of legitimacy; and (*d*) an area of relative freedom in which that legitimate alternative may be pursued.

This brief and selective treatment of a few of the factors which have contributed to the African nationalist awakening suggests certain avenues which might be profitably explored and more fully developed by subsequent research. Specifically, what is the relationship between the nature and intensity of nationalism and the degree of urbanization, the degree of commercialization of agriculture, and the size and geographical distribution of the wage-labour force and salariat? In short, what is the causal connection between 'detribalization' and nationalism? Certain aspects of such an inquiry could be subjected to statistical analysis, but the results could only be suggestive, and in some instances might be positively deceptive. In the case of urbanization, for example, the highly urbanized and agriculturated Yoruba peoples of Nigeria for nearly a decade lagged far behind the Ibo peoples in nationalist vigour and *élan*. Ibadan, the largest urban centre in tropical Africa, has been until recently one of the most politically inert towns of Nigeria. Again, in terms of the proletarianization of labour and urbanization resulting from European industrialism and commercial activity, the Belgian Congo was one of the most advanced territories, but one in which nationalism was least in evidence.[1] Freetown, Sierra Leone, one of the oldest non-traditional urban centres, became a haven of respectability and conservatism, being eclipsed by the less-developed Protectorate in the push towards nationalist objectives. Urbanization has been an important ingredient in the nationalist awakening, but it has been a certain type of urban development – mainly the impersonal and heterogeneous 'new towns' – which has occurred in conjunction with other equally decisive factors.

In the case of the relationship between the degree of commercialization of land and labour and the degree of nationalism, the figures set forth for Ghana in Table I suggest either a causal connection or a parallel development. Yet in turning to similar figures for other territories – especially the Belgian Congo and Nigeria – it is clear that the relationship between commercialization and nationalism, important though it may be, must be considered and interpreted in the light of other variables.

Again, the fact that the nationalist movements have been organized and led by intellectuals and the so-called middle class suggests a relationship between nationalism and the number of Africans with higher education, the size of *per capita* income, the degree of the individualization of land tenure, the size of middle-class and professional groups (i.e. independent traders, produce middlemen, farmers employing labour, chemists, lorry

---

[1] The Belgian policy of stabilization of labour in the urban centres of the Congo, in which 83 per cent. of the men have their families with them, was one of the several factors which may help to explain this.

owners, lawyers, doctors, etc.), and the degree of vertical mobility within the emergent socio-economic structure. In any event, the insights of an economist are indispensable for a complete anatomy of African nationalism.

The Christian missionaries have been blamed frequently for their ruthless assault upon native religious systems and the thoroughgoing Europeanization, conscious or implicit, in their evangelization. This has suggested the formula: missionaries = detribalization = nationalism. Yet the post-war figures shown in Table II do not bear out this assumption.

Table I

COMMERCIALIZATION AND NATIONALISM IN CERTAIN AFRICAN TERRITORIES

Territory	Percentage of Cultivated Land Used by Africans for Commercial Production (1947–50)*	African Wage Earners as Percentage of Total African Population (1950)†	Degree of Overt Nationalism
Ghana	75	9·0	Advanced
Former Belgian Congo	42	7·6	None
Nigeria	41	1·2	Advanced
Uganda	33	3·9	Nascent
Kenya	7	7·6	Nascent

* E. A. Keukjian, 'Commercializing Influence of the Development of Exports on Indigenous Agricultural Economics in Tropical Africa', unpub. diss. (Harvard University, June 1953); United Nations, Economic and Social Council (15th session). *World Economic Situation, Aspects of Economic Development in Africa.* New York, Document E/2377, 20 March 1953.

† United Nations, Department of Economic Affairs. *Review of Economic Conditions in Africa (Supplement to World Economic Report, 1949–50).* New York, Document E/1910/Add. 1 Rev. 1-ST/ECA/9/Add. 1, April 1951, p. 76.

Missionaries have been important catalytic agents in the transformation of African societies, but the causal connection between their activities and nationalist assertion cannot be established by mere quantitative analysis. The figures in Table II hint at a possible causal relationship between preponderant Protestant evangelization and advanced nationalism (viz., Ghana and Nigeria) and preponderant Catholic evangelization and the absence of nationalism (viz. Portuguese Angola and the former Belgian Congo). Yet this connection must be examined in the light of other relevant factors, such as the degree of control and direction extended to missionary societies by colonial governments; the freedom allowed such societies to establish schools – particularly secondary schools – and to determine the curriculum; the tolerance accorded anti-white or anti-colonial sects (e.g. the Jehovah's Witnesses are permitted in most of British Africa but proscribed in non-British Africa); the latitude allowed African sects of a

Table II

CHRISTIANITY AND NATIONALISM IN CERTAIN AFRICAN TERRITORIES

Territory	Percentage of Christians to Total Population	Percentage of Protestants to All Christians	Percentage of Catholics to All Christians	Degree of Overt Nationalism
Former Belgian Congo	37	29	71	None
Malawi	26	49	51	Nascent
Ghana	15	58	42	Advanced
Angola	15	22	78	None
Kenya	10	51	49	Nascent
Nigeria	5	67	33	Advanced

syncretistic, revivalistic, or puritanical character; the extent to which evangelical bodies have *Africanized* their church organization, the priest-hood, and the propagation of the gospel; and, finally, the strength of Islam.

The corrosive influence of Western education has been a significant ingredient in the rise of nationalism. Yet the Belgian Congo claimed a higher percentage of literacy than any other colonial territory in Africa.[1] In order to establish a relationship we must move beyond the superficial analysis of literacy statistics and ask the following questions:

1. *The nature of the curriculum.* Has it been and is it literary and based upon the model of a European grammar school, or is it practical and designed to train the student to be a good farmer, artisan, or clerk in European employ, and incidentally to limit his sophistication and contact with unsettling ideas? Is instruction conducted in the vernacular or in a European language?

2. *Opportunities for post-primary education.* Are secondary schools (particularly those operated by missionary societies or by enterprising and nationalist-minded Africans such as Eyo Ita in Nigeria or Jomo Kenyatta in Kenya) allowed to mushroom into existence, or are they care-fully planned and rigidly controlled by the colonial government as to both number and curriculum? What are the opportunities for study in universities abroad? What is the latitude granted students to determine their own careers? Here we touch upon a crucial factor – in 1945, Free-town, Sierra Leone, and Lagos, Nigeria, each had more Western-type secondary schools than all of the non-British territories in Africa com-bined. In 1952 over 4,000 Africans from British territories were studying

[1] United Nations, *Non-Self-Governing Territories.* Vol. III: *Special Study on Education.* New York, Document ST/TRI/SER.A./5/Add. 2, January 1951.

in universities and technical schools abroad and nearly 1,000 in territorial universities in Africa, whereas only a handful had such opportunity or inclination in Belgian and Portuguese Africa. This is in part a reflection of the existence of a larger African middle class in British Africa, but it is also the result of the unique British attitude regarding the relationship between higher education and emergent African leadership. French policy and practice, despite differing assumptions, most closely approximate those of the British.

3. *Openings of careers for the talented.* The stability of any political or social order is determined by this factor. Is there any planned relationship between the output of the schools and opportunities for satisfying employment or careers ? In French and Belgian Africa, colonial governments have maintained a stringent control over the supply-demand situation as between *post-primary* schools and the requirements of government and the developing economy. In British Africa there are hundreds of thousands of unemployed or underemployed 'Standard VI' boys clustered in the coastal towns and urban centres of the interior.

The most potent instrument used in the propagation of nationalist ideas and racial consciousness has been the *African-owned* nationalist press. In Nigeria alone nearly 100 newspapers or periodicals have been published by Africans since the British intrusion, of which 12 dailies and 14 weeklies – all African owned – are currently in circulation. The crucial role performed in the nationalist awakening by African journalistic enterprise on the British West Coast is well known.[1] Until the publication of *Afrique Noire* (organ of the *Rassemblement Démocratique Africaine* of French West Africa) there was nothing in non-British Africa which even closely approximated this development. And even this journal is no match for the pungent criticism and racial consciousness one finds in the pages of Dr Nnamdi Azikiwe's *West African Pilot* in Nigeria.[2] Needless to say, the nationalist press is one of our major sources of data regarding nationalist motivation, objectives, and organization. It is not the number of newspapers published which is significant, but rather the volume of circulation and areal distribution, the news and editorial content and the nature of the

[1] Compare with the number of *African-owned-and-edited* dailies and weeklies (combined total) in the following territories : British Africa: Ghana (17), Uganda (8), Sierra Leone (7), Gambia (3); *French West Africa* (10); and none in so far as is known, in Belgian, Portuguese, or Spanish Africa; or in Kenya, the territories of the Central African Federation, or in the Union of South Africa.

[2] On the other hand, there appears to be no newspaper in British West Africa comparable with the European-owned-and-edited journal of French West Africa entitled *Les Echos de l'A.O.F.*, which 'week after week passionately attacks the administration. . . .' See Thomas Hodgkin, 'The Metropolitan Axis', *West Africa*, 9 January 1954, at p. 6.

appeal, the types of readers, the existence of competitive papers sponsored by colonial governments, the financial stability of the paper, and other factors which would reflect its impact and influence upon the ideas, aspirations, and activities of those literate groups predisposed towards nationalism.

These are but a few of the more important factors in the rise of nationalism which require evaluation and weighting before the student of comparative colonial nationalism can go beyond the mere description of the history and anatomy of a particular nationalist movement. There is a great danger in doing a disservice to scholarly research in Africa if one generalizes on the basis of observations made and data assembled in one territory. As has been suggested, there are certain general predisposing and precipitating causes of modern nationalism which are applicable to the whole continent; yet once these are mentioned, it is necessary to examine each area of nationalist activity for that special combination of factors which explains the origin, strength, and orientation of its nationalist movement.

Normally, a colonial nationalist movement directs its efforts towards the attainment of two main objectives: (1) the achievement of self-government, and (2) the creation of a cultural or political sense of nationality and unity within the boundaries of the area of the nation to be. Nationalists are obliged to adopt the second objective because imperial powers either did not or could not establish political boundaries which embraced only one self-conscious cultural unit; and certainly those powers made no conscious effort to build nations. The nationalist dilemma is that in most cases pursuit of the primary goal (self-government) lessens the likelihood of achieving the secondary goal (cultural and political unity). Put another way, the drive behind African nationalism in many instances is not the consciousness of belonging to a distinct politico-cultural unit which is seeking to protect or assert itself, but rather it is the movement of racially-conscious modernists seeking to create new political and cultural nationalities out of the heterogeneous peoples living within the artificial boundaries imposed by the European master. Their task is not only to conduct a successful political revolution and capture power, but also the painful job of national political integration. And as Professor Crane Brinton has shown, the lessons of history are that nation-building is the product of both consent and coercion, and usually the latter.[1] It is the colonial power, of course, which has had a monopoly over the means of coercion.

The major factor conditioning the development of a particular nationalist movement, therefore, is the degree of internal politico-cultural unity, tolerance, or compatibility amongst the peoples of the area moving into

[1] Crane Brinton, *From Many One* (Cambridge, Mass., 1948).

its national era. Disunities can exist in a given territory for a variety of reasons:

1. Traditional pre-colonial hostilities and cultural incompatibilities such as exist between the Kikuyu and Masai peoples of Kenya, or the Ibo and the Tiv peoples of Nigeria. In some instances these have been exacerbated as a result of imperial policies; in others as a consequence of the mere fact of lumping them together and endeavouring to impose territorial uniformity.

2. Tensions between groups resulting from unevenness in development, acculturation, and the acquisition of modernity. These can be the product of original cultural differences (i.e. the variations between groups in their receptivity and adaptability to modernity – e.g. the Ibo and Hausa); historical circumstances (i.e. differences in the duration and intensity of the European impact – e.g. the Creoles of Freetown *v.* the Mende peoples of the Protectorate of Sierra Leone); or of constitutional reforms pointing towards African self-government. One could argue that Ibo-Yoruba hostility in Nigeria is the product of all three factors. Just as the advance towards independence precipitated a cleavage between Muslims and Hindus in India, so has the development of nationalism and the move towards self-government in Africa brought to light a multitude of disunities. Fear of domination by the more advanced and acculturated groups – European or African – is one obvious explanation.

3. Tensions between the Westernized *élite* – the nationalists – and the traditionalists and the masses. This nationalist disability has tended to be exaggerated in the past, usually by imperial spokesmen endeavouring to repudiate the nationalists or to isolate them from the traditionalists. The intensity of the cleavage varies widely according to circumstances. In several areas such as Sierra Leone, the Northern Territories of Ghana, Western and Northern Nigeria, amongst the Kikuyu in Kenya, and in Zambia and Malawi the educated nationalists and some leading traditionalists have co-operated in varying degrees.

4. Differences within the ranks of the Westernized *élite*. These disagreements – and one is struck by their persistence, strength, and virulence – may arise from several causes, including normal competition for power and prestige or honest differences over aims, timing, or methods to be employed in the nationalist drive. Such differences as separate Messrs Fily-Dabo Sissoko and Mamadou Konaté in the former French Sudan; Lamine Gueye and Léopold Senghor in Senegal; Felix Houphouët-Boigny and Kouame Binzeme in the Ivory Coast; Prime Minister Kwame Nkrumah and Dr J. B. Danquah in Ghana; the Sardauna of Sokoto, Obafemi Awolowo, and Dr Nnamdi Azikiwe in Nigeria; Eliud Mathu

and Jomo Kenyatta in Kenya; and Harry Nkumbula and Godwin Lewanika in Central Africa, have very materially affected the course and strength of nationalism in the territories concerned.

These nationalist disabilities are the product of a complex mixture of hard historical and cultural facts, of changes introduced and differentials created by the Western intrusion, as well as of the provocations of the nationalist drive itself. The success of any nationalist movement will in a large measure depend upon the extent to which these internal tensions are softened or dissipated. The latter will depend, in turn, upon the degree of repressive opposition, or unwitting or intentional co-operation, of colonial governments; upon the development of pan-territorial political associations, the membership of which is rooted in all ethnic groups and in which there is free vertical mobility into the 'upper crust' which that membership constitutes; upon the emergence of pan-territorial economic-interest groups (e.g. middle-class associations or labour organizations); and upon many other sociological processes (out-group marriages, commonsality, etc.) which Professor Karl W. Deutsch has suggested are essential building blocks of any new national community.[1]

It would be naïve and unhistorical to argue that a large measure of politico-cultural integration is required – as distinguished from being desirable – in order for a nationalist movement to succeed in wresting self-government from an imperial power. Most successful colonial nationalist movements have been organized and led by small minorities which have been able either to gain the support of the masses or to capitalize upon their inertia and apathy. It would be unrealistic, however, to contemplate the success of a movement which did not have at least a minimum of unity or tolerance within the 'upper crust', even though it be of the sort displayed by the unstable truces negotiated from time to time between the Sardauna of Sokoto, Mr Obafemi Awolowo, and Dr Nnamdi Azikiwe, the regional leaders in Nigeria.

Some of these forces contributing towards integration are measurable and provide rough indices upon which the research scholar can base predictions of the development of a particular nationalist movement. In an interesting new theory regarding the growth of nations, Professor Deutsch has suggested certain criteria which might be profitably employed in seeking to determine the prospects of success of a nationalist movement in its nation-building endeavours.[2] His central thesis is that cases of successful political integration in history show a number of patterns which seem to

[1] The Growth of Nations', *World Politics*, Vol. 5, pp. 169–96 (January, 1953).
[2] Ibid. See also Deutsch's *Nationalism and Social Communication* (cited in note 5), pp. 81 ff.

recur. As he puts it, a nation 'is the result of the transformation of people, or of several ethnic elements, in the process of social mobilization'. The prospects of success are indicated by the completeness of that transformation and the intensity of social mobilization around the symbols of the new national community. A nation is not only a subjective affirmation of will of zealous nationalists; it is also the product of the operation of powerful objective forces, several of which have been mentioned.

Thus far it has been assumed that the leaders of nationalist movements in Africa will seek to build new national communities out of the diverse human materials located within the artificial boundaries of the existing colonial territories. This was precisely what happened in Latin America (Spanish imperial provinces), in the Middle East (European and Turkish regions), and in South-east Asia (Dutch Indonesia, Burma, and in a qualified way, British India). In the case of British Africa, where nationalism is most advanced, this same tendency for nationalism to follow boundaries established by the imperial power rather than those coincident with pre-colonial socio-political groups is in evidence (e.g. Ghana and Nigeria). On the other hand, in many areas the situation is still relatively fluid. Togoland nationalism has been predominantly an Ewe affair, and the Ewes are a trans-territorial group stretching from the Gold Coast to Dahomey. Separatist sentiment in Northern Nigeria is an example, *par excellence*, of incomplete social mobilization. This, when coupled with growing Yoruba and Ibo self-consciousness, suggests that earlier pan-Nigerian nationalism may be eclipsed and Nigeria may ultimately become three or more states. Until the recent decision to give the Southern Cameroons greater autonomy within the emergent Federation of Nigeria, Cameroonian nationalists were wavering between remaining an integral part of the Eastern Region of Nigeria, or seceding and joining with the nationalists in the French Cameroons in an endeavour to create a Kamerun nation based upon the artificial boundaries of the short-lived German Kamerun.[1] In Kenya, Mau Mau and all earlier proto-nationalist movements have been predominantly Kikuyu endeavours, even though the name Kenya has been employed. In Tanganyika, the Chagga Co-operative movement may be the basis for a Chagga separatism; and in Uganda, it is questionable whether pan-Uganda integrative forces can erase the 'national' separatism implicit in the Buganda Kingdom. Again, in Central Africa, will the territorial separatism symbolized by the Northern Rhodesian and Nyasaland National Congresses be eclipsed by the common sentiment and institutions growing out of the New Federation?

In the case of French Africa, dissimilarities in colonial policy (i.e.

[1] *West Africa*, p. 87 (30 January 1954).

assimilation and direct rule) have tended to produce a somewhat different situation. Yet since the reforms of 1946, as a result of which each of the territories of the two federations of French West Africa and French Equatorial Africa received their own representative assemblies, territorial nationalist movements have tended to eclipse the pan-French African *Rassemblement Démocratique Africain* in much the same fashion as Nigerian, Ghanaian, and Sierra Leonian nationalist movements have replaced the earlier National Congress of British West Africa. Thus one finds the *Parti Républicain de Dahomey*, *Parti Progressiste Sudanaise*, *Union Démocratique du Tchad*, and similar organizations in each of the territories. The future 'national' orientation of nationalist forces in French Africa would seem to depend upon the extent to which pan-Federation forces and institutions, such as the *Grand Conseils*, or the assimilationist forces of the French Union, such as the metropolitan parties and labour movements projected overseas, operate to retard the growth of territorial symbols and sentiment. One thing, however, seems certain: French Africa – because of the French policy of assimilation and direct rule – is less likely to encounter such movements as the *Egbe Omo Oduduwa* of the Nigerian Yorubas, the Kikuyu Central Association in Kenya, and the *Bataka* movement of Uganda.

In general, it would seem that where nationalism manifests itself in considerable strength it is evidence that disintegration of the old and social mobilization around the symbols of the new order have occurred on a scale sufficient to weaken or destroy attachments and loyalties of the nationalists to pre-colonial socio-political units, either because they have been crushed and are beyond memory or because they are unattractive or manifestly unsuitable as 'nations' in a modern world of nation-states. The European presence has done much towards the creation of new nations, the 'national' sentiment of the nationalists being a reflection of this.

A few of the many factors which might be observed and evaluated in order to determine the probable success, as well as the territorial implications, of an African nationalist movement or nation-building endeavour are as follows:[1] (1) the degree of internal social mobility, economic interchange and interdependence, intermarriage and commonsality, and the intensity and level of social communication among the ethnic groups comprising a given territory; (2) the location of population clusters and 'core areas', as well as of 'sub-national' regions of more intense economic

---

[1] For several of the concepts used here the author is indebted to the works of Professor Karl W. Deutsch, previously cited. See especially his *Nationalism and Social Communication*, pp. 15–45.

interchange or of cultural focus; (3) the powers and functions of 'sub-national' political institutions (i.e. regional, tribal, etc.), and the degree of *meaningful* participation in them by the Western-educated elements; (4) the rate at which 'national' institutions and activities are capable of attracting and absorbing new social strata from all ethnic groups into the 'national' life (e.g. the ethnic composition of the central administrative and technical services); (5) the centrality and nationalness of educational institutions, particularly the professional schools and universities; (6) the degree of pan-territorial circulation of nationalist newspapers and literature and the extent to which these play up 'national' events and personalities; (7) the differentials in the material development, *per capita* income and wealth, the acquisition of modern skills and knowledge, and the concentration and capacity for accumulation of capital amongst the differ-ent sub-national areas and ethnic groups;[1] (8) the ethnic make-up of the Western-educated categories and particularly of the active membership of nationalist or proto-nationalist groups (9) the development and extent of usage of a trans-tribal pan-territorial language, be it English, French, Portuguese, Swahili, or Hausa; (10) the compatibility of the 'detribalized' basic personality types produced by the indigenous cultures; (11) the extent to which the territory concerned embraces total cultural groups, or, put another way, the degree to which artificial colonial boundaries have bifurcated ethnic groups whose division may be the source of later irredent-ism; and (12) the rapport between the Western-educated nationalist ele-ments and the traditionalists, including the existence of nativistic tensions or economic grievances which the nationalists could manipulate or exploit in their mobilization of mass support.

Results obtained from inquiries along these lines would go far to explain the present orientation of a nationalist movement, as well as possible future trends. And yet an emphatic note of caution should be sounded: objective forces of integration and disintegration are powerful determinants in the nation-building process, but so also are subjective factors.[2] By all laws of geography and economics Northern Ireland should belong to Eire, and East Pakistan to the Republic of India; but they do not. By the same laws,

---

[1] It could be argued, for example, that apart from historical and cultural factors, the difference in the *per capita* income of the three regions of Nigeria (£26 for the Western Region, £16 for the Northern Region, and £23 for the Eastern Region) is of no little significance in the recent and current drive for greater regional autonomy. See A. R. Prest and I. G. Stewart, *The National Income of Nigeria*, abridged ed., pp. 14–16 (Lagos: Government Printer, 1954).

[2] Given suitable conditions, including a politically favourable milieu and the proper techniques, there would seem to be no reason why subjective factors such as loyalties, attitudes, and attachments to national or 'sub-national' symbols, could not to some extent be measured.

the Gambia should belong to Senegal, French Guinea to Sierra Leone and Liberia, Mozambique to the former Central African Federation, and so forth; and yet present trends suggest that such will not be the case. The principal forces currently operating to shape Africa's emergent nations are either tribalism or a nationalism following artificial imperial boundaries; and, with few exceptions, neither of these is directed towards the creation of political units which the geographer or economist would classify as ideal. In this respect, of course, Africa is not unique.

The foregoing raises the crucial question of whether it is possible for the peoples of Africa – in their own interest – to avoid the balkanization implicit in the full application of the national principle to their continent. So long as the rest of the world is organized according to that principle, and so long as the national idea universally embodies aspirations which cannot be satisfied by other forms of human organization, the answer would seem to be in the negative. The quest for racial equality and acceptance is as important an ingredient in the African revolt as is the desire to determine one's own destiny. Rightly or wrongly, self-government within the confines of the sovereign nation-state has become the supreme symbol of the equality of peoples. The only possible alternative would be broader Euro-African political groupings or self-governing plural societies in which emergent African leaders could play what they would feel to be an equal role. In the light of the persistence of national self-determination as a symbol, and particularly in view of the growing strength and contagion of African nationalism, the future of such multi-racial experiments will depend in a large measure upon the rapidity with which European governments and leaders provide for such a role.

17

The Rise of African Nationalism: the Case of East and Central Africa[1]

Robert I. Rotberg

The nationalism of East and Central Africa was handicapped in a way the West was not: namely by the presence of large numbers of white settlers. The climate and land of the area were more conducive to European farming and consequent settlement. The largest number of settlers – mainly from Britain and the Union (now the Republic) of South Africa – went to Southern Rhodesia. Their number and power was great enough by 1923 for the colony to be granted full internal self-government, with the status, unique in the British Empire, of 'self-governing Colony'. The British government retained, as well as control over defence and foreign policy, certain reserve powers to prevent racially discriminatory legislation; but through disuse in practice these powers soon atrophied into ineffectiveness. In 1962 they were largely relinquished in exchange for a constitutional revision which for the first time admitted Africans to the Southern Rhodesian legislature, where they are still outnumbered 3 to 1 by whites. In Northern Rhodesia and Nyasaland it was not clear until the late 1950's that Africans were clearly destined to prevail over local Europeans. In 1953, Northern and Southern Rhodesia with Nyasaland formed, under pressure from local settlers supported by the British government, the Federation of Rhodesia and Nyasaland. The Federation, professedly based on a loosely defined philosophy of 'partnership' between the races, was dominated throughout its brief life by white politicians. It met with complete hostility from African opinion in Northern Rhodesia and Nyasaland and was finally dissolved, having never achieved full independence, at the end of 1963.

The smaller number of settlers in Uganda and Tanganyika have never been politically powerful – in the latter country many of them worked with the Tanganyika African National Union (TANU), the African nationalist party. In Kenya, however, the settlers had considerable power until the late 1950's in spite of a famous declaration by the British government in 1923 that should their interests conflict with those of the Africans the latter were to be paramount.

One of the results of the power of white settlers in these countries has been that, since Africans' political destinies looked less clear and their political advance was blocked, the feeling of protest took other forms more often than in West Africa. One of these was the formation of independent African religious organizations – the Mau Mau of Kenya might be considered as an extreme example of this. These methods were more appropriate

[1] Reprinted from *World Politics*, Vol. XV, October 1962.

largely because of the presence of white settlers and the consequent discriminatory political and social systems of these countries.

Colonialism almost everywhere in the non-Western world produced reaction, and where this reaction could not be expressed directly, or where healthy protest failed to bring about any appreciable amelioration, the conquered people expressed their rejection of colonialism religiously. Sundkler views the formation of African independent religious bodies as inevitable whenever there are no other outlets for protest available.[1] The Bantu quasi-Christian movements also permit those who are ambitious to come to prominence without direct reference to the colonial context. Furthermore, as Mair has rightly concluded, the separatist sects and prophet cults of Africa (like the related cargo cults of Oceania and the ghost groups of Indian America) demonstrate the need for 'a religion that corresponds to widely held aspirations'.[2]

In East and Central Africa one may differentiate two varieties of anti-colonial religion. The separatist sects have seceded from mission churches or have simply been formed by a small cadre of dissatisfied adherents. They emphasize African control of the present (not necessarily the future) and they model themselves on the prevailing Protestant mission form of organization (although the BaEmilio Church of the Sacred Heart of Jesus, of Northern Rhodesia, represents a Roman Catholic schism). These separatist sects have always asserted strong claims for African self-government within the congregational context.[3] They have baptized readily, revised the orthodox rules of mission Christianity to permit polygyny and beer-drinking and, wherever conditions were ripe, led overt, sometimes violent, and always abortive revolts against colonial authority.

The second variety, African versions of chiliastic cults so common to the Western world, depends on the inspiration of a prophet or a mystic.[4] Their members are converts from mission churches or from the ranks of

---

[1] Bengt G. M. Sundkler, *Bantu Prophets in South Africa*, p. 297 (London, 1948).

[2] Lucy Mair, 'Independent Religious Movements in Three Continents', *Comparative Studies in Society and History*, I, p. 135 (January 1959). cf. George Eliot, who writes of '. . . eager men and women to whom the exceptional possession of religious truth was the condition that reconciled them to a meagre existence, and made them feel in secure alliance with the unseen but supreme ruler of a world in which their own visible part was small.' – *Felix Holt*, p. 42 (London, 1866).

[3] The literature of separatism in Africa is extremely varied in scope and quality. In addition to Sundkler, see Katesa Schlosser, *Propheten in Afrika* (Braunschweig, 1949) and *Eingeborenenkirchen in Süd und Süd-West Afrika* (Kiel, 1958); F. B. Welbourn, *East African Rebels* (London, 1961); George Shepperson, 'Ethiopianism and African Nationalism', *Phylon*, XIV, pp. 9–18 (March 1953). See also Jomo Kenyatta, *Facing Mount Kenya*, pp. 269–79 (London, 1961).

[4] An excellent theoretical discussion is Bryan Wilson, 'An Analysis of Sect Development', *American Sociological Review*, XXIV, pp. 3–15 (February 1959).

non-believers. Their organization is loose and unstable, their dogma is frequently non-existent, and their ritual is usually syncretic, spontaneous, and highly emotional. They emphasize confessions, faith healing ('Only pure water will do'), drumming, dancing, speaking with tongues, intercession by mediums and communication with ancestors or gods, divining, purification, elimination of sorcery and witchcraft, a fraternity of the elect who are sanctified by being 'born again', and baptism by total immersion.[1] They are millennial. With the apocalypse will come a new and totally black Jerusalem. No longer will Africans be hewers of wood and drawers of water for the white man. These movements represent a reordering of daily life in preparation for the apocalypse and a structuring of a black godly pantheon or, in some cases, the deification of the local prophet as a Son of God to replace Christ or Muhammed in African minds.[2]

Religious separatism in Bantu Africa dates from the formation of the Tembu National Church in 1884.[3] By 1900 it had reached Barotseland, transmitted by Sotho evangelists, and Nyasaland, where it was furthered by the Australian evangelist, Joseph Booth. The sequence of events that led via Booth to the formation of John Chilembwe's Providence Industrial Mission in Nyasaland, the first dynamic African separatist church in Central and East Africa, has been thoroughly described by Shepperson and Price.[4] By 1915 Chilembwe, backed by American Negro money, had brought about a unique religious experiment that was exclusively African. More intelligent or courageous than most other separatist sect leaders, or perhaps simply more persuaded of his own understanding of Africa's destiny, Chilembwe was active in opposing any government measures that he deemed an affront to Africans. He protested against the employment of African troops in Ashantiland, Somaliland, and against the Germans. He championed the cause of Nyasaland's landless proletariat. He opposed tax increases. Foreshadowing similar activity years later in Kenya, he established a chain of independent schools in the Shire Highlands (Nyasaland). Eventually he saw himself as the leader of an independent black Nyasaland, and he directed his Christian followers in a brief, bloody, and wholly unsuccessful rising against European rule.[5] Most other separatist churches

[1] For some examples, see R. I. Rotberg, 'The Lenshina Movement of Northern Rhodesia', *Rhodes-Livingstone Journal*, XXIX, pp. 63–78 (June 1961).

[2] See Raymond Leslie Buell, *The Native Problem in Africa*, II, pp. 601–12 (New York, 1928).

[3] Sundkler, 38 ff. See also G. M. Theal, *Basutoland Records*, II, pp. 184, 229–31, 241 ff (Capetown, 1883).

[4] George Shepperson and Thomas Price, *Independent African* (Edinburgh, 1958).

[5] Ibid., pp. 265–320. cf. Nyasaland Protectorate, *Report of the Commission Appointed . . . to Inquire into . . . the Native Rising within the Nyasaland Protectorate* [6819] (Zomba, 1916).

have, since Chilembwe, confined their activities to more peaceful paths (governments have been more wary), although the Watu Wa Mngu in Kenya and the Lenshina movement of Northern Rhodesia have had clashes with the police.[1] Even where the independent churches have failed to demonstrate violently, they have remained in continual opposition.

Chiliasm in Africa is an American export. But Russell's 'millennial dawn doctrine',[2] popularized by the Watchtower Bible and Tract Society, has been improved almost out of recognition by the African genius of the cult. Elliott Kenan Kamwana Achirwa preached the coming of the Kingdom wherein Africans would soon have full independence and control of taxes. The government would go. 'We shall build our own ships; make our own powder, import our own guns.'[3] Mwana Lesa, the self-styled Son of God, promised his followers immediate entrance into the select circle of believers and a reserved seat in the Garden of Eden. He proposed first to rid the earth of witches. At one performance a spirit seized him, '. . . for his eyes were red as coals of fire, and on his lips flecks of foam were appearing. He swayed and tossed his arms about like a mountain tree in the grip of a tempest, and the women of his retinue were swaying and moaning as though in fear and terror. . . .'[4] The African Watchtower movement that frightened Northern Rhodesia after World War I taught the immediate end of the world. It followed that there was no need to obey chiefs or government, to cultivate or to work; it was only necessary to be baptized – and baptism was easy – and to wait expectantly for the millennium. But in the meantime disobedience impelled conflict between white government and African anarchy. It led to warfare and to the eventual imprisonment of large numbers of tribesmen possessed of a simple eschatology.

Government treated separatist sects and chiliastic cults with amusement, a measure of contempt, and some fear. Orthodox missionaries always sought to persuade their governments to forbid independent churches, and for long administrations limited the dissemination of religious propaganda and the spread of most independent African churches. In Northern Rhodesia the government unsuccessfully tried legal subterfuge to curb the influence of the Lenshina movement, and to eliminate the Ethiopian Catholic Church in Zion. Government feared the millennial movements more, however, and prohibited most Watchtower literature, censored the

[1] Rotberg, ibid., p. 76.

[2] Charles Taze Russell, *Studies in the Scriptures*, 7 vols. (Allegheny, Pa., and Brooklyn, N.Y., 1886–1904).

[3] Quoted in George Shepperson, 'The Politics of African Church Separatist Movements in British Central Africa, 1892–1916', *Africa*, XXIV, p. 239 (July 1954).

[4] Carl Von Hoffman, *Jungle Gods*, p. 53 (London, 1929). Also Frank Melland in *Glasgow Bulletin*, 14 January 1939.

rest, and generally invoked sedition laws whenever prophets became too important. Prophets thereby became martyrs and objects of subsequent veneration by national political parties.

What has been the contribution of these religious movements to the development of African nationalism? Most important, the many cults and sects have helped to revive African self-respect. They have shown that change is indeed possible and that Africans are capable, given some solidarity, of asserting a measure of influence within the colonial context. They have diffused new, often heretical ideas about the importance of Africans for Africa. They have provided an alternative to total submission to white power, and they have brought about ties that substituted mutual belief and purpose for traditional kinship arrangements. Together with the proliferation of associations, the religious movements helped to make possible the rapid rise of modern nationalist parties.

I I I b : Politics and Government

The readings in this section are concerned with the development and functions of political parties in Africa, with recent apparent trends towards single-party rule and with the various movements towards political unification. Since we shall return to this last crucial question in the final section of this book, in this introduction we concentrate on the problem of one-party rule since it illustrates many political phenomena unique to the African continent. In addition, it is a feature of African politics which gives rise to slightly uncomprehending concern in non-African countries.

The most obvious problem facing an African government emerging from alien rule is its choice of a form of government. It is natural that in the West, with its democratic ideals, and involved as it is in a Cold War with states which it regards as undemocratic, this choice is predominantly seen as one between democratic and undemocratic forms of government. An aspect of the African scene on which attention has been lavished by Western writers in the last few years is the supposed decline of democracy and trend towards one-party rule; yet it remains one of the least well understood features of Africa. It is certainly true that since their independence, and indeed before it, many countries in Africa have shown a tendency towards one-party rule and in some cases 'authoritarianism'; although there are so far few, if any, cases where 'authoritarianism' has arisen that has not been rooted in a more or less widely based political party. A common political feature of many under-developed countries in South-east Asia, and especially in the Middle East and Latin America, has been military government, generally following a sudden *coup*. There is already some evidence that certain countries in tropical Africa may follow a similar pattern.

The single parties we are concerned with in Africa are by no means always of the extreme left or right (normally associated in Europe and the

West with one-party rule): in the formerly French African colonies (Senegal and the Ivory Coast, for example) they have often been parties of the centre or moderate right in terms of the European political spectrum. This fact points to two conclusions. First, that it is unwise to transfer European and American ideas of what is 'left' and 'right' to African politics; second, that it is not in political ideology but in features common to the countries concerned that we should look for an explanation of this trend. Our search for an explanation should be in two directions: on the one hand, in common historical features of the countries concerned; on the other hand, in common contemporary problems.

It is often asserted that Africans are accustomed in their traditional tribal way of life to authoritarian rule by chiefs and that, consequently, authoritarianism is likely to result in their modern national governments. Because there is no tradition of organized opposition it is suggested both that authoritarian leaders find it easier to assume power and that the people as a whole make little effort to oppose their rulers. This is perhaps the least convincing of all explanations; on the one hand chiefly rule is very different in kind from rule by a national government in that its acceptance by the people is based on a multitude of common traditions and features of cultural and political organization within the tribe which do not enter into the attitude of people towards a state; on the other hand it is by no means true that traditional rule in Africa has been entirely or even predominantly authoritarian. Even the most powerful chief must take account of tribal councils.

A much more significant historical explanation is the effect of colonial government. For many years Africans have become used to the authority of rulers whom they did not elect; the contact of the average African with his government today is sometimes not very different in kind from his contact with the old colonial governments. Besides this, where independence has been given pragmatically, territory by territory, as was the case in British-ruled Africa, the colonial government has often used political disunity among the Africans as an excuse for delay in granting independence (in Kenya and Uganda for example). Thus since close political unity has been an accelerating influence in the gaining of independence, the predominance of a single party has been encouraged. That one party has been firmly entrenched in power at the time of independence partly explains why it should continue to predominate; but it does not explain why the tendency should be strengthened.

What then are the common features of independent Africa which tend to make for one-party rule? An argument which is now commonly accepted by those sympathetic to African development is that national unity within a country whose boundaries were arbitrarily drawn by the European scramblers for Africa in the nineteenth century and which contains often a large diversity of peoples, requires strong rule and the unifying effects of a single party with which citizens can identify themselves. Wallerstein, and others, have gone further and suggested that since the state of Africa today is analagous to a state of 'siege', in the sense that the forces making for national disunity and poverty are so powerful, a large degree of central government authority may be the only means of defence against them. It is only when these forces begin to be conquered that Africa will have time for what the West calls political democracy.

It is often very unclear what is meant by democracy. Is it a term used only for systems where there is an effective opposition – even perhaps reserved for two party systems? Alternatively does democracy have more salient characteristics? There is often a confusion as to whether the most relevant criterion for democracy is the existence of a real choice of parties or whether it is the existence of a real line of communication between the people and their government – in other words, whether what people *think* is relevant to the way in which they are governed. The first criterion may be misleading if the parties which can be chosen are competing oligarchies, equally out of touch with the people; and Africa measures up better to the second criterion than to the first. In Ghana, Guinea and Tanganyika, among others, great efforts have been made to improve and strengthen the communication between government and people and the most effective means of doing this has usually been through the party. The single party is certainly not seen always as an instrument of oppression; its numerous educational and social functions have tended to encourage the image of an approachable and responsive party. It would be wrong to transfer the Western image of a political party unchanged into the African context. The facts that the means of communication to the centre have not always been effective, and that there has been much corruption, do not belie the intentions of the leaders. This suggests that the argument which attributes the emergence of one-party systems to the traditional familiarity with chiefly authoritarianism, besides being wrong in its assumptions, is trying to explain a phenomenon which may not in fact exist. To argue that there is no *a priori* reason to identify one party rule with lack of democracy is not to whitewash African one-party systems completely. In some cases there have occurred what seem unnecessarily harsh and thorough suppressions of political opposition: doubtfully harmful individuals have been imprisoned; political parties, Communist, conservative and tribal, have commonly been banned when to informed outside observers, at least, they scarcely seemed a danger to the integrity of the state. Concern has been expressed that the pursuit of such policies has sometimes been reinforced, as in Ghana, by a careful propaganda of a quasi-religious nature to glorify the party and its leader. Such propaganda has at times been bizarre if not positively sinister. Nevertheless, whether or not such concern is misplaced, patriotism and the adulation of leaders is often in Western countries overladen with religious fervour of doubtful authenticity.

Most political movements, especially those of protest, develop a mystique, half true, half idealized, as a justification for their aims. There is nothing peculiarly African about this. In Africa such 'theories and myths' arose largely out of a feeling of imposed inferiority created by the various myths which colonialism, no less than African nationalism, required to sustain it. This reaction by Africans has created an interest in pre-colonial African history, albeit sometimes a rather idealized one. It has created a new African literary tradition greatly preoccupied with negritude. These examples of 'Africanism' do not deserve the cynicism with which they are sometimes greeted; for the colonial myths and the actions which they sustained were not conducive to a sense of dignity or self-respect. New nations require powerful ideological weapons as bastions of their own self-confidence and to bolster their feeling of nationhood. This is especially true of Africa where the colonial boundaries were often drawn with scant regard for pre-existing political divisions.

It has already been suggested that democracy as we know it in the West may be a luxury which Africa cannot yet afford. Bearing in mind the enormous problems which any African government must face, Africans are not much impressed with the potentialities for achieving the necessary radical changes through a two- or multi-party 'Western' democratic system. That the New Deal in the U.S.A. was more effectively implemented than the New Frontier, that de Gaulle solved problems which the Fourth Republic in France could not, must in large measure be attributed to the fact that at those times these two countries faced a 'state of siege' not dissimilar to that of Africa today. There is no doubt that many Africans are greatly impressed with the enormous changes wrought in Soviet Russia in the last forty-five years. Yet for this progress some Soviet citizens have paid a high price. Most Africans do not wish such a price to be paid in Africa. Hence the concern of the most thoughtful African leaders to establish a new approach to political action neither Western nor Eastern – nor even a middle way, but an African way.

A further point worthy of discussion is the relation between strong centralized rule and political stability. There is a tendency, in the U.S. and in Britain at least, to associate political stability with a democratic party system. But the experience of the Fourth Republic in France shows that this is not a necessary connection. It thus appears that there may be a contradiction within African politics: in view of the many regionalist forces latent in most African states, a weak government at the centre may be conducive to political instability; and yet the stronger the government at the centre becomes, the greater may be the countervailing forces which build up and the more severe in consequence may be political instability if such a government is overthrown. This danger may be accentuated if the military emerges as a political force; although in fairness it should be noted that in the Middle East and Latin America, military coups have usually taken place where rule at the centre was not strong.

Although the problem of one-party states seems of most concern to Europeans and Americans, this is much less the case with Africans. Many African political leaders have tended to take as axiomatic some of the arguments presented above in justification of one-party rule. It is not something which they feel embarrassed to justify.

We have dealt with this at length largely because it is an important problem of *attitude* on the part of observers. Africans tend more to regard their major political problems as:

(*a*) the building of national unity and the diminishing of the centrifugal tendencies in African states;

(*b*) the rapid improvement of the level of skills, educational achievement and administrative ability to secure the conditions for administrative efficiency and economic and social development;

(*c*) the consolidation of the political freedom already gained and the elimination of all 'neo-colonialism';

(*d*) the attainment of a more important position for Africa in the world which is often taken as being synonymous with the achievement of Pan-Africanism.

We do not propose to deal with all of these in this section but, together with the readings, they should provide plenty of issues for profitable discussion. These and other issues lead naturally to a consideration of the economic alternatives facing Africa to which we shall come in Section IIIc.

18

Welfare Activities of African Political Parties[1]

Thomas Hodgkin

The functions of political parties in Africa are many. We have already learned something of their major role in bringing independence. But after this is accomplished the role of a responsible political party is crucially changed – from the promotion of propaganda hostile to alien rule and the disciplining of a widespread movement of protest into the agent of a government concerned to educate the state politically and to modernize a backward nation.

When independence came to most African countries they had not been ideally equipped to perform the functions of a modern state – welfare and educational services were under-developed and the burden of filling these gaps fell more than is usual upon the political parties since they were the only existing organizations accustomed to organizing the people on a local level. Functions, therefore, which in western countries are performed by the machinery and personnel of the state have in Africa been exercised by the party – a fact which further strengthens the trend towards identification of party and state and so to single party systems. This reading shows how African parties perform these activities.

WELFARE, ADMINISTRATION, AND PATRONAGE

I have already stressed the importance of the social-service aspect of African party functions. In this respect African parties in general, and the mass parties in particular, belong to the category which Professor Neumann has labelled 'parties of social integration', parties, that is to say which seek to provide for the social needs of their members and supporters 'from the cradle to the grave'.[2] There are various reasons why African parties have tended to assume 'welfare' functions, of which imitation of European parties of the Left is probably the least important. What is most evident is that pre-colonial African societies, like pre-capitalist societies in other parts of the world, had as a rule a well-developed system of mutual aid, which ensured that the resources of a community, limited though they might be, were available to its members, above all in periods of crisis, personal or collective: birth, marriage, and death, plague, pestilence, and

[1] Reprinted from *African Political Parties*, Penguin Books, 1961.
[2] S. Neumann, *Modern Political Parties* (Chicago, 1956).

194

famine. This traditional system of mutual aid, though it has by no means been destroyed during the colonial epoch, has been made much less effective as a result of processes with which we are all familiar: urbanization, the growth of a proletariat, mass migration, the imposition of a framework of alien insitutions, the spread of competitive values, and so forth. At the same time modern African man has to deal with crises of new types. The resulting need for new institutions which will provide the individual with protection, support, and a sense of fraternity, has been met by organizations of various kinds – Tribal Unions, Improvement Associations, Burial Societies, Dancing *Compin's*, and so on. It has also been met, in some territories most effectively met, by the political parties.

There are other reasons why mass parties are likely to take a special interest in social needs. One is that their members deliberately run risks of a special kind, during the period of nationalist struggle; their activities are likely to lead to clashes with the police, arrest, trial, imprisonment. Hence parties like R.D.A.,[1] Neo-Destour, or Istiqlal, which have had to face long periods of administrative *répression*, have been obliged to pay a great deal of attention to the provision of legal aid for those arrested, and the raising of funds to provide for the maintenance of the dependants of those imprisoned or killed. During long strikes, such as those which occurred in French West Africa during 1953, the parties, as well as the trade unions, have been responsible for organizing the supply of food from the villages to the families of the strikers in the towns. In addition they have constantly been involved in case-work, dealing with the innumerable minor problems arising from administrative disapproval: for example, transfers and dismissals of party members who are also civil servants.

Moreover, the mass parties are better equipped than other African organizations to provide for social needs because, at least during their more flourishing periods, they are relatively rich. This is particularly true of territories like Ghana, the Ivory Coast, and Senegal, where parties have been able to tap the resources of a sizeable bourgeois class. Dr Schachter describes the pre–1950 R.D.A. in the Ivory Coast as 'easily the richest, financially the most self-reliant, and . . . . the most generous of all West African political parties', and quotes M. Léon's remark – 'If Houphouet asks the Baule today for 5, 10, or 20 million [francs C.F.A., i.e. £10,000, £20,000 or £40,000], he will have them in twenty-four or forty-eight hours.'[2] Such special appeals for funds, made by the party leader to his own Baule community, were in addition to the party's regular income,

[1] Rassemblement Démocratique Africain.
[2] Ruth Schachter. *The Development of Political Parties in French West Africa*, unpub. Oxford D.Phil. thesis, 1958.

based upon an annual subscription of fr. C.F.A. 50 (2s.) and an estimated membership, in 1950, of 850,000 card-carrying members. There are also various forms of practical assistance – foodstuffs, or the use of lorries, for example – which such parties can call on their bourgeois supporters to provide.

Another advantage which mass parties possess is that, even where they do not enjoy power, so long as they are legal, their leaders normally have access to the seats of power. Even during the period from 1947 to 1950, when the R.D.A. was in total opposition to the French Administration, 'a deputy who had access to the French Government might succeed in having governors or administrators replaced or reprimanded'.[1] The party leader who is also a member of the legislature in a colonial State must include in his responsibilities the effort to remedy acts of administrative injustice or stupidity affecting his constituents and supporters, and such cases naturally tend to be channelled through the party.

The responsibilities of African parties in regard to individual grievances and problems are much larger than those of European parties. The British, for example, do not normally regard their Government, as Africans during the colonial period came to regard the Administration, as essentially hostile, an 'instrument of coercion', so that even its constructive and social services tended to be suspect. Sékou Touré makes this point, contrasting the functions of the State in former French Guinea with its functions in the new independent Guinea:

> One of the characteristics of the régime of domination was that it gave supremacy to political force over moral force. . . . The colonial régime means simply that. . . . Hence it is easy to recognize that the Judiciary, the entire system of repressive institutions, the department of Water Supplies and Forestry [*Eaux et Forêts*], the local guards of the old régime, the police, the gendarmerie, the Army – all these had only one purpose, to maintain the supremacy of force, to restrain the trends towards emancipation.[2]

In these circumstances Africans have looked for assistance to the mass party, which was felt to be friendly, and in a sense their own creation, rather than to the colonial State, which was alien and imposed.

What sort of services do the mass parties provide? Partly, as I have indicated, they are concerned with case-work – combining the functions of Citizens' Advice Bureaux and the National Council of Civil Liberties in

[1] Ibid.
[2] Sékou Touré, *Cinquinerre Congrès National du Parti Démocratique de Guinée: rapport de doctrine et de politique générale* (trans. as 'Toward Full Re-Africanisation'. Paris, 1955).

Britain, but supplementing these with a conscious agitational purpose. Dr Schachter gives some examples of typical day-to-day instructions issued to local R.D.A. leaders:

Tell Abdoulaye his daughter cannot be forced to marry the old chief.
Tell the peasants not to sell the crops at that ruinous price.
Defend Pango's palm trees against destruction by the forestry service.
Speak up for Binta's right to cultivate the land the chief claims.[1]

Second, while it is normal for parties to assist party members and their families in situations of special need – sickness, unemployment, victimization, imprisonment, overseas education, death – some parties or their peripheral organizations have concerned themselves with 'welfare' in a more systematic way. I have quoted elsewhere the instance of La Goumbé, in Treichville, Abidjan, a mixed, Muslim, predominantly Dioula, youth association, linked with the local R.D.A., which combined the activities of 'emancipating young women from family influences, assisting the process of matrimonial selection, providing on a contributory basis marriage and maternity benefits (including perfume and layettes for the new-born), preserving the Dioula tribal spirit, and running an orchestra.[2] La Goumbé was organized on a tribal basis. But parties can also meet an important need by knitting together tribal groups in a new social setting. Dennis Austin makes this point in regard to Tema, Ghana's new port, where the C.P.P. was concerned with 'finding jobs, finding homes, settling disputes, because among the immigrant population the party was felt to be a more friendly, approachable, familiar body than the Labour Office, the Housing Officer, or the Magistrate's Court'.

Third, mass parties frequently organize their own police forces, primarily to preserve order at meetings and rallies and on public occasions. In areas where the population clearly prefers party justice to justice administered by officials, magistrates, or chiefs, they may also undertake judicial functions. Thus in the Ivory Coast:

in the village of Bopri . . . an R.D.A. tribunal, judging according to customary law, examined 200 cases during 1947–9. Tribunals of this type operated during this same period in the *cercles* of Mau (Guéré), Daloa, and Dimbokro.[3]

Finally, a mass party may come to exercise administrative functions; in particular areas it may effectively govern. This, no doubt, is most liable to occur in a near-revolutionary situation – but not only in such cases.

[1] R. Schachter, ibid.
[2] T. Hodgkin, *Nationalism in Colonial Africa* (London, 1956).
[3] P. Decraene: *le Panafricanisme* (Paris, 1959).

It is possible for a *de facto* party administration and an official colonial administration to achieve, for a time, a form of peaceful coexistence, making mutual adjustments to one another. I have seen this type of relationship existing between the Spanish administration and Istiqlal's administration in the little enclave of Ifni during 1956. G. Bédos describes a comparable situation in the Ivory Coast during the period from 1947 to 1951, where:

'Officials', who held their mandate only from the R.D.A. tended to replace chiefs and local authorities appointed by the Administration. Before the decline of its influence in 1951, the R.D.A. made efforts to bring these Government-appointed authorities over to its side; where this seemed impossible it set up local committees in their place. In some areas in the bush (in the District of Mau, for instance) the local party leaders offered their help to the Administration, which sometimes accepted it. This, however, was not always the case; hence situations arose in which authorities designated by the Administration, lodging continual complaints about the usurpation of their functions, coexisted with R.D.A.-appointed 'officials' who had found no difficulty in securing the support of the local population.[1]

Mass parties do not necessarily lose their welfare functions once independence has been achieved. Indeed, one of the main interests of the party leadership after independence is to redirect the party's resources and energies away from the negative task of destroying the old system and towards the positive task of constructing the new. Thus in Tunisia in 1957, a year after independence, Neo-Destour and its youth organization were involved in a variety of socially useful activities: building local schools, carrying on a campaign against trachoma, fighting locusts, reclaiming waste land, planting eucalyptus trees beside the roads, establishing 'Bourguiba Homes' for abandoned or destitute children, and providing for the needs of Algerian refugees and wounded.

In the administrative field, however, problems are apt to arise. What should be the relationship, in an independent African State, between the local leaders of the dominant party on the one hand and the elected local councils and administrative officials on the other? This is an old problem, but it has presented itself in a variety of new forms. 'The dualism existing between the political authorities and administrative authority' was discussed in the Guinea context, with particular clarity, by Sékou Touré at the second national conference of P.D.G.[2] *cadres* in November 1958. Broadly speaking, his conclusion was that a certain dualism, and consequently a certain tension, was necessary and healthy; but that the absolute suprem-

---

[1] G. Bédos and M. A. Dejammet, 'Le Rassemblement Démocratique Africain'. Association Française de Science Politique, Table Ronde (March, 1959).
[2] Parti Démocratique de Guinée.

acy of the party must be reconciled with the relative freedom of action and initiative of the *conseils de circonscription* and the new African professional administrators. The fact that both the leaders of local councils and the administrators are likely at the same time to hold posts of responsibility within the party naturally tends in practice to limit the tension here.

Another problem confronting the mass parties after they have achieved power is that, without ceasing to be 'parties of principles', they inevitably become also 'parties of patronage'. In some respects this tends to increase the party's strength and effectiveness. It is of the nature of a mass party to 'reward its friends and remove its enemies'. The enjoyment of power vastly extends the range and increases the value of the rewards which the party has to offer to its friends, allies, and *militants*. Dennis Austin has pointed out how, in the case of the C.P.P.

> Patronage is used as an additional cement of party unity: e.g. C.P.P. candidates who lost the 1956 election were given diplomatic appointments abroad, directorships on the public corporations, jobs in the Builders' Brigade or in regional commissioners' offices, or scholarships to study law.[1]

Similarly the Cocoa Purchasing Company, which Krobo Edusei once picturesquely described as 'the atom bomb of the C.P.P.', undoubtedly helped the C.P.P. to win, or retain, the support of those farmers who were assisted with loans.

The difficulty is that, though patronage can be regarded as a special form of 'welfare', which a party in power uses to reward loyalty and past services (somewhat in the same way as the former colonial governments used to reward 'loyal' chiefs and intellectuals), the rewards which it has at its disposal, even in a relatively wealthy territory like Ghana, are limited. They can be numbered, perhaps, in thousands, whereas party members can be numbered in hundreds of thousands, and supporters – in times of maximum strength – in millions. Hence patronage, as the leaders of governing parties are well aware, is a two-edged weapon. While in some respects it may strengthen party unity, in others it may tend to weaken it, by creating a new division between the beneficiaries of patronage within the party – those enjoying middle-class salaries, expense accounts, cars, official houses, 'offices of profit' – and the mass of members and supporters who do not enjoy the material fruits of power.

What is difficult to decide is how far this use of government patronage has weakened the party's earlier enthusiasm and idealism – and how far

[1] D. Austin, 'The Convention People's Party in Ghana'. London Univ. Inst. of Commonwealth Studies Seminar, 1958.

it may prevent the party from keeping in touch with mass rank-and-file opinion.[1]

It is clear that the use of patronage by a governing party tends to promote the transformation of the party leadership, or a section within the leadership, into a new ruling class; and that this in its turn tends to stimulate the growth of a puritan, reforming opposition, either within the party or outside it. Whether the mass parties now in power, and likely to obtain power, in the various African States will be able to find ways of counteracting this tendency, and reasserting their egalitarian principles, remains to be seen.

[1] D. Austin, 'People and Constitution in Sierra Leone' (*West Africa*, 13 September–11 October 1952).

19

African One-Party States[1]

Gwendolen Carter

This reading shows how colonial governments have influenced the rise of the single-party state in Africa and how this trend has been reinforced by the needs of the new African states as seen by their leaders. The tendency to change constitutions after independence in the direction of presidential rule has continued since this was written; Mr Julius Nyerere has returned to office as the first President of Tanganyika; and in Ghana presidential rule has been further strengthened by President Nkrumah to the cost of the judiciary – the Chief Justice of Ghana was dismissed in December 1963 after his acquittal of three men accused by the government of plotting to overthrow the state. Nigeria too has become a republic with Dr Nnamdi Azikiwe as its first President, although the Nigerian constitution retains the chief executive power in the hands of the Federal Prime Minister.

This reading is taken from the introduction to a book which discusses the single-party systems of Liberia, Tunisia, Guinea, Senegal, the Ivory Coast and Tanganyika.

Never before have so many countries become independent within so short a space of time as in Africa between 1956 and 1962. Their independence was the culmination of a major movement in human history that is no less significant because of the brevity of its time span and, with rare exceptions (notably in the former Belgian Congo), its lack of violence and basic dislocation. As the result of this movement, some two-thirds of the people of the world's second largest (though most unevenly populated) continent ceased to be part of the last great area of colonial control and came under locally based governments headed by their own leaders.

The emergence of so many newly independent states has had an obvious impact in the realm of international affairs. It should have no less an impact in the fields of theoretical and practical comparative government. Within a few years has been compressed a variety of techniques and practices in the transfer of political power that offers rich opportunities

---

[1] Reprinted from *African One-Party States*, edited by Gwendolen Carter, copyright, 1962, by Cornell University, used with permission of Cornell University Press.

for comparative analysis. So too do the evolving structures and ideologies of the new African states. The concepts of traditional comparative government were developed for the most part out of an analysis of the governments of the United States, Great Britain, western Europe, and the Soviet Union. This led to a theoretical dichotomy, between democracy and dictatorship, between the so-called 'free world' and that of totalitarianism, whether fascist or Communist, that is more rigid than a rigorous consideration of even these mature political societies can sustain. The wealth of political practice in the developing countries suggests the need of a still more searching reconsideration of fundamental concepts, particularly when the latter are based on governmental structure rather than on practices and attitudes.

The structure and the ideology of a new African state are inevitably affected by its pre-colonial and colonial background but possibly still more by its leaders' own experiences and their evaluation of their country's particular needs. Thus even those countries that have experienced a common pattern of colonial rule are already diverging widely in their approaches to political decisions, their techniques of control and direction, and their goals, not only internally but also within the continent of Africa and in the international community. To provide interpretation and understanding is, hopefully, one of the contributions of theoretical comparative analysis to the practical conduct of affairs.

Few forms of organization have given rise to more differences of opinion than that of the one-party state. In traditional comparative analysis the number of political parties in a country has been considered a sound index to the character of its rule. One-party control is associated not only with dictatorial but also with quasi- or wholly totalitarian rule. This judgement seems to be confirmed by the experience of one-party régimes in Nazi Germany, the Soviet Union, and the 'people's democracies' of eastern Europe. Yet the fact that so many of the new states have a dominant or single political party but are clearly not totalitarian suggests a revision of at least this part of the prima-facie argument. Moreover, the representatives of many of these states also claim that they are democratic rather than dictatorial in character since their governments are selected, or at least endorsed, by popular election, they rest on mass party support, and, in addition, there is considerable interplay between groups within these mass parties as well as a broad base of popular participation and consent.

To make a definite choice at this moment between these interpretations of the character of newly developing states may be to do a disservice to them and to ourselves. To term them democratic when they provide little or no chance for an opposition party to play a role within the governmental structure would be to violate a basic criterion of a democratic system – that it institutionalizes public criticism of governmental measures and provides a method for the peaceful change of leaders and of ruling groups. Yet to overlook the possibility that such institutional arrangements may develop within their structures may be equally misleading, for their present form is an obvious result of their drive for independence and of their current concentration both on building national unity and on promoting economic development.

In most instances the single or dominant party in a developing state is an outgrowth of the mobilization of persons and groups in the pre-independence period. In the former British territories, the existence of a cohesive political party under a dominant leader was a *sine qua non* for the transfer of political power to local hands. Since the British were empirical, reacting to and through a 'process of interrelated pressure', to quote Sir Andrew Cohen,[1] the conditions for extension of local power remained relatively common while the timing differed. In the former French areas, it was the timing of the transfer of powers that was common while local conditions often varied widely. Broad policy decisions, like the passage of the *loi cadre* in 1956 (which made possible the decentralization of power to the territorial assemblies of French African countries and thus to their controlling party groups), and the transformation of the French Union into the Franco-African Community in 1958 through the referendum on the constitution of the Fifth (or de Gaulle) French Republic generalized the change in the *de facto* possession of power and subsequently in status. None the less it was the post-war extension to Africans of representation in the French National Assembly, the Council of the Republic, and the Assembly of the French Union that gave rise to the interterritorial R.D.A. (Rassemblement Démocratique Africain), and within the more advanced units of French West Africa, the local R.D.A. branches also developed in the pre-independence period the cohesive party organization and dominant leaders that the British regarded as the passport to responsible government and ultimate independence. Thus both colonial régimes stimulated, though by different means, the mass dominant parties, which form the decisive link between the pre-independence and post-independence periods.

Although the single or dominant party under a strong and popular leader is closely associated with the progress toward independence in a high proportion of the newly independent states, it has also seemed to provide both stability and continuity after independence. In contrast, a multiplicity of parties in the Sudan and in Pakistan (to take two widely separated

[1] *British Policy in Changing Africa*, p. 41 (Evanston, Ill.: Northwestern University Press, 1959).

countries) and the lack of strong leadership led to impending disorders which gave rise to army rule. It is true that in India and Nigeria the combination of strong linguistic or tribal divisions and a federal structure has provided more pluralistic systems which may well have still greater possibilities of persisting unity than the nonfederal one-party states. But even India has one dominant party, the Congress Party, while Nigeria has a dominant party in each of its regions and one, the Northern Peoples Congress, which can hardly be left out of any federal government coalition.

The stabilizing and, commonly, centralizing role of the dominant party within a new state seems indisputable, but this fact is only one of those which need to be taken into account in evaluating the character of one-party states. At present the existence of a dominant or single political party in a number of states is associated not only with stability but also with mass popular support. Whether this situation is a temporary one or has elements of permanence, whether it is associated only with the first generation of leaders and the early flush of nationalist fervour or can be transmitted through established channels, and whether it can survive in the face of the pressures for rapid economic development are long-range questions whose answers demand a far wider and more long-term investigation than can be attempted in this volume. Even the experience gathered together on these six states suggests, however, that one-party states can differ widely in origin, practice, and objectives and that no one category should encompass this diversity.

Of the six states with which this book is primarily concerned,[1] only one, Liberia, has had a long experience of independence. Liberia also provides an almost classic example of oligarchic one-party rule by the descendants of what was once an alien and remains an unassimilated group, the Americo-Liberians. Liberia is unique on the African continent in the passivity of its majority tribal people who as yet have neither used their numbers to gain local political control, as has happened in what is the most nearly comparable situation of Sierra Leone, nor reacted against local minority control either through violence or by appeals to the United Nations, as have Arabs in Algeria, Africans in Kenya and in the Rhodesias and Nyasaland, and Africans and Asians in South Africa.

The other five countries achieved independence late but under widely varying circumstances, none of which were free from strain. Tunisia had by far the oldest and best-established nationalist movement, one which operated for substantial periods outside the constitutional system and did not win full acceptance by the French until 1954. Houphouët-Boigny's Ivory Coast branch of the R.D.A. was under somewhat comparable

[1] Liberia, Tunisia, Guinea, Senegal, the Ivory Coast and Tanganyika - Eds.

restraints between 1949 and 1950, when he made peace with the authorities both within his own territory and in Paris. The Guinea branch of the R.D.A. suffered no such ostracism in its own territory in the comparable period, but subsequently Guinea's decision to vote 'no' on the referendum that determined membership in the Franco-African Community and its difficulties in securing acceptance of Guinean independence created a rupture with the former *Métropole* unparalleled in any other transfer of power. Senegal experienced its own particular problems over independence not because of tension with France but because of the break-up of the Mali Federation. The Tanganyika nationalist movement, which began later than any of the others, suffered some slight harassment by colonial authorities, and its leaders had less experience with party organization and political techniques than those of any of these other countries since its first election was held barely three years before independence on 9 December 1961.

Despite these problems, there has been a remarkable degree of continuity between pre- and post-independence periods, not only in local governing groups but also, with the exception of Guinea, in relations with the former *Métropole*. One of the most remarkable features of almost all the former French African states is the degree to which they have continued to depend on French officials (still paid for by France) as administrators and as technical aides and on French subsidies for their economic development. The British, in contrast, have tended to cut off, or sharply to reduce, their economic aid when a former colony becomes independent and to expect the newly sovereign country to assume not only the expense of the salaries of those former colonial officials who become members of local administrative and technical staffs but also to help in providing compensation to those who retire from such services. None the less all the African territories that have graduated from British colonial control have sought to retain a considerable number of the former colonial administrators (though rarely in as obvious positions as in the French-speaking territories), turn first to Great Britain for economic aid, and have acquired membership in the Commonwealth of Nations. Liberia has had something of the same kind of assistance in technical aid and in financial support from the United States in the postwar period.

The continuation of these types of contact undoubtedly has some effect on the character of local rule but far less, it would seem, than local conditions, organization, and goals. Liberia remains oligarchic, with only slight and gradual infiltration of tribal peoples into the governing group. If this process is encouraged by the example of mass parties in surrounding territories, the latter may have borrowed something from the

205

strongly presidential structure of Liberia. Apart from Senegal, in which there is both a President and a Prime Minister, all the French-speaking territories (except the former Belgian Congo) have centralized the executive authority in a President. So, too, has Ghana under its new constitution. Tanganyika, Nigeria, and Sierra Leone, in contrast, have retained the characteristic division of the parliamentary system between the titular and the real executive. None of these three,[1] as yet, has established a republic although at least the first two can be expected to do so. In Tanganyika and Sierra Leone the titular executive has little obvious influence at this stage, but it seems likely that there is already some division of authority in Nigeria between the Prime Minister, Sir Abubakar Tafewa Balewa, and the colourful national leader, Nnamdi Azikiwe, who became the first Governor-General. This balance might swing still further toward the presidential office when the republic is declared. The same might also become true in Tanganyika, particularly if Julius Nyerere becomes the first President. If this development should take place in Nigeria and Tanganyika, the situation of the executive in these countries would then more nearly approximate that in Senegal, where Senghor commands the mass support and exercises ultimate authority but leaves organization and administration in the hands of his Prime Minister, Mamadou Dia.

The political dominance of a single personality is not confined to developing countries, but it is strongly evident within almost all of them. In none of the six countries treated in this volume is there so strong a cult of personality as in Ghana, but Bourguiba, Houphouët-Boigny, Tubman, and also Senghor have become national symbols as well as decisive leaders. Sékou Touré's position is somewhat different because of the Guinean insistence on the primacy of the party, but the role he plays differs less in practice from that of the others than it does in theory. Seemingly most divergent from the pattern is the situation in Tanganyika, where Julius Nyerere stepped down from his office as Prime Minister so shortly after his country achieved independence. It seems possible, however, that in the perspective of the counter-pressures among different groups within Tanganyika and the slightness of party cohesion Nyerere can become more of a focus for national unity through his organizational work for the Tanganyika African National Union than through holding a governmental office.

---

[1] Both Nigeria and Tanganyika (now part of Tanzania) have become republics since this was written. Nigeria maintains the Office of Prime Minister together with the titular office of President. In Tanzania the President is the executive head of the Government.

There is an obvious interrelation between the dominance of a single person and the discipline and structure of party organization, but this relationship may take different forms of major importance for the character of the regime. In Mali, but only there, party organization is so dominant and, in a sense, pure that it has excluded the emphasis on personality so obtrusive elsewhere. The intensity of Malian organization and discipline helps to explain why the country was so ill-matched a partner to more pluralistic Senegal. If organization can be a substitute for personal leadership, as in Mali, it is rare, however, that the opposite can be the case. Personal leadership, like that of Houphouët-Boigny and Senghor, may be combined temporarily with a loose party structure. But it is noticeable that much more attention is now being devoted to strengthening the Ivory Coast's party organization than was the case in the period either before or immediately after independence. Bourguiba has found the same need in Tunisia and encountered the same kinds of pressures from younger persons within his party. It is in Senegal and Tanganyika that the dominant party has the least well knit structure, partly because of counter-ethnic loyalties, group demands, and rural-urban divisions and partly because of lack of dynamic drive. Liberia's True Whig Party does not even seek, much less possess, the mass base of the other parties here described and is content to secure much of its cohesion from personal family relationships.

As long as strong personal leadership continues, mass loyalty (if it exists) tends to be directed to the single figure rather than the party structure. Party orders and party efforts to rouse popular enthusiasm for national or local development plans may suffer in consequence as even Guinea has discovered. The problem of succession is accentuated. Yet the alternative of loyalty to a régime and a country rather than to a person or group of persons requires a national orientation that a country with the deep roots of Tunisia finds easier to evoke than the newer entities of sub-Saharan Africa.

None of the new African countries, except Nigeria, places great emphasis on the governmental institutions through which measures are formally enacted into law. The lack of representation in their assemblies of more than one political party makes opposition highly unlikely and proceedings dull. Indeed, although Ghana is widely criticized for its restrictions on the opposition, the nine opposition members still vocal in its assembly in 1962 made that body far more lively than were most other African legislative bodies. Not only are discussions rare in most of these assemblies, but also there is little public interest in what takes place. Yet there is still a major difference between the insistence in Guinea that the party ranks higher than any governmental institution and the appearance maintained by the others that the party works through, but is not above, governmental institutions. By this means, the framework and an ideology are maintained which leave the way open for institutionalized opposition that may no longer be considered dangerous if a national consensus can be achieved.

It will take more than a change in the attitude of the dominant party, however, to provide the kind of institutionalized interaction between rival political groups which is taken so much for granted in Western democratic countries. The role of the loyal opposition is a difficult one to play. No party in newly independent Africa has yet accepted its discipline. In Ghana, Togo, and elsewhere, at least some opposition groups have plotted assassination as the means to remove the ruling figure from office. If frustration over the possibility of gaining power by any other means may help to explain these plots, they provide the governing group with ample excuse for measures of restraint, arbitrary detention, and exclusion from political activity. None of these six countries have been wholly free from such dangers, though Tunisia and Tanganyika have been the least obviously affected by them. Nowhere among any of them is there any open encouragement to diversity of political expression.

Moreover, most French-speaking states of sub-Saharan Africa have adopted an electoral device which effectually shuts out representation in an assembly by an opposition party. First instituted by Guinea and then widely copied, this device turns the whole country into an electoral district within which the winning party takes all the seats. Even a 50·1 per cent. of the vote yields 100 per cent. representation under such a scheme, though it must be noted that most of the newly emergent countries, and all five included in this volume, have mass parties which secure a high percentage of the total vote.

But even in those rare African countries where an opposition can still win a few seats in an election, the deprivation involved in their exclusion from a share of the powers and opportunities that are afforded the governing group provides them with a powerful incentive to unity. It is sometimes said facetiously that 'the opposition is either in gaol or in the government'. Increasingly the latter is the case. Most of the dominant African parties have demonstrated a remarkable capacity for absorption of former rival or antagonistic groups and a quite surprising willingness to elevate their leaders thereafter to important government posts.

The result of these mergers in Tunisia, Senegal, the Ivory Coast, and even Guinea has been to develop political parties which are themselves composed of the kind of diverse groups that might be expected in a Western country to form two, or even a series of, political parties. Something of the interaction and compromise hammered out between political parties in the congressional or parliamentary system goes on within these African political parties though without the publicity which is one of the healthiest aspects of public interchanges. These African intraparty debates may even bear some resemblance to that which goes on within the Republican or the Democratic Party. This is not formal, structural democracy, but it can provide for the airing of issues, the awareness by the people at large of the policies that are to affect them, and the consideration by leaders of the sentiments of their followers.

Officially, Guinea has adopted 'democratic centralism' as the method of interaction between followers and leaders. Plans can, and indeed must, be discussed widely until decisions have been made. Thereafter no debate and no divergence are permitted. Within these limits, much is being done to bring new ideas and information, particularly to the rural areas. The mass party is looked on in Guinea, as in Tunisia, the Ivory Coast, Senegal, and Tanganyika, as the purveyor of plans and precepts, the stimulator of new projects, the educator of the young and of the peasants, and the emancipator of women. Apart from Liberia, the political party has far more, therefore, than a governing role, for it sees as additional objectives the liberation of the people of its country from poverty, illiteracy, and apathy. In such tasks many Africans feel, with more than a little justification, that there is no room for disagreement or divided efforts.

20

Authoritarian and Single-Party Tendencies in African Politics[1]
Martin L. Kilson

This reading further examines the causes and prospects of single-party trends. In a part of the paper not reprinted here the author distinguishes between two meanings of 'single-party rule': (1) where only the governing party is allowed to exist – this applies, among others, to the Parti Démocratique de Guinée (P.D.G.), the Union Soudanaise in Mali, the Parti Dahoméen de l'Unité (P.D.U.), the Parti Démocratique de la Côte d'Ivoire (P.D.C.I.), the Union pour le Progrès du Tchad (U.P.T.) and the True Whig Party in Liberia; (2) where 'the governing party has an overwhelming majority and employs its legal, police and political powers to restrict the competitive position of opposition parties and groups' – this applies, among others, to the Convention People's Party (C.P.P.) in Ghana, the Sierra Leone People's Party (S.L.P.P.), the Tanganyika African National Union (T.A.N.U.), the Northern People's Congress (N.P.C.) in Northern Nigeria and the Union Progressiste Senegalaise (U.P.S.).

The author identifies five causes of single party tendencies: (1) type of political party; (2) Marxist ideology; (3) political instability stemming from tribal conflict or unrest; (4) political insecurity stemming from real or supposed external threats and (5) traditionally oriented ideological preference for a slowly changing *status quo*. Through lack of space we reprint here only his concluding note on patterns and prospects.

PATTERNS OF SINGLE-PARTY EVOLUTION AND PROSPECTS OF OPPOSITION

1. Patterns

Four rather distinct patterns may be delineated, though normally more than one of these is operative in any given state: (1) extra-parliamentary restrictions on opposition parties; (2) government dissolution or outlawry of opposition parties; (3) regroupment or a united-front process; and (4) a voluntary merger of the opposition with the ruling party.

Extra-Parliamentary Restrictions and Outlawry. The first two patterns of single-party evolution are best considered together because they in fact

[1] Reprinted from *World Politics*, Vol. XV, No. 2 (January 1963).

occur together, and they are more widespread than the other patterns. Extra-parliamentary or extra-legal restrictions against opposition parties have occurred at one time or another in all of the nineteen African states where the single-party tendency is dominant.[1] A variety of government measures have implemented these restrictions, among which have been imprisonment of opposition leaders, repression or censorship of newspapers, limitations on rights of assembly, and intimidation by police and/or party activists of the governing party. Imprisonment of opposition leaders has occurred in nearly all the African states noted above, and in three instances it involved charges of conspiracy to assassinate the head of state (viz. Ghana in 1958, Dahomey in 1961, Togo in 1961).

Restrictions on rights of assembly and the ability of opposition parties to agitate have also been relatively widespread. Indeed, if the claims of opposition parties themselves are accepted, such measures are wellnigh universal, not merely in states where the single-party tendency is dominant but also in competitive situations like Western Nigeria, where opposition groups have complained of restrictions by government bodies.[2] In some instances, government simply refuses permits for holding political rallies, as in Tanganyika, where in 1961 the Minister of Home Affairs banned political rallies of the opposition Tanganyika African National Congress (T.A.N.C.) on grounds that, in the Minister's words, Congress's speakers 'disregarded the conventions of public speaking.'[3] In this particular instance, another type of restriction on opposition parties was apparent in the T.A.N.U. government's refusal to permit the Youth Wing of T.A.N.C. to register as a political organization – a method of restricting political groups that is also used elsewhere in Africa. It should be noted, moreover, that this method of control over the formation of political groups (and also over non-political groups like welfare associations, tribal unions, etc., which often become *political* in African politics) is a continuation by African states of a power exercised by colonial governments. Given the peculiar problems of nation-state formation confronted by African states, some have utilized this power to prevent the establishment of particularistic parties – e.g. in Ghana, as already noted, or in Ivory Coast, where the Constitution holds any group whose purpose is 'particularistic propaganda

[1] These nineteen states are: Congo (ex-French), Central African Republic, Dahomey, Gabon, Ghana, Guinea, Ivory Coast, Liberia, Mauritania, Mali, Niger, Northern Nigeria, Senegal, Sierra Leone, Tanganyika, Tchad, Togo, Tunisia, and Upper Volta.

[2] See *Daily Times* (Lagos, 4 October 1961), 1; ibid, p. 10 (2 January 1962).

[3] Quoted in Tony Hughes, 'Tanganyika on the Eve', *Africa South*, p. 71 (October–December 1961).

of racial or ethnic character' to be beyond the law.[1] Ivory Coast and Ghana governments have even outlawed personal, physical acts of tribal identification, such as facial scarification, etc.

Restrictive measures involving the press have been less frequent than imprisonment of leaders and limitations on rights of assembly and agitation, but have been utilized in several states. In Tunisia, the opposition paper *al-Sabah* was suppressed in 1957 by the Neo-Destour government, presumably for its Pan-Arab tendency;[2] in Ghana the *Ashanti Pioneer* Control Act of 1960 placed the main opposition paper under government censorship; and in Dahomey the P.D.U. government passed a law in 1961 permitting seizure of newspapers for incitement to misdemeanours and for other reasons.[3]

As for outlawry of opposition parties, this has been a pattern of single-party evolution in all but five of the nineteen states listed above, these five being Northern Nigeria, Sierra Leone, Mali, Tanganyika, and Gabon. An important feature of this pattern has been the simultaneous deportation or otherwise forced exile of leaders of outlawed organizations, even though they were citizens of the state concerned. Thus, in Ivory Coast, Ghana, Niger, Upper Volta, Liberia, Tchad, and Senegal, leaders of outlawed parties or unions have been deported.

One feature of the dynamic of the foregoing methods of single-party evolution is that there would appear to be some relationship between the type of ruling party on the one hand, and the specific government unit executing restrictive measures against opposition groups. Thus, in Ghana, Tanganyika, Guinea, and Ivory Coast, it has been the central government and its organs that execute these restrictions. This is partly due to the natural centralizing tendency of mass-type parties, reinforced in the case of Ghana and Guinea by the government's adherence to a variant of the Marxist pattern of development. On the other hand, in Sierra Leone and Northern Nigeria, where caucus-type parties rule, a major part of the restrictions against opposition has been executed by local government bodies, or more particularly by Native Authority Councils, Courts, and Police. Since the governmental consequence of a caucus-type ruling party has been a significant devolution of government power to local units associated with the traditional ruling *élite*, the latter has been capable of using this power to harass opposition groups.

[1] *Constitution de la République de la Côte d'Ivoire, 1960*, Article 6. Cf. Professor Coleman's emphasis upon ethnic and tribal pluralism as an obstacle to the rise of authoritarian African governments, in Gabriel A. Almond and James S. Coleman eds., *The Politics of the Developing Areas*, p. 368 (Princeton, 1960).

[2] See Neville Barbour, *A Survey of Northwest Africa*, pp. 318–19 (Oxford, 1960).

[3] See *West Africa*, p. 263 (11 March 1961).

Voluntary Merger and Regroupment Process. Voluntary merger has been the least current pattern of single-party evolution, the best examples being the merger of opposition parties in Guinea with the ruling P.D.G. in 1958, and of the *Parti Soudanais du Progrès* with the *Union Soudanaise* in Mali in 1959. The regroupment or united-front process is somewhat similar to voluntary merger, especially in so far as both patterns have involved the grant of ministerial and other senior government posts to leaders of parties that merge or regroup with governing parties. However in such instances of regroupment as occurred in Mauritania in 1961, Sierra Leone in 1960, Congo Republic in 1961, and Gabon in 1961, this pattern of single-party development has been preceded by a period of major restrictions against opposition groups by the government. Thus the extent to which the regroupment process has been 'voluntary' would appear much less than the two instances of voluntary merger, properly so-called, in Guinea and Mali. Even in the latter states – and especially in Guinea – the post-merger period has witnessed government limitations (imprisonment and outlawry) upon groups tending or wishing to break away from the single-party system.[1]

It should also be noted that the regroupment type of party merger has tended to occur in the context of a national election, taking the form of all parties establishing a national union electoral list that occasionally involves one candidate standing for a given office, and particularly the office of President. For instance, the Presidents of Ivory Coast, Mauritania, Gabon, Congo, and Togo were elected at national elections in which, through national union lists, they were the sole candidates for the office.

2. Prospects

Generally, the immediate future of effective opposition parties in African politics does not appear particularly bright. Even when they are not subjected to extra-parliamentary measures, they tend to be weak institutions, lacking the financial and other resources necessary for effectively competing with governing parties. The latter, on the other hand, in addition to their aura of nationalist legitimacy (a not inconsiderable advantage), have access to government apparatus as a means of perpetuating their rule, and African governing parties seldom hesitate to employ government funds, transport, and other equipment for electoral campaigns and other political activities. For instance, in February 1962 a Ghana government

[1] Cf. Philippe Decraene, 'Guinée An IV: La Révolte des Intellectuels', *Le Monde*, p. 4 (29 December 1961). Cf. also *Afrique Nouvelle*, p. 4 (27 July–2 August 1962), for an account of the Mali government's handling of 'those who have manifested their opposition to the monetary decision [i.e. the nationalization of the Mali franc] of the party and the government'.

loan of £497,860 to the Guinea Press – which publishes all C.P.P. organs – was written off for 'services rendered by the Press'.[1] In Nigeria, where a relatively competitive party system prevails and formal expression is given to Western-type democratic procedures, government funds amounting to £2,000,000 have found their way into the service of the governing party in the Western Region, the Action Group, through the indirect method of transference to the party of a part of government loans to a private Nigerian firm (the Nigerian Investment Properties Corporation).[2] Similarly, in the Ivory Coast the P.D.C.I. government grants subvention to folklore and youth groups connected with the party, as well as to an array of voluntary associations unrelated to it.

Another aspect of the use of government for party purposes that prevails in most French-speaking African states is the direct participation by civil servants in party politics as party members, officers, activists, etc., thus giving the governing parties a significant advantage over their rather weak opponents. In the Ivory Coast, this situation has even taken the form of organizing 'une commission politique' of the P.D.C.I. in the departments and ministries of government in order, among other things, 'to control the conformity of the authorities to the directives of the party. . . .'[3] Ghana has moved along similar lines, commencing the formation of C.P.P. branches in government ministries in January 1962.[4] Thus, when these situations are combined with those I have analysed as major causes of the tendency towards single-party rule, there would not appear to be very much in African politics to make one especially sanguine about the prospects of opposition parties.

As some observers have argued, it may be that such a prospect is neither necessary nor desirable at the present stage of African political systems, which function within nation-states still in process of becoming internally coherent. These observers also suggest that the single-party system is capable of sustaining an important measure of democracy, by which they mean widespread participation, active and free discussion, etc. – all of which constitute influence by the *demos* upon the decision-making process.[5] This proposition, however, has not been taken very much beyond the realm of assertion, still wanting empirical demonstration and conceptual definition. What *kind* of decisions, for instance, are influenced by

---

[1] Quoted in *West Africa*, p. 215 (24 February 1962).
[2] See *Daily Times*, pp. 1, 3, 9–10 (Lagos, 9 August 1962). See also *West Africa*, p. 1027 (15 September 1962).
[3] Philippe Yace, 'Le Parti', *Fraternité*, p. 8 (Abidjan, 4 August 1961).
[4] *Evening News*, p. 8 (12 January 1962).
[5] Cf. Immanuel Wallerstein, *Africa: The Politics of Independence*, pp. 161–7, *passim* (New York, 1961).

participation and discussion in parties, like P.D.G., C.P.P., T.A.N.U., and *Union Soudanaise*? How real is the choice of candidates for party and government office given to the masses in these single-party situations? What are the limits of opposition politics in these situations; that is, what is meant by 'opposition' within a single party when there is no assumption of a right to carry it to its logical conclusion (to *organize* one's opposition) when one's demands are not satisfied?[1] It simply is not enough to say that one index of democracy in a single-party situation is the prevalence of 'conditions in which opposition can be expressed.'[2]

I should note here that my own reading and analysis of the single-party situations in African politics suggest a more sceptical view as to their democratic character, *but I am not particularly convinced that this is the most meaningful yardstick for appraising them.*[3] Although I myself have used this measurement in much of this article (e.g. my characterization of methods of single-party development as 'authoritarian'), I am inclined to look at other functions of African single-party systems besides the democratic one; and my analysis leads me to believe that the governing parties and their leaders do not consider it supreme. More specifically, I tend to concur with Mair's keen observation that 'Since the unity of the new [African] States is so precarious, it may well be that their rulers cannot at present afford that tolerance of opposition which is the ideal of representative democracy. . . . The crucial problem for the new governments seems likely to be how to be authoritarian enough to maintain stability and carry through their modernizing policies, and yet not so obviously oppressive as to provoke active or passive resistance.'[4]

I should point out, finally, that some observers hold that use of the term 'authoritarian' in analysing African single-party systems may not be appropriate, especially where mass-type parties are concerned, given the large-scale participation provided by such parties, their role in national integration, etc. Thus, Professor Wallerstein maintains that 'the one-party system in the African context is often a significant step toward the liberal state, not a first step away from it. . . . The one-party structure is an interim system of African states which they are maintaining for the present.'[5]

[1] Cf. Ruth Schachter, 'Single-Party Systems in West Africa', *American Political Science Review*, LV, pp. 304-7 (June 1961).

[2] Ibid., p. 304.

[3] Cf. H. B. Mayo, *An Introduction to Democratic Theory*, p. 220 ff. (New York, 1960).

[4] L. P. Mair, 'Social Change in Africa', *International Affairs*, XXXVI, p. 456, italics added (October 1960). Cf. Carl J. Friedrich, *Constitutional Government and Democracy*, pp. 8 ff. (Boston, 1941); 'In the evolution of our Western World . . . national unification had to precede constitutionalism.'

[5] Wallerstein, *Africa*, pp. 163, 166.

Interesting as this proposition is and *perhaps* true for the long run, it is not particularly apparent in the thinking of the leaders of single-party states, and certainly not among the leaders of Guinea, Mali, and Ghana, where an effort is being made to employ political power for a revolutionary reconstruction of society. Note, for instance, Touré's adumbration of his view of liberalism and thus, presumably, of the liberal state: 'The enemy of revolutionary firmness is liberalism which, from compromise to compromise, drives a party into incriminations and anarchy. The best [liberal] arrangements and the most clever compromises only lead to general discontent and could not possibly preserve the higher interests of the people since they subordinate them, wholly or partly, to the selfish interests of groups or individuals; they could only maintain inequalities and increase antagonisms; they perpetuate confusion and doubt, distrust and discouragement.'[1]

Nevertheless, whatever the correct term may be for classifying and measuring African single-party systems – as against other political arrangements – their reversal is not particularly imminent. And this appears true despite such developments as the grant of amnesty to political exiles on the part of the Ivory Coast and Ghana governments, overtures of such amnesty made by Niger and Upper Volta to their political exiles, the release of political prisoners in Ghana and Ivory Coast, or Ghana's revocation of the *Ashanti Pioneer* Act of 1960, censoring that newspaper. Such grants of amnesty to political exiles are primarily an astute response to the manner in which the keenly contested politics of Pan-Africanism may affect the internal political stability of participant states (e.g. the use of an exile for political purposes by the exile's host-state). The latter strategy – i.e. lifting of censorship laws, etc. – may be a unique feature of African politics whereby, once the purpose of a restrictive measure has been secured, its continuation as a formal legal measure is considered an unnecessary demonstration of restrictive intent. In other words, once the intent is accepted as second nature to the political system and its participants, statutory expression of the intent is not required. This does not, however, necessarily alter an African single-party system. It may well strengthen the system.

[1] Sékou Touré, 'Message to the Nation . . . on the Occasion of the New Year, 10 January 1962', in *The International Policy of the Democratic Party of Guinea*, VII, pp. 218–20 (Conakry, n.d.). This 'Message' is not printed in the French edition of this volume; see Touré, *La Politique Internationale du Parti Démocratique de Guinée*, VII (Conakry, 1962).

21

Larger Unities: Pan-Africanism and
Regional Federations[1]
Immanuel Wallerstein

The problem of African unity is coming increasingly to dominate political discussion and policy in Africa. This reading tells the story of the movement towards greater unity up to about 1961. Since that date the distinction between Casablanca and Monrovia powers has become increasingly blurred; and since the conference of independent African States at Addis Ababa in the summer of 1963, these two groupings seem to have lost most of their earlier importance. The results of that conference will be further discussed in the Introduction to section IIIf.

The drive for larger African unity, Pan-Africanism, is probably stronger than similar movements elsewhere in the world. It is not strong enough to assure immediate success, perhaps not even ultimate success. But Pan-Africanism seems likely to loom large as an active issue in African politics in the near future.

Pan-Africanism is a very loose term and covers several different movements, which it would be well to distinguish. Pan-Africanism may be said to have arisen first as a protest movement of American and West Indian Negroes who were reasserting their links with Africa and the achievements of African civilizations. Its precursors were the early back-to-Africa movements which led to the creation of Liberia and Sierra Leone, movements which reached their high point in the remarkable spread of Garveyism in the United States in the 1920's.

In 1919, during the Versailles Peace Conference in Paris, the American Negro leader, W. E. B. Du Bois, organized the First Pan-African Congress, presided over by Blaise Diagne, first Negro deputy from Senegal in the French parliament. Du Bois organized four more such congresses between then and 1945, earning the title of 'father of Pan-Africanism'. The Fifth Congress was held in Manchester in October 1945, at the end of the Second World War. Du Bois was chairman. The joint secretaries were George Padmore, West Indian Negro and latter-day theoretician of Pan-Africanism,

[1] Reprinted from *Africa: the Politics of Independence* (Random House, New York, 1961).

and Kwame Nkrumah. The assistant secretary was Jomo Kenyatta.

The 1945 meeting marked a shift of emphasis in Pan-Africanism from a protest movement of Western hemisphere Negroes seeking racial equality, allied with African intellectuals, to a tool of African nationalist movements fighting colonial rule. One of the organizations that grew out of the Manchester meeting was the West African National Secretariat, whose secretary was Nkrumah. It was established in London in 1947. When Nkrumah was called to the Gold Coast in 1948, the Secretariat ceased to function. There were no serious organizational developments from this point until 1957, when the Gold Coast (Ghana) became independent.

Ghana's independence and the first Conference of Independent African States, held in Accra in April 1958, once more changed the charter of Pan-Africanism. It was still a tool in the African colonial struggle, although now a complication arose. Who would direct and control this movement? Whether independent African nations had some greater right to wield this tool than the nationalist movements in countries not yet independent would become an issue. However, as more and more African countries gained their independence, the central question became rather the unification of sovereign states.

Thus, Pan-Africanism has had at least three political objectives, which to some extent can be seen as occurring in three successive periods. First, it has been a protest movement against racism, largely of American and West Indian Negroes. In this capacity, Pan-Africanism still continues. It is an interesting and important story, but we shall not tell it here. Second, Pan-Africanism has been a tool in the hands of African nationalist movements struggling for independence. It probably has not been the most important tool in this struggle. It has played some role, but one far less important than internal party organization and, as a rallying force, it has been no more important than territorial nationalism. At some points, it has even caused strains and hence, perhaps, setbacks for particular nationalist movements.

Third and most recently, Pan-Africanism has been a movement to establish a supranational entity or entities encompassing various independent African states – at its most hopeful, the United States of Africa. In this last aspect, Pan-Africanism has perforce had only a short life, much too short for us to be able to evaluate its achievements properly. Yet in its short history, the Pan-African movement has had some important successes and suffered some serious setbacks. Perhaps in reviewing these experiences we shall discern what motivations lie behind Pan-Africanism and what structural factors affect its possibilities of success.

Why larger unities? On the surface, this goal seems to make little sense.

Larger Unities: Pan-Africanism and Regional Federations

We have seen how nationalist movements have struggled to create a sense of nation, to establish political and economic institutions within a national framework. Why break down this entity the moment it is set up? Yet large numbers of African politicians cry out against the 'balkanization' of Africa, which they say must be overcome. For many people the slogan of the anti-colonial revolution was not 'independence' but 'independence and unity'. According to their standards the goal of the nationalist movements has not been achieved by sovereignty; they require African unity as well.

African nationalists feel that in a real sense their struggle is an unfinished business and will continue to be so until unity is achieved. The objective of nationalism was not independence. This was only a means – one of two possible ones, as we have seen – to their real goal: political equality. At one level, independence assures equality in that each nation is sovereign and is legally free to pursue its own national interest. On another level in the international arena, small and poor nations are scarcely able to compete on equal terms with big powers. Thus there appears an old political theme: in unity there is strength. If we can achieve African unity, it is argued, then we shall really have control over our own society. We shall then be able to remain apart from the quarrels of others; and we shall then be able to obtain assistance from the outside. This, of course, is not an irrational analysis.

The economic case for larger unities, to be sure, is strong. It was used for a long time by colonial governments to justify the establishment of federations of which they approved, such as the Federation of the Rhodesias and Nyasaland. Essentially the argument is that a larger internal market is necessary to stimulate industrial and commercial development, and that a larger geographical area contained within one political framework makes for more rational economic planning. Some claim that economic co-operation is both a justification for Pan-African unity and a means through which it can be achieved. Others oppose larger unities because of the economic detriment to their countries (this is true of some relatively richer countries).

Basically, though, Pan-Africanism is a political (and, as we shall see, cultural) movement. Economic arguments have proved insufficient to accomplish anything positive. But in the political arena, the quarrels over the pace and method of decolonization since 1957 on the one hand have destroyed some old possibilities of unity and on the other hand have created some new and unexpected channels for unity. In fact, decolonization has caused major political realignments in Africa, largely around the issues of Pan-Africanism.

Colonial governments created units larger than the individual territories.

Units such as French West Africa or French North Africa, British West Africa or British East Africa existed as institutional structures or at least as well-defined regions with common problems. The degree of administrative unity varied, although usually at least functional organs of co-operation existed, such as the West African Currency Board, East Africa Literature Bureau, the Institut Français d'Afrique Noire. These limited co-operative enterprises at the administrative level were matched by early nationalist groupings that were similarly organized on a regional level. Examples include the early National Congress of British West Africa, the Association des Etudiants Musulmans Nord-Africains, and most impressively, the Rassemblement Démocratique Africain, a French African political movement, at some point or other organized in what are now twelve independent countries. There were structures, then, that brought together political parties, trade unions, youth and students' groups on an inter-territorial basis; but before 1957 these did not exist on an all-African basis, nor did they exist outside the framework of the colonial administrative structure, although the nationalist groups chose the widest structure available. The only all-African meeting ground before 1957 had been the Pan-African congresses, and these were intermittent, inadequately representative, and without a continuing structure.

Decolonization in Africa, although occurring within a relatively short span of time, seldom occurred simultaneously in different territories, even those in the same area. Thus in British West Africa, Ghana became independent before Nigeria which became independent before Sierra Leone. In French West Africa, Guinea became independent before the Federation of Mali, which became independent before the four states of the Conseil de l'Entente (Ivory Coast, Upper Volta, Niger and Dahomey). Sometimes, as in French West Africa, the very pace of decolonization became a major issue *between* various African countries. The first ones to become independent in a group of territories were reluctant to remain in joint administrative structures with territories that were still colonies. Thus, in 1957, Ghana withdrew from such joint enterprises as the West African Airways Corporation. After Guinea's independence in 1958, she was excluded from the French West African inter-territorial structures, which were to disintegrate completely by 1959. The administrative dismantling was sometimes matched by partial collapse of the inter-territorial nationalist structures during this period. This was notably true in French black Africa. Between 1958 and 1960, as a result of quarrels over the methods of decolonization, the integrating nationalist structures on the party, trade union and youth levels were all seriously weakened. While Guinea and Mali and the Entente states argued over methods and immediate goals, each was afraid to be associated with inter-territorial voluntary structures which might be of a different political tendency than its own. So each pressed its internal groupings to break ties with inter-territorial groups of opposite tendencies.

In British East Africa and Central Africa a different type of dismantling of unified structures was occurring. Here inter-territorial administrative structures had come into existence against the express wishes of the African population and with the assent of a white settler population. This was notably the case in the establishment of the Federation of the Rhodesias and Nyasaland (Central African Federation) in 1953. This was also largely true of the East African High Commission and its correlative agencies. In both cases, African opposition to unity was based on the fear that a unification of territories would tend to result in the prevalence throughout the larger entity of the policies of the most settler-dominated territory (Southern Rhodesia and Kenya, respectively). Unity in a colonial settler context was seen as a retrogressive step, one that would delay rather than speed up African liberation. In East Africa, African nationalists successfully opposed the creation of a federal structure. In Central Africa, the primary demand of African nationalists since 1953 has been the dissolution of federation.

In spite of their opposition to federation in settler areas, in organizing themselves to pursue their own aims. African nationalists have created the Pan-African Freedom Movement of East and Central Africa (PAFMECA) and have stated quite explicitly their goal of a federal structure for their states, once they have obtained independence and universal suffrage. In 1960, mindful of the experience of West African decolonization and its impact on unity, Julius Nyerere of Tanganyika announced the willingness of his movement to accept a short delay in its then imminent independence in order to enable Kenya and Uganda to receive their independence simultaneously with Tanganyika. His hope was that this would enhance the possibility of creating a single federal state.

A situation similar to that of East and Central Africa may be seen in South Africa. There the three so-called High Commission Territories – Basutoland, Bechuanaland, and Swaziland – which are governed by the United Kingdom Colonial Office, had resisted incorporation into the Union of South Africa, an issue which had been discussed since 1907. In South-West Africa, a former mandate which the Republic of South Africa has refused to place under United Nations trusteeship, African nationalists call for the recognition of the trust status of the territory as a step toward ultimate independence. Here again, as in East and Central Africa, Africans are against unity in so far as it means subjection to white-settler rule. The economic arguments put forward are scorned. The political reality is primary. On the African organizational level, however, a different picture is seen. The African nationalist organizations of both South-West Africa and the Republic of South Africa find themselves together since 1959 in the South Africa United Front. There is very close collaboration between the Basutoland nationalist groups and those in the Republic.

The picture on the north-eastern Horn of Africa is somewhat different, but it also stresses the significance of the timing of independence. In this region live the Somali people, who during the colonial era were found in five areas: Italian Somaliland, British Somaliland, the southern half of French Somaliland, the Ogaden district in eastern Ethiopia, and the north-east corner of Kenya. There has long been a pan-Somali movement to unite this people. The largest single group is found in Somalia, which was Italian Somaliland, an Italian trust territory which long in advance was promised its independence in 1960 by the United Nations. When the date of independence approached, the United Kingdom responded to pressure in British Somaliland by granting this territory independence four days before Somalia, with the express expectation that the two would merge, which they did.

Still another variant occurred in North Africa, the Maghreb. Here Tunisia and Morocco received their independence in 1956, while Algeria was still fighting for hers. The long struggle of Algeria strengthened the moves for Maghreb unity, as various attempts were made by independent Tunisia and Morocco to assist Algeria. At an early point in the struggle, Tunisia's Bourguiba proposed to France that Tunisia (and Morocco) should retrocede some of their sovereign powers to a new French-North African confederation, provided that Algeria first was allowed to enter on an equal basis into a North African federation. Here is the same simultaneity principle advocated by Nyerere in East Africa, applied to somewhat different circumstances. This move failed, and in 1958 the governments of Tunisia and Morocco, and the Provisional Government of the Algerian Republic proclaimed a confederal structure, which was not seriously implemented because of the continuing French rule over Algeria. This was a clear case of utilizing unity as a weapon in the fight for independence.

The vagaries of the decolonization process, in so far as they have affected the possibilities of African unity, have not been entirely fortuitous. Colonial governments were not entirely indifferent to these questions. On the contrary, it can be argued that France was systematically, although not outspokenly, hostile, the British to a limited degree favourable, and the Belgians veered sharply between extremes.

Between 1956 and 1960, as French black African territories went from colonial status to autonomy to independence, the French seldom threw their support to elements favourable to larger political unities. The reason was very simple. Those who most strongly advocated unity were also those who most strongly pushed the advances toward independence. French repudiation of the goal of independence led to deep suspicion of the goal of unity. This was true of their attitude toward the moves made in this period to establish strong federal executives in French West Africa and French Equatorial Africa. The same was true of their attitude toward the reunification of both Togo and Cameroun with their British trust counterparts. It was true, as well, of their view of the pan-Somali movement in French Somaliland. And of course the French would never sympathize with moves for North African unity because these moves were predicated on the assumption of Algerian independence from France.

The British position was less clear-cut. In the early colonial era, they too sought to divide and conquer. But once they came to terms with the nationalist movement in a particular area, they looked with favour on achieving larger unities, chiefly on the grounds that larger entities showed more potential for stability and economic development. We have already mentioned the case of British Somaliland. There, having long opposed Pan-Somali tendencies, the British surprised everyone, including the Somalis, by timing British Somaliland's independence to coincide with that of Somalia. In Nigeria, the British bore much responsibility for the rise of regionalism. But once having decided to go forward to independence, the British, between 1956 and 1960, were one of the important forces working toward the establishment of the strongest possible federal state for an independent Nigeria. In the settler territories of East and Central Africa, the Colonial Office was historically a stalwart supporter of moves toward federation, imposing its point of view on the Africans and to some extent even on the settlers. Nevertheless, by 1960 British support had somewhat abated as a result of the persistent African opposition. At this stage, having once again decided to go forward to independence (with universal suffrage), the British sought means of preserving the federal link (tainted by its association with white-settler domination) between the future independent African states. The work of the Monckton Commission in Central Africa and the Raisman Commission in East Africa are illustrations.

The factor that has made for the greatest difference between the British and the French attitudes towards larger unities in Africa has been the British willingness to acknowledge the legitimacy of the goal of independence. This has enabled the British, during the transition period, to look ahead to the post-independence period and plan their policy accordingly. They have thus always been able to take a more relaxed view of African unity than the French.

The Belgian policy has been quite different from both the French and the British. The Belgians had always ruled the Congo as a unitary state with some administrative decentralization. When they decided to grant the Congo its independence, they were eager to retain this unitary character. They feared that separatist movements would destroy the strong economy of the Congo in which they intended to remain involved.[1] Shortly after independence, when it appeared that Belgium's continuing political and economic relationship with the Congo was threatened by the strong supporters of the unitary state, the Belgian government veered to a strong support of separatist, indeed secessionist, elements.

The policies of the colonial powers in relation to larger African unities can be seen to reflect their views of their own interests. That Britain, France and Belgium analysed these interests differently does not detract from the reality of this motivation. Even in so far as colonial powers were favourable to unity, it was a unity within the family, so to speak. When it came to moves for Pan-African unity that cut across the traditional colonial divisions, even the more sanguine British hesitated occasionally. Yet, of course, African unity will have real meaning only in the degree to which the new entities will cut across divisions of European language and demarcations of European colonial spheres.

What concrete achievements can be pointed to as evidence of the reality of Pan-African aspirations? There were, first of all, the Conferences of Independent African States, in Accra in 1958, in Addis Ababa in 1960. These were among the several successors to the Pan-African Congresses. Up to now these assemblies have been largely resolution-passing bodies, but they have been able to secure the adherence of all the independent states.[2] The one permanent structure to grow out of these Conferences was the African bloc at the United Nations which, by regular meetings of the permanent representatives of the African states, forged an impressive unity between 1958 and 1960. With the admission of sixteen more African nations in the 1960 session of the United Nations and the divisive explosion of the Congo, this unity at least temporarily disappeared.

Parallel with these Conferences of Independent African States have been

[1] However, during this period, 1959–60, the *French* government, characteristically, gave tacit encouragement to the Bakongo separatists led by Joseph Kasavubu.

[2] Except the Union of South Africa, which was actually invited to the 1958 Accra Conference but refused to come because the colonial powers were not invited also.

the meetings of the All-African People's Conferences (A.A.P.C.), another of the successors to the Pan-African Congresses. The A.A.P.C. groups include nationalist political parties and trade-union federations of both independent and not-yet-independent African countries. Hitherto, the major concern of the A.A.P.C. has been the liberation of the remaining colonial Africa. The first meeting was held in Accra in 1958, followed by one in Tunis in 1959, and a third in Cairo in 1961. The A.A.P.C. has set up a continuing machinery, a secretariat whose headquarters is Accra. The first secretary general was George Padmore, Trinidadian and close collaborator of Nkrumah, with whom he was joint secretary of the 1945 Manchester Pan-African Congress. When Padmore died in 1959, he was succeeded by Adboulaye Diallo, Guinea's resident minister in Ghana and former trade-union leader in French West Africa.

It is important to note the close links, through personnel and ideology, between the Conferences of Independent African States and the All-African People's Conferences. The latter have been the non-governmental parallel to the inter-governmental body,[1] and have had a certain flexibility of manoeuvre, structure, and even language from which the exigencies of government protocol restrain the former. It is also important to note that both these structures have joined together black sub-Saharan Africa and Arab North Africa. This has been not peripheral but central to the conception. Indeed, thus far, these structures have been better at bringing together black and Arab Africa than at bringing together French-speaking and English-speaking Africa. The structures thus far have not been able to involve some of the significant groups in French-speaking black Africa, despite the fact that the North African participants are largely French-speaking. This was because, as we explained earlier, some of the French Africans have resisted greater African unity.

Many of the forces behind the A.A.P.C. have attempted to create an All-African Trade Union Federation (A.A.T.U.F.) as a concrete method of furthering African unity. Here there has been an added complication: Some African trade unions today are members of the International Confederation of Free Trade Unions (I.C.F.T.U.), a non-Communist body.[2] One of the forces behind A.A.T.U.F. has been the Union Générale des Travailleurs de l'Afrique Noire (U.G.T.A.N.), an inter-territorial group

---

[1] The same double structure of inter-government meetings on the one hand and inter-party, inter-trade union and inter-student organization meetings on the other hand has been used on a smaller geographic scale in North Africa.

[2] A few less important unions belong to the International Federation of Christian Trade Unions; also a very few belong to the Communist-dominated World Federation of Trade Unions. Finally, there are a large number affiliated with none of these internationals.

whose base was in former French West Africa.[1] U.G.T.A.N. achieved internal unity in 1957 by getting all the constituent members to break ties with internationals – 'positive neutrality' on the trade-union scene. U.G.T.A.N. leaders and others have thought that such international non-affiliation should be the basis of the projected A.A.T.U.F. Some trade unions affiliated with the I.C.F.T.U., notably those of Tunisia and Kenya, have argued that they do not wish to cut their ties with the I.C.F.T.U. This quarrel has made the realization of A.A.T.U.F. difficult. But here again it should be noted that all the preparatory meetings for A.A.T.U.F. have included both North and sub-Saharan Africans, both French-speaking and English-speaking black Africans, and the divisions over international affiliations have cross-cut the geographical and language differences. Similar efforts in the field of youth and students' groups have been even more tentative.

On the inter-governmental level, the chances for unity, as we have seen, were affected by the decolonization process. We have mentioned the real, if partial, success of the Pan-Somali movement, as well as the more limited results of efforts to create a unified North Africa. There has also been the reunification of Cameroun with the southern half of the British Cameroons, as well as the earlier federation of Eritrea with Ethiopia.

In French black Africa, we have shown, decolonization worked against unity. This was particularly evident in the attempt to create a federation of French West Africa. Though originally there were eight territories, an attempt to create a structure called the Federation of Mali could rally only four, of which two failed to ratify the constitution and the remaining two, after a year and a half of coexistence, broke apart in August 1960. One move intended to counter the Federation of Mali was the Conseil de l'Entente, a loose confederation of sovereign states. The Conseil de l'Entente was as much a move designed to prevent unity (of the federal Mali variety) as one to promote unity. Another attempt in former French Equatorial Africa to found a federal Union des Républiques d'Afrique Centrale (U.R.A.C.) – similar in conception to Mali – foundered before it was ever ratified. As for plans to establish unities that transcended colonial spheres, the proposal of the Abbé Boganda for a United States of Latin Africa (to group Cameroun, Congo, Angola and the four states of former French Equatorial Africa) and the plans of the Senegalese for Senegambia (to incorporate the tiny British colony of the Gambia into Senegal or, at one point, into the Federation of Mali) never got beyond the talking stage.

[1] The headquarters were in Conakry, Guinea, and the president of U.G.T.A.N was Sékou Touré, President of the Republic of Guinea, who started his political career as a trade-union leader.

On the other hand, out of the destruction of French West African unity caused by the process of decolonization came the construction of one political unity that does transcend colonial language barriers, the Ghana-Guinea Union in 1959.[1] Ghana and Guinea do not have contiguous frontiers, and the Union has no structure beyond the fact that the two countries exchange not ambassadors but resident ministers, who have the right to attend the cabinet meetings of the partner. The Union has neither common institutions, common language, nor common currency. And yet it would be rash to discount it. For the Union has brought together two dynamic countries which, despite many common attitudes, had almost no contact until the very time of the Union. The Union may be thought to be nothing but a very strong alliance, which is all it amounts to in terms of structure. But its significance lies in the fact that it symbolizes the possibility of transcending the 'language barrier' and, by this very fact alone, is a force of attraction for Pan-Africanists throughout Africa.

Ghana and Guinea both separately and together are major pressures toward African unity. Their force lies in their internal strength and dynamism, their vigorous positions on international affairs, their neutralism, their constant efforts to promote liberation in colonial territories and to support, financially, and otherwise, Pan-Africanist elements. The North Africans represent another such pressure, not always a united one. Presenting an image of themselves as Africans first, Arabs second, they are working very hard to see that African unity includes them, although they may conceive of this unity as a coalition of regional frameworks (such as North Africa, West Africa, East and Central Africa, etc.).

The United Arab Republic (U.A.R.) is often credited with being a major force in Pan-Africanism. Actually, despite money expended both in propaganda and in assistance to various nationalist movements in their anti-colonial struggles, and despite the fact that at various points some nationalist leaders (for example those of Algeria, Cameroun, Uganda) have had bureaux in Cairo, the U.A.R. has played only a minor role. The reason is that their image of themselves, as well as that which other Africans have of them, is of a country primarily interested in Arab unity and only secondarily concerned with all-African unity.

It is more significant to ask what are the present and future roles of Nigeria and the Ivory Coast. Nigeria, Africa's largest country in population, enjoys the prestige and power of its size and the fact that in itself it represents an achievement in terms of African unity. Thus far, the need to maintain the balance of internal unity has kept it from playing the

[1] To which the *Republic* of Mali adhered in 1960, making it the Union of African States.

downstage role of Ghana in the Pan-African movement. However, the very fact that Nigeria considers Ghana's role an exaggerated one may push her to advocate pan-African doctrines even more strongly. The Ivory Coast, by contrast, has shown itself cool to larger unities which would impinge on her own autonomy and development. Unable to fight Pan-Africanist forces alone, the Ivory Coast has taken the lead in creating the Entente, as well as a co-operative arrangement of a larger group of French-speaking states (Abidjan, Brazzaville, and Yaoundé Conferences of 1960–61).

The Congo crisis temporarily divided most of the half of Africa which was independent in 1960 into two camps: the strong pan-Africanists who attended the Casablanca Conference, and the advocates of a milder form of unity who attended the Brazzaville Conference. This crystallization into separate units is only momentary, however. As East, Central and South Africa attain independent governments based on universal suffrage, the crosscutting alliances should begin to make the realization of African unity a reality.

It is clear from this discussion that not all Africans and not all African states are equally Pan-African in their enthusiasm. What should be noted is that there is some correlation (not a perfect one) in each African state between those elements who are modernizing and centralizing and those who are oriented to Pan-Africanism. The strength of the Pan-African drive can be attributed precisely to the fact that it is the weapon of the modernizers – those throughout Africa who are most radical in their nationalism, most vigorous in their demands for equality, most conscious of the primacy of political solutions to the problems of Africa. Pan-Africanism may one day be divorced from modernization in Africa. It is not so today. To the extent, then, that Pan-Africanism fails, modernization too is set back.

22

Political Power in South Africa[1]

O. D. Schreiner

In most ways, economic, social and political, the Republic of South Africa represents a special case. It is easily the most industrially advanced of all countries on the African continent, it is the seat of intense racialism and the focal point of attack by all the newly independent African States, it is the only sovereign State still under white domination and, in terms of national wealth, it is the richest country in Africa.

It is impossible to leave South Africa out of any volume which purports to deal with Africa yet, traditional factors apart, it presents different problems from those of other areas and different conditions in which they have to be solved.

We therefore include this extract from the balanced and informed series of Presidential Addresses delivered over the past three years to the South African Institute of Race Relations by Dr Schreiner. Here is set forth an overall factual summary of the situation together with some positive suggestions, made by an authority who is himself – unlike so many writers on the subject – a resident South African.

There are certain basic facts that stand out in the South African scene today. Non-Whites outnumber Whites by more than 4 to 1 and increase more rapidly. Apart from a small group representation of Coloured persons in the Cape Province, the non-Whites are voteless and all political power is by law concentrated in the hands of the Whites. The racial groups, though predominating respectively in different areas, are thoroughly mixed up throughout the country, both territorially and economically. Earlier by custom or contract and later by law, residential and to some extent business, separation has been brought about in the urban areas, and the whole country is apportioned for ownership and occupation between Africans and persons other than Africans. But there is nothing approaching a complete separation of the racial groups, and all the country's activities – farming, mining, transport, secondary industry and commerce – are carried on by the brains and muscles of persons of every racial group,

[1] Extracts from his Presidential Addresses, 1962–4, to the South African Institute of Race Relations.

working in association and ordinarily living at no great distance from each other. On the consuming side of course, everyone who can pay for what he buys is welcome everywhere, and increasingly the prosperity of White businesses depends on their ability to attract non-White purchasers.

The ground is now prepared for a consideration of certain features of the apartheid policy, in order to see whether they, and consequently the policy as a whole, are realistic in the first or proper sense of the term. The first such feature to be examined is the legislation against mixed marriages and extra-marital miscegenation. This legislation is fairly recent. Mixed marriages were first made unlawful in 1949. Extra-marital intercourse between White women and Africans had been prohibited by some pre-Union legislation in 1902 and 1903, but it was not until 1927 that Parliament, during the first government of General Hertzog, prohibited intercourse between all Whites and Africans. In 1950 this was extended to cover intercourse between Whites and all non-Whites. In 1957 the prohibition was extended to include immoral and indecent acts, and enticing, soliciting or importuning were specially provided for. The maximum penalties were at the same time increased from five years' to seven years' imprisonment and male offenders became liable to a whipping of up to ten strokes.

In such circumstances it is inevitable that some Whites should become increasingly obsessed with the belief that race differences are more important than any other differences, such as those of character or belief. Miscegenation has, among them, been elevated into a crime so atrocious as to make all other crimes seem relatively venial.

I turn now to certain features of apartheid which are closely related to the economic structure of our country. The first is generally referred to as the Bantustan policy. The idea is to build up the reserves, originally created or recognized under the Natives Land Act, 1913, and since then somewhat augmented, into areas of self government for Africans, where eventually, it is hoped, a much larger proportion of them would live than do so at present. The aim is to attract or impel Africans, who, or whose ancestors, came from those areas, to return to them, and there enjoy a system of tribal control by chiefs, headmen, and councillors similar to that under which they lived before the White man came to the country. This is a large subject, with wide ramifications depending, among other things, on how far it is contemplated that the breaking up of South Africa is to be carried – whether, for instance, there would eventually be African states inside our existing boundaries, with their own police and armed forces of all kinds and customs barriers between themselves and the rest of South Africa, and with the right to make treaties with other countries. At the present stage the principal feature of the project appears to be the attempt to restore the power of the chiefs and headmen, and the tribal group loyalties, which had become weakened under the impact of western civilization. The economic development of the reserves is intended to go on side by side with the restoration of tribalism, but such development is not to be done with private White capital but only with African owned capital which is, and for long will be, substantially insignificant, or with money provided by the government. Industries in which White capital is invested are to be confined to places outside the reserves. Such industries are to be attracted to the exterior fringes of the reserves by advantages of various kinds, including perhaps the relaxation of colour bar restrictions. It seems even to be possible that by some permit system capitalists who wish to start industries anywhere in the country will be put under pressure to start them in the fringe areas.

Today the official idea is apparently to expand the carrying capacity of the reserves considerably not only by continued soil conservation but also by large-scale developments, with substantial towns, water and electricity schemes and greatly improved communications. These somewhat vague designs are alluring in the abstract and no one would lightly decry projects which, even if their main purpose is to draw off some of the African population from the rest of the country, would have the effect of improving the lot of Africans in the reserves. But apart from the uncertainty as to what steps would be taken to get Africans to return to the reserves, these schemes if carried out, would cost a very great deal of money. If that money was going to be spent because, for good reasons, it appeared to be economically desirable from the point of view of the country as a whole, the projects would no doubt be justifiable. But it seems to be clear that the governing object is to change the population ratios in the rest of the country, and it has not been suggested that, from the point of view of economics, the kind of development of the reserves that is now proposed is the best, or anything like the best, way of spending the money. The decision to build up the reserves is not an example of economic planning for the country as a whole. Looked at as a matter of economics the only doubt appears to be whether the economic disadvantage will be merely great or whether it will be enormous. With enough capital one can grow bananas at the poles and edelweiss on the equator, but it is not likely to be good business.

Similar in broad design to the Natives Land Acts are the Group Areas Acts, the first of which was enacted in 1950, as an extension of the Asiatic Land Tenure Act, 1946, and other laws restrictive of the rights of Asians, to own and occupy land. The Acts have grown into a code distributing limited rights to own and occupy land, for residential and business purposes, between all the racial groups, the Whites coming off much the best. It is a very complicated code involving an extensive interference with vested rights. The catalogue of hardships which these Acts have inflicted is a long and dismal one, but with that aspect we are not at the moment concerned. For present purposes the important feature is that large sums of money have been and are being spent in dislocating a working economic set-up, not in order to achieve any economic benefit for the country as a whole, but in order, putting it at the highest, to achieve ideological aims of racial separation to which the non-Whites, the persons by far the most detrimentally affected, have throughout been steadfastly opposed. An expensive bureaucratic machine has been set up to carry out these dislocations and the direct and indirect cost to the country must already be enormous, and, of course, will go on growing. If unyieldingly pursued, the Group Areas policy must increasingly interfere with the normal play of forces on which the economic health of the country depends. However aptly realism in its second sense may describe the Group Areas Acts, they are certainly not examples of laws that are economically advantageous to the country as a whole.

The next matter to be considered – and it is of the greatest importance – is the use of our manpower, and the related problems of the colour bar and the education of the non-White population. It is a fact that barriers exist which secure to Whites, substantially, a monopoly of skilled work in South Africa. These barriers are not in general the result of legislation directly imposing them, but on the other hand they are not a mere matter of custom, the employer, normally White, preferring to employ Whites on skilled jobs. There exist legislative provisions for restricting employment about mines, works and machinery to persons who are not Africans, and other provisions for reserving certain jobs to members of particular racial groups, which means as a rule, in practice, the White group. These provisions are in actual use and in some cases undoubtedly result in less efficient persons having to be employed in positions for which more efficient members of another race are available. But more widely operative is the indirect colour bar based upon such statutes as the Apprenticeship Act and the Industrial Conciliation Act, which are generally effective to make skilled work the preserve of the Whites. Non-Whites are hardly employed in the large and growing civil service, save in departments specially associated with their own non-White group, or as unskilled workers.

In this way the Whites are, as a group, treated as if they were disabled persons in need of sheltered employment because of their inability to face free competition with the members of other races. They are not, of course, in general incapable of competing with non-Whites, though some individuals no doubt are. But the supposed need for protection arises out of the belief that the standard of living of the Whites, as a group, has to be protected against the competition of persons whose standards of living are assumed to be permanently at lower levels.

In effect the apartheid principle, operating through all forms of the colour bar, means that employers, including the government, are, by law or by the power of trade unionists armed with the vote, precluded from employing the best man for the work to be done, that the skilled and responsible work of the country is being done by persons chosen from only a fifth of the population, instead of from the whole, that there is a constant shortage of people to do such work, and that the Whites, through being sheltered from the competition of the non-Whites, are without the stimulus to hard work and self-improvement that they otherwise would have.

A major effect of the colour bar is to keep the wages of non-Whites depressed. As is well known, the gap between skilled (mainly White) and unskilled (mainly non-White) wages is far wider here than elsewhere. Recently there has been substantial unanimity among the employing classes – the government, industrialists, merchants – supported by bankers and economists, that non-White, and especially African, wages ought to be increased considerably. No doubt in many cases there is a humanitarian basis for the support given to the proposal but the more effective argument in its favour has been the fact that, as things are, the bulk of our population is being artificially, i.e. by the colour bar, prevented from earning, not only the minimum needed for efficiency, but also enough to provide the markets that our industries require, particularly in view of the shrinking of our foreign markets owing to the unpopularity of the apartheid policy abroad. That policy harms our industries, both externally, by reducing our foreign markets, and internally, by reducing our internal market.

It is interesting to observe the difficulty which is being experienced in raising non-White wages. One factor may be the depressing effect which the gold mines are said to exercise on African wages and which is said to flow unavoidably from their fixed price product, since the mining companies cannot raise the price of gold to meet a general rise in wages. But this, though it may be an important contributory factor, is not the ultimate one. The difficulty is more deep-seated. Everyone professedly wants to raise non-White wages, but substantially everyone is impotent. The final spur to action is lacking. If suitably qualified non-Whites had votes and, if, consequently, non-White workers had effective trade union support, a solution to the problem of raising non-White wages would certainly be found. The much-emphasized risks of inflation and unemployment, if wages were raised without a corresponding increase in productivity, would no longer present insuperable difficulties. Nor, for municipal employees, would the principle seem so nearly inviolable that assessment rates must not be raised in order to raise wages. These obstacles would disappear in the course of negotiations in which on both sides an element of power was mixed with reason. It would no longer be necessary to prove, what it is in fact impossible to prove, at least to everyone's satisfaction, that higher wages, would lead to increased productivity. It is by free negotiations, including arbitrations, between employers' organizations and trade unions representing all employees, with collective power, as well as collective responsibility, and with the State as third party in the background, that conditions of labour are generally established in the free world.

The education of African children, on which it will be convenient to concentrate attention, is now governed by the Bantu Education Act, 1953. In continuation of the previous trend, more African children are now becoming literate than was the case some years ago, and that by itself is all to the good. But on the other side of the balance there are serious defects. The system has been made over-rigid and over-centralized. Non-governmental teaching has been unduly interfered with. The standard reached by the great majority of African children remains extremely low. Apart from other considerations it is difficult to see how such a system can produce the requisite supply of properly equipped teachers. If, however, despite the present low level, the prospects of improvement were good the new system might still prove to be better than the more elastic one which it superseded. But the prospects do not seem good. A main obstacle to improvement is the fact that the African children are being taught as far as possible through the medium of the African languages used in their homes, or, if their home language is English or Afrikaans, through the language of the tribes to which they belong or are deemed to belong. Before the new system was introduced, the great majority of African children who received schooling – it was practically all given at State-aided mission schools – were taught through an African language only for so long a period as was necessary to enable them to follow teaching through one of the two official languages, usually English. This gave the children the immense advantages of having a wide range of good school books and of gaining access to the world of thought that is embodied in European literature. The educated African adults of today have almost all had those advantages and the home language of their children is doubtless often English or Afrikaans. But now African children, many of whom are the teachers of the future, are being compelled, for as long as the authorities think it possible, to learn through the vernacular, in which school books are rare and inferior. They are in this way, moreover, being excluded from the mental enlargement that comes from a good knowledge of a language with a wide vocabulary and a great literature, past and contemporary. If the new system continues without substantial modification, our African children will, despite the greater wealth of our country, be at a serious disadvantage compared with those in the High Commission Territories, the Federation[1] and indeed a large part of the African continent.

The only other feature of our educational system that requires mention here is the ban, imposed in terms of Act 45 of 1959, on the admission of non-Whites as students to those universities which were prepared and accustomed to receive them.

It is quite impossible to enumerate all the features of apartheid that fill the non-Whites with a sense of injustice and resentment, but examples in plenty can be collected, not only from the items that have already been mentioned, but also from such features as the pass laws, influx control and the discriminations in regard to amenities that were legalized by the Separate Amenities Act, 1953. Non-Whites resent generally the fact that legislation, which vitally affects them and much of which puts them at a serious disadvantage as compared with the Whites, is enacted without their having any share in making it law. It is, of course, true that it is mainly the more advanced in education and living standards who feel strongly about the unfair operation of the policy of apartheid. But though this is true it is not important. Everywhere the better equipped set the tone for their less advanced fellows. This is only natural. It does not change the fact that there is a widespread sense of injustice and consequently of resentment at the operation of apartheid.

An obstacle to the growth of non-racial parties in multi-racial countries has, I believe, been the tendency to try to secure separate representation in Parliament for different racial groups, by communal voting or some other device.

The present position in South Africa is that only White persons can be elected to Parliament and that, with one exception, only White persons (all Whites, male or female, who have reached the age of eighteen years) have the vote. The exception is that Coloured males in the Cape Province elect four White members of Parliament, the province being divided into four constituencies for that purpose. Thus of the total number of 160 members of Parliament (including, since 1949, six from South-West Africa) one-fortieth are elected by the Coloured people, who form about one-eighth of the population, while none at all are elected by the Asians (about one-thirtieth) or by the Africans (about two-thirds). The Whites,

[1] i.e. Zambia, Malawi and Southern Rhodesia – Eds.

numbering less than one-fifth of the population, elect all but four of the members of Parliament.

. This position has been reached by the following steps. At the time of Union the vote in the Transvaal and the Orange Free State was confined to White males of the age of twenty-one or over. In Natal of the total electorate less than 1 per cent. were non-White, including a very few Africans. Asians in Natal ceased to be registrable as voters in 1896. Coloured persons in Natal were registrable on an income or property qualification until Act 46 of 1951 came into operation. In the Cape there was no colour distinction, there being low educational, income and property qualifications for all persons. In the result about 15 per cent. of the Cape registered voters were non-White. White women were first given the vote in 1930 throughout the Union and on the same basis as White males. By legislation passed in 1936, usually referred to as the Hertzog legislation, Africans in the Cape Province were removed from the common roll and given communal representation. This was taken away in 1960. By Act 46 of 1951, passed in 1951 and becoming operative in 1956, Coloured persons including Asians in the Cape Province were removed from the common roll and given communal representation. In 1958 the minimum age for White voters was reduced from twenty-one to eighteen.

The National Party, which constitutes the Government, has been mainly instrumental in bringing about the present position and is, it seems, resolved to maintain it. Perhaps because it realizes that the present arrangement is, to all appearances, most unfair to the non-Whites, the party seeks to justify the position by linking it up with that part of the general doctrine of apartheid which is usually referred to as the 'Bantustan' policy. This policy plans to divide the whole country between the different racial groups and give the members of the groups exclusive voting rights in the areas allotted to them. The Transkei is to be the first of the non-White areas. There the Xhosa tribes are to be in complete control and there Xhosas from all over South Africa will be able to vote for a local legislature. It is unnecessary to go into the formidable practical difficulties in the way of creating such Bantustans. The economic disadvantages are obvious and serious. But it is said by Government supporters that there are higher considerations than economics. This may be accepted, though economic factors continue to operate even when they are disregarded, and their neglect may cause serious social evils. One must at least be sure that the overriding considerations are in truth higher, that is, juster or socially and morally better. Assuming, however, that the practical and other objections to the Bantustan policy can be overcome, there remains the insuperable objection to the compensation argument, that a vote for members of a Bantustan legislature, however attractively ornamented, could never, while the Bantustan remains part of the Republic of South Africa, provide a real share of political power. Nor could any reasonable person be persuaded to imagine that it did. The legislature of a Bantustan that remained part of South Africa would be a local, subordinate body, wielding, in a poor, rural area, delegated authority that could be withdrawn at will by the White controllers of the Republican Government and Parliament. It is highly unlikely that even for a short time voting for such a subordinate body would be regarded by non-Whites in South Africa or by the rest of the world as adequate compensation for the absence of the parliamentary vote. But even if it could be assumed that some temporary stay of the attacks on the retention of all political power in the hands of the Whites could in this way be gained, it could not provide a durable settlement.

Bantustans, in other words, are to be places where votes can safely be exercised by non-Whites without influencing the balance of power in the country. From the point of view of real, legal power, which rests solely on the control and exercise of the parliamentary franchise, the ballot papers in a Bantustan election might as effectively be dropped into a well as into a ballot box. It has been authoritatively stated that further Bantustans on the Transkei model are not contemplated for the present. There is clearly no scope for more of them without a major re-apportionment of the land, a vast increase of the share to be assigned to Africans and large allotments to other non-Whites. But the Government has stated that there is to be no increase in the area of the African Reserves beyond their present 13 per cent., approximately, of the whole country. The Transkei is therefore likely to remain the only detached part of South Africa to wear the trappings of independent statehood, though less elaborate forms of local government could be furnished with a voting system that could also be put forward as a substitute for the parliamentary franchise. In any event there is no essential difference between the large Reserve that looks like a province and might conceivably at some future date receive sovereign independence, and the small Reserve that looks like a local authority area and could never receive more delegated power than that of a health board or divisional council. In the case of both types of Reserve, to say that those who live or have lived there, or whose ancestors, or some of them, came from there, are compensated by voting rights, based on this so-called homeland association, for the absence of any share of real power seems to be playing with the word 'vote'. So long as one has a vote, it is in effect asked, how can it matter much for the members of what body you are voting? The pith of the matter is that all Africans are to be deemed to have

237

a 'homeland' of their own, which will suffice to disentitle them from ever becoming qualified to exercise the parliamentary vote, the only vote that really counts.

The contention, based on various calculations, that any qualified franchise must lead in ten, fifteen, twenty-five or thirty years to a non-White majority, and should therefore be ruled out, has an appeal to some White persons who look at the matter superficially. The argument has formal validity only on the assumption that you can never get away from voting on solidly racial lines. But if you are always going to have a situation like that, there is no hope for our future, whether we are Whites or non-Whites. It simply means unlimited hostility for all time. Continuance of that racialist way of thinking must lead to bigger and bigger white police and military forces and more and more underground anti-White activities on the part of non-Whites. That is no sort of prospect for our country. It is not even necessary to go into the question of how particular qualifications work out over particular periods. One can put it quite shortly – because the non-Whites are increasing faster than the Whites the only safe thing for the latter is to refuse the former any share of political power. It is easy to put oneself into that impossible sort of position. But one comes back to the fact – it is a fact – that the position is impossible. Very few Whites who apply their minds to the matter really have any doubt that it cannot last indefinitely. If that is so, the sooner we get away from it the better, and the best way to reach a fair and practicable solution, one that could be reasonably and confidently defended before any impartial tribunal, is to accept an individual, non-racial, qualified franchise on a common roll as essential, and get down to working out the details.

23

Modern Political Ideas[1]

Colin Legum

We have now learned something of the nature of African politics, their history and the issues with which they are concerned. The reading which follows presents us with a closer glimpse at the vocabulary of African politics and its atmosphere.

Pan-Africanism has produced a language of its own which conditions the thinking and the politics of the entire continent. It cuts across the English-French language barrier, and across the Sahara. Emotions have been converted into ideas, and ideas into slogans. It matters little today whether a Pan-African speech is being made in Cairo or Capetown, Dar-es-Salaam or Dakar; the political language, with its slogans and appeals, is immediately identifiable. Here is one striking example:

> We know that even after our independence has been achieved that *African Personality* which we would build up will depend upon the consolidation of our *unity*, not only in sentiment but in fact. We know that a *balkanized* Africa however loudly it might proclaim to the world its independence and all that, will in fact be an easy prey to the forces of neo-imperialism [*neo-colonialism*]. The weak and divided can never hope to maintain a *dignified independence* however much they may proclaim their desire to be strong and united; for the desire to unite is a very different thing from actual unity. One can foresee the forces of neo-imperialism manipulating these little states in Africa, making them complacently smug in this mere sentimental desire to be one, and at the same time doing everything possible to prevent the realization of that unity. . . .[2]

Some of these sloganized concepts have never been clearly defined; they have simply developed. Their meaning emerges from their context. Not infrequently they contradict each other in the sense in which they are used. But such contradictions are not peculiar to Africa. What does *democracy* mean when used in Europe or America ? The point is that there

[1] Reprinted from *Pan-Africanism, Short Political Guide* (Pall Mall Press, 1962).
[2] Statement by Julius Nyerere to the Second Conference of Independent African States, 1961.

239

is a common understanding to which particular words or concepts are related even when they are being used for different purposes. For example, *non-alignment* is interpreted in widely different ways; but few can doubt its essential meaning.

NON-ALIGNMENT

How the *positive neutrality* of Delhi and Bandung evolved into the narrowly defined *non-alignment* of Cairo and Belgrade has already been told. What follows is an attempt to reflect the dominant attitudes that have developed around this concept, but without trying to relate precept to practice.

Non-alignment expresses freedom of decision and of choice in deciding each international issue on its merits; in effect an united and independent policy.

> We say what we believe whether this pleases or displeases. (President Nasser.) We do not tend to support one bloc against the other, but we are bent on finding the best solutions to the problems pressing on us, whether it be colonialism, disarmament, atomic tests or Germany. We shall study all existing views and we shall express ourselves in support of those providing for the most objective settlements. (President Modeiba Keita.)
>
> Our standing in the eyes of the world will be greatly enhanced if we consistently express our views on international disputes, without fear or favour, and act in accordance with the moral dictates of our conscience. (President Osman of Somalia.)
>
> We consider it wrong for the Nigerian Federal Government to associate itself as a matter of routine with any of the power blocs. . . . This freedom of action will be an essential feature of our policy . . . our policies will be founded on Nigeria's interests and will be consistent with the moral and democratic principles on which our constitution is based. (Prime Minister Sir Abubaker Tafawa Balewa.)
>
> The gravamen of any policy endorsed by us should be based upon an independent and not a neutral attitude, especially with reference to issues which affect the destiny of Africa or the people of African descent no matter where they may live. (Dr Nnamdi Azikiwe.)
>
> Non-alignment implies for each nation the right to establish the type of government it desires, to freely choose its régime, its economic and social system, and its way of life – in short, to act in accordance with its own guiding spirit unhampered by any pressure from outside. (Ben Yousseff Ben Khedda, President of the Algerian Provisional Government.)

Non-alignment is *not* neutrality.

> This policy . . . must not be confused with *équilibrisme,* with a balancing act which takes up no fundamental position and which aligns itself now with one, now with the other, of the two blocs according to circum-stances. . . . We examine international problems in the light of our national

interests and of the interests of Africa, and at the same time in the light of our desire for peace and for the peaceful coexistence of all countries, and we decide our policy in the light of these principles alone. If our policy then coincides with that of the Eastern or Western bloc, this is entirely a matter of chance and not the result of calculation. A balancing *équilibriste* policy causes a country to lose its entire personality. It can be blackmailed by both blocs. . . . (Modeiba Keita.)

Ghana stands for positive neutralism and non-alignment as against what I might describe as negative neutralism [which] believes that armed conflict between the Great Powers can only bring misery and destruction to those who participate in it. I consider this view to be unrealistic. Those who hold it believe that in the world of today a State can secure its safety if it withdraws itself entirely from the international problems of peace and war and avoids taking a definitive stand on issues which affect the balance of power in the world today. (Dr Nkrumah.)

Nor is non-alignment isolationist. It is not fearful of becoming involved in world affairs. On the contrary, it demands to be involved, but not on the Great Powers' terms.

We should remain in constant touch with the two conflicting military camps, since non-alignment does not mean that we isolate ourselves from problems; it means that we should contribute positively to the consolidation of understanding, and to the opening of channels for the passage of ideas and thoughts across the deep chasms caused by crises. (Colonel Nasser.)

We, the small nations, cannot stand aloof from this suicidal race . . . of armament. It is our duty to the world to put the Great Powers wise to the dangers of their activities. (President Abboud of the Sudan.)

Our neutralism does not mean isolation or detachment from one part of humanity; on the contrary, it means the search for and acceptance of whatever is true and just in the sum total of human thinking. Our neutralism is dynamic and alive; its sole concern is to save human values and to promote the peace and progress of the human race. (The King of Morocco.)

Non-alignment rejects the view that Africa must inevitably end up by falling into either the camp of the West or the East.

. . . The West always talked about the dangers of Communism infiltrating into Africa. We think this is not a danger. It was not really a question of the newly-independent African States being Communist or capitalist. People used to say that I was a Communist. Now we read the same thing about Guinea and Sékou Touré. (Colonel Nasser in an interview.)

We must stress that our enemies often attempt to have it believed that Africa is being taken in tow either by the West or by the U.S.S.R. – in any event that it obeys a foreign force or concept. . . . Of course Africa is not unaware of the existence of two blocs which influence world politics. What is of interest to know today is the doctrine of Africa. The East-West conflict often makes one lose sight of the necessity of putting this question to Africa, at least for those who are not aware of whether or not this Continent has its own views and its own doctrine, and consequently whether it represents a coherent system distinct from the other systems. (Sékou Touré.)

The people who anxiously watch to see whether we will become 'Communist' or 'Western democrats' will both be disconcerted. We do not have to be either . . . but we have the lessons of the East and the West before us, and we have our own traditions to contribute to mankind's pool of knowledge. (Prime Minister Julius Nyerere.)

I will not become the stooge or satellite or pawn or hireling of anybody. (Colonel Nasser.)

As we would not have British masters, so we would not have Russian masters. (Dr Nkrumah.)

Non-alignment looks to both blocs for economic and technical aid, but expects it to be united.

When certain nations grant aid . . . they are surprised that the receiving countries do not follow their policies in international affairs. . . . (Modeiba Keita.)

Soviet bloc aid comes without strings; U.S. aid carries unacceptable conditions amounting to control. Communist aid helped us to survive and to escape domination from the West. (Colonel Nasser.)

[We shall develop] . . . with the interest and support of the West or . . . be compelled to turn elsewhere. This is not a warning or a threat, but a straight statement of political reality. (Dr Nkrumah.)

As a result of its economic weakness the non-aligned world has become a stake that is to be won by the granting of economic assistance, a stake in the hands of the great Powers, each of which is attempting to secure political support, strategic strong points, and sources of raw materials and markets. The non-aligned world is aware of its strength and unity and is refusing to become the instrument of alien designs. (The King of Morocco.)

Bilateral international assistance . . . has been based on political propaganda, and not on social and economic concepts. . . . The endeavours of the underdeveloped countries to liquidate the old economic forms which gave rise to the present-day disparity in economic development, requires the co-operation of the rich countries . . . in this great international effort. . . . It is needless to state that, under no circumstances, shall we accept assistance from any country which may be tinged with any conditions that will infringe on our sovereignty and independence. . . . (General Abboud.)

Non-alignment does not constitute a third *bloc*, though it is sometimes spoken of as a third *force*.

The non-aligned countries have no intention of forming any bloc. (Colonel Nasser.)

We are not here to constitute ourselves into a third bloc, yet by this very conference we are constituting ourselves into a moral force and influence between the East and the West in the cause of peace. (Dr Nkrumah.)

The purpose of this conference should not be to organize ourselves into a third bloc. (President Osman of Somalia.)

Non-alignment allows for the development of friendly feelings towards both blocs; it feels free both to praise and to criticize them.

I believe that there is a great fund of goodwill for Africa in the United States of America and we in Ghana will certainly do all we can to foster good relations. (Dr Nkrumah.)

The United States . . . should be the first to appreciate the realistic reasons why we as a small country should endeavour to preserve normal relations with the two other great powers of the world today—the Soviet Union and China. (Dr Nkrumah.)

The Governments of the U.S.S.R. and Ghana declare that they resolutely condemn imperialism and colonialism in all its forms and manifestations, and express their firm confidence that, at present, given the unity of all the progressive forces in the world there exists prerequisites for doing away with the system of colonial oppression and exploitation for good. (A joint declaration.)

. . . Colonialism may come to us yet in a different guise, not necessarily from Europe. (Dr Nkrumah.)

Local Communist parties . . . always work to seize power . . . their objectives are dangerous – and that is why the Communist Party is illegal in Egypt. But our people do not have to like Communism to feel friendship and sympathy for Russia. (Colonel Nasser.)

I am aware that . . . such a conference for non-aligned States is an attempt unwelcomed and disapproved by several Powers hostile to peace, foremost among which are the colonial powers wishing to stifle all voices of conscience and extinguish every torch of freedom, if only they could. (Colonel Nasser.)

Guinea condemns colonialism and not countries or people. It wants the equality and unity of peoples and of men, without consideration of colour or religion. It remains totally aware that fraternal co-operation, peaceful coexistence and peace between peoples, constitute a clear indication of human progress in work, justice and democracy, and express the wish that all the peoples of the world commit themselves firmly to the harmonious development of the destiny of mankind. . . . We are of the generation of Africa which holds out fraternal hands to all peoples to advance towards the greater and real happiness of man. . . . (Sékou Touré.)

We have noted – I am telling you the conclusions reached by Africans and Asians and I must report them to you objectively – that the countries of the Eastern bloc, whatever many be their reasons, unreservedly support the peoples struggling for liberation from the colonial yoke. . . . Moreover we have found that help from the Eastern bloc is always immediate help and does not offend the susceptibility or the dignity of the receiving country . . . we have come to the conclusion that the countries of the Western bloc are timidly trying at present to revise their attitude with regard to the *tiers monde,* where they are always outpaced by the countries of the Eastern bloc. (Modeiba Keita.)

President Modeiba Keita of Mali said . . . that world crises could be settled if Premier Khruschev showed the same spirit of goodwill as President Kennedy demonstrated this week. . . . Mr Keita expressed the hope that there would be an 'echo' of the President's attitude from Mr Khruschev's meeting with President Nkrumah and Prime Minister Nehru.

Non-alignment implies non-participation in military alliances with Great Powers (denying the right to maintain bases). This is laid down in the definition adopted at the Cairo preparatory conference for the Belgrade meeting.

This right (to chose one's own system of government) and freedom of choice are incompatible with any participation in a military alliance. (Ben Yousseff Ben Khedda, President of the Algerian Provisional Government.)

Non-alignment is often presented as being in the interests of the West itself.

The policy of aligning with the West creates a burning issue for Communists. So long as they have a legitimate issue to fight, persecution only adds fuel to the flame. Paradoxical as it may sound, the safest way of aligning with the West is not to align with the West. (Dunduza K. Chisiza, Parliamentary Secretary of Finance, Nyasaland.)
   . . . I think the best thing to do, for those of us who have achieved independence, and for the West – especially for the West, with its ideology based on freedom and human dignity – is to play down a bit this business of national pride. . . . (President Bourguiba of Tunisia.)
   In foreign affairs my Government intends to practise a policy of neutrality. We believe that an underdeveloped country . . . cannot sensibly do otherwise. But it goes without saying that our links with Western countries are much closer than those with Eastern countries are ever likely to be. (President Sylvanus Olympio of Togo.)
   After talking with President Kennedy in March 1961, Nkrumah declared his preference for the United States over the Communist camp, and warned Americans not to equate anti-colonialism with Communism.
   The Indo-Chinese, the Madagascans and the Guineans repeat unceasingly 'we love and we always want to love France, but we cannot in any way merge our love for France with infidelity to our own country. Constraint kills love: liberty expands and enriches it'. (Jacques Rabemananjara.)
   We have said that independence does not mean a rupture with France, that it does not mean an end to co-operation with France whose culture and language will continue to serve the Guineans. . . . From the moment of our independence, without acrimony, without preconceived ideas, we have held out our hands to France. What we wanted, and what we still want, is that new relationships may be established between the French nation and the young Guinean nation to the greater advantage of both peoples. (Sékou Touré.)
   President Keita said that at present technicians in Mali were mainly French. If however relations between Mali and France did not return to

normal and the French in Mali were threatened by the French Government with the loss of their nationality if they remained in Mali, the Republic of Mali would seek the technical assistance essential to her survival from all countries of the world.

AFRICAN PERSONALITY

No phrase is in more constant use than *African peronality*; yet it is seldom defined: Aimé Césaire illustrates the vagueness with which it is often used when he discusses Sékou Touré's answers to the question of how Africa will find the 'ways and means' for its growth and development.

With regard to the economy, for example, Sékou Touré would say it must 'rediscover its *African personality*'. With regard to law, that it must be worked out on the basis of 'the *African personality*'. Of education, that its mission is 'the rehabilitation and blossoming of the *African personality*'. Always the same word, always the same fundamental requirement, Africa; and the same endeavour to dislodge the 'spirit of singularity' in all places at the same time.

Explaining the significance of the first Conference of Independent African States Dr Nkrumah said: 'For too long in our history, Africa has spoken through the voice of others. Now, what I have called an *African personality* in international affairs will have a chance of making a proper impact through the voices of Africa's own sons.' Mr Tom Mboya says: 'The *African personality* would be meaningless unless it were to be identified with the noble things Africa fought for. . . . She has a clean past and a new start, and instead of joining any of the present power blocs or forming just another bloc, she should concentrate on establishing her own personality in the context of dedication to basic individual freedoms and civil liberties.'

The clearest definition is that offered by the writer Alioun Diop: 'The *African personality*, which is the basis and foundation of our humanism, aspires . . . to being freed from the Western grip. *It requires that our people should speak through us*. . . . Our peoples only mean to give expression to what they alone can show forth: how they see themselves, how they identify themselves in the context of the world situation and of the great problems of mankind. . . .'

NEO-COLONIALISM

By *neo-colonialism* we mean the practice of granting a sort of independence with the concealed intention of making the liberated country a client-state, and controlling it effectively by means other than political ones. What has happened in the Congo is an example. (Alex Quaison-Sackey, Ghana's Representative at the U.N.)

Neo-colonialism emerged attempting to attain the same aims of exploitation as the old colonialism, using new methods which outwardly appear to be more in line with the spirit of the age. In this domain, military pacts are directed more against internal fronts of nations seeking to free themselves . . . rather than against foreign aggression. In the same way aid and trade were used as a veil to dominate the resources of nations and exhaust them to the benefit of the exploiters. The policy of economic and monopoly blocs was equally directed to this end. (Colonel Nasser.)

The Imperialists of today endeavour to achieve their ends not merely by military means, but by economic penetration, cultural assimilation, ideological domination, psychological infiltration and subversive activities even to the point of inspiring and promoting assassination and civil strife. (Dr Nkrumah.)

. . . The European Common Market . . . is but the economic and financial arm of *neo-colonialism* and the bastion of European economic imperialism in Africa. The Treaty of Rome, which brought into being the European Common Market, can be compared to the treaty that emanated from the Congress of Berlin in the nineteenth century. The latter treaty established the undisputed sway of colonialism in Africa; the former marks the advent of *neo-colonialism* in Africa. In another sense it may be said that the Treaty of Rome, particularly in its effects on Africa, bears unquestionably the marks of French *neo-colonialism*. Indeed, the former French Investment Fund for Economic and Social Development has become the Fund for Financial Assistance and Co-operation, and the European Fund claiming to help newly-independent African States economically and financially are now one and the same thing. The Fund . . . simply reduces that territory to the position of an exclusive market for the economy of the metropolitan country. (Dr Nkrumah.)

Although *neo-colonialism* recognizes the danger that new forms of subjection may come from sources other than Western, its commonly accepted meaning is of a threat by the former colonial powers to establish 'backdoor colonialism'. It derives principally from a suspicion of Western intentions based on the history of former colonial relationships. It is quick to point to the fact that out of approximately £185 million granted by France for spending in Africa in 1962, more than £57 million is for French military forces and installations.

'BALKANIZATION'

The first application of this term to Africa is attributed to President Senghor. It is the favourite running-mate of *neo-colonialism*.

The colonialists are ready to 'finance' as much independence as one wants; they are ready to flatter African Governments and to wax enthusiastic before the three million free Guineans, before the thirty million

Nigerians, etc. . . . . But their Machiavellian plan still aims at dividing the African in order to remain master of the Continent. (Sékou Touré.)

We are convinced that the States of Africa will never be independent, in the full sense of the word, if they remain small States, more or less opposed one to another, each having its own policy, its own economy, each taking no account of the policy of the others. (Modeiba Keita.)

The *balkanization* of Africa is a source of weakness to our Continent. The forces of imperialism and of neo-imperialism will find their own strength in this basic weakness of our Continent. Surely, one would have expected that if we have a chance to undo part of the harm that has already been done by this *balkanization* of our Continent, we would not hesitate in taking that chance. (Prime Minister Nyerere.)

As the former colonial territories become independent, new dangers await us. The European colonial powers, although they are now being compelled by the force of African nationalism to grant independence, are none the less planning to continue to dominate Africa by a new system of foreign domination, namely the *balkanization* of Africa. They are ready to grant independence, but under certain conditions, such as the negotiation of defence agreements, and the guarantee of economic advantages such as would satisfy the demands of African nationalism. By this means, they. expect to be able to create a large number of small independent States, but which shall continue to be dependent upon the former colonial powers perpetually for their economic, technological, social and cultural development. (Ako Adjei, Foreign Minister of Ghana.)

Instances of *balkanization* frequently cited by sections of African leaders are the secession of Katanga; the separate independence of Mauritania, and Togo; and the break-up of the Mali Federation. The leaders of these three countries, and their supporters, naturally take a different view.

Dr Azikiwe, too, has given a different perspective to this question.

From the evidence at our disposal it would appear that whilst European nations may be rightly accused of *balkanizing* Africa in the nineteenth century, yet they have atoned for it by federating many African territories, which are now being *balkanized* by African nationalists on the attainment of the independence of their countries. The British West Africa, French West Africa and French Equatorial Africa are examples of *balkanization* by African nationalists, and the Central African Federation is an example of *balkanization* in process brought about by the racial segregation and discrimination practices by a small minority of European settlers against the African majority who are the owners of their countries.

Closely allied with *balkanization* are the popular current ideas about tribalism and federalism *versus* strong central government, puppet rulers, and African unity.

The Congo provides a striking example of how federation can be used as a cloak to conceal new colonialism. In fact this type of federalism is not federation at all. It is separation. It does not unite, it *balkanizes*.... Fundamentally the reason African ethnic groups failed to maintain their independence and succumbed to colonialism was that they were too small and not economically viable. The whole history of the colonial penetration of Africa was the history of the colonial powers supporting one ethnic group against the other and exploiting African differences so that, in the end, all came equally under the colonial yoke.... The masses who struggled for independence did not do so in order to put a handful of puppets into power.... But we have, or should have, an effective answer to *balkanization*, and the answer is African unity. (Dr Nkrumah.)

AFRICAN DEMOCRACY

Rejection of dictatorship and belief in the democratic ideal are attitudes common to virtually all African leaders.

If I thought Africans could not produce a democracy I would leave politics. (Leopold Senghor.)

With the failure of parliamentary democracy in many newly-independent countries, it has become fashionable for a school of political philosophers to assert, sometimes with an air of superiority, and often with that of finality, that democracy cannot be exported.... Some ... even assert that the African or the Asiatic (*sic*) is basically authoritarian and dictatorial. It would seem that these philosophers do not appreciate the difference between the failure of parliamentary democracy on the one hand and the failure of democracy on the other; the Westminster brand of democracy, or what has been referred to as 'cricket' democracy, is one method of ensuring democracy as a form of government. If that method fails, another might succeed.... The failure of parliamentary democracy in a newly independent country should therefore be regarded rather as a temporary aberration than as a permanent deviation from the democratic ideal. (Sir Abubaker Tafawa Balewa.)

Every mortal blow that is struck by an independent African nation at the vitals of democracy is rationalized by [these] theorists as the African's peculiar method of adapting democratic usages to his barbaric and primitive environment.... The outrageous declaration by an African leader that a one-party system is in accord with the democratic way of life has been ably defended by [these] spokesmen of the Western democracies.... But it is an affront to the African race to suggest that they are incapable of applying these principles.... Communists have laid down dogmatic methods for the practice of Communism. Any deviation ... is condemned and denounced.... There are no dogmas for the practice of democracy; and democrats cannot and must not censure any nation on the grounds of deviationism. But they must at least have the courage and honesty to insist that a flagrant departure from the ideal of democracy is not an acceptable variant of the most beneficent and ennobling form of government which mankind ... has evolved. (Chief Awolowo, Leader of Nigeria's Opposition.)

I must say that . . . I have my own doubts about the suitability for Africa of the Anglo-Saxon form of democracy. (Julius Nyerere.)

There are two ways of governing a country. In the first way, the State may substitute itself for all initiative, all men, all consciences. At that moment it deprives the people of their liberty of initiative, places them under conditions and in consequence passes itself off as omniscient by trying to solve general problems and problems of details simultaneously. Such a State can only be anti-democratic and oppressive. We have adopted the second way and chosen to be a democratic State. (Sékou Touré.)

DEMOCRACY BY DISCUSSION

Democracy is essentially government by *discussion*. . . . (Sir Abubaker Tafawa Balewa.)

To the ancient Greeks 'democracy' meant simply government by discussion. . . . But not all the people assembled for these discussions . . . those who took part in them were the 'equals'. . . . The two factors of democracy which I want to bring out here are *'discussion'* and *'equality'*. Both are essential to it, and both contain a third element 'freedom'. (Julius Nyerere.)

Democracy, the freedom of all the supporters to exert themselves in the conception of the problems, in the *discussion* of the problems, and in the choice of solutions to be carried out. On the other hand, the leadership of the Party for its part, has complete freedom in the achievement of the tasks decided upon, and in the judgement of the forms of action appropriate to the objective conditions of this achievement. (Sékou Touré.)

FOR AND AGAINST THE ONE-PARTY STATE

An organized opposition is *not* an essential element. . . . An organized opposition may arise, or it may not; but whether it does or not depends entirely upon the choice of the people themselves and makes little difference to free discussion and equality in freedom. (Julius Nyerere.)

I can understand that some countries may find a second party superfluous if nearly everyone is agreed on the essentials. In this case, what is important is that minority opinion should be able to express itself, independently or within the party, without intimidation. I would agree with my friend Julius Nyerere . . . that the test of a democratic régime in Africa might not necessarily be the actual presence of a second party, or several parties, so much as whether or not the régime tolerated individualists. This is a crucial point, for societies are not built or improved by conformists. (Sylvanus Olympio.)

Opposition parties must develop not because the text books say so but rather as a normal and natural process of the individual freedom of speech and freedom to criticize government, and the right of a people to return a government of their choice by use of the ballot box. . . . In practice when a country has just won its independence . . . [there will be room only] for a very weak and small opposition . . . at least in the initial period. Unless a split occurs in the ranks of the new nationalist Government, this situation may continue for ten or even more years. This does not mean the abandonment of democracy, but it is a situation which calls for great vigilance on the part of the people in respect of their individual freedoms. (Tom Mboya.)

Leaders of opposition parties, who may have fought for independence just as valiantly as anybody else, find themselves the recipients of practically nothing. Herein lies the rub. It is only natural for these people to feel they have been given a raw deal . . . they are almost certain to despise and denounce their opponents. . . . Their opponents will regard this as mischievous detraction. . . . And so the stage is set for full-scale mud-slinging which sometimes culminates in the governing party clamping down on their opponents with the force of law. . . . The problem we are facing here is how to make it possible for leaders of opposition parties to share in the gratitude and admiration which the masses lavish on their rivals in the early years of independence. For this there seems to be no better idea than that during the first ten years or so there should be 'national' Governments. . . . (Dunduza K. Chisiza.)

The greatest danger to the survival of the Opposition arises where the Government has an overwhelming majority. The party which 'brings in' independence . . . almost invariably gets overwhelming support at the start of independence . . . the Government party is often tempted to rule without regard to the rights or views of the Opposition. Some countries even go to the length of being hostile to the Opposition and their supporters. This . . . is undemocratic. (Chief H. O. Davies, Q.C.)

Both the Government and the Opposition must be strong to survive. But they must not crush the Opposition. One must be pragmatic like the English. When the Opposition is within the law, allow it; but when it is against the law, don't stand for it. (Leopold Senghor.)

Democracy and a one-party system of government are, in my opinion, mutually exclusive. Under a one-party system the party in power arrogates to itself the right to be the only ruling party for all time. . . . (Chief Awolowo.)

Unless an Opposition, as a 'Shadow Cabinet' which is capable of replacing the Government, exists democracy becomes a sham. . . . Failure to tolerate the existence of an Opposition party would be disastrous to the existence of democracy. (Dr N. Azikiwe.)

DEMOCRATIC CENTRALISM

Although we have only one political party . . . free democratic practice is respected at our meetings. All opinions are expressed and that which gains the most votes is considered to be the right one and consequently the one whose policy is applied. . . . (Modeiba Keita.)

Modeiba Keita's description is that of *democratic centralism* to which he, Sékou Touré and Dr Nkrumah subscribe. Its basis is that the Party and the State are the same; both rest on the people's will, and they must be democratically consulted in the *formulation* of policy.

Democratic centralism carries the following principles: (*a*) All responsible men in the Party are directly and democratically chosen by the supporters who enjoy total liberty of conscience and of expression within the Party. (*b*) An affair of the State of Guinea is the affair of all the citizens of Guinea. The programme of the Party is democratically discussed. As long as no decision has been made, each is free to say what he thinks or what he wishes. But when, after extensive discussion in congress or in assembly, a decision has been arrived at by a unanimous vote or by a majority, the supporters and the leaders are bound to apply it correctly. (*c*) The responsibility for leadership is not shared. Only the responsibility for a decision is shared. Thus, no distortion of discipline should be permitted. (Sékou Touré.)

In our Party all are equal regardless of their race or tribe. All are free to express their views. But once a majority decision is taken, we expect such a decision to be loyally executed, even by those who have opposed that decision. This we consider and proclaim to be the truest form of *democratic centralism* – decisions freely arrived at and loyally executed. This applies from the lowest to the highest level. None is privileged and no one shall escape disciplinary action. (Dr Nkrumah.)

AFRICAN LAW AND JUSTICE

The question is to transform, to renovate, to reconvert the *matter* as well as the *spirit* of Justice . . . It is not to African peoples that one needs to speak about Justice because there is not one African, not one coloured man who, since his coming of age, has not longed for real justice . . . because in the course of history . . . coloured people, through incomprehension, self-ishness, wickedness, have been bullied, humiliated, discredited, dis-qualified. . . . The qualitative change in our judicial practices and political behaviour of our magistrates are the two elements of a single problem: Justice – rapid, democratic and humane. (Sékou Touré.)

The Government believe that the courts of law should be absolutely independent of the Executive, and should be a bulwark for the defence of the rights of the individual. . . . Unfortunately it is impossible to include fundamental rights . . . in the Independent Order in Council, but it is the Government's intention to include these fundamental rights in the con-stitution once Independence has been granted. (Dr Nkrumah.)

The Law of Lagos 'to safeguard and advance the will of the people and the political rights of the individual' was enacted at a conference on the Rule of Law organized by the International Commission of Jurists in the Nigerian capital in January 1961. It was attended by 194 judges, members of the legal and academic profession from twenty-three African countries. One of the questions the Conference discussed was Preventive Detention.

Almost unanimously they condemned its practice, while at the same time recognizing the difficulties faced by newly-independent countries.

> The most crucial issue in the discussions was the concern felt by all the participants for the observance of the fundamental human rights and the limits within which these should be fostered with due regard for the security of the State. Most participants deplored all attempts by Governments to muzzle criticisms of their actions by well-disposed persons anxious for the supremacy of the Rule of Law, and everyone felt that there should be real freedom of expression and of the Press, but that the need for State security should not be overlooked. (Dr T. O. Elias, Attorney-General and Minister of Justice, Nigeria.)
>
> Some of the participants questioned whether specifically African needs do not call for the recognition of a specifically African legality. This may be recognized without falling into contradiction, for there is a universal principle of legality according to which all political, economic and juridical institutions should be conceived for man and not vice versa, while there are at the same time principles of legality peculiar to Africa. . . . In Africa the liberation of man . . . cannot be obtained except through observance of the essential requirements of independence, unity, democracy and economic development. Similarly, principles of law applied in Africa must achieve a synthesis between more recent and customary law. (Gabriel d'Arboussier, Minister of Justice, Senegal.)

In his proposals for establishing 'a concert of Africa', Dr Azikiwe has put forward the idea that it should promulgate 'an African Convention of Human Rights as an earnest of their belief in the rule of law, democracy as a way of life, respect for individual freedom, and respect for human dignity. This convention of human rights should declare categorically the faith of the Members of the concert of Africa in freedom under the law.'

SUMMING-UP

No African leader believes that the Anglo-Saxon or Westminster model of parliamentary government can be transplanted to Africa. All *say* they believe in democracy, although this need not necessarily be parliamentary democracy (Abubaker, Nyerere, Olympio, Nkrumah, Sékou Touré, Modeiba Keita, Mboya). Some, however, insist on the model of parliamentary democracy, because they believe in the essential safeguard of an organized Opposition (Awolowo, Azikiwe). The right of an organized Opposition to exist is also recognized by those who do not necessarily subscribe to 'parliamentary democracy'. (Abubaker, Nyerere, Mboya, Olympio, Senghor, Chisiza, Bourguiba). But not everybody in this latter category accepts that an organized Opposition is essential to the working of democracy, at least not in the early stages of independence. (Mboya,

Nyerere, Olympio). There is a widespread belief that because of the nature of the circumstances in which many African States come to their independence, a period of *national government* might be the right answer (Chisiza, Mboya). A special category of leaders either believe in, or subscribe to *democratic centralism*.

How have these diverse views worked out in practice in the independent African States? Of the twenty-eight States (excluding South Africa), seven have established Coalition or National Governments while permitting the existence of political parties and of elections (Cameroun, Chad, Congo (Brazzaville), Congo (Leopoldville), Dahomey, Gabon and Somalia).

Eight maintain one-party States in which no other political parties either exist or are allowed to exist (Central African Republic, Guinea, Mali, Ivory Coast, Mauritania, Niger, U.A.R., Upper Volta).

Six have Governments in which a single party controls all, or virtually all, the seats; but allow for opposition parties to organize themselves and to participate in elections (Ghana, Liberia, Senegal, Tanganyika, Togo, Tunisia).

One has military rule (the Sudan); one has Imperial rule (Ethiopia); one has semi-Imperial rule (Libya); and one has a mixture of Imperial rule and party political freedom (Morocco).

Only two maintain a system of parliamentary democracy (Nigeria and Sierra Leone).

AFRICAN SOCIALISM AND MARXISM

In the language of the left-wing of African nationalism, socialism and Marxism are seldom differentiated as between 'Marxist socialism' and 'democratic socialism'. The emphasis is always heavily on 'African socialism'.

> The Marxism which served to mobilize the African populations, and in particular the working class, and to lead that class to success, has been amputated of those of its characteristics which did not correspond to the African realities. (Sékou Touré.)
>
> Socialism is based, by definition, not only on race, but also on geography and history – political and economic. It is these values, especially the cultural values of sentiment, which constitute the contribution which the new Negroes can make to the rendezvous of giving and receiving: to the convergent current of socialism, in a word to the 'New Directions of Socialism'. . . . We have developed co-operation, not *collectivist*, but *communal*. For co-operation – of family, village, tribe – has always been honoured in Black Africa; once again, not in collectivist form, not as an

aggregate of individuals, but in communal form, as mutual agreement. (Leopold Senghor.)

These aims [of the C.P.P.] embrace the creation of a welfare state based upon African socialist principles, adapted to suit Ghanaian conditions, in which all citizens, regardless of class, tribe, colour or creed, shall have equal opportunity . . . our party also seeks to promote popular democracy based upon universal suffrage – on 'one man one vote'. (Dr Nkrumah.)

Arab socialism repeats the same theme.

The Arab socialist feels free to be inspired by all that has been created by human thought. He feels free to construct and to add to his heritage. While the communist strictly obeys the principles which are the basis of his indoctrination, the Arab socialist is a faithful adherent to the history of the problems and realities of his people and his country. (Mohammed Hassanine Heikal.)

The [Egyptian] Revolution laid down for itself six principles, declared in the name of the people to achieve Arab socialism. These principles were inspired by the past – its errors and its sins – and by the present with its positive strides, and by both the foreseeable and the far-off future. These were: eradication of imperialism and its agents; eradication of feudalism; eradication of monopoly and the control of capital over the Executive; setting up a strong national army; establishing social justice; setting up a sound democratic life. (Aly Sabry, U.A.R. Minister for Presidential Affairs.)

'African socialism', is in its essence *deviationist*.[1] It permits 'borrowing' of ideas, but rejects the importation of international communist ideology. Although Sékou Touré, Dr Nkrumah and others talk about the 'working class', 'the peasants', etc., they quarrel *a priori* with the class war. Sékou Touré's draft of the C.G.T.A.[2] manifesto 'rejects the class struggle because of African social groups' identity of living conditions and lack of differentiation into antagonistic classes, and because of the economic and political alienation to which the peoples of tropical Africa are at present subjected.' 'We have rejected from scientific socialism, atheism and violence, as being fundamentally contrary to our nature . . .' (Leopold Senghor.) In his *Autobiography* Dr Nkrumah describes himself as a 'Christian Marxist'.

---

[1] See *Karl Marx in Africa*, p. 104.
[2] Confédération Général des Travailleurs d'Afrique.

IIIc: Economic Change and Development

INTRODUCTION

We have seen that most African economies have retained a 'colonial' pattern of production, concentrating on the production of primary products for export and importing most of their manufactured needs. While there is still some doubt as to how fast demand in the developed countries will increase for Africa's primary products, most economists are agreed that some diversification of African economies is both sensible in the interests of efficiency and necesssary if Africa is to grow at anything approaching the pace it desires. There is, however, much disagreement as to the means whereby this may be achieved. In so far as there is a 'conventional wisdom' of African development it seems to be that the largest returns are likely to come from concentrating investment on education, agricultural improvement and transport. This has been a theme of several reports of the International Bank for Reconstruction and Development and is suggested also by many Western economists. Most African countries seem to accept readily the stress on educational investment, which usually takes a major portion of government expenditure – often as much as 30 per cent., and in the Eastern and Western Regions of Nigeria nearly 50 per cent. In those Western European countries which have a predominantly state-run education system the proportion is nearer to 10 per cent. The rationale for such high expenditure in Africa is the continent's appalling shortage of skills at all levels – especially at the higher levels of administration and management. Large numbers of Europeans are still working in independent African countries in many of the senior administrative posts (especially in education) despite the increased desire of these countries to 'Africanize'. Thus investment in the higher levels of education, necessary to train Africans to fill these posts and new ones which may arrive, seems an imperative of African development; so also is education at lower levels to facilitate training in other important skills in agriculture and industry.

It is in the agricultural sector of African economies where it is probably

255

possible to obtain the most spectacular returns from small investments. The introduction of fertilizers, insecticide sprays and small scale irrigation could increase both the quality and variety of crop as well as its yield by allowing more intensive cultivation. Land reform may also be a problem, although some parts of Africa have large areas which might be brought under cultivation in settlement schemes without much difficulty. There is no doubt that even at the present state of the African economy demand can easily be found for considerable increases in marketable agricultural output if the variety were sufficient. It is ironical that at present a continent as rich in agricultural potentiality should import a large proportion of its basic food requirements. Thus increased agricultural output could perform valuable service in reducing food imports leaving the valuable foreign exchange for more urgent needs. Also, if industrialization and consequent urbanization continue to increase, there will be further need for expansion of the output of the agricultural sector.

A major factor at present in curtailing marketed agricultural production is the shortage of transportation, hence the stress on transportation investment. Also, through improved transportation the market for manufactured goods can be expanded to a much wider area. The two forces will reinforce each other since each will create demands for the products of the other. By widening the accessible market, transportation may allow the economies of large scale production to be reaped not only within individual countries but also between countries. At present the extent of trade between African countries is very small indeed.

There is no doubt, therefore, of the wisdom of stressing the crucial importance to the economy of more investment in these three sectors – education, agriculture and transportation; and power (usually hydro-electric) is often added to the list. Nevertheless when African countries are advised to concentrate their investible resources on these, protests are commonly heard from Africans that industrialization (we use the term to refer to manufacturing industry) is ignored; rapid industrialization, they often say, is the real solution to Africa's poverty and excessive dependence on primary production. Such protests are often dismissed as the result of semi-Marxist ideological predilections; nevertheless in spite of what we have said about the 'conventional wisdom' these protests seem to us to possess solid economic justifications.

The stress on investment in education, agriculture, transportation and power is too often based on an erroneous but common view of economic development, namely that a developing country must go through a stage of establishing the pre-conditions for self-sustained economic growth. The four sectors we have mentioned are supposed to provide the essential

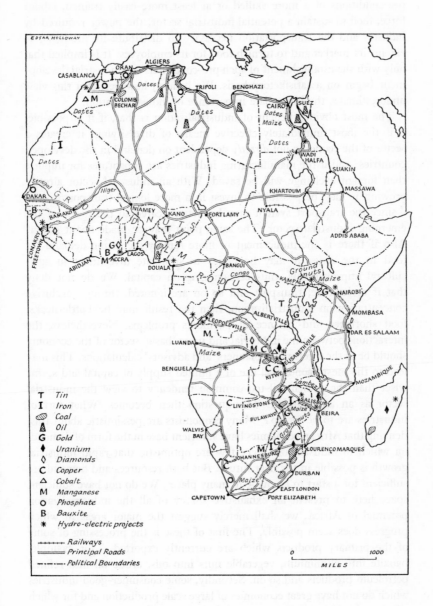

pre-conditions of a more skilled or at least more easily trained, labour force, food to sustain a potential industrial sector, the power required by industry and the transportation necessary to distribute its products, to extend its market and to furnish food for its employees. It is implied that only with the establishment of such pre-conditions can industrial development begin on a satisfactory basis. We believe, however, that this view underestimates the immediate importance of industrialization.

The most obvious benefit of industrialization is that, if it is possible, it is the most immediately effective means of diversifying; it creates a sector of the economy not *directly* dependent on demand in the developed countries; and if the manufacturing industries are substitutes for imports then foreign exchange will be saved. With an industrial sector already growing it may be possible to invest in a more logical transport system – since the transport system may be better geared to the needs of the emerging industrial sector. The same point may be made about power. Also if there is the inducement of more rapidly increasing demand for food in the cities it may be easier to stimulate investment in agricultural improvements, thus economizing on capital. We do not deny that if agriculture, transport and so on are ignored, through exclusive concentration on industrialization, then the result may be bottle-necks, food shortages and balance of payments problems. Nevertheless, the interactions between the industrial and more 'basic' sector of the economy should be in the forefront of planners' and advisors' calculations. This may lead to the most economical use of a limited supply of capital and seems wiser than the present all-too-common tendency to view the industrial sector as an afterthought. The question then becomes 'What sort of industries are to be set up ?' Many economists are pessimistic about this, denying that African economies have sufficient base in the form of demand, on which to industrialize. Very few are optimistic that rapid industrial growth is possible in the near future. But both resources and demand are sufficient for a start to be made in many places. We do not have sufficient space here to present an exhaustive survey of all the industrialization potential of Africa; we shall merely suggest the major areas in which progress does seem possible. The first of these is the processing of some of the primary products which are currently exported – for example, bauxite into aluminium, vegetable nuts into oils, crude oil into refined petroleum products and so on. Secondly, some consumer-good industries which do not have great economies of large scale production and for which some demand already exists, may be started – things such as shoes, some textiles, soap, food processing and canning, etc. At present these would mostly be for the home market though some might be exported; but prospects for African encroachment on the markets for cheap consumer goods so successfully exploited by Japan and Hong Kong do not at present seem bright. Although such developments may economize on foreign exchange if they substitute for what is now imported, there may be counteracting elements in that some of the manufacturers may require imports in the form of raw materials and machinery for their production. The third type of industrialization which may now be possible is in goods in whose production there are great economies of large scale production; while this may not be directly feasible in many individual African countries, it may be possible to set up profitable plants to assemble parts of such goods – bicycles for instance – rather than actually to produce the goods. Transport costs and foreign exchange may thereby be saved. A car assembly plant has already been set up in Southern Rhodesia – although there the demand was expected mainly from the small but wealthy white community. All of these three types of industrial production may require temporary artificial support before they become fully established. There is, therefore, in some cases a strong argument for temporary subsidization or tariff or quota protection for such industries in the early stages. We do not propose to discuss this fully except to say that most economists accept in some circumstances the economic justification for such temporary support. If, however, after a fairly generous time such industries still cannot compete with foreign produce, then there would be little to gain by continuing such support – and to the consumers quite a lot to lose.

Many economists, however, have used broader, more dynamic arguments for protecting industry. They argue that the 'infant industry' argument, outlined above, is based on the assumption of a given and static endowment of productive factors, especially capital; protection over a wide range of industries, however, may reduce uncertainty about markets which inhibits investment and so encourage a greater amount of domestic capital formation. There is no doubt that arguments of this kind are strong ones; but they are double-edged weapons in the sense that such a policy, if based on little more than an enthusiastic hunch will have grave results if it fails. The issue of protection, therefore, is one which requires careful research in each particular case and needs very delicate manipulation of the various policy tools – tariffs, subsidies and so on.

The readings in this section raise, though they do not answer, three crucial questions of African economic development: the problems of industrialization which we have discussed above; the question of private incentives *versus* government control; and Professor Berg presents some of the evidence on which decisions about economic integration must be based. We shall now consider these two further questions.

The question of private incentives very soon takes us into the discussion of the comparative merits of political and economic systems not strictly related to African economics as such. Consequently we shall restrict ourselves here to presenting some of the reasons why a considerable degree of central economic planning and government participation in the economy is likely to exist in most African countries:

1. Most public utilities (power, railroads, etc.) are already in government hands in most countries and are likely to remain so.

2. Large public works projects (such as dams to provide power and irrigation) require such large investments and often long periods of waiting for results that private capital is unlikely to finance them. Often in fact they will be financed by foreign government loans to the African government in question.

3. Both Eastern and Western nations have shown a preference in giving economic aid for financing government owned projects within the framework of a national plan.

4. Considerations of economic independence may encourage African governments to nationalize foreign corporations operating in their country, especially if a large proportion of current profits are repatriated instead of invested in the African country. Profits are sometimes repatriated not because there are no profitable vacuums for investment locally, but because a foreign corporation is unwilling to expand its field of activity within the economy. A government active in many fields within the economy would not have this problem.

5. There may be reasons to nationalize foreign financial corporations (banks, etc.) if they discriminate in their loan policies against indigenous investors who could in fact make profitable use of the loans to the benefit of the economy as a whole.

6. Fears of nationalization may discourage private investors, foreign and domestic, from taking up potentially profitable opportunities; if the capital is to materialize at all in that case it must come from the government.

7. In an economy undergoing major structural change from subsistence production to a monetized modern economy it may be necessary for active interference by government agencies to smooth the frictions of change and to prevent the suffering which may result from that change. For instance a movement of labour to the cities may leave traditional agriculture in no position to feed the population without government encouragement of modernization in the agricultural sectors. In some areas of Zambia, for example, a large part of the harvest has sometimes been marketed by traditional producers to finance immediate consumption of other goods; but too little of the crop has been retained and a severe food

shortage has resulted before the next harvest. Problems such as these may be inevitable in a rapidly changing economy but must if possible be guarded against by a vigilant central authority which tries to relieve some of the frictions of economic change.

8. Where there is a predilection for strong central government in the interests of modernization, development and national unity, this centralization must involve economic as well as other activities.

Incentives based upon private motivations will still have their place even in a centrally planned economy but for the reasons outlined above as well as others it is unlikely that many African economies will for long remain private enterprise economies as they progressively embark on the voyage of economic development.

9. These arguments, and the doctrine of neo-colonialism (or neo-imperialism) which we discuss in the Introduction to section IIIf, have offered major props on which to build ideas of African Socialism. There have been several prophets of doctrines which have gone under this name, including Presidents Touré of Guinea, Nkrumah of Ghana and Senghor of Senegal. There is as yet no generally accepted doctrine of African Socialism and the emphases of various statements have differed considerably. But all of them draw heavily on Marxian socialism and the democratic socialism of Europe while making adjustments which seem to them appropriate before transplanting them to the African context. Those who draw mainly on democratic socialism find much of the democracy inappropriate for Africa. And several African Marxists have stressed the inapplicability of Marxist doctrines of the class struggle, which were devised for nineteenth-century Europe. The common feature of all the doctrines, however, whatever their source, is the importance given to state action in the spheres of social and economic policy.

So far we have discussed African economic development as if it were always to take place within the existing national units. Larger industrial projects however, which require moderate or large-sized markets before they can produce economically, such as steel production, have little promise of success in African countries (which are predominantly small as well as poor) at present. This fact has led to suggestions that the answer to the demand for rapid economic development is the establishment of larger economic units by African countries. These units may take one of three main forms:

1. Free trade areas, where tariffs are abolished between the constituent units but each of them is allowed to pursue independent tariff policies towards the rest of the world.

2. Customs unions, where tariff barriers between member nations are

removed and a unified tariff with respect to the rest of the world is adopted by the whole area.

3. Closer economic unions, which may include elements of 1 and 2, reinforced by joint economic policies with respect to public utilities, investment, taxation, planning or any combination of these or other items of economic policy.

The advantage of economic unions of any of these kinds is a controversial subject on which the facts (such as they are) are ambiguous and economic theory unhelpful. The potential advantages of the larger market may be limited initially by transportation problems. In addition there may be 'economies of scale' in things other than production – for example in administration or in education; in these cases the costs and benefits may be even harder to identify adequately in advance. But the most important disadvantage is that when a customs union or free trade area is established without any fiscal mechanism to redistribute income within the union, it is often found that the already comparatively developed areas within the union receive a disproportionate amount of further investment and the union fails to have any great impact on the less-developed areas. This has already been the case to a certain extent in East and Central Africa with Kenya and Southern Rhodesia respectively being the main beneficiaries – although there were some non-economic reasons in both these cases. We see a case of the opposite in French West Africa in the last reading in this section. In this case the richer, more developed unit (the Ivory Coast) gained as a result of the break-up of the federation because the redistribution of income in favour of the poorer regions was more than enough to offset the gains which the Ivory Coast made in other ways by virtue of Federation. In the same way Zambia is likely to gain as a result of the break-up of the Federation of Rhodesia and Nyasaland at the end of 1963 since in that case the income redistribution went, perversely, to Southern Rhodesia the most developed of the three countries in the Federation; Southern Rhodesia was subsidized by Zambia's immense copper export earnings; Zambia's own development was almost certainly set back by her involvement in an arrangement of this kind. Now that the countries of East Africa are all independent, negotiations are proceeding which may lead to a Federation of Kenya, Tanzania and Uganda. Uganda's apparent lack of enthusiasm in these negotiations is governed partly by a belief that, being the least developed of the three territories and in need of the access to the sea which the others provide her, she must try to secure redistributive fiscal transfers in her direction or some other *quid pro quo* for joining, if the economic benefits of Federation are not all to go to the other territories, especially to Kenya.

From these examples it is clear that in order to balance the gain
losses of economic union to the satisfaction of all parties, and to provid
means by which the arrangements can be adjusted if necessary, fairly
strong central economic control may be necessary both to direct investment
and to exercise redistributive taxation functions. Consequently if the
potential gains of a customs union are to be reaped, centralized political
control over groups of countries may be needed. This will involve a great
deal of complex and hard political bargaining. Should economic unions
emerge in spite of these difficulties, regardless of their economic consequences, they will at least be monuments to successful inter-African
co-operation in the face of great difficulty.

Besides the possibilities of regional economic integration, co-operation
is already taking place in a number of ways in a continental scale through
the Economic Commission for Africa (E.C.A.), a regional agency of the
United Nations. This co-operation has not yet been of great practical
significance but is likely to become more important. Arrangements are
now under way for the establishment of an African Investment Bank under
the auspices of the E.C.A.; this bank may become an important source of
international capital for African countries.

It is still too early to say whether the new spirit of unity exhibited at the
Conference of African States in Addis Ababa in 1963 will produce concrete results in the form of economic co-operation; it has already had
practical effects in other fields as we shall see in the Introduction to
section IIIf.

24

frican Economic Problems[1]

Benveniste and W. E. Moran, Jr.

This general survey of economic problems shows how closely economic issues are related to every aspect of government policy. This is, of course, true of all modern countries but for the underdeveloped nations of Africa and elsewhere it has a special significance. Such countries, poor by European or American standards, lack many of the things which serve to increase a nation's wealth – capital, education and skills of all kinds. Yet at the same time the economic values of African countries tend to be modern ones: the opportunity for education to the highest level is regarded as a social necessity for which the state should if possible provide; so are social services of other kinds – health, unemployment benefits and other welfare measures. In poor countries such social aims press upon policy from both sides: on the one hand, humanity and liberal values demand more spending on these items; on the other hand the desire for rapid growth to be produced from limited resources may demand that some of these worthy ends must be sacrificed for the time being. Western nations are rich enough for a good deal of education to have become a consumption commodity; in poorer countries it must still be regarded as an investment commodity.

In fields other than education, alternative economic policies are ringed around with important political consequences; it is hard to pursue 'developed' social and other policies on a poor and underdeveloped economic base. This and other general problems are outlined in this reading.

INTRODUCTION

Large-scale foreign influence on African traditional society is recent, dating back only sixty years. Except for traders, mostly limited to coastal settlements, victualling stops for the Orient trade, and a few slave raiders, the Continent remained isolated until the middle of the nineteenth century.

Algeria was conquered by France in the 1830's, but Tunisia was not taken over until the 1870's, and Morocco in 1912. The Niger Basin was explored in the 1830's; the Zambesi and the great lakes in the 1850's and 1860's; the Congo Basin as late as the 1870's. Large parts of Africa were still unexplored by Europeans at the beginning of the twentieth century.

[1] Reprinted from *Handbook of African Development*, Frederick A. Praeger (1963).

African Economic Problems

The partition of Africa south of the Sahara took place in Berlin in 1885.

The settlement of substantial white minorities in Kenya and the Rhodesias took place in the twentieth century. The economic penetration inland from coastal trading posts dates from the beginning of the twentieth century. For example, the railroad from Lagos to Kano was not opened until 1912.

By and large, the African way of life is still predominantly traditional. In most African countries, European influence is very limited. 95 per cent. of the population does not live in urban centres or even close to the few means of communications established by colonial administrations. Africans live the way their ancestors did before them. Generally, 70 to 80 per cent. of the African population lives in a subsistence economy, with only occasional participation in the market economy.

Although European ways of life have not replaced African ways, European influences have had a devastating impact on the traditional way of life. This impact has resulted first of all from the changes instituted by the colonial administrations. These changes, directed at replacing the old order with more modern forms of government, resulted in the weakening of traditional authority. The introduction of Christianity and education weakened the belief of the people in old forms of religion and education. Perhaps of greater importance have been the three by-products of colonial conquest – the African revolution of rising expectations, the independence movement, and Pan-Africanism. In many ways, these three social forces have dealt the principal death blow to traditional control and order.

THE DUALITY OF AFRICAN ECONOMIES

In those countries where there has been European domination and substantial economic development, there are two distinct economies – modern European and traditional African. The Europeans first introduced trade to secure ivory, gold, and slaves, then tropical products, and finally minerals. This modern-market sector of the economy, oriented toward exports, was monopolized by the European community. Africans benefited from this sector of the economy through employment, rarely above the labour or clerk level. Africa did not develop many entrepreneurs to promote the growth of an African market economy alongside of the European market economy. The exceptions, such as the 'mammy' traders of West Africa and the cocoa farmers of Ghana, were rare. The great mass of the African people remained in the traditional subsistence economy.

Until very recently, the whole continent, except the Union of South Africa, Southern Rhodesia, Egypt, Ethiopia, and Liberia, remained in a state of political tutelage. The essence of colonial status was that economic power, as well as political sovereignty, was in alien hands. Banking and commerce, such processing as developed, shipping currency and credit, taxation and public expenditure, were all dominated by citizens of the colonial powers. Even where local initiative had developed, or where, for economy, some people of the country were being trained in subordinate skills, policy decisions were made by the colonial establishment which formed a governing *élite*.

Raw materials were produced for export, and sometimes processed, by entrepreneurs from the European country wielding political power over a particular territory. These exports went to the metropolitan country in large measure for consumption or re-export to the rest of the world.

Colonies were operated as part of a foreign economy, that of a colonial empire. No attempt was made to make the individual colony a national economy viable on its own. Colonies in Africa were not developed in terms of African or regional possibilities or requirements but in terms of their place in the colonial scheme.

REORGANIZATION OF AFRICAN ECONOMIES

The newly independent African countries must now develop their economies in the light of their own needs, their relationships to their African neighbours, and their relationships with the rest of the world. This is the reality of independence which the Africans now seek. The most difficult and most important problem is the expansion of the market economy so that Africans, most of whom still live in a subsistence economy, can make a greater economic contribution to the economic growth of their own countries. Economic growth is essential to meeting the cost of the services Africans are demanding.

African leaders find that most Africans still live in traditional ways, while the few educated and a growing number of other people want to achieve non-traditional goals. To achieve these new goals, the new African leadership inherits a few modern structures imposed during colonial days. In some cases, the structures may be adequate as a starting point for new African programmes of economic development. In all cases, there still is the problem of reorganizing largely traditional tribal societies into new social structures to permit the achievement of the new African goals. This reorganization of African social and economic life presents the newly independent states and the West with a variety of problems.

The Africans feel they are in a precarious position because the market economy, the only source of substantial revenue, is in the hands of foreigners. The new states have already shown their intention to change their relationships with the foreign investors who predominate in their market economies. In some cases, this intention is shown by demands for new means of sharing the profits of ventures, particularly in the case of minerals. In other cases, it is shown by demands for an equity participation by Africans in these ventures, either by individuals or the state. Quite apart from this, there is the demand that Africans participate personally to a greater extent in the operation and control of these ventures – the demand for Africanization.

The newly independent states are anxious to expand industry and trade, but the change from colonialism to independence and difficulties such as those which have arisen in Guinea and in the Congo are causing many foreign private investors to hesitate investing in this expansion. These new states have expressed their interest in foreign private investment to help with the expansion of their economies, but cannot be expected to forego such development if those investors do not come forward. Most of the new states have taken steps to determine the character of the new industries they want and to establish institutions to seek out investors. These institutions include a number of new development corporations and banks. When they have not been able to find interested private foreign investors, some of the new states have already moved toward the promotion of state-owned industries.

The leaders of these new states are Western educated and are oriented towards Western economic methods. They can be expected to face their problems from this point of view, but because they believe they must develop their economies in the light of African conditions, they will have to use new approaches. For example, in many newly independent countries, the large mass of the people in the subsistence sector of the economy and the people with low-level earnings in the market economy have very limited savings. Low-money incomes result in a very limited tax base, and government revenues are generally low. Foreign private investment is slow to move, and foreign aid is not sufficient to counter these limitations and provide all the resources necessary to the kind of development desired. The idea of mobilizing the unused time of the people as a means of promoting development is attractive. This idea is the basis of experiments in community development, such as those in Ghana, and human investment programmes similar to the Chinese model, as proposed in Guinea.

There is no doubt that Africans will evolve new ways of life that will be principally African. To do this, they will want to experiment with many approaches, some Western oriented, some new and original. The characteristics of the societies evolved will depend in part on the contracts, assist-ance, and comprehension accorded by non-Africans.

PREVALENCE OF SUBSISTENCE ECONOMIES

Most Africans live in subsistence economies. They grow their own food and fibre or barter with their neighbours. They make only limited or occasional forays into the market economy to sell their products or services and buy some desired article. The standard of living of this great mass of people is quite low. There are important differences between those few countries, such as Ghana and the Ivory Coast, where an important agri-cultural export crop like cocoa is produced by the local people for sale, and the economy of most of the African countries where export production has not been substantially developed or is in the hands of Europeans.

Figures on national income or national product are rudimentary at best because little has been done to measure the real value of subsistence production. As shown in Table I, the figures can only indicate the rough order of magnitude of African poverty. The figures for some countries

Table I

PER CAPITA NATIONAL PRODUCT

1956–7

Country	U.S. Dollars
Algeria	221
Egypt	109*
Tunisia	179
Ethiopia	30
Kenya	78
Madagascar	119
Uganda	57
Tanganyika	48
Belgian Congo	76
Rhodesia and Nyasaland	132
French Equatorial Africa	126
French West Africa	133
Ghana	194
Nigeria	69
Sierra Leone	70

* Estimated 1954 prices.

Source: *Economic Survey of Africa Since 1950*, p. 16 (United Nations, E/CN/14/28, New York, 1959).

should be treated with care, particularly for those countries with a substantial European population. For example, the relatively high figures for Algeria result from the fairly large incomes of one million Europeans in that country. As shown by the data in Table II, the average Moslem income in Algeria is substantially lower than European income. Thus, despite the relatively high level of per capita income shown for Algeria, the estimated average annual income for Algerian Moslems in agriculture is $40 and corresponds more to the $30 shown in Table I for Ethiopians than to the $194 for Ghanaians.

Table II
ANNUAL INCOME PER CAPITA IN ALGERIA

	Agriculture	Other than Agriculture
European	U.S. $1,440	U.S. $650
Moslem	40	92

Source: *The Economic Development of Algeria*, p. 16, I.S.E.A. (Paris, March 1960).

POPULATION AND FOOD

In the last few years, there has been a sudden spurt in the rate of population growth. As shown by the data in Table III, the rate has been increasing for a long time. The estimated increase in this rate during the 1950–75 period is far greater than the increase in the 1925–50 period.

A truly unprecedented situation has come about in recent years. It is now possible, by fairly inexpensive and simple public health techniques,

Table III
ESTIMATED POPULATION GROWTH IN AFRICA
1925, 1950, 1975

	Population (millions)			Percentage Increase	
	1925	1950	1975	From 1925 to 1950	From 1950 to 1975
North Africa	29·0	42·7	70·4–76·4	47	65–70
South Africa	8·7	13·9	22·5–24·4	60	62–76
Rest of Africa	109·0	142·0	202–230	30	42–62

Source: *The Future Growth of World Population*, p. 28, United Nations Department of Economic and Social Affairs (New York, 1958).

to drop the death rate to low 'modern' levels without first raising the economic productivity of a 'traditional' society. In the Western world, the population growth of modern times was accompanied by an economic development which made it possible to accommodate the increasing number of people at higher standards of living, but in many underdeveloped countries today, a rapid population growth is taking place before economic growth can even get well under way.

Most of the countries of Africa where population explosions are taking place are not too densely populated. But population growth rates of 2 per cent. a year, already quite common in Africa, are a heavy handicap in the struggle of these countries to provide more food, clothing, and education per person. If strenuous efforts to achieve economic and social advancement result in little more production growth than is necessary to keep up with population growth, frustration of hopes will ensue.

This problem is illustrated by the fact that in all of Africa (except Libya, Sudan, and the United Arab Republic) the *per capita* food production appears to have gone down. As shown in Table IV, some statistics published at the first F.A.O. Regional Conference for Africa in Lagos, Nigeria, November 1960 indicate that 'the rate of increase of agricultural production, and especially food production in the African region, appears to have slowed down considerably in the last few years. For 1959–60, the latest season for which data are available, provisional estimates indicate that there was a slight fall in production from the level of the previous year. On a *per capita* basis, food production appears to have fallen below the pre-war level for the first time since the immediate post-war years. Similarly, if allowances are made for changes in imports and exports the improvements over the pre-war level of *per capita* food supplies that had been achieved earlier also seem largely to have been lost in the last few years. The production statistics for basic food crops and livestock products in Africa are subject to a considerable margin of error, however, so that these data can be regarded as no more than approximate indications of the trends that have probably occurred.'[1]

Because there is no measure of production and consumption in the subsistence sector of the economy, it is difficult to determine how far this trend applies. It is, however, clear that Africa, which should be a net exporter of foodstuffs, is not even organized to meet its own food needs. This failure means that scarce funds, which could otherwise be used for development purposes, must be used to pay for imported food.

[1] *Review of the Food and Agricultural Situation in the African Region (Except Libya, Sudan, and United Arab Republic)*, p. 1, First F.A.O. Regional Conference for Africa, Paper ARC 60/2(a) (Lagos, November 1960).

Table IV

PER CAPITA FOOD PRODUCTION IN AFRICA

1952–3 to 1956–7 = 100

Pre-war average	96
1948–53 average	96
1953–4	101
1954–5	100
1955–6	99
1956–7	101
1957–8	96
1958–9	96
1959–60 (Preliminary)	92

Source: *Review of the Food and Agricultural Situation in the African Region (Except Libya, Sudan, and United Arab Republic.* First F.A.O. Regional Conference for Africa, Paper ARC 60/2(a) (November 1960).

SCIENCE AND TECHNOLOGY

The experience of introducing modern methods in Africa has clearly shown the need for adaptive invention if these methods are to be of any use. For example, the introduction of Western agricultural techniques has been successful in such parts of Africa as the coastal plain of Algeria or the plateau of Kenya where they were compatible with the climate and soil, and where the white man has settled and put them into practice. There has also been successful adaptation in tropical areas for large-scale European-type plantations. Little has been done successfully to increase the agricultural productivity of African farms even where European farms have been successful. In some areas, there is the additional problem of redistribution of land and of agricultural reform. In most areas, there is need for new social techniques to interest and persuade African farmers to adopt new ways and methods of cultivation.

Western farming methods cannot be adopted in Africa, but must be adapted to the peculiarities of African soils and climate. Much is being done along scientific lines to improve knowledge of African soils and techniques of cultivation, but much remains to be learned. What is not being done, at least not sufficiently, is the study of the social aspects of the problem of African agriculture, the means of effectively applying new techniques in African conditions.

There have been interesting experiments along the lines of co-operative effort, community development, and agricultural extension services in some countries, particularly in Ghana, Kenya, Uganda, Morocco, and some of the French Community states. In such countries as Kenya and the Congo a substantial part of the efforts which have been made in the post-war period have been directed toward improvement of indigenous agriculture. But, taking into account the dimensions of the problem, massive help is still needed.

Communal approaches to agricultural development may be well suited to the traditional patterns of land ownership of some African tribal societies. Many Africans are interested in these experiences of Israel, Mexico, India, Yugoslavia, Japan, and China. Israel has been providing assistance along these lines to some African countries, notably Ghana. The French government has created a special aid group to assist African governments in initiating village aid and agricultural communal services,[1] and it is reported that the Chinese are assisting the government of Guinea in similar efforts. Since African governments are interested in the experience of Israel or Mexico, it would seem most important that some way be found to make this experience available to these governments. The West should think in terms of the vast resources of the non-Communist world.

INDUSTRIALIZATION

Until now, industrialization has been largely export oriented and European controlled. The general lack of African markets has resulted in the creation of export-oriented activities and industries based principally on the exploitation of mineral and agricultural resources.

Export industries do have a very crucial role to play, particularly as a source of the foreign exchange needed to achieve economic growth, but foreign-owned industries are limited in this regard, and they offer only limited employment opportunities. It is not surprising that independent African governments want to create and protect local industries for the processing of locally produced raw materials either for export or to meet local needs. African economies will, to some extent, disengage themselves from the economy of the ex-metropoles unless they can find better opportunities for such development within the old relationship than they have in the past. This disengagement may in some cases include the gradual withdrawal of African countries from European monetary zones and attempts to create regional groups to provide large internal African markets on which expanded industrialization could be based. Guinea has called for the creation of an African monetary zone of which the Guinea-Ghana

---

[1] This is the Bureau pour le Développement de la Production Agricole d'Outre Mer (B.D.P.A.) which has worked in Madagascar, Soudan, Algeria, Republique Centrafricaine, Côte Française des Somalis under the auspices of the French programme of co-operation with the Communauté states.

union would serve as the embryonic beginning. One of the first declarations of M. Modibo Keita upon taking direction of Mali, formerly French Soudan, was to state that to insure protection of his country's economy he would consider eventual participation in an African monetary zone.

Most of the industry in Africa is concentrated in a few cities such as Salisbury, Bulawayo, Elizabethville, Leopoldville, Dakar, Algiers, and Casablanca. The rest of the continent is relatively unaware of their existence, and indigenous agriculture has often failed to benefit from these investments.

In the Congo, the major industry is mining, but there are also such industries as cement, textile, beer, soap, margarine, shoe, brick, tile, sanitary ware, furniture, ceramic, and cigarettes. The Congolese people want to see a higher level of industrialization to provide some of the many products which must still be imported.

Prior to independence, the Belgian government was obliged under the original Congo Basin Treaty to follow an open-door policy toward trade in the Congo. This meant no discriminatory treatment in favour of any one nation. It resulted in a very low-tariff structure and little or no protection within which an incipient Congolese industry could grow. In other countries in Africa, where the open-door policy did not prevail, the growth of local industry was often impeded because it would have been competitive with industries in the metropoles.

Given adequate internal demands through which sufficient economies of scale could be reached, there are bound to be new opportunities for African and non-African entrepreneurs to create new secondary industries in newly independent Africa. But even so, it may be some time before these opportunities are taken up. Rapid growth of local industry is bound to be impeded by the smallness of African markets and by the absence of African entrepreneurs and trained cadres.

THE REVOLUTION OF RISING EXPECTATIONS

Poverty and the lack of opportunity for self-government that it implies have been the lot of ordinary people in most of these countries for centuries. Although poverty is not new, there is a new factor – the awareness of poverty, the realization that it is not the inevitable lot of man, and the determination to do something about it.

This new awareness, often referred to as the revolution of rising expectations, has come about in Africa largely as an indirect consequence of colonial domination. First, the wealth-producing capacity of the Western world, demonstrated in the metropolitan countries, proves that dire poverty for the masses is not inevitable. Second, the greatly improved means of communication, including radio, film, and world travel, brought this demonstration to the attention of an increasing number of people in Africa.

This revolution can be characterized as a demand for improvement of living standards by large sectors of the populations who still live in static social patterns and are not in a position to contribute greatly to the change they demand. This demand for an accelerated transition and transformation causes many strains and pressures throughout the social organism; dealing with these strains and pressures often requires the utmost in wisdom.

In Africa, the revolution of rising expectations sometimes takes racial overtones that further complicate the problem. Africans have rarely known poor Europeans, and for the uneducated, it is sometimes natural to assume that once independence comes, the white man's riches will come with it. Africans educated abroad realize that riches and power do not necessarily go with a white skin.

As Thomas Kanza of the Congo wrote, 'Before coming to Europe we thought it would be . . . like Paradise. From our experience in the Congo, we had the erroneous impression and belief that it was enough to be white and European to have an important position and high income. . . . We did not understand that it could be different in Europe. We imagined it as the "land of riches" where one could only find intelligent, beautiful, and happy white men.'[1]

Little has happened to make it clear that the improvement in well-being elsewhere was the result of great social changes and followed increases in production made possible by new social organization.

The independence movements in Africa were built, nevertheless, on such hopes. The leaders of the newly independent countries are now faced with a large portion of their populations expecting that with independence these hopes will be realized. The inability of the great mass of these people to make any substantial contribution to the revenues or manpower required to bring about the change and the great social changes required before they will be in a position to, pose grave difficulties.

If one or two years after the excitement, after the first euphoria of freedom, young governments have not been able to show results, if there are belt-tightening programmes, if most Africans are still poor, and there are still white men (technicians) brought in by the government at much higher living levels, there will be discontent.

[1] Thomas R. Kanza, *Alta NDELE*, p. 18 (Brussels, 1959).

THE APPEAL OF COMMUNISM

The problem of reorganizing traditional subsistence economies into modern market economies is complex. The new governments must find a way of putting their potential resources to work. They are having a hard time finding a way within the existing framework of private enterprise. Bringing about the necessary social changes and creating the necessary institutions, for example, institutions for agricultural demonstration and credit, marketing and distribution, and savings and investment, begins to seem an impossible job. Some new governments have been attracted to the Israeli experiment as a possible method. Many are beginning to listen to the siren song of the Chinese who claim they have found a way.

It is important to distinguish between techniques of economic development and the Moscow-dominated communist movement. It would be quite dangerous for the West to equate the first with the second. Many African leaders are interested in new social techniques, particularly those dealing with communal approaches to increased agricultural productivity. In that limited sense, many African intellectuals may be 'communizing'. This does not mean these leaders want to join the Moscow-dominated communist movement. It is therefore important to assist these leaders in evolving new social techniques. The Sino-Soviet bloc can be expected to promote their methods and ideology. The West should make available to Africa the Free World experience such as that of Israel, India, or Mexico.

African countries will deal with the East if only to demonstrate the reality of their independence. If the West refuses to help because of this or is slow or less effective, the East will reap the advantage.

The Russians, the East Europeans, and the Chinese have been active in Africa for some time. The Institute for Ethnography in Moscow has been concerned with African problems for many years. Many other Russian centres are publishing studies on Africa, on its culture, history, its languages, and on its political structures. An unknown number of Chinese, Czechoslovakians, Poles, and Russians are becoming familiar with Africans and with African languages.

Many African students and trade unionists are being trained in Moscow, Prague, or in Peking, and many African leaders have visited the Iron Curtain countries. There are perhaps 10,000 or 20,000 official members of communist parties in Africa, and an unknown additional number in countries where the parties are not legal. Ever since the United Arab Republic received arms shipments from Czechoslovakia in September 1955, Africa has become clearly aware of the possibility of Sino-Soviet aid.

The Soviet Union, its satellites, and China have established full diplomatic missions in many newly independent countries, and through the theme of Afro-Asian Solidarity, through such means as radio broadcasts, unions, student organizations, and youth movements, they have begun to explain what their solutions may mean in the African reality.[1]

After France refused to continue providing aid when Guinea selected independence, a vacuum was created which was rapidly filled by the communists. In 1959, the Soviet Union signed an agreement for economic co-operation with Guinea and undertook to extend that country a line of credit amounting to $35 million. This loan was followed by one of $25 million from China. The Soviet Union, East Germany, Poland, and Czechoslovakia are establishing a polytechnical institute, a major broadcasting system, and a very large modern printing plant in Conakry.

It was not until September 1960 that the U.S. government was able to negotiate the basic agreements necessary before any U.S. aid could be furnished. President Sékou Touré has allegedly taken the position that the proposed American agreement, required more in the way of formal undertakings than the Russians asked, and that the United States offered far less in the way of aid.

Guinean trade has been gradually shifting toward the Soviet bloc, jumping from 3·2 per cent. of total exports in 1958 to 16·8 per cent. in 1959.[2] Trade with the Soviet bloc is expected to reach about 65 per cent. of Guinea's total trade in 1960. This expectation reflects Guinea's decision to leave the franc monetary zone in the beginning of the year, and the accompanying difficulty of trading with the West because of an unacceptable currency.

NEEDED: A NEW APPROACH

African leaders are generally concerned with the problems of economic development they now face. They are generally hopeful that the West will be able to provide effective help in the coming years. They have definite opinions about some of these problems; they have definite attitudes. Probably the most important of these is that they want to have a predominant voice in what is done or proposed to assist African economic development.

[1] See 'De la Propagande et de l'Infiltration Communiste dans les Regions Sous-Developpées', by Peter Sager in *Un Defi à l'Occident*, pp. 113–123, Cours d'été au College de l'Europe Libre (Strasbourg, August 1958).

[2] 'Le Commerce Extérieur de la République de Guinée en 1959'. Banque Centrale des Etats de l'Afrique de l'Ouest, Note d'Information No. 58 (Paris, May 1960).

African Economic Problems

The West is confronted with a new reality in Africa. This new reality calls for new goals, new intentions, and new approaches. The question that must be answered by non-African countries is how can effective co-operation be provided to the emerging African nations. What is now being done? How can outside help be provided so that Africans can better solve their own problems? How can enough men and money be sent to Africa to help Africans start on economic development while their own people are being trained? What is now being done? Will private initiative have a role to play in Africa? How can private initiative, both African and non-African, be assisted to be more effective in Africa? What is the outlook for African export trade? What is the significance of African export trade to its future economic development? These are the problems that independence, African aspirations, and the realities of peaceful economic competition with the Communists make urgent.

25

Migrant Labour in Africa: an Economist's Approach[1]

Walter Elkan

One of the consequences of 'colonial' economic development and dualism was the widespread emergence of a system of migrant labour: people from the villages worked for a time in mines, plantations or in the cities. Migration was usually within countries although in Southern Africa there was a good deal of boundary crossing: many Malawians worked, and still work, in Southern Rhodesia or in South Africa. Originally most of these migrants returned to their villages and a permanent urbanized proletariat developed only slowly. Sometimes, to persuade unwilling workers to move, colonial governments imposed poll taxes on the rural population; they were thus forced to join the money economy, at least for a time, to earn sufficient to pay these taxes. It was widely believed by employers and colonial governments that these taxes were necessary because Africans were insufficiently responsive to wage incentives and so there was no point in raising wages to attract labour; many economists now doubt whether this was true. Colonial governments were also slow to acknowledge that a permanently urbanized population was developing and this belief often led to an unwarranted delay in the provision of social services for these urban dwellers.

This reading describes the nature of this labour migration and some of the issues about it which have concerned economists and governments.

If there is one feature of the African labour scene which is universally recognized, it is that wages, particularly for unskilled work, are very low indeed when compared with the wages for similar work in more developed regions. In few tropical African territories do unskilled workers receive so much as $15 per month, and even on the most optimistic assumptions about the cost of living, wages of that order cannot conceivably afford their recipients much of a livelihood.

Explanations of the low level of wages usually attach importance to the imperfect specialization in Africa between wage labour on the one hand and farming on the other, which inhibits efficiency and thus causes labour productivity to be low, and it may be therefore worth while to examine in some detail, and from the vantage point of our own discipline, the nature of this imperfect specialization between wage labour and farming.

[1] Reprinted from the *American Economic Review* (May 1959).

Migrant Labour in Africa: an Economist's Approach

It is in most parts of Africa the common practice to seek only temporary employment in mines or towns or on plantations and sooner or later to return to homes on peasant farms in the countryside. This is in contrast with European and North American experience. It is true that there have been times and places in Europe and North America when farmers have taken up temporary employment away from home, but in general this has never been a significant feature in the structures of our economies, except perhaps for the supply of seasonal labour, whilst in Africa and other underdeveloped regions it has become a dominant and truly distinguishing feature. In most tropical African territories there are now a few permanent wage earners but their number is still generally very small.[1]

It is, of course, difficult to discern the degree of permanence of a labour force, particularly when this labour force is, itself, expanding rapidly. No two territories collect figures on a comparable basis and it is hard to devise a satisfactory measure of permanence or stability in wage employment. One cannot hope to obtain a satisfactory answer to direct questions about people's future plans so that the degree of permanence can only be assessed on the basis of past behaviour, for instance, by asking people what period of their total working life they have spent in employment. In this way a recent survey of unskilled workers in Kampala, Uganda, revealed that those who had lived in town continuously for five years or more accounted for less than 20 per cent. of the whole, and the Carpenter Report, which is probably the most thorough inquiry into these problems in Africa, states that in Nairobi, Kenya, only 11 per cent. of African employees had completed five years' service with their current employer (although this is not of course the same as continuous residence). Such figures as are available all confirm the more or less transitory character of large sections of the labour force.[2] Even in the Copperbelt of Northern Rhodesia where specialization has perhaps gone further than in other parts of British Africa, it is reported by a competent observer that African labour is still principally migratory.[3]

This difficulty of documenting the extent of impermanence is not at all a matter of chance. It springs, I believe, from the fact that both economists

[1] Tropical Africa here excludes the Republic of South Africa where it has been estimated that there were in 1951 some 1½ millions who had in some sense become permanent town-dwellers. See Summary of the 'Tomlinson Commission', p. 28. Report U.C. 61/1955 (Government Printer, Pretoria, 1955).

[2] *Patterns of Income and Expenditure of Unskilled Labourers in Kampala*, East African Statistical Department, Nairobi, 1957, and *Report of the Committee on African Wages* (Carpenter Report) (Government Printer, Nairobi, 1954).

[3] J. Clyde Mitchell, 'Africans in Industrial Towns in Northern Rhodesia' in *Report of the Duke of Edinburgh's Study Conference*, Vol. II, p. 3 (Oxford Univ. Press, 1957).

and governments tend to regard short-term migration as essentially a transitional thing – simply as one of the many strains and stresses to be endured by a young industrial economy developing painfully out of primitive conditions. It is perhaps to be hoped that it will indeed be transitory; but before settling to the main task of this paper, which is to examine the causes likely to make for its persistence, let me record my view that observers of the African scene have tended to understress this particular problem in favour of others resembling more closely the problems with which Europe and America had to deal in early industrial revolution times. Much attention has been given, for instance, to the questions of creating a large enough labour force and also to the growth of attitudes and aptitudes which will enable African workers to participate satisfactorily in industrial life. These are old and familiar problems in a new setting: how old and familiar, may be illustrated by recalling that Andrew Ure, writing in the early nineteenth century, stressed the need to train human beings 'to renounce their desultory habits of work and to identify themselves with the unvarying regularity of the complex automaton';[1] and he attributed Arkwright's success less to his knowledge of machines than to his skill in devising and administering a successful code of factory discipline.

Again, much of the energy of labour economists from the older industrialized countries has been devoted to the study of labour movement, of trade unions and other institutions affecting the determination of wages and the supply both of labour as a whole and of particular grades of labour. Such studies are both important and relevant in Africa, provided – and it is an important proviso – that it is realized that these apparently familiar institutions are part of a basically different economic setting. There is some danger of institutional studies being done without due cognizance of two things: first, that the economic setting displays certain genuinely novel characteristics, of which short-term migration is one, and, second (which follows from this), that institutions growing up within the labour force, such as trade unions, may really be extremely different in function and character from the institutions which bear the same name in other economies. In other words, our economic training in countries where a specialized labour force seems, as it were, to be part of the order of nature is an advantage only if we are prepared to give due weight to those factors in the African situation which are not only new to us but which are also the dominating and basic facts about that situation. Temporary labour migration, which I would call the dominating problem in the African industrial scene, derives directly from this particular

[1] Andrew Ure, *Philosophy of Manufacturers*, p. 15 (London, 1835).

set-up which is not found in the experience of Europe or America.

Industrialists and governments are rightly concerned to devise policies which will bring about a more perfect specialization between farming and wage earning. They consider the present lack of specialization is wasteful in several ways. In the first place, where movement between the two sectors involves, as it often does, long-distance migration, manpower is wasted in long and arduous journeys. Second, it is a waste to give much training to men who regard employment as merely temporary and so the labour force remains perpetually unskilled. Third, it retards progress in farming by removing from the farms at any one time a varying proportion of young adult men.

Why does temporary labour migration persist? In Europe the growth of towns was associated with the growth of a new category of people: the urban industrial working class. In Africa, too, the towns are growing rapidly, but, although some of their houses may be built to last a lifetime, those who live in them seldom stay for long. Sooner or later they return to their original homes. The explanations of this state of affairs which have been advanced fall broadly into two groups. The first, which may be amply documented from many sources, attributes men's unwillingness to sever permanently their ties with the countryside to an innate taste for an easy life. It is said – curiously – that Africa is blessed with a bountiful nature and that since a minimum of effort affords an ample sustenance there is no inducement to work hard and continuously. Given this view, the explanation of temporary migration in search of work then becomes simple: men work only long enough to acquire the cash needed to buy those things which only cash can buy, and when they have earned enough they leave employment and return to subsistence farms. Those who advance this explanation often refer to men as target workers, and the idea of the target worker has been widely canvassed.

There is by now too much evidence of the positive desire of Africans in most parts to enjoy a higher standard of life, but though one would therefore have to reject the idea of rigidly limited wants, it is not necessary to dismiss the whole concept of the target worker. If we define targets not in terms of particular objects like bicycles or particular sums of money but more generally as means to attaining a permanently higher standard of life, the concept is still useful and can indeed serve to throw light on the reasons why people engage in employment only temporarily. Their purpose, or target, in seeking employment is not to enjoy an immediate increase in their standard of life but rather to save as much money as possible in a more or less given time with which to increase the productivity of their farms. They seek the fruits of their work in town, not in the form of an immediate increase in consumption, but rather in the higher yield of better equipped farms. They save to be able to buy a waterproof roof for their houses and storage sheds, to acquire large solid bicycles on which to carry their crops to market, or to be able to pay the bride-price for wives whom they will expect to do the major part of the work in the fields. Observers of temporary town workers notice that, low though their wages are, they appear not to use them all for day-to-day living and they conclude that their wants must be very restricted, whereas money is in reality saved in order to satisfy a broader range of wants at a later time. We may, therefore, accept a modified concept of the target worker while rejecting the general hypothesis that African workers lack 'wants'. The target aimed at may not be at all clearly defined in terms of either goods or money but ought to be thought of more in terms of a limit to the time available. Given the fact that people look upon employment only as a means to higher incomes later, when they return to the country-side, they will not stay in employment indefinitely even if they find that they have saved less than they had hoped. Changes in wages, which increase or diminish the amount that can be saved in a given time do not, therefore, greatly affect the length of time that migrant workers will spend in employment. This fact, of major importance in the framing of management policies, often gets less than its due weight.

A second explanation for the persistence of temporary labour migration would be the view that labour migration is simply an initiation rite. Schapera and other anthropologists have found in the societies which they have studied that young men are not regarded as eligible to marry until they have spent a period of time away from home. Men, therefore, simply enter employment as aspiring doctors might enter a medical school, and they naturally leave again just as soon as they have served their time. The views of anthropologists command respect. Too few economists have followed the spirit of Professor Tawney's injunction to acquire a 'stout pair of boots' (and go see for themselves), and this places them at a disadvantage *vis-à-vis* anthropologists, who for months or years are prepared to live the life and learn the language of villagers in remote rural areas. But research at that depth may lead to too great a respect for the statements of informants in the tribe. Anthropologists have means of checking the internal consistency of data gathered on family structure, social custom, and religious belief. They are apt to be just a little less critical when it comes to economic matters. The idea that a spell of employment in town is part of the process of initiation, or the 'done thing', may be largely a rationalization of simple economic motives. Certainly it is most unlikely to be the whole story, and I would argue that it never can be the most important part of the story. To accept the proposition that labour migration is mainly a cultural requirement would be to deny that changed economic circumstances could directly alter it and thus one would have to regard as pure coincidence the fact that in Uganda, for instance, the practice of seeking temporary employment is most deeply rooted in those areas where young men have least alternative opportunities of earning an equivalent income in other ways, and that in some areas where the practice was at one time almost universal, the coming of alternative opportunities has caused it to melt away like snow.

This brings us to a third view, which sees the persistence of temporary labour migration as a consequence of low wages and unpleasant conditions of life in town and other centres of employment. It is probably this view which is most widely held today and therefore warrants the closest examination. Its exponents maintain that the conditions and wages in the towns are not sufficiently attractive to persuade immigrants to stay for longer than a year or two at the most; and that wages are based on the needs of bachelors and that the lack of houses capable of accommodating families, and the absence of protection against sickness, unemployment, or old age obstruct an assumed natural tendency to come to work and live in the towns. Bad conditions and insecurity explain why only the young will come to town and why men are reluctant to bring their wives or families.[1] Since labour migration is correctly regarded as wasteful, the remedy has seemed to lie in making urban life more attractive, by policy measures designed to raise wages, by providing suitable houses at reasonable rents, and by instituting schemes of social insurance. We need not be concerned here with the cost of these measures or the propriety of paying for the amenities of workers in the towns (who are often less heavily taxed than peasants) with money collected from peasants in the countryside whose income may be smaller. If short-term labour migration is indeed wasteful and if improvements in the town will overcome it, they may soon pay for themselves in the form of higher productivity. Nor need we question the assertion that in most African towns wages are low or that life is unpleasant. These things are unfortunately beyond dispute, although there are variations from place to place and few tropical African towns exhibit the grinding poverty and demoralizing apathy with which visitors to Calcutta and other Asian towns have become familiar. If people are to live in towns or even to spend only a short time in them, there rests a responsibility on the authorities to see to it that conditions there are tolerable and that people get enough to eat. But here I am concerned not with the desirability of improving wages and conditions, which seems to me

[1] Cf. L. P. Mair, *Studies in Applied Anthropology*, p. 78 (London, 1957).

axiomatic, but with the question of what effect improvements are likely to have on the practice of temporary migration. The question is not trivial, for a great deal of social policy in Africa takes it for granted that improvements will automatically bring about the desired end of greater specialization. Thus the Carpenter Committee in Kenya, which undertook a very thorough investigation of these matters, concluded that 'the immediate basic conditions for stabilising labour are seen to be – the payment of a wage sufficient to provide for the essential needs of the worker and his family; regular employment; a house in which the worker and his family can live; and security for the worker's old age'.[1] This led them to recommend large increases in wages, better provision of houses, and schemes for the provision of security against the normal hazards of industrial life, and thereby make it possible for men to sever their connections with the countryside and 'get away from the enervating and retarding influences of [their] economic and cultural background' (p. 138) and to live with their families in town. This view is widely echoed in other parts of tropical Africa.

There is unfortunately reason to doubt whether these policies by themselves will be effective. Whilst in the collieries at Enugu in Eastern Nigeria and in the copper mines of the Congo they appear to have met some success, it is reported from the former French West Africa that improved housing has in no way affected temporary migration, and in general the evidence is conflicting.[2] It is conflicting because certain vital factors tend to be forgotten by an approach which sees stabilization as mainly a problem of what happens to people while they are in employment and which regards stability as simply a function of the income from employment. The migrant worker, unlike anyone who studies him only during his brief masquerade as an urban proletarian, views his own life as a whole and is well aware that his income consists not solely, or even necessarily mainly, of wages and other benefits of employment, but also of the income which his family draws from farming in the countryside. This farm income may be only a subsistence income, from crops that are grown for consumption on the farm, but often a surplus is grown either of these subsistence crops or of others that are grown especially for sale and in that case the farm income may consist in part of cash. Whatever form it takes, this farm income is a part of the family income no less than the wages earned in employment. The size of this farm income varies greatly from place to

[1] *Report of the Committee on African Wages,* loc. cit., p. 139.
[2] Inter African Labour Institute. *The Human Factors of Productivity in Africa – A Preliminary Survey,* Chap. 8 (C.C.T.A., 1956) and V. Thompson and R. Adloff, *French West Africa,* p. 494 (Allen & Unwin, 1958).

place. Where land is plentiful, as it still is in many parts of Africa, and where there are opportunities for the sale of crops, the farm income may well exceed the bare demands of subsistence. In other parts, land is now scarce and high population densities may prevail; here the income from farming may hardly suffice to support a family at all. Yet even here people cling to their farms tenaciously, because if they did not they would forego part of this income.

This tenacity with which people cling to their land is partly to be explained by feelings and emotions which go beyond the realm of economics; but partly it arises out of forms of land tenure, which, however diverse in many ways, have this in common, that they restrict the opportunities for obtaining, and parting with, land. Terms like ownership and tenancy must be used carefully when we consider systems of land tenure other than our own, but it is quite certain that hardly anywhere in Africa can a man obtain real compensation for vacating a farm. Either he has no individual claim to his land or, if he does, there is no market for his farm, since land of equal value still lies untilled. Even in Buganda, which has the most 'Western-like' system of land tenure, a tenant can claim no compensation for improvements, and although an incoming tenant pays a premium, this goes to the landlord or his agent, not to the outgoing tenant. In Kikuyu country, where land is scarce, farmers do sell their farms even though such sale has no legal sanction; but partly for that reason and partly because Kikuyu are poor and cannot borrow, farm prices bear little relation to their value as measured by the income which they might be expected to yield over a period of years.

The terms on which land is held are more commonly discussed in relation to agricultural policy but they are highly relevant to the persistence of labour migration. If the future income of a farm, however small, cannot be capitalized, the farm must exercise a strong pull. So long as a man cannot obtain compensation for vacating his land and, on the other hand, cannot normally maintain his right to it unless he or his family are in actual occupation, he has no inducement to vacate it and he is therefore bound to regard employment as in some sense temporary. It is sometimes argued that the compensation for abandoning the land comes in the form of higher wages which a long period in employment is bound to bring him, that low wages are the consequence of low productivity, and that productivity is caused by the fact that men have not committed themselves to employment. Such reasoning is naïve. An individual's wage is not determined in such simple ways, and Africans who work for wages are less easily deluded by such comfortable moral theories than their employers or their governments. It is one of those hypotheses which are true in general and in the long run; it is not a consideration which could influence very potently an individual about to make a choice. At present, if a man were to withdraw permanently from the countryside, he would be giving up both a part of his income and also a form of insurance against unemployment or ill health. If there were provisions against these risks, such as those envisaged by the Carpenter Report, the value to a man of his farm would be correspondingly diminished, but the farm would still yield him an income, and this is so irrespective of whether the wage he earns in town is high or low and whether or not family houses are available in town. Unless a permanent withdrawal from the countryside is actually made a condition of employment in the town, workers will tend to hold on to their farms. In the Belgian Congo withdrawal from the countryside is now in a sense made a condition of certain kinds of employment. To quote Hailey's *African Survey*, 'recruiting conditions now insist upon the labourer being accompanied if possible by his wife and family'.[1] Once an entire family leave their holding in the countryside it ceases to be theirs and it ceases to afford them further income or security. The success of stabilization policies in the Belgian Congo may therefore be attributable as much to this compulsory severance from the land as to the positive inducement of employers. It is also possible that, although a farm may yield an income, residence in the countryside is sufficiently unpalatable, perhaps because of the power exercised by the authorities, for income to be sacrificed in exchange for the relative freedom enjoyed in the towns. This, too, is said to operate more strongly in the Belgian Congo than elsewhere in tropical Africa.

There are other reasons why a loss of income may be countenanced. We have dismissed as *simpliste* the notion that a man's wage must inevitably rise if only he will commit himself to urban life. This does not, however, preclude the possibility that a man who has already happened to attain a high wage may not then decide that a relatively small sacrifice of income is worth the pleasure of living a normal family life in town and it is then that it becomes important that this ambition should not be thwarted because suitable housing is not to be obtained. But in practice, such a sequence of events still appears to be rare, and, as in pre-industrial England, the successful town-dweller's first impulse seems generally to be to augment rather than diminish his assets in the countryside. Moreover, leaving a family at home or on the farm is, in Africa, not incompatible with conjugal life in town and many of the ties which those who can afford it form with women in town have about them a semblance of stability.

Parallels are sometimes drawn between nineteenth-century English

[1] Lord Hailey, *An African Survey, Revised 1956*, p. 1392 (London, 1957).

history and recent developments in Africa. In regard to migration, it may be as instructive, by way of summary, to point to some contrasts. The English towns of the nineteenth century drew their populations not from small peasant farmers but very largely from agricultural labourers who owned no land and were already entirely dependent on wages before they entered the urban industrial labour force.[1] They stayed in the towns, not because they found the conditions there attractive, but because, unpleasant though town life may have been, it was preferred to the life of an agricultural labourer. People stayed put in the towns, not because they afforded them adequate wages and security, but because, in the words of the East Africa Royal Commission, this was 'their most economic choice'. In most parts of tropical Africa it clearly is not.

I have attempted in this paper to relate the question of short-term labour migration to the very simple and fundamental economic proposition that a man – whether he be an African man or some other sort of man – would sooner have a higher income than a lower one. This fact, which leads us at once to consider the agricultural as well as the industrial structure, should never be lost sight of, for other factors, important as they may be, are secondary to it.

---

[1] A. Redford, *Labour Migration 1800–1850, passim.* The Irish immigrants and some of the Scottish Highlanders were an exception, but the farm they left had become so small as to be worthless.

26

Problems of Economic Development[1]

Mark Karp

Heavy dependence upon a few export commodities and the fluctuations in world prices of these tend to produce wide fluctuations in overall export earnings from year to year and consequently add complications to long-term planning. Two suggestions have been made to eliminate this problem: world-wide agreements to stabilize the prices of primary commodities, and diversification through industrialization. These have already been discussed in the Introduction to this section; this reading points, through examples, to some of the difficulties inherent in both these approaches. It shows also the additional problems which African countries face by virtue of the persistent 'colonial' pattern of their economies.

It is a curious but readily observable fact that for most African countries whether politically independent at this time or not, the task of framing basic economic policies is still largely carried on outside the countries themselves. Several factors may lie behind this phenomenon, one of the most obvious being the difficulty of breaking habits and traditions formed long ago in a colonial institutional setting. But the importance of the phenomenon lies not so much in the reasons for it as in its consequences. For it is practically inevitable that, when formulated at a considerable distance from the area to which it is to be applied, economic policy should be characterized by a high level of abstraction. This makes it hard to avoid conceptual ambiguities which in turn cause a wide gap to develop between the policy's initial formulation and its eventual implementation.

The nature of this problem may be illustrated by considering briefly three goals of economic policy that are being widely discussed today with reference to African countries – stabilization, industrialization and diversification.

The concept of stabilization is fraught with several difficulties. To begin with, the concept may refer to prices, money incomes, or real incomes. The stabilization of any one of these does not insure the stabilization of the

[1] Reprinted from *New Forces in Africa*, edited by William H. Lewis, Public Affairs Press (Washington, D.C., 1962).

other two and, under certain conditions, may even cause them to be de-stabilized. This is particularly true of agricultural commodities. When a crop is short, prices normally tend to rise, thus compensating the producer for the smaller crop. The stabilization of prices in these circumstances will necessarily lead to the de-stabilization of producer incomes.

A second difficulty is that of deciding whether small and frequent changes represent a greater or lesser measure of stability than relatively large and infrequent changes.

A third difficulty arises out of the dualistic nature of African economies. Most African countries are characterized by fairly large subsistence sectors that exist, alongside smaller, though far more productive, monetized sectors. Under these conditions, the process of economic development is practically synonymous with the enlargement of the money economy at the expense of subsistence production methods. Since market prices perform important social functions of guidance and control, there is a genuine risk that stabilization policies, which ordinarily cause producers to lose contact with market forces, will interfere with these functions and thereby tend to preserve economic dualism.

Stabilization as a policy objective is being pursued in African countries that belong to the sterling zone as well as in those that belong to the franc zone, but the mechanisms employed in the two groups of countries are significantly different. Broadly speaking, in the sterling zone a system of marketing boards has been created which compels producers to sell export crops at prices that are below market levels. The losses thus incurred by producers are partially offset by a fairly liberal tariff policy with respect to imports. In the franc zone, a system of *caisses de stabilisation* is employed which allows producers of export crops to receive the full benefit of market prices and, in many instances, of prices that are substantially above market levels. On the other hand, imports are subjected to highly discriminatory tariffs in favour of French producers. Since 1958, tariff barriers on imports have been gradually lowered for the benefit of France's European Common Market partners, but high duties have been maintained on goods originating from third countries. As a consequence, living costs in African countries that belong to the sterling zone are generally lower than in those that belong to the franc zone. Another important difference is that the burden of stabilization tends to fall upon producers in the former and upon consumers in the latter group of countries.

Despite differences in the mechanisms employed, the difficulties inherent in the concept of stabilization have similar effects in both monetary areas. Since Professor Bauer has already analysed these effects with respect to sterling zone countries in his celebrated study of economic concentration in the former British West Africa, I shall limit my observations to the operation of stabilization schemes in the franc zone.

In Senegal, where the economy depends heavily upon exports of peanuts to France at prices that range from 10 to 30 per cent. above world market levels, a fairly rigid stabilization scheme was put in operation a few years ago. During the period 1956–60, consequently, producer prices changed only once, while money incomes and real incomes tended to fluctuate from year to year. Thus, producer prices were stabilized at 100 during the first three years of the scheme, and rose only four percentage points in 1959–60. On the other hand, money income rose 14 percentage points in 1957–8, declined in 1958–9, and increased 11 points in 1959–60. During this four-year period, real income fluctuated only three percentage points.

In view of the highly artificial basis upon which the Senegalese peanut trade rests, it is not possible to compare fluctuations in producer incomes with those that would have occurred in the absence of stabilization. A comparison of this kind can be made, however, in the case of coffee and cocoa stabilization schemes operated in the Ivory Coast.

Most of the Robusta coffee produced in the Ivory Coast is sold in France at prices above market levels, but a small part of the annual crop is sold on the world market, chiefly in the United States. The *Caisse de Stabilisation*, which has been functioning since 1955, fixes the producer price for unroasted coffee delivered at Abidjan on the basis of estimates of the average annual price expected to be derived from the combined sales on the two markets. If prices actually obtained are higher than those fixed by the *Caisse*, sellers must turn over the difference in proceeds to it; conversely, if realized prices are lower, it is the *Caisse* that pays out the difference in proceeds to sellers. This method of stabilization makes it possible to compare actual prices and incomes with those that would have obtained in the absence of intervention by a statutory body. If we compare changes in actual and potential average prices and money incomes of Ivory Coast coffee producers during the period 1955–9, for example, we find that: (*a*) actual producer prices rose 35 percentage points – 19 per cent. in 1956–7, 17 per cent. in 1958–9; (*b*) potential producer prices rose 18 percentage points – 18 per cent. in 1956–7, rose another 22 per cent. in 1957–8, and declined to the 1956–7 level the following year; (*c*) actual money income increased 37 percentage points during the four-year period; and (*d*) potential money income fluctuated between 41 percentage points in 1957–8 and 19 points in 1958–9.

It will be noticed that during the first two years the pattern of changes in prices and incomes was not disturbed by the operations of the *Caisse*. Thereafter, prices appear to have been stabilized to a degree. Actual incomes, on the other hand, showed no material improvement over potential incomes in terms of stability, while the direction of change was significantly altered; that is, incomes fell when they would have risen in the absence of intervention by the *Caisse* and vice versa. The *Caisse*, in other words, was able in this period to stabilize prices in some measure, without thereby stabilizing incomes; at the same time, the effect of its operations on price and income movements was strong enough to cause producers to lose contact with market trends.

Somewhat similar results were achieved with respect to the stabilization of cocoa. During the period 1956–9, for example, producer prices rose approximately 29 percentage points, while potential producer prices rose 108 points. Actual money income fluctuated greatly during the period, dipping 31 points in 1957–8, but rising 11 points above the 1956–7 base year index of 100 in 1958–9. Potential money income, on the other hand, registered a steady growth attaining 79 percentage points in three years from the 1956–7 base period.

Most of the cocoa produced in the Ivory Coast is exported to France at world market prices. A *Caisse de Stabilisation*, modelled along the lines of the *Caisse* for coffee, was set up in 1956, a year that saw a temporary but sharp fall in cocoa prices. The *Caisse* fixed the initial producer price at a level slightly above that of the market and to do this it was forced to borrow funds in France. Thereafter, prices on the world market recovered, but the *Caisse*, though it raised producer prices, kept them at a level markedly below that of the market, partly to recoup losses suffered during the first year of operation, and partly out of a desire to accumulate sufficient reserves that would enable it to meet similar contingencies in the future.

It may also be noted that coffee and cocoa prices in the Ivory Coast were allowed to change more frequently than those of peanuts in Senegal. It is not possible to determine, however, which of the two methods in fact achieved a greater measure of stability.

The concept of industrialization presents almost as many difficulties as that of stabilization. It may refer to the establishment of light manufacturing industries, heavy industries, or merely industries for the processing of agricultural commodities. It may refer to export-creating or import-replacing industries. Furthermore, policy statements about industrialization are of little value when made without reference to feasibility. In this respect it may be instructive to note that a preliminary three-year study recently completed in Madagascar to determine the feasibility of import-replacing industries on that island gave the following tentative conclusions: 5 per cent. of the goods normally imported could be produced locally with relatively small investments; 30 per cent. could be produced locally, but would necessitate fairly heavy investments; 45 per cent. could not be produced locally, either because of technical difficulties or because of unfavourable profit expectations. As for the remaining 20 per cent. no determination could be made without further and more detailed investigations.

Much more research along these lines is obviously needed before any meaningful policies can be elaborated for the industrialization of African countries.

With respect to diversification of trade, the principal difficulty here usually lies in the failure to make sufficiently clear the nature of the gains that are to be expected from it. Once again it seems convenient to refer to the case of Madagascar, where highly varied environmental conditions have tended to encourage the diversification of exports.

Official sources for Malagasy export statistics list twenty-eight principal commodities. In 1960, coffee represented about 32 per cent. of the total value of exports. Livestock products, rice, sugar and vanilla took up less than 10 per cent. each. Eleven commodities (cloves, essential oils, graphite, mica, peanuts, peas, pepper, raffia, sisal, tapioca and tobacco) took up less than 5 per cent. each, while the individual share of the remaining twelve items on the list was less than 1 per cent. When these figures are compared with those for Senegal, where peanuts during the same year represented a share of 86 per cent. of total exports, or for Ghana, where cocoa's share was 62 per cent., or for the Central African Federation, where copper's share was 59 per cent., or for the Ivory Coast, where coffee's share was 51 per cent., to cite but a few examples, the relatively high degree of diversification of Madagascar's export trade becomes more than apparent.

Since individual prices tend to move unequally, diversification has benefited Madagascar in that it has helped to minimize losses in periods of falling prices. On the other hand, it has prevented the country from maximizing gains in periods of rising prices. In other words, diversification has been beneficial in terms of security, but not in terms of development. There is no evidence to suggest that Madagascar has fared any better, in terms of development, than African countries with undiversified export trade patterns. On the contrary, it is probable that the dispersion of human effort, particularly in agricultural production, that has resulted from diversification has tended to act as a drag on economic progress.

From what has been said so far, it does not follow, of course, that stabilization, industrialization, or diversification do not represent appropriate goals of economic policy. The foregoing analysis was intended only to show that an economic policy that is formulated in the abstract can be neither meaningful nor effective. The difficulties inherent in such an approach to economic policy might be avoided, or at least minimized, if steps were taken so that African countries could frame their own policies. Such an undertaking would probably run into many technical, administrative and financial hurdles. But there is little reason to believe that they would prove to be insuperable.

27

The Economics of Independence in French-speaking West Africa

Elliot Berg

In the Introduction to this section we suggested that the question of economic integration of countries in Africa was a major one. This reading shows what happened when an economic union in West Africa disintegrated after independence. The Federation of French West Africa was more than a customs union since fiscal transfers occurred and government expenditure was biased towards the poorer regions. This description of the effects of economic union and disintegration raise some of the problems which we mentioned in the introduction to this section. In this area it is doubtful whether the richer region (the Ivory Coast) will again be enthusiastic about making the economic sacrifices, even short-term ones, which would be necessary to make economic union attractive to the poorer regions. Yet in other areas of Africa as well as this one, such sacrifices may be essential to the achievement of economic unions which may in the long run be beneficial to all parties.

It is now almost two years since most of the French-speaking states in West Africa became independent, and over three years since Guinea voted itself out of the French Union. This is not much time as economic affairs go. But one trend is already clear: the economic unity that once character-ized relations between the states of French Africa has begun to disinte-grate. For most of these states this has meant new obstacles on the path to economic development; for one of them – the Ivory Coast – it has been a boob.

For over fifty years prior to 1958 important political and economic ties bound together the eight French colonies which made up the Federation of French West Africa. Within the Federation each of the territories had some administrative autonomy, and after 1946 each had its own political institutions. But economic institutions and policies were the same in all. They formed a single market area within which goods, capital and labour circulated freely. They had a common tariff system, a common currency, common fiscal policies. And in the Federal Government in Dakar they had not only an institution for the co-ordination of economic policy, but

[1] Reprinted from *West Africa* (10, 17, 24 March 1962).

294

an agency which provided centralized public services to each of the territories.

Two main consequences followed from the economic unification of this area and its integration in a federal system. Firstly, there developed a certain degree of interpenetration of economic activity between the territories, both in product and in labour markets. Secondly, the federal budget became an instrument of economic policy, redistributing income from richer to poorer states.

Judged by the volume of inter-territorial merchandise trade the degree of integration of product markets was not great. Excluding transit trade (imports flowing through coastal territories to territories in the interior), inter-territorial trade was a minor part of the total trade of the area – probably less than 10 per cent. Though relatively small, this figure does represent a significant amount of integration, for Senegal particularly. Dakar became a centre not only of public administration, but of ancillary services for the private economy throughout the Federation. Also, such secondary industry as developed in each of the territories tended to establish its capacity on the basis of markets (and, in some instances, raw material sources) in other territories of the Federation.

The inter-territorial relationship was closer in the labour market. Two kinds of movements of labour have been traditional in this area. One is the movement of unskilled migrant labourers – perhaps a quarter of a million annually. About 50,000 come from northern Guinea and western Mali to work as seasonal sharecroppers on African peanut farms in Senegal; perhaps 200,000 more move from Mali, the Upper Volta and Niger to work in the Ivory Coast (and Ghana). In addition, there has traditionally been in West Africa a high degree of mobility of skilled and educated people. Senegalese, Dahomeyans, and Togolese – better educated than their counterparts in the other territories – worked throughout West Africa.

The second consequence of economic unification – the role of the Federal Government as income redistributing agency – was of greater significance to most of the territories than was the network of economic interdependence which grew up. Economic development in this area, as in most of the under-developed world, has been very unevenly distributed geographically. The coastal areas and their immediate hinterlands have tended to outstrip by far the huge areas of the interior. National income estimates give some indication of these geographical differences in degrees of development. In 1956 the gross domestic product of French West Africa, excluding the value of subsistence output, amounted to about $1·4 billion (converted at the rate of 210 overseas francs equal one dollar), or about

$60 for each of the 23·5 million people in the area. Senegal and the Ivory Coast, with about one-quarter of the people, produced over 50 per cent. of the marketed output. The four interior states (Mali, Niger, Upper Volta, Mauritania) with 60 per cent. of the total population, produced less than a quarter of total marketed output in 1956.

The two relatively advanced territories (and particularly, since 1949, the Ivory Coast), paid in taxes to the federal government more than they received in public services or rebates. These two territories and, in the post-war period, Metropolitan France, financed most of the federally-provided services in West Africa. They also contributed, through the federal budget, to the budgets of the Sudan (now Mali), Upper Volta, Mauritania, Niger and Dahomey. (Guinea tended to come out about even.) In 1954, for example, the locally-raised part of the federal budget was about 25 billion C.F.A. francs. The Ivory Coast contributed 10 billion and Senegal another 10 billion. Mauritania, the Sudan, Upper Volta, Niger and Dahomey, with 60 per cent. of the Federation's population, contributed 10 per cent. to net Federal receipts. Although federal services were not distributed evenly among the states, these poorer areas certainly enjoyed substantially more than 10 per cent. of them.

The past several years have seen a breaking-down of this framework of inter-territorial economic co-operation and integration. The process of economic disengagement got its initial impetus in 1956. Political reforms introduced by the *Loi Cadre* of that year substantially reduced French control over the area. In part because of French influence, and in part because the Ivory Coast adamantly pushed for it, all decision-making power was passed to the individual territories, none to the Federation. After 1957 the institutions of the Federation were rapidly dismantled. It was officially dissolved in April 1959.

In many respects, political independence did not change the old economic relationships; in 1960 the economic unity of the area remained largely intact, except for the disappearance of the Federal Government. The area still formed a single market. All the French-speaking states including Guinea (until March 1960) and Togo were part of the Franc Zone. Out of the wreckage of the Federation several groupings had emerged: The Mali Federation formed by Senegal and the Sudan, and the *Conseil de l'Entente*, consisting of the Ivory Coast, Upper Volta, Dahomey and Niger. While the Mali Federation was constructed on a genuinely federal basis, the *Conseil de l'Entente* was much more informally structured; it involved no common political institutions, but was to co-ordinate fiscal and other economic policies and to provide for a 'solidarity fund' fed by 10 per cent. of the custom revenues of each of the four countries and distributed according to need. The Ivory Coast agreed in this way to carry on the Federation's function of subsidizing the Upper Volta, Niger and Dahomey.

By 1960, then, the Federation of French West Africa – the foundations of French-speaking West African economic integration – had crumbled, but many of the walls still stood. It did not take long, however, before even they began to fall. In August 1960 the Federation of Mali split up. The reasons were mainly political differences between the ruling parties in Senegal and the Sudan. The economic consequences were severe for both states, for not only did they abandon political ties; they cut all formal economic relations as well, and their economies were more deeply integrated than those of most other states in the area. Their transport systems were unified. The port of Dakar handled 250,000 tons of Sudanese trade – about 5 per cent. of the total, and some 40,000 tons of Sudanese groundnuts were exported annually through the Senegalese river port of Kaolack – a large share of that port's total tonnage. The Dakar-Niger Railway, connecting Dakar and the coast with Bamako, depended on Sudanese traffic for more than half of its revenue. In wholesale and retail trade the major firms with head offices in Senegal serviced the import-export trade of the Sudan. And in manufacturing, Senegal's sprouting industry had developed on the basis of markets throughout the old Federation of French West Africa, but especially in the Sudan. According to some estimates, the Sudan took 30 per cent. of the total processed goods output of Senegal, 50 per cent. of its sugar and 40 per cent. of its textiles. The break-up of the Mali Federation therefore demanded a drastic reconversion in the economic relationships of the two countries.

The *Conseil de l'Entente* survives. But its effectiveness has been limited and it too has been shaken by separatist trends. Its councils have been the scene of much squabbling. The Upper Volta and Dahomey have charged that the Ivory Coast, contrary to the original agreement, has altered its tariff schedules and fiscal policies unilaterally. More important, the Upper Volta and Ivory Coast have been in steady dispute over the proportion of total customs revenue collected in the Ivory Coast which is attributable to imports of the Upper Volta. Upper Volta dissatisfaction over this question was a major factor leading to an agreement with Ghana in the middle of 1961 eliminating duties and all barriers to trade between the two countries. Unlike the Ivory Coast, Ghana was generous in estimating the customs revenue collected in Ghana on imports destined for the Upper Volta. For the last six months of 1961 Ghana granted on this account a global sum of $5.6 million at low interest, with repayment in fifteen years beginning after five years. The full implications of the Ghana-Upper Volta arrangements are not yet clear. But it surely represents a serious strain on the structure of the *Entente*.

The labour market also shows evidence of the contracting area of economic integration in French-speaking West Africa. The movements of unskilled labour do not yet appear to have been significantly affected, though the disruption of transport between Senegal and Mali, and recent attempts by Guinea to stabilize its migrants locally, may affect Senegal's future peanut labour supply. It is with respect to inter-state movements of skilled manpower that restrictive tendencies are sharpest. In 1958 some 20,000 Togolese and Dahomeyans fled the Ivory Coast, following riots and violence directed at them by local inhabitants. More recently there have been a series of incidents reflecting deep ill-will and resentment – some aimed at Senegalese working in Mauritania, others at Dahomeyans working in Niger.

Cracks have appeared, finally, in the structure of the Franc Zone. In March 1960 Guinea suddenly withdrew from it, and set up its own currency system. Then, after the disruption of the Mali Federation, Mali (the ex-Sudan) insisted on regulating capital transfers even between Mali and other Franc Zone arrangements. Finally, the Ghana-Upper Volta accord of last summer is not fully consistent with the Upper Volta's continued membership in the Franc Zone, for it permits the Upper Volta to import freely from the Sterling Area, contrary to the exchange control regulations of the Franc Zone. No action has yet been taken by France to deal with Mali's and the Upper Volta's refusals to live by the rules of the monetary game. It may be that the effects are not significant enough to induce any action. But it is hard to see how Mali and the Upper Volta can continue over the long run to be both in and out of the Franc Zone.

Centrifugal tendencies have not shattered all links between French-speaking West African states. The *Entente* still exists. A common currency still prevails everywhere in French-speaking West Africa except Guinea. Among these states there remains in operation a West African Customs Union. Wider organizations designed to stimulate economic co-operation have been created: the Ghana-Guinea-Mali Union, an African and Malagasy Organization for Economic Co-operation, and others. From this activity, however, few concrete economic results have materialized. It has certainly not counterbalanced the opposing trend toward economic fragmentation.

The effects of economic fragmentation have been harmful for all the French-speaking states except the Ivory Coast. Senegal has been hardest-hit. It has lost significant portions of its market for manufactures and services, and has seen its role as centre of public administration dwindle.

Senegalese industry, it is true, has managed to weather the crisis. The development of new industrial enterprises (begun before 1960), the protection of established industry by the imposition of a new range of high tariffs, and a bumper ground-nut crop in 1961 – all of these combined to prevent economic catastrophe as a result of the closing of the Mali market. But industrial expansion slowed down in most sectors; in some (matches and textiles) output in the second quarter of 1961 was 10–15 per cent. below output in the similar period a year earlier. And nothing could be done to help the floundering Dakar-Niger Railway. The loss of the Mali traffic resulted in a decline of 70 per cent. in freight receipts and 45 per cent. in passenger receipts in 1961.

Nor did Mali escape unharmed, though the statistics are lacking to define the nature and extent of the damage. Its imports now come through the Ivory Coast, where it also sells most of its cotton and rice. The price of imports, as well as the regularity of delivery, has been affected by the use of a new and circuitous outlet to the sea. Crucial heavy construction materials have been particularly affected; the price of cement in Bamako rose nearly two times between August and December 1960.

The poorer states as a group have all suffered from the loss of the aid formerly provided through the budget of the Federation of French West Africa. They have been thrown back more on their own resources, and on aid from France or other non-African countries. Most are finding even the support of their relatively expensive civil services a burden barely supportable by locally-raised resources; the capital investment allocations in their budgets are negligible or non-existent. To take but one example: Dahomey's 1961 budget of some $25 million contains no capital expenditure provisions, yet it anticipates a deficit of about 15 per cent. Despite a 10 per cent. cut in civil servants' salaries, salaries absorb $18 million, or almost the entire amount of revenue raised from local sources.

The Ivory Coast alone among the West African states has come out ahead as a result of recent changes. Relief from the obligation to contribute to the federal budget, combined with rising revenues, have meant that the resources available for its own public use have soared – from an average of some $40–50 million annually in the mid-fifties to nearly $120 million in 1960. Its port facilities and transport system have enjoyed the benefits of new traffic to and from Mali; rail receipts in the first half of 1961 were almost 70 per cent. higher than in the first half of 1960. With the withdrawal of Guinea, the Ivory Coast share of the protected French market for coffee, bananas and other tropical products has expanded; it now has over 15 per cent. of the French banana market, as against 8 per cent. in 1958. New investment has flowed in not only to provide for the growing market.

but to produce goods and services formerly supplied from Senegal. France has continued to be generous with its aid.

The collapse of the world coffee and cocoa markets after 1958 – cocoa prices fell by 50 per cent. between 1958 and 1961, and coffee prices by 60 per cent. – obviously threatened the Ivory Coast's position; coffee accounts for half of the value of its exports and cocoa for another 25–30 per cent. The Ivory Coast, however, has taken these declines in its stride, for two reasons. Its output of coffee has increased at an extraordinarily rapid rate – from an average of about 100,000 tons a year in the period 1955–7 to about 150,000 tons in 1959–61. Total income from coffee sales, therefore, even at much lower prices per ton, have remained high or increased. More important, the degree of support given by France to Ivory Coast coffee has reached astonishing proportions. Throughout most of 1961 the price of Ivory Coast coffee was about twice as high in Le Havre as in New York. Although there was some difficulty finding room in France for Ivory Coast coffee output at these prices, most of the crop has been marketed there. Thus the Ivory Coast, the world's third largest coffee producer, has so far healthily survived the worst coffee crisis since the 1930's. It has done so largely because the French have been willing to support their price and hence provide an exceedingly large indirect subsidy.

With this kind of helping hand, the Ivory Coast economic performance since 1958 has been slightly short of phenomenal. Between 1958 and 1960 the value of exports rose 20 per cent. and during the first seven months of 1961 40 per cent. again, as compared with the similar period in 1960. The value of industrial output rose 21 per cent. in 1959 and 24 per cent. in 1960. Construction is booming: employment in the building industry grew 40 per cent. in 1960, and the number of licences granted for new industrial construction in the first half of 1961 more than doubled over the comparable period in 1960. From the government's new affluence all parts of the public sector have benefited, but particularly the educational system. Between 1958 and 1961 the number of students in schools almost doubled; the rate of school attendance bounded from 27 per cent. to 36 per cent. in three years. Secondary school attendance also doubled during this period, to almost 12,000. Well over a thousand Ivory Coasters are in universities, and the country's own university is well established.

The course of recent economic events in French-speaking West Africa suggests two general observations relating to the problem of political and economic integration in West Africa. The Senegal and Mali story indicates that in matters of the unification of states it may be better not to try at all than to try and fail. The severance of economic relations between

Senegal and Mali was unnecessary; it was the bitter offspring of anger and frustration. Had the two states remained politically separate, they could have retained their considerable economic integration with profit to both.

The Ivory Coast experience has implications with possibly ominous overtones for the future of African political unification. In part, that country's remarkable advance of the past three years is due to its political separation from its sister states in the Federation of French West Africa. Relieved of its heavy share in the costs of federal government, it has been able to spend locally most of its revenues. This has contributed to the buoyancy of its economy and the enlargement of its own network of social overhead facilities and public services. Also, its own industrial advance has been hastened by the tendency to reduce the place of Senegal's exports in the Ivory Coast market. Viewed from Abidjan, federation hardly appears to have been an economic advantage.

Is it possible to put forward as a general proposition that relatively richer states would do better to avoid political unions with poorer neighbours? Such a proposition is contrary to the general direction of thinking on the economics of integration. This body of thought tends to underline the advantages of union that accrue to the richer, more advanced regions; it warns of the danger that the poorer, more backward regions may be overwhelmed by the industrial head-start of the richer partners and remain permanent poor cousins – as in the American South, Southern Italy or, some have claimed, Uganda.

It does none the less seem that in West African conditions, a serious degree of political unification may not be economically advantageous to the relatively richer states. For such political unification is likely to mean some redistribution of available public investment resources from rich to poor regions. The poorer regions need schools and roads even more than the richer ones, and have less capacity to provide them. In West Africa, moreover, the poorer regions tend also to be more heavily populated, which would affect their political influence within the unified body. Within a politically unified state these regional demands would be presented with insistence, and, in the name of nation-building as well as equity, it can be expected that they would be met – to some extent at least.

With political and economic unification, then, the poorer regions will probably grow faster, but the richer ones more slowly than if they were not unified. Whether the overall rate of economic expansion of the area as a whole will be greater or less depends on many complex factors, about which little is yet known: the size of the public sector and possibilities for economies of scale in public services, the extent to which income redistribution is likely to occur, the extent of the differences in productivity of public investments in richer and poorer regions, and many others.

All of this indicates that exclusively economic considerations will not carry the argument for political integration in West Africa. It is just as well to recognize this from the outset, to recognize that the essential motor of political unification lies outside the economic realm. Unification represents a political act of faith which must be its own justification.

IIId: Social Change

In a civilization which has existed with few important basic changes, and none which can compare in scope with the industrial revolution, there has remained a closer and more constant reaction among the institutions of society. Where conflicts occur, modifications have been gradually evolved at a rate which has posed no real danger to the fundamentals of social organization on which (comparatively) harmonious social living must be based. Nevertheless, corporate life, like individual life, is never static, but is always changing, and such is the complexity and sensitivity of human life that these changes may appear to constitute, even to a stable society, a threat to its very existence.

Thus, the effects of automation on the distribution and functions of labour, or the so-called 'new morality' in sexual relations among the younger generations of post-war Western Europe, are examples of changes in relatively isolated sectors of social life which nevertheless seem disruptive and dangerous to the society concerned.

During the twentieth century the civilizations of Africa have been faced with comprehensive and radical changes to their entire social structures that, in their extent and range, are perhaps without parallel in the history of man. Furthermore, these changes have been by outside forces, and it is only more recently that we find adjustments and re-evaluations developing from within African societies themselves. The extent and remorselessness of social change is to be found in every sphere of human life. In religion, Islam came in from the East and, more recently, Christianity from the West, each with its own ethic, divine sanction and institutional framework. These touch not only upon belief, but influence the moral content of behaviour, the structure and values of marriage, and man's conception of himself, each profoundly related to the quality and content of social, as well as personal, life. In economics, as we have already seen, the values of the industrial market and the needs of the centralized machine have been superseding the need to produce only in order to live and the simpler values of dispersed villages of individuals. With this has come, among many other things, the intensification of the desire to possess and the gradual divorcement of man from the land. Mobility of labour, partly due to this desire to earn more in order to possess more, and partly to the rapid expansion of modern industry and the need for centralized (sometimes seasonal) labour forces, has inevitably affected family life. The whole structure of government has changed, as the centre of gravity moves away from tribal organization towards the one-party State. Modern science infiltrates the continent, demonstrating pragmatically the power of a different way of thinking about nature and its manifold problems.

The traditional, rural, tribal agriculturalist or pastoralist finds himself, almost overnight, employed by modern industry and living in an impersonal modern city. These changes, involving the meaning of life itself and man's relationship with his fellows, touch every aspect of existence, bringing problems, personal and social, parochial and national, that an observer from another continent finds it almost impossible to fully comprehend. The wonder is not that so much social change is occurring but that the African seems able to assimilate so much. Yet, in the countries where the progress of change has been most rapid, the exciting stage has been reached when the process of the new having displaced the old is almost completed, so that what is happening now is the development of new variations to modern problems that are uniquely African.

28

Some Problems of Social Change[1]

George Kimble

This summarizes the major characteristics of social change, its magnitude, speed, uneven incidence and superficiality.

To the African, all the blessings of the white man, his high standards of living and material comfort, his full employment (for so it seems to an African), the social ease of his life, all these things would be inherited as soon as 'independence' arrived. This is the first of several readings which demonstrate why this unhappily remains an African dream.

The most advertised characteristic of African social change is its magnitude. Students of the social sciences are constantly telling us that there is scarcely a tribe or a family in the whole of tropical Africa that lives today as it did a generation ago, or a field of investigation that does not repay a periodical going over for the evidences of change it discloses. Some of these evidences have been referred to in Volume 1: the break-down of old food taboos; the rise of new trades, towns and means of transport, and the new physical and economic mobility that results from it; the modification of indigenous cropping practices, and of the land tenure systems that went with them; the less general but significant modification of such indigenous practices as the keeping of cattle for currency, and pastoral nomadism; the increasing importance of women in commercial life; and the development of new forms of association, such as the co-operative society.

But the scope of the change is much wider than this. Consider the African's home, for instance. While most homes continue to be fashioned of traditional materials in the traditional way and pattern, increasing numbers, even in remote villages, are being built in the style of the simple European home. Single-storey dwellings with two or three rooms, they are made of brick or cement slab, galvanized iron, plaster, planed or pressed wood, equipped with some plumbing and perhaps electric light, and furnished with beds, chairs, a kitchen table, and dresser, curtains and linoleum. In the better-class African homes, in such towns as Léopoldville,

[1] Reprinted from *Tropical Africa*, Vol. 2, Twentieth Century Fund (New York, 1961).

Accra and Dakar, it is not unusual to find a kitchen range, an icebox, a shelf of books, and a radio or a portable gramophone with powers of endurance equalled only by the nerves of those who listen to it. Even in the bush it is exceptional to come upon a home that does not have some untraditional feature, such as an iron bedstead, pages from an American news magazine used as wallpaper, or cast off petrol tins used to brew native beer.

Consider, too, the personal and family life of the African. True, the impress of the past upon it is still plainly seen in most groups – in such diverse 'cultural traits' as lineage systems, age groups or sets, fertility rituals and rituals relating to puberty, marriage and the other great epochs of life, prayer to one's ancestors, hair styles, and the decoration of clay pots and dug-out canoes. But its outlines are becoming blurred, at some points to the extent of being hardly recognizable. The clothes an African wears are, with rare exceptions, no longer those of his own making or design. At least part of the food he eats is likely to have been raised by hands other than his or his family's; and some of his most highly prized panaceas are likely to be pills and potions no witch doctor ever thought of. Instead of having two or more wives, he may have but one. The work he does for at least part of the time is of a kind for which there is no tribal precedent; it is of a kind, moreover, that frequently needs to be done away from home and in company with men of other tribes.

It follows that for part of his time a man is *dépaysé* if not detribalized, footloose if not fancy-free, and able to forget his status role – often with results as damaging to his health and integrity as to the cohesion of his family. As for his wife, the chances are that she works harder than if she were in a polygynous household because there are fewer hands to help her; that she has little in common with her husband since his concerns are no longer solely those of the local clan; and still less in common with her children, who, most likely, spend part of their early years pursuing the white man's learning, of which she has no more than an inkling.

Of course, not all wives stay at home these days. Numbers of them go along with their husbands, living at or near their place of work. In Léopoldville alone there are quarters for more than 40,000 married couples, and many of them have been occupied by the same tenants for years on end. For the women, as for the men, the move to a town or a mining compound means more than a change of place. It means new ties and relationships, and difficulty in making them because of linguistic and sociological differences; new ways of doing things, such as drawing water from taps, washing the baby with soap, and disposing of human waste in a flush toilet. Often it means no way of doing things that have always been done by women, such as growing the family's food and running initiation schools and other kinds of secret organizations. Inability to do these things can result in a considerable loss of prestige.

The changes in home and family have been accompanied by changes of similar magnitude in the community. The kind of society desired by most modern African governments calls for co-operation on a bigger scale and in more ways than were needed in the days of tribal autonomy. The administering of public programmes, such as the building of roads, bridges and dams, the securing of watersheds against erosion, and the control of mosquitoes, locusts and other pests, call for co-operation by large inter-tribal groups, rather than small clans. So does the raising of money to finance such programmes. So also does the organization of peasant cash crop economies capable of competing, as they must, with the highly capitalized and well-run economies of older lands. What is true of these largely non-political concerns is true of political ones. Democracy may begin at home – in the grassroots of the family, clan and tribe – but it needs the winds and rains of a wider domain to make it strong. In these days especially, democratic governments need all the good men they can find to come to the aid of the party, and no one tribe has enough of them.

All of this helps to explain the coming into existence in recent years of the local district council and treasury, the voluntary self-help association, the mass literacy and adult education movement, the co-operative society, the political party, and both regional and federal forms of government.

SPEED

A no less striking characteristic of African social change, in the opinion of many, is the speed with which it has come about. Certainly it is not difficult to find supporting evidence. Thus, it is still less than a hundred years since David Livingstone witnessed (1871) the massacre by slavers of 300 to 400 market people – mostly women – on the banks of the Lualaba River. It is less than seventy years since the British came upon the last evidence of wholesale human sacrifice in Nigeria (1897 in Benin City). It is less than sixty years since the last slave caravan was intercepted (1903) in what is now the Federation of Rhodesia and Nyasaland. And there are Africans still living in that territory who clearly remember seeing the man who fathered the Federation, Cecil John Rhodes.

There is scarcely a theme of African life on which some rapid changes have not been rung. An instance may be cited from education. A few miles outside Nairobi there is a boarding school – the Alliance High

School – for 200 African boys, drawn from all parts of Kenya. In eleven years down to 1955, only one boy had failed to graduate, and the next year he passed the graduating examination – which was the same as that sat for by thousands of the brighter products of British schools. Nearly half the graduates, averaging fifty a year, received the equivalent of a straight A. In such matters as athletic, musical and theatrical ability, industry, courtesy and courage, nearly all of them, in the opinion of the headmaster, would have stood comparison with their European counterparts. But what is perhaps most significant from our standpoint is the fact that nearly all of them were only one generation removed from total illiteracy. Until they went to this school they knew practically nothing of the meaning of money. Few of them came from homes where either books or newspapers were regularly read, or where there was any intelligent conversation beyond that necessary for the conduct of domestic affairs. And this school, though a leader in its field, is by no means untypical of what has been happening elsewhere, in almost every territory. To cite another instance: down to the early 1940's there was only one institution in the whole of tropical Africa where students could do work of university calibre, namely, Fourah Bay College, at Freetown, Sierra Leone. Today more than a dozen such institutions exist in almost as many territories.

Similarly impressive statistics can be gleaned in the field of health and health services. Whereas at the turn of the century less than half of all West African children are believed to have lived to their first birthday, today the ratio is nearer seven out of ten, and in some areas (e.g. Lagos, Nigeria) more than nine out of ten. And whereas in the first five years of the present century the number of people killed by sleeping sickness in Uganda was of the order of 100,000, in the first five years after mid-century the number killed by it in the same territory was almost certainly less than 100.[1] Several other territories can point to equally dramatic declines in a wide range of diseases.

In the field of government administration there have likewise been changes as conspicuous for their speed as for their size. It goes without saying that at the beginning of the present century there were no ballot boxes, no political parties, and, beyond Liberia and Ethiopia, no autonomous governments. No Africans held posts in any colonial administration, and very few in any civil service above the rank of clerk. And there was

---

[1] *Notified* deaths from sleeping sickness during this quinquennium averaged less than two a year, according to the *Annual Report of the Medical Department [of the Uganda Protectorate] for the year ended 31st December 1955*, p. 14. Government Printer (Entebbe, 1957).

as yet no serious talk of partnership, let alone self-government. Today, regular elections are held in a score of the major territories; there are 10 million qualified electors in Nigeria alone, and in the region as a whole not less than 40 million. Of the major territories, five (Liberia, Guinea, Ghana, the Republic of Sudan and Ethiopia) are sovereign (1959). Five (Nigeria, the French Cameroons, Togo, the Belgian Congo and Somalia) became sovereign in 1960. Several other territories are self-governing entities of the French Community; Southern Rhodesia is a self-governing British colony. Most of the rest have at least a measure of control over their internal affairs. In almost all of them the Africanizing process in the civil service, business industry and the professions is proceeding about as fast as the supply of 'Europeanized' Africans will allow. Many of the leaders thrown up by these rising political tides would scarcely be recognized by their own fathers. Some of them would have difficulty in recognizing themselves as they were ten or twenty years ago, so great is the change wrought in them by the changes around them.

What is frequently as striking as the speed of social change is its acceleration. In the 1920's and 1930's the speed of change in education, social welfare and government was barely more than a trot, even on the fastest African courses. It was fast only by comparison with the customary tempo of African life. Since World War II, on the same courses, it has become a gallop that gives the spectators almost as much to think about as the riders, and keeps the backers in a state of nerves. And more horses are getting into the field all the time.

Statistics of change, like those of horse racing, are apt to obey the law of diminishing returns. But, since it is impossible to measure acceleration without them, one or two more must be cited. For our first example we take the growth of what the Belgians call the *population extra-coutumière*, the population living outside the tribal area. At the beginning of the century not a single Congolese African, it may be safely said, resided outside his tribal area. Not only would he have been scared to, but he would have had no way of making an honest living outside. As late as the outbreak of World War II fewer than a million Congolese were living extra-tribally. By 1951, however, 2 million, and by 1959 more than 3 million – approximately 25 per cent. of the total African population in the Belgian Congo – were living away from their tribes.

For a second illustration we go to Uganda, and to an expression of change that is perhaps as much economic as social, namely, the growth of the co-operative movement. The figures speak for themselves: the number of co-operative societies (exclusive of producers' marketing unions) increased from 118 in 1947 to 1,423 in 1957; membership surged from 7,447 to 136,172 between the same years; and working capital grew more than fivefold, from less than £20,000 to more than £100,000.[1]

But one must not get the impression that everyone – African, Asian and European alike – is happy about the changes taking place, or that everyone has been greatly changed by them. On the contrary; if there are two things as certain as the magnitude and speed of the changes taking place in the social life of tropical Africa, they are the patchiness of the change and the superficial look of much of it.

UNEVEN INCIDENCE

Some areas show far fewer evidences of social change than others. Put a traveller down among the tribal peoples of the great escarpment country of Ethiopia and he might think that he was back in the sixteenth century with Pedro de Covilham and his Portuguese colleagues who wrote of them. If he should see these people coming toward him with garlands of flowers round their necks and playing pan pipes, he might feel even more at home reading a book of Greek mythology. A traveller would also have no difficulty in finding 'stubborn unlaid ghosts' in such out-of-the-way places as the southern shore of Lake Rudolf in northern Kenya, where the El Molo tribe, one of the smallest in Africa, seemingly prefers extinction to change; in the Kalahari Desert, where the Bushman still uses the cupid's bow in his love-making ritual and often manages still to live without any of the white man's aids; and in the Lobi country deep in the interior of the Ivory Coast, where the custom that sons murder either their fathers or mothers to prove their manhood is still honoured when the authorities aren't looking.

Nor would a traveller need to go as far as this from 'civilization' to find the past. He could find it on the airfield at Malakal in the Sudan, if by chance a Dinka had chosen to graze his herd around its margins; for a Dinka continues to make few concessions to the Western view of propriety and none where clothing is concerned. He could find it in the Aberdare Mountains of Kenya, within sight of Nairobi on a good day; for it is here that the Mau Mau had their hide-outs and conjured up the witches of a pagan past. He could see whole panoramas of the past from the windows of a train running through the Middle Belt of Nigeria or the back country of Angola.

On the other hand, put a traveller down in Léopoldville's western suburb of Kalina and no amount of familiarity with Stanley's travels would

[1] *Co-operative Information Bulletin for the British Commonwealth*, various issues (published by the Co-operative Union Ltd., Manchester, England).

enable him to identify it as the place where the explorer persuaded some 400 Congolese chiefs to sign treaties of friendship. For almost everything about Kalina except the climate is a cultural import. Its houses and apartments are built in the style favoured in Palm Beach and Miami. Its streets are well paved and lined with shade trees – as few indigenous village roads are. Its shops are stocked with high-quality products of European and North American factories. Its restaurants feature the finest in imported foods. Its places of worship, and its schools are of Belgian design and Palestinian inspiration.

Or put the traveller down in Kampala, Uganda, near the Kabaka's Enclosure, with a copy of John Hanning Speke's *Journal of the Discovery of the Source of the Nile*, and about the only things to strike him as familiar would be the fence of 'tall yellow reeds of the common Uganda tiger grass' around the palace, the regal hauteur of the womenfolk about its gates, and the very general liking for a potent native beer known as *pombe*. As to the rest – the four-storeyed Bulange (the parliament building of the Kabaka's government) equipped with electricity and a public address system; the hilltop cathedrals, Prostestant and Catholic; Makerere College with its many-styled halls of learning and leisure rampant on a field of green, its English-speaking student body drawn from eighty tribal backgrounds and living in the manner hallowed by centuries of British academic convention; and, not less important, the business quarter, where Europeans, Asians and Africans match wares and wits, stir the poor man's imagination with pictures of plumbing and flatter the rich man's pride with talk of the latest in fashions for himself and his wife – all this and much more is out of Speke's world.

The same could be said of any of a hundred other cities. And not of cities only; there are countrysides in which the traveller of earlier days would be hard put to it to find his social bearings.

In much of the Kikuyu country of Kenya, for instance, dispersed settlement has given place to nucleated settlement. This 'villagization' programme, originally intended as a security device against Mau Mau terrorists, has proved so widely acceptable that a whole new way of African life is being built around it. To reduce the walking time to and from the characteristically scattered bits of farm land (which was increased for most farmers as a result of the programme), the Kenya government has been pushing through a parallel programme of land consolidation by exchange. Many hundreds of square miles of Kikuyuland have already been divided into compact small holdings to which owners have a clear title and on which they can more readily apply the principles of good husbandry and so make more money to support, among other things, the greatly improved services

311

now being made available to the villagers. Each of the larger villages has a health clinic, a clean and reliable water supply, a school, a recreation centre and church. The shops are much better than those found in the bush, where the turnover is slow and consequently the range of offerings small. In most villages babies – formerly back-loaded almost everywhere – can be left at day nurseries in charge of trained sitters while their mothers are at work in the fields. Many villages have facilities to train women in hygiene, housekeeping and – greatest innovation of all! – ball playing. For the men the 'villagization' programme means change, too: more scope for the leaders among them to show their quality, and more reason for the led to see that the quality is good; closer touch with the outside world by means of radio, news-sheets, pep talks, and the comings and goings of neighbours; firmer discipline, but more distractions; more problems, but higher hopes.

Many other rural communities provide equally notable evidences of change. Some, like those of the Gezira in the Republic of Sudan and the upper Niger valley in the Sudanese Republic (formerly French Sudan), virtually owe their existence to the white man's initiative. Frequently the only things the people attracted to such developments have in common are their tiredness, poverty, wretchedness and yearning to be free. The welding of such people into cohesive groups inevitably calls for social improvisation. Other communities have undergone an economic metamorphosis – in the case of the Kipsigis of Kenya, from nomadic pastoralists to sedentary farmers. No community can make such a break, involving its internal and external relationships, without rewriting parts of its social testament. Then there are many communities, mostly small, that have embraced Christianity as a living faith. In them, the New Testament has become the guide to both belief and conduct. And any community that takes the New Testament for its guide quickly finds itself in the midst of social change of the most radical kind.

SUPERFICIALITY

When we have said all this, however, the fact remains that we have been talking only about 'minorities', and that among these much of the evident change has a superficial, or 'topped-up', look about it. As for the 'majorities', in most cases they continue to think of themselves as belonging to the old social order. To most of the cattle-keeping Masai, for instance, the world of class-room, clinic, lathe, legislative assembly and Christian church is still as foreign as the world of their crop-raising neighbours, the Kikuyu and Chagga. They want to have as little to do with either as possible, and as a rule they have their wish. So, too, the pygmies of the Congo basin forest. From time to time they may do some light work for the local *commandant*, but they show little desire to live like him, or to trade the seclusion of their hutments for the exposure of his housing projects. Nor is this point of view held only by herders and hunters. Tens of thousands of cultivators find that the newcomers' homes, offices, workshops, mines and plantations where they sometimes work as labourers are new jungles – sources of food and excitement, but also of fear and trouble, frequently coming to them in the guise of sickness. As soon as they can conveniently do so, they go back home, taking with them such symbols of their prowess as they have managed to come by. They have been in the new world, but they are not of it; to all appearances, they are not much interested in becoming part of it.

But what of those who have come to think of themselves, or to be thought of, as changed men, and as being the product of the white man's world as much as of their own? Of these, it is arguable that many – perhaps a majority – are still commuters, citified Westerners one week, bush Africans the next, their permanent address and roots being still deep in the country. They may live as Europeans do, work as they do, and worship as they do, but after a while the European mantle slips from their shoulders and they are children of the African earth again – until they weary of the role or are forced to abandon it temporarily. Many miners, machine shop workers, clerks and artisans 'commute' in this fashion; many doctors, lawyers, teachers and other professional men find it easy and pleasant to do the same, though not, it would seem, without impairment of their skills.

And what of those who have done with the bush, who never leave the world of the European? They may be lost to the tribe, but rarely are they lost to the world of the tribe and rarely do they seek to be. Peter Abrahams, himself an African-born negro, makes this point very clearly in his *A Wreath for Udomo*. Set in a west African territory called Pluralia, and reading in places like an eye-witness account of social change in the Gold Coast of the early 1950's, the story is largely framed around the 'dual personality' of a promising young politician, Mhendi, who could never forget that there were two Pluralias. He was born between two worlds, 'that of the cities and the white men and that of the countryside and the old tribal ways. And though I had been to school in the cities, and had gone to Europe, I was still a son of the tribe. They couldn't think of me as anything but a son of the tribe. I couldn't outrage my old father's great dreams.'

Meanwhile it seems that plenty of Africans are less fastidious, taking what they fancy from the foreigner and also keeping what they fancy of their own, much as children do when faced with a supply of new toys which they have not space to stow. And as with children, the things they fancy frequently provide the student with a wonderful field for sociological and psychological inquiry. More important, they frequently provide the advocate of early political autonomy with a shock. For no man is greatly changed by acts of parliament, by grant of licence to teach or to practice law, by adoption of another man's dress, or even by the rite of baptism into another man's religion. How he is changed 'in depth' – in his thinking and feeling, his values and judgements – is beyond our competence to tell; but of one thing we can be sure: time is a factor in the process. In most of tropical Africa, there apparently hasn't yet been enough time.

29

From the Old Culture to the New[1]

Guy Hunter

This reading, which follows logically from the last, sets out in further detail the content of the general problem created by so much change happening so quickly to so many.

'Industrialization is a way of life as well as of production and distribution. . . . Each culture emphasizes certain values which determine the way of life of a people.'[2]

SOME CONTRASTS

African political leaders have accepted with enthusiasm the aim of economic development. But African societies, shaped by their earlier and quite different necessities, still contain within them, as living forces, the personal attitudes and social institutions of the older world. If we are to understand a little better the outlook and behaviour of Africans, of the men who may come as applicants for a job in a factory or a bank, it is necessary to break down this clash of values into the realities of everyday life. What does it feel like to live, not between two worlds, but simultaneously in both of them?

Here generalization is particularly difficult. Both geographically and culturally, the spread of Western influence has been so uneven. Some African societies, not in deepest forest or desert but just off natural communications, remain to this day extraordinarily isolated. The aeroplane from Kariba to Livingstone passes over the valley of the Gwembe Tonga, now largely flooded by the rising lake. Elizabeth Colson has described how, after the withdrawal of the Mission stations in the 1930's:

> It was almost twenty years before the Valley would again have Europeans resident within it. . . . No roads led into it. Access could only be had by footpaths, and these, as they wound through the rugged escarpments,

---

[1] Reprinted from *The New Societies of Tropical Africa* (Oxford University Press, under the auspices of the Institute of Race Relations, 1962).

[2] K. A. Busia, 'The Impact of Industrialisation on West Africa', Nigerian Institute of Social Research Conference, 1960.

were of such a nature that a bicycle was a hindrance rather than a help. (p. 31.)

Until the coming of the roads in 1950, everything had to be transported on the back or head or occasionally on donkey-back, and the nearest source of trade goods was some two or three days' travel from the Zambesi. . . . Since 1950, imports have increased, and the people are becoming progressively more dependent upon them. But there are still many women who have never struck a match, never held an electric torch or threaded a needle. People yearn for clothing and salt, and will work to obtain them. Other items seldom enter into their immediate calculations. (p. 36.)[1]

Some cultures, though not inaccessible, have resisted change far more strongly than others. This is true of the strong Islamic cultures of the West African savannah, and of some groups, such as the Pakot (Suk) of East Africa, who have a highly specialized culture centred on a single occupation. Again, some of the strongly structured political systems have been able to absorb change within a traditional framework of institutions, while others, less coherent and definite, have tended to disintegrate.[2] The reasons why one local culture rejects change which another will accept, or abandons one custom while clinging to another, are too complex and various for description here. It is enough to say that a similar European impact may have quite different results on two African groups not fifty miles apart.

Again, some African peoples, particularly on the West Coast, not only had longer European contacts but had evolved an urban and commercial life of their own which was perhaps more easily blended with the Western system when it came in full force. By contrast, in much of East and Central Africa, the money economy scarcely existed as late as 1900, save in the Indian and Arab trade of the East Coast ports.

In addition to these differences of geography, culture and intensity of modernizing influences (whether from European or African leadership), there are differences within any single group, mainly between those with some formal education and the rest. But this is by no means the single cause. Men who have migrated to employment, soldiers or traders who have travelled widely may become deeply influenced by new ideas and patterns of behaviour.

Thus the rate and depth of change can only be measured by careful analysis of individual areas and of the life history of special groups within them. But there is a single *direction* of change which is applicable as to

[1] E. Colson, *The Social Organisation of the Gwembe Tonga* (Kariba Studies, Manchester University Press for Rhodes-Livingstone Institute, 1960).

[2] See studies of Rwanda and Urundi by Ethel M. Albert, 'Socio-Political Organisation and Receptivity to Change', University of New Mexico, *South Western Journal of Anthropology*, Vol. 16, no. 1 (Spring 1960).

some factors all over Tropical Africa and as to others at least over very wide areas. The traveller in East, Central and West Africa cannot fail to be struck by the repetition of certain situations in every one of a dozen countries on his route. Whether the process is far advanced or barely started and with all the variations of custom and environment and influence it moves always one way. This chapter will consider some specific aspects of this change, the groups to whom it chiefly applies, and finally some of the social problems which result.

One measure of change lies in the degree to which everyday events are ascribed to rational or scientific causes rather than to spiritual or magical influences. Jacques Maritain once argued that until the Church had conquered animism in Western Europe, the age of science could not begin – the electric telegraph could not come if a powerful spirit was believed to sit on every pole.

The situation in modern Africa is extremely complex. On the one hand there are the traditional African religious beliefs, usually called animism, very widely connected with religious reverence and service to the spirits of ancestors. 'Ancestor worship' – a phrase which is apt to carry wrong implications of idolatry in Western ears – represents a strong belief in the continuing power and influence of the spirits of the dead, and it has had, as in many advanced cultures such as that of China, many beneficial effects in the support of tribal ethics; it is connected, though in widely differing ways, with parallel beliefs in the existence of God and of other superhuman spirits. Alongside religious belief there has also been belief in magic. Magic is usually distinguished from religion in that the religious believer petitions for help, which he may not receive, while the man who uses magic believes that he has a key to certain occult forces which are compelled to act if the right formula is used. Into this situation have come two new and major religions, Christianity and Islam, both very widely propagated and accepted. It is probably safest to say that, for the majority of African people who have come in contact with these new religions, three elements of belief continue to exist simultaneously – the cult of ancestors, magic and either Christianity or Islam. Dr Mair observed in Buganda: 'As regards the recourse to magic for supernatural aid, my impression is that with the Baganda Christianity has neither discredited nor replaced the traditional methods.'[1] Claude Tarditz[2] observes that in many Christian families of Porto Novo the customary ceremonies of the ancestor cult were

[1] L. P. Mair, *An African People in the Twentieth Century* (London, Routledge, 1934).

[2] Tarditz, op. cit. Dr Field also points out that the frequent 'confessions' (self-accusations) to witchcraft which occur in mental disturbance help to confirm popular belief in the existence of witches.

observed in addition to a Christian burial service; and in the Cameroons it has been noted that although 74 per cent. of African plantation workers gave their religion as Christian, both animist and magical practices were almost universal.[1] In Ghana Dr Margaret Field[2] observed that many of those who came to consult local priest-oracles at their shrines were Christians.

Probably each of the three elements of belief fulfils a need. The ancestor cult is so deeply interwoven with tribal customs and rituals and rules of family life that to abandon it altogether would mean the most painful severance from the family and community. In honouring such observances the highly educated and Christian African would be showing a certain piety towards tradition and towards other, less sophisticated, members of his family; they may arouse in him the same recollections of childhood and the unity of a community which an urban agnostic in Europe would feel at a funeral in his old village church. Islam and Christianity provide for the need of a higher religion, which includes the promise of life after death, and both have a certain prestige value, since in both cases they were associated with conquering civilizations. Finally, magic remains a living reality, never far beneath the surface. Many anthropologists[3] have pointed out that magic tends to be associated with situations of uncertainty, lack of knowledge, lack of security in personal relations. In consequence it is apt to grow, rather than decrease, in urban situations where Africans are cut off from the support of their home community and feel insecurity in most acute form. Indeed, there is a tendency in modern Africa for the best of the traditional religion to be degraded into magical practices; an improvement in the stability and conditions of town life could probably do most to halt this. Many employers in Africa could testify to the fear of magic among employees – we were told of one man in the Copperbelt who had reached one of the highest ranks open to Africans with some education who abandoned his job with its accumulated long-service rights to return to his village because he feared that his life was threatened by witchcraft.

Superstition, as we know in Europe, never dies completely, and is particularly liable to reappear in times of war, or insecurity and anxiety. It is a form of extra insurance. Indeed, those in Europe who have abandoned all living Christian belief will treat Christianity as a superstition – a mother who believes far more firmly in the efficacy of a 'polio' injection

[1] E. and S. Ardener and W. A. Warmington, *Plantation and Village in the Cameroons* (London, Oxford University Press, 1960).

[2] M. J. Field, *Search for Security* (London, Faber and Faber, 1960).

[3] e. g. Malinowski, Firth, Richards.

than in Baptism will have her child baptized to be on the safe side; and here Christianity is in a similar relation to science as animism to Christianity in Africa. In terms of the entry of African peoples into a modern economy it is not the ancestor cult as such which is likely to be a hindrance; belief in magic, with its inhibiting effects on ambition (for success invites jealousy and ill-will) and its results in irrational behaviour is far more serious.

A second, and vital, index of change lies in the degree to which obligations inside 'Western' relationships, and outside the family, are felt to have binding force. A factory or County Council or the Civil Service demand special forms (not degrees) of moral behaviour which are sometimes strange to African values and sometimes conflict with them. The primary, overriding, obligation to the family, the custom of bringing a chief a small present or 'dash' when asking assistance, are deeply embedded in African custom. But the factory personnel officer should not, in Western eyes, give all the jobs to his relatives; the Councillor should not expect a 'dash' if he presses a constituent's complaint; confidential information is supposed to be held in trust for the institution and cannot be passed on to relatives. Africans understand well enough that a man may have different roles in society – as head of family, as chief or in a ritual capacity. But the number of roles was small, and each had its morals attached to it. The new circumstances introduce many new roles – manager, District Councillor, civil servant, trade unionist. To Africans who grasp these new opportunities their own tradition does not supply any corresponding set of rules and their behaviour may conflict with what seems to a European to be the elementary demands of the role. In the field of financial honesty, the issue has been clouded by the presence of Europeans. Both white individuals and their institutions were felt to be almost infinitely rich. They would not really miss a few pounds, and indeed, had they been African, they would have been under some obligation to help the poor. Moreover, they were an alien group, to which the rules for internal behaviour in the African community might not apply. There are many signs that where wholly African institutions are involved, a different attitude is shown. It has apparently been no disgrace to defraud a County Council which is felt to be part of 'government', but to steal the funds of a tribal association or a cotton co-operative primary society is likely to bring the offender into most serious trouble with his own people. The growth of commercial honesty and of the other qualities which are needed in the new social economy will depend both on a much fuller identification of the African with institutions felt to be genuinely his own, and on a gradual training in the moral systems which attach to the new roles.

It is hard to overstate the importance of the family relationship in African society. Africans invest in personal relationships,[1] because they supply their ultimate security. When the Wankie[2] Coal Mine dismissed 7,000 African workers in a week in the 1931 slump, they 'just disappeared' – in fact, to relatives and people who had obligations to them. Until an alternative system of social security appears, family obligations are likely to remain paramount, even where they conflict with the obligations of the new type of society.

The recognition of authority is another point of difference. Most Tropical African societies recognize authority in age, in traditional office, in high lineage or sometimes in another tribal group felt to be superior. The industrial hierarchy is built upon technical skill, experience and seniority in employment, which have little to do with age and nothing with lineage or tribal history. The African who finds himself within such a hierarchy is in a very strange world.

Closely related – but not identical – with concepts of authority are those of status. The new westernized society introduces new status ranks – to have Cambridge Overseas School Certificate is a high status symbol, particularly in rural society. These new symbols tend to replace the older ones, or at least to coexist with them. Professor Nadel records how a young, educated African in Bida (Northern Nigeria) remarked to him: 'All our native ranks and titles mean nothing today; what has meaning are only offices under the Native Authority, posts which carry real influence and wealth.'[3] This is a deeply significant – and probably exaggerated – remark, since Nupe society, which Professor Nadel studied, was firmly divided by various ranking systems, as well as by slavery and patronage, as were other sections of the Fulani empire.[4] The caste system in Senegal (nobles, freemen, artisans, freed slaves, griots, slaves, in descending order) is another example of a status system which cannot be fitted into a Western pattern of education, free opportunity and technical hierarchies. It is easy for Europeans to forget how complex such systems are, and how far down in the social scale they run. Even the humblest official of the westernized administration may hold a very high ranking in relation to the African villager.[5]

The relative emancipation of women will provide another obvious

---

[1] See Elizabeth Colson in *Africa Today*, supra. [2] Near Livingstone, Rhodesia.

[3] S. F. Nadel, *A Black Byzantium* (London, Oxford University Press, 1942).

[4] M. G. Smith, *Government in Zaggan* (London, Oxford University Press, 1959).

[5] 'Le facteur des postes d'Oran apparait effroyablement privilégié par rapport de la masse de la population, alors qu'à Arras ou ailleurs il se sent au contraire une personnage très modeste.' M. de Schryver, *L'avenir politique du Congo Belge* (Brussels, Institut Belge de Science Politique, 1960).

conflict between the old culture and the new. But it would be easy to read into this a quite false idea of the status of women in a great many traditional African societies. Apart from the strict Muslim groups, there are many peoples in Africa – for example, the Yoruba of Western Nigeria – where women have by tradition a strong element of economic and social independence; nor are these only the matrilineal[1] societies. Perhaps in almost all African societies, the woman has a 'kingdom' of her own, with both its obligations and its recognition. She frequently has responsibility for cultivation of land; for the preparation of food, with all its customary significance; for rituals concerned with fertility; and in settling a host of questions concerned with the marriage of young people and the obligations connected with it. 'It is because she bears a heavy responsibility that her position in the family and with her husband is a secure one.'[2] Emancipation, in the sense of adopting a Western pattern of behaviour, may in fact deprive the African woman, at least temporarily, both of her duties and her honoured place, particularly if she is living in a large mixed town, far from the ritual of the hearthstones and the ceremonies which helped to express and formalize her place in village life. Only a few have broken right through to a full education and a fully westernized 'professional' life.

Attitudes to work may again show a profound difference between the old and the new culture. Professor Biesheuvel[3] has noted the almost compulsive attitude to the virtues of hard work which colours European society. Whether or not this springs, as Max Weber suggested, from the Protestant ethic, it has certainly been deeply imprinted by the further development of our competitive and technical society. Work is seen, not only as the condition of progress, but as a positive moral good, so that missionaries were constantly preaching 'habits of industry' and 'the dignity of labour'. Certainly, such an attitude is far removed from that of the older African way of life. Europeans have constantly declaimed against the 'apathy', the incorrigible laziness of African tribesmen, sometimes with moral condemnation pure and simple, sometimes with excuses of hot climate, malnutrition or debilitating disease. But if African life was leisurely, if there was time to gossip under a shady tree, to have a three-day beer-drink, to go off hunting more for fun than for any real expectation of a bag, it was partly because life did not offer great vistas of possible headway and achievement. Africans were not pursued by the Western devil called 'Time is Money', nor the anxiety to 'go places' when there was no

[1] i.e. tracing descent through the female line. It does not imply a matriarchy.

[2] D. Westermann, *The African Today and Tomorrow* (London, Oxford University Press for International African Institute, 1949).

[3] S. Biesheuvel, *Race, Culture and Personality* (Johannesburg, South African Institute of Race Relations, 1959).

place to go. Even hunger might not be worth the extra effort of forethought and labour needed to avoid it.[1] Work was necessary for subsistence, to fulfil tribal and family obligations, to amass bride-price or perhaps gain a mark of status: it had no personal moral connotation.[2] To avoid its boredom, it might often be done in company, with song and mutual encouragement. 'Probably the greatest shock to the newly educated African in paid employment is that he has to work all day and every day.'[3]

The African attitude to land, so different from the commercial attitude, has been mentioned already. It is the symbol of a world where access to land, and therefore to food, is the basic security, however poor the land may be. The transition from a society where security is based on land (with its dangers of floods and famines) to one where it rests on social organization (full employment – with its dangers of disorganization or breakdown) is a profound change and one which stirs deep emotion and fears.

Another field of contrast in the early period of contact between the Western and the African traditional culture has been that of African attitudes towards economic exchange and the use of money. It has sometimes been said that at least some African peoples altogether lack an economic sense. Cyril Ehrlich[4] quotes a case in Uganda where a cattle owner, who would refuse 600 shillings for a beast, is prepared to exchange it quite happily for a 300 shilling bicycle; or where Baganda peasants would sell trees worth 100 shillings for 10 shillings. Dr Mair[5] has noticed similar cases in Uganda and Elizabeth Hoyt[6] in Kenya. In fact, the main proposition only makes sense in relation to a particular stage of society. Professor Polyani,[7] in a symposium on the nature of the market in early civilizations, has pointed out that modern conceptions of the economy are entirely strange in societies which redistribute goods through multiple reciprocal obligations based on kinship and other ties.

The disembedded economy of the nineteenth century stood apart from the rest of society, more especially from the political and governmental systems. In a market economy the production and distribution of material

---

[1] See particularly Richards, *Land, Labour and Diet in Northern Rhodesia*. The last pages have a balanced assessment of this particular situation among the Bemba.
[2] For a detailed analysis of attitudes to work in a primitive community outside Africa (Tikopia, Solomon Islands), see Raymond Firth, 'Work and Community in a Primitive Society' in Report of H.R.H. The Duke of Edinburgh's Study Conference, 1956, vol. II (London, Oxford University Press, 1957).
[3] Field, op. cit.   [4] Ehrlich, op. cit.   [5] Mair, op. cit.
[6] E. Hoyt, 'Economic Sense and the African', *Africa*, XXII, 1952.
[7] Karl Polyani, Conrad M. Arensberg and Harry W. Pearson (Ed.), *Trade and Market in the Early Empires* (Illinois, The Free Press and The Falcon's Wing Press, 1957).

goods in principle is carried on through a self-regulating system of price-making markets. It is governed by laws of its own, the so-called laws of supply and demand, and motivated by fear of hunger and hope of gain.

In contrast, in societies regulated by status rather than contract, and relying on reciprocity:

> The elements of the economy are here embedded in non-economic institutions, the economic process itself being instituted through kinship, marriage, age-groups, secret societies, totemic associations and public solemnities. The term 'economic' life would here have no obvious meaning.

Thus land, or cattle, or goods would pass at betrothal or marriage, marking a change of status, gifts or food would move from person to person according to the rules of the social situation. Nor is there an exact quantitative measurement – 'reciprocity demands adequacy of response, not mathematical quality'.

Firth,[1] in a different context, makes the same observation:

> In a primitive society, there is no relationship which is of a purely economic character. . . . Therein lies the strength of primitive society, in that it enlists the binding forces of one aspect of society to support those of another.

Finally, Dr Mair[2] illustrates very well the difference in approach:

> When one compares the reason why cattle are desired with the reason why backcloths are desired, it becomes clear that different commodities are valued from points of view so different that the values cannot be reduced to a single common denominator . . . the possession of most goods is prized for its own sake, rather than for the sake of other goods which might be acquired by disposing of them.

These quotations help to explain the exchange of a cow for a bicycle in what seems an 'uneconomic' way. They do, however, represent the pure theory rather than the changing facts of the present situation. Even in status systems, fairly precise numbers of cattle or other goods become recognized as the right quantity for bride price or other transactions; and as soon as some form of currency becomes common, there is a gradual move towards reducing transactions to a single common standard. The naïveté of early (1910) Baganda cotton-growers,[3] who are said to have delivered their cotton at the collecting point and walked off

[1] R. Firth, *Primitive Economies of the New Zealand Maori* (New York, E. P. Dutton and Company, 1929).

[2] Mair, op. cit.

[3] See P. G. Powesland, *Economic Policy and Labour* (Ed. W. Elkan), East African Studies, no. 10, 1957.

without waiting for payment (presumably regarding it as a form of tax) does not last long in modern circumstances. While it is important to remember that many African societies are still only beginning to separate out 'economic' from other activities, it would be utterly false to assume that in some way 'Africans' lack economic sense. Professor William O. Jones[1] has demonstrated, over a wide field, that where Africans have a real chance of understanding the issues involved, they have a shrewd sense of economic advantage; and indeed from personal observation, it is difficult not to be struck by the amazing, if sometimes misplaced, ingenuity with which many Africans will snatch at the smallest economic opportunity.[2] As will appear later, some well-intentioned agricultural settlement schemes and some incentives used in industry have come to grief for the very reason that the Africans concerned have worked out what will pay them best more accurately than their employers. The transition from single calculations of what pays to the more complex economic sense which involves calculation of capital, depreciation, ton-miles or machine-utilization obviously will take time and formal education, as it does in the West.

Finally, at the level of more personal life and of institutions such as marriage, the transition from old to new ways is often painful and difficult. There is much evidence, particularly among middle-class Africans, of a movement by both men and women towards accepting the Western monogamous pattern, and towards a much more personal relationship between husband and wife – a movement from a contract between families to a companionship between individuals. An inquiry among Ghanaian students showed that 73 per cent. of the sample thought polygamy 'definitely backward', and that 87 per cent. (80 per cent. of males and 94 per cent. of females) thought that 'love' was the most important factor in marriage.[3] The same group were predominantly hostile to the traditional matrilineal pattern by which a maternal uncle assumes responsibility for children. In the same way, and for more commercial reasons, matrilineal inheritance (by the wife's lineage, not by the husband's children) is becoming increasingly unpopular, since a man who builds up a business cannot hand it on to his sons.[4]

[1] W. O. Jones, 'Economic Man in Africa', *Food Research Institute Studies*, vol. I, no. 2 (Stanford University, May 1960).

[2] For instance the man who obtained free from a bank a large packet of folders, with captioned illustrations showing the virtues of a savings account, and sold them at 2*d*. each as a simple English Primer.

[3] T. P. Omari, 'Attitudes in West Africa towards Marriage', *British Journal of Sociology*, vol. XI, no. 3 (September 1960).

[4] Peter Garlick, *African Traders in Kumasi* (University College of Ghana, 1959). See also 'The Matrilinear System and Business Enterprise' (N.I.S.E.R. Conference, 1960).

These changes in personal life are far more important than the somewhat trivial 'proofs' of them which can be given in a few statistics. It is a fundamental quality and attitude to life which is at issue. In the old world, the community comprehended the individuals within it, supported and sanctioned them, surrounded them with a cocoon of fine-spun relationships, related them to the ancestors of the tribe and to its posterity. In return, it exacted certain disciplines and obligations – the choice of marriage partners which would best serve the harmony and propriety of family life, the duty to contribute in work and wealth to the common good. Against this world must be set the Western emphasis on the free individual, free to develop capacities and powers, to choose his friends and his wife, to move beyond his home community into a wider society, to insulate himself against demands from less successful relations or neighbours – but free also to fail, and to find little but the impersonal support of State charity if he does. The new opportunities carry with them the new burden of individual freedom to the deepest level of personality. They involve personal moral responsibility. They involve the strength to live without dependence.

30

The Status of African Women[1]

H. J. Symons

The position of women in tribal society is ambiguous. Although they shoulder a greater burden of manual work than, comparatively, is the custom in most modern societies, they nevertheless exert considerable influence and authority, as was pointed out by the late Dr Herskovits.[2] But in matters touching upon the development of new ideas and patterns of action consequent upon the arrival of the industrial revolution in Africa, they remain far behind their menfolk. This is particularly true in those areas of life, among them education and all positions of *formal* social authority, where they have traditionally had little or no part to play.

In other respects, too, the position of women in changing African society is a difficult one. Urbanization has often resulted in the dispersion of the family unit and the weakening of family ties, in both of which women stand to lose more than men. Then again, their economic function having weakened and in some places having disappeared altogether, their self-respect has suffered.

In the present paper Dr Symons examines some of these problems as they have been developing in South Africa particularly.

The change taking place in the status of African women is one of the important things affecting South Africa. It is misleading to say that the women are 'emerging' from a state of servitude, or even of submissiveness, for in their traditional society, they were not secluded in any kind of oriental purdah or trained to be docile and subdued. Indeed, they hold important positions in some tribes, such as the Swazi, where power is shared by the king and his mother, or the Transvaal Lovedu, who are governed by a line of queens, the Mujajis, widely famed as rain-makers, and the inspiration of Rider Haggard's story of 'She-who-must-be-obeyed'. Even ordinary women had the right under tribal law to sue or be sued, control arable land, and possess property acquired by work and as gifts. Venda women use such property to give as bride-wealth for women who become their so-called 'wives' performing for them some of the same

[1] Reprinted from *Africa in Transition*, The Bodley Head (London, 1958).
[2] In Reading 2.

duties as women who are married to men – a practice that European courts have declared to be immoral and contrary to public policy.

Nevertheless, the family in South African tribes – as distinct from matrilineal peoples like the Bemba farther north – was polygynous, patriarchal and patrilineal, that is to say, male-dominated. Girls left their village at marriage to join the husband; and a man might establish his own homestead after marrying and having children, but the patriarchal group was much more self-contained, closely knit and stable than the family in European or present-day African society. Functions were divided between men and women, each sex exercising leadership in its own sphere, and where these clashed it was the man who formally and legally, if not actually, took decisions and acted on behalf of all. Public affairs, the business of settling law cases, the big tribal gatherings to discuss policy, and the making of war were also reserved to the men.

Now in the modern and increasingly Westernized society African women are beginning to claim and fulfil many of the roles and functions previously held by men, and to think of themselves as individuals and not only in terms of their relations to families and kinship groups in which men play the leading part. This process is, however, considerably held up by certain conflicts between these facts of social change and the legal systems which operate and regulate the status of women.

It is these difficulties which I am going to consider; and the first thing to say is that (in South Africa) for Africans, three different legal systems are operative, and these systems do not speak with one voice. They frequently command different courses, or express different moral values, and many an individual is caught up in bewilderment and personal disaster.

The first system is the customary law of the tribe to which every African is presumed to belong, though many thousands of men and women today actually have no tribal affiliations. Tribal systems are varied, and I shall avoid going into detail about them. It will, perhaps, be obvious that many of the customary rules affecting women are not suitable today, or desired by women who are breaking away from tribalism, whether they have left the rural areas or not. Such women are discovering through education, Christianity and hard experience as breadwinners that they suffer disabilities as women under their own tribal laws.

The second system, known here as Native law, is based upon European interpretations and amendments to tribal laws. It is applied, exclusively to Africans, by the Native courts, which are presided over by European administrators. Legislatures and courts have set themselves the aim of freeing the tribal law of what in European eyes are blemishes: the punishment of sorcerers, marriages arranged by family heads for their children, or the transfer of children from one family to another in settlement of marriage debts. Both bride and bridegroom must now consent to marriage; widows cannot be forced to bear children in the name of their deceased husband. These are changes inspired by the reformer anxious to rescue women from subjugation, but there are other modifications that bear the imprint of a juristic concept drawn from the individualistic society of the West and imposed on the very different kinship and economic pattern of the tribe. It is something of a paradox that under this Westernized version of tribal law, women's rights have been whittled down in important respects.

The third system is European law, the common law of the land, which in South Africa is Roman-Dutch law. For the individual African this often acts as a kind of safety-valve; its application to Africans dates from a more liberal past, when policy was framed with a view to assimilating Africans and Europeans into a common economic, legal and political system. It is one of South Africa's anomalies that whereas all African women are denied the vote, they have the right to avail themselves of the common law, by which they may, without restraint, achieve the status of European women in matters of marriage, guardianship, contracts and proprietary capacity.

The conflict between this Roman-Dutch law and Native law will be apparent when it is realized that generally speaking, and ignoring local variations, under Native law women are treated as perpetual minors. They may not own, inherit or bequeath property. They may not enter into contracts. They may not enter into a Native law marriage without the consent of their father, brother or other male guardian. They cannot exercise rights of guardianship over their children even if unmarried, widowed or divorced.

Now it may be claimed that in respect of the guardianship over women Native law does not differ substantially from most systems of tribal law. It is true that in the traditional society the widow in most South African tribes would be taken care of by one of her late husband's brothers, if she had no son, or if her son was a minor. The brother would have to provide her with land and help her as though she were his wife. Indeed, under a custom known as *ukungena*, meaning 'to enter', he or some other relative of the deceased was expected to have children by the widow, these being regarded sociologically and legally as the legitimate offspring of the dead man. The tribal attitude was that a widow's reproductive capacity or sexual needs should not be neglected because of her husband's untimely death. This attitude and emphasis is different from that which regards the women as a perpetual minor. The results might often be the same, were it not, again, for the fact that the tribal way of life even in rural areas has changed considerably, and in important ways.

Nowadays, for example, *ukungena* tends to fall into disrepute, partly because missionaries and their converts think it is immoral, and partly because of the shortage of land. Heirs are eager to take possession of the plot occupied by the widow and her daughters and often neglect and harass them so as to drive them off the land and take occupation themselves.

If the widow is a Christian and was married by Christian rites she cannot enter into a *ukungena* relationship. Her prospects of remarriage are comparatively small. Consequently a great number of widows are found in both rural and urban areas without male guardianship even where Native law continues to treat them as minors.

In the old social order, now rapidly disintegrating, neither men nor women lived independently of a family group. There were few unmarried women or men. A woman had security, and an assured social position within the family, whether as daughter, wife or mother. Property was not for the most part individually owned, but was attached to the domestic group under the care of the head who administered it in the interests of all members, women as well as men.

This collective and co-operative kinship group has been greatly disorganized under the pressure of Western individual economics, education and religion. Not more than 10 per cent. of African husbands have more than one wife today, for polygyny has become a luxury. With the decline of polygyny has gone the large extended family of the old society. We are witnessing the emergence of the simple monogamous family group that seems to be the universal type of domestic unit in our present industrialized and urbanized civilization.

Other changes are the growth of individual ownership, and reluctance to accept kinship obligations. Large numbers of young men and women leave home to earn an independent living as domestic servants, factory workers, nurses, teachers and traders. Contrary to the old standard, there are many unmarried, widowed, divorced or deserted women who, in fact, exercise power of guardianship and act as heads of households in both town and country.

Many individuals in a state of transition from tribal culture to a new type of society observe customs drawn from both sources. Africans combine the *lobola* institution (the practice of handing over cattle or other valuable consideration to the bride's father) with a Christian or civil rites marriage. It is not uncommon for men to be married at one time to different women under European and Native law, although the Native law marriage in such circumstances is not valid.

The coexistence of two types of marriage in one society gives rise to conflicts and anomalies. Take the instance of a polygynist with four or five wives who is converted to Christianity. The missionary tells him to put aside all his wives except one whom he must marry in the Church. He then has the problem of disposing of the other, now ex-wives. Native law or tribal law as interpreted by the Courts to suit this new situation (which obviously could not have arisen in the old society) says that the husband has a duty to maintain and care for the ex-wives as long as they remain in his village or homestead, under his tutelage, but he may not, of course, co-habit with them.

These occurrences are not to be construed as 'reversion to the primitive'. The 'mixed culture' situation is the result of a conflict between two dissimilar ways of life and an imperfect adjustment to conflicting values.

Segregation perpetuates the migrant labour system, which greatly affects marriage and family life. Half a million adult men, two-thirds of them between eighteen and forty years, are at any one time temporarily absent from their homes in the reserves. The number of women temporarily absent is very much less. The urban population, in consequence, has a surplus of 700,000 males, and the reserves a surplus of 600,000 females. The unbalanced sex ratio, together with the instability of migrant communities and the insecurity of African life in urban areas, is playing havoc with the family organization. Reliable figures are lacking, but it is certain that a large proportion of couples in the larger towns are not married by either Native or European law, and that there is a widespread practice in some reserves of dispensing with all formalities at marriage and resorting to the *Ukuthwala*, a form of elopement or abduction.

It is evident that the tribal law, meaning here both customary and Native law, no longer corresponds to reality. Whatever it says, women are not subject to perpetual guardianship. They work, earn wages and acquire property, and in the course of so doing enter into contracts. They do marry without the consent of their parents; or, failing that, enter into extra-marital unions. They do exercise guardianship over their children.

Women, however, have a trump card to play which they are bound to use with increasing effect. This is their growing influence in the national organizations. Here their services are valued by their menfolk, and the more important they become in the movement for the removal of the colour bar and segregation laws, the more they will press their claims to the removal of the disabilities they suffer as women. We must, therefore, anticipate the growth of a feminist movement within the framework of African nationalism. The pressure for feminine emancipation is bound to stimulate and accelerate the pressure for political emancipation.

330

But this very fact, whereby the women's political activities become a strong weapon against the conservatism of African men, also, on the other hand, leads them into increased political and legal difficulties. An African woman was recently convicted for living in Cape Town without a permit and deported under police escort to her home in the Transkei. She left her three children with her husband, to whom she had been married for sixteen years. The Crown alleged that she had not lived in Cape Town for the full fifteen years required by law to establish a legal defence against eviction from an urban area.

Here, as in Europe, the decisive factor is likely to be the role of women in public affairs and as wage-earners. Early attempts to emancipate them by legal reforms failed because they were premature and lacked the appropriate social basis. With the decline of liberalism, a policy of 'legal segregation' was practised which, combined with a narrow and rigid formalism, led the courts to depress women's status in many respects below that of the old tribal laws. Now it is the Native law that lags behind social practice. There is as yet no concerted movement to make the law conform to usage, partly because the disenfranchized African population has no power to decide such matters, and partly because the men, being in the more favourable position, are not inclined to sponsor such a movement. But the discordance between law and practice is only one ingredient in a complex situation resulting from a great social upheaval, which is uniting a multiplicity of small, intimate social groups into an urbanized, mechanized multi-racial state. I do not doubt that tribal culture – magic, ancestor worship, polygyny, clans, a subsistence economy, chieftainship – all this will be dissipated and erased in the process, and that African men and women will embrace the ideals of human dignity and equality that have always inspired the emancipator.

31

The African Urban Milieu: a Force in Rapid Change[1]

Peter S. C. Gutkind

The phenomenon of city life is nothing new in Africa, in parts of the Sudan trading cities have existed for several centuries. What is new is the growth of modern, industrialized conurbations at a speed that the growth of accommodation and other necessary social amenities cannot match.

The fact of living in a modern city carries implications that have long been known to sociologists. In the present reading, these implications are examined as they occur and develop within an African context.

THE GROWTH OF TOWNS

Fundamentally, African urban areas expand for much the same reasons as towns in any other part of the world, i.e. because of the drift from the rural areas rather than a high natural increase in the urban population. Specifically, Africans, like others, come to live in towns in order to seek employment, education and better environmental facilities or to escape from traditions the force of which they find disagreeable. In short, Africans, whether driven by rural poverty or because towns act as magnets for the ambitious, come to live in towns because of the search for alternative forms of subsistence. Yet it is manifestly impossible to single out any one single reason which motivates the migration of people from one habitat to another and to suggest that the pull is stronger than the push. Certainly we are quite in error in thinking that population movements coincide with demands for labour as a result of the European penetration of Africa. We may lack the careful documentation to support the view that tribal movements were extensive long before European contact, yet even a cursory glance at the diversity of physical types, cultures and languages found in Africa, indicates a mingling of peoples often from very diverse stock and background.

Today migration is of vital importance to African well-being. For many the ability and right to move about has the function of a safety valve, the absence of which could spell doom to many an African population. Yet for

[1] Reprinted from *Civilisations*, 12, 2, 1962.

long both administrators and social scientists felt that migration had far-reaching inimical consequences for the tribe. More recently, however, Van Velsen and Watson have shown that labour migration and participation in a Western-type of economy can be a positive factor in African life and that urban life does not invariably result in the complete rejection of traditional values, although the adoption of new values and participation in new associations, taking the place of old kinbased forms, is no substitute in avoiding certain undesirable consequences which flow from migration and urban life. Despite any possible deleterious consequences, the East Africa Royal Commission had this to say about the migrant labour system:

> In the existing situation the migrant labour system appears to be the only one through which a considerable section of the African population can meet its needs . . . [it is] the most economic choice which the African can make, however socially deleterious or otherwise it may be. Notwithstanding these disadvantages the system brings about an improvement in the economic condition of those who go out in search of paid employment.

The causes of rural-urban migration, the mechanism that brings about urbanization, are manifold and not very clearly understood. It is a process that can be more easily described in its results than in its operation. Naturally, a heavy turn-over of temporary urban residents hardly contributes to the development of stable institutions and of important corporate groupings which can aid in the adaptation of those from rural areas to a hitherto alien way of life. It is certainly useful for our understanding of different types of urban areas, or parts within such areas, to follow the distinction set up by Wilson between 'temporary urbanization' and 'permanent urbanization' although his observation of conditions at Broken Hill, Northern Rhodesia (in 1941) that the 'African male workers in town are, typically, migrant labourers . . . is not now typical at all',[1] may not be shared by students of other areas. Certainly the percentage of those born in urban areas in East Africa is small, ranging from 5 to 10 per cent. Thus the population of virtually all the urban areas is made up and increased through migration.

Certainly the most powerful magnet drawing Africans to the towns is the prospect, even if short-lived, of regular and paid employment. Unless employment is possible in the rural areas as estate or plantation workers, or unless cash crops are extensively grown, the prospects of steady employment in the country is small. In towns, however, the choice of jobs is often considerable and the strangeness of the place and the inconveniences suffered take second place to possible long-range rewards. No doubt,

[1] See p. 346, G. Wilson.

333

were it not for the fact that the new towns of British East Africa were predominantly peopled by young men between the ages of fifteen and thirty-five, the conditions of congestion and overcrowding, poor housing, lack of privacy or excessive regimentation would hardly be tolerated by older persons. Certainly, urban conditions for Africans are far from ideal, as a good many recent urban studies have indicated. Yet these conditions are tempered by what Steel has called a 'real enthusiasm and zeal for urban life' that may well be responsible for the 'remarkable way in which predominantly agricultural and rural peoples are adapting their activities and ways of life to a considerable degree of industrialization and urbanization'. Certainly nearly every town, even during times of economic growth and prosperity, can point to reserves of labour 'surplus to requirements'. It is to a large extent this human surplus in search of employment, plus those suffering prolonged periods of under-employment, who shape urban conditions and give colour to a distinctive urban milieu.

This urban milieu, so clearly to be seen in almost any African town and often vividly characterized either by an observer such as Marris in his study of Lagos[1] or through the words of the residents themselves, nevertheless has an elusive and ephemeral quality. Moralists not infrequently deplore the social problems, which are, in any case, not confined to Africa, yet systematically ignore what we have learned to understand, if not accept, for ourselves, namely that a large number of people seek out, enjoy and prefer the kind of life which is characteristic of Asian urban life, particularly the freedom of relations between the sexes, the drifting from one job to another, the freedom of mobility and the lack of regimentation found in those areas not under the control of municipalities, central governments or companies. It is, of course, far too early to tell what kind of life and communities will emerge in the new towns of East Africa now that in most cases control has passed to all-African governments both local and central. Will the new towns take on a distinctly African expression and harbour ever increasingly peoples of different tribes unable and perhaps unwilling to associate more closely for the common good? Or will the growing urban *élite* impose its views of how law and order is to be achieved? How will the endless number of acute problems be resolved? That it should be the aim of administrators and others 'to build up integrated urban communities' in East and Central Africa and that there is 'no alternative but to make every effort to create the conditions which need to be created if Africans are to lead satisfactory lives as permanent town dwellers' seems now agreed upon by all.

---

[1] See p. 346, P. Marris.

334

CONTEMPORARY PROBLEMS OF THE NEW URBAN AREAS

It is often quite mistakenly assumed that the economic social and environmental problems of Africa's new towns differ radically from those in urban
areas anywhere else. In substance, whatever the extent and intensity of the
problem, a large concentration of people from different backgrounds
competing for limited facilities is the core of any problem in any urban
area. While in Western European and American cities the population, or
certain sections at least, have lived in towns for many centuries and have
learned to live with the enigma which their environment provides for
them, over much of Africa there is no urban tradition and hence virtually
no experience to draw on for either the newly arrived urban resident or the
administrator in coping with the wide range of problems which inevitably
arise. Added to this are problems characteristic of a tropical environment
which is the source of special difficulties in sanitation and health, work and
productivity, housing and transport. While it is easy to cite the problems
we still lack a great deal of precise information, a condition which lends
itself easily to exaggeration of many complex situations and hinders the
formation of policy. Penetrating studies dealing with the social pathology
of African urban areas have yet to be carried out although most urban social
surveys have paid some attention to such matters as overcrowding, disease,
delinquency, crime, heavy drinking, prostitution and dependency of the
young, the unemployed and the disabled. However, a number of special
studies have been carried out, although they are rather thin on theory.

Not only are the urban problems rooted in the consequences of mere
numbers, but also in the very nature of the composition of the urban
population. Not only do Europeans, Asians, Coloured, Arabs and Africans
live in the same urban areas – a setting which reflects the complications of
social and culture contact – but within each ethnic community there are
innumerable language, educational, occupational, status and class differences. In this respect, as well, such differences are based on education,
residence-location, specialization of functions and income as in most
cities of the world. What then might be considered some of the major
and perhaps distinctly African urban problems?

(i) The Physical Setting

Apart from the fact that African towns have to cope with the special
conditions imposed by a tropical environment, not all of them are sited at
the most suitable places. Thus it is not uncommon for the most desirable
parts of an urban area to be occupied by non-Africans and the least
desirable parts, often low-lying areas difficult to drain, by Africans,

335

Asians, and other non-white groups. Thus even if such African areas were not infrequently heavily congested, problems of water supply, sewerage, and control over sanitation generally is often exceedingly difficult. Should there be permanently paved roads in such African areas, stormdrains are rarely adequate at times of torrential storms. Most difficult, however, to enforce are adequate measures controlling health conditions and the very minimum of acceptable housing standards.

Physically, urban growth is so varied that it is difficult to detect a common pattern except in as much as the inhabitants impose on the physical development their traditions regarding lay-out, zoning and facilities. Unless there is some rational authority imposed on the gradual expansion of the towns, a tightly knotted urban centre tends to develop. Subsequently roads and residential and commercial development spread out from the centre rather like a spider's web which grows until it engulfs even the more distant 'suburbs' of the non-Africans and those areas where industry had been established some years earlier. Not infrequently, as in the case of Kampala, Uganda, the University College of East Africa, once two miles distant from the city centre, is now surrounded by intensive residential and light commercial development. Thus the time is drawing to a close when non-African areas were of low density and marked by high building and maintenance standards.

In all the three East African territories serious efforts are now being made in creating conditions of greater uniformity of sanitation and building standards. Zoning laws and town planning schemes are designed on the basis of somewhat more rational grounds than race and wealth. There is a shift from the emphasis on low-cost renting on housing estates to owner-occupier areas. Most territories have begun in a modest manner to clear slums and reduce heavy overcrowding. Even if very high density areas cannot be cleared, 'urban renewal' is often effectively carried out by means of paving existing roads, cutting new highways and access roads, re-siting markets, providing a more adequate water supply and public transportation and other amenities such as street lighting, the latter having an important effect on the sense of security of the population. Obviously, much needs to be done to bring the opportunity of greater privacy to many an overcrowded African urban area. Yet not all experiments in re-settlement result in satisfactory communities as established ties of kinship and association are broken, an observation recorded in England and in Nigeria.

(ii) The Economic Setting

The most marked feature of the new towns of East Africa is the poverty of the African urban masses; the urban worker is often far less privileged than is realized by those who set out on their migration to the towns. It is the opportunity to find employment which is a major incentive in the rural-urban migration and it is urban employment which is primarily responsible for the 'urban way of life' and the rhythm and milieu of this distinctive type of human grouping. While it is remarkable how the new African urban areas have been able to absorb large numbers of Africans and even provide some kind of employment for some of them, the most outstanding characteristic of the urban labour problem is the huge disparity in wages between Africans and non-Africans and, perhaps, more recently, even within the African community itself where a very small political and economic *élite* is forging rapidly ahead of the mass of Africans. Apart from the economic implications of this disparity, such characteristics not only feed nationalist aspirations but could be the substance of serious mass discontent in the years ahead. Thus, it could be that the new African territories will pay more attention to income and wages policies on a national level in an effort to help the growing disparity of financial reward.

To the vast majority of Africans, the cost of maintaining themselves either as single or family men is considerable. Food is costly and rent-profiteering is common, particularly in slum property. As zoning laws have often removed Africans far from their places of employment, the cost of transportation is not infrequently a heavy additional burden. If it is difficult for the majority of Africans to make ends meet even for absolute essentials, the urge to purchase some small luxuries is very great, with the the result that many Africans find it difficult to arrive at a satisfactory allocation of priorities of needs and wants. Baeck has pointed out that 'group reference functions' underlie consumption patterns among Africans as much as among peoples in Western Europe or elsewhere. Baeck concludes:

> The attraction exercised by an implanted consumption pattern coming from a more developed economy affects the traditional consumption behaviour in the sense that it provides a reference schema to all income strata and that in relation to the immediate upper income level.[1]

Many expenditure studies have revealed that urban Africans spend large sums on items which many observers would consider unessential and that the influence of a modern money economy may have a serious and detrimental effect on diet, a fact explained by Hoyt who writes:

> Where people are plunged all at once into a situation away from home in which they have no choice but full-time earning for money, they have lost their familiar anchorages and are without experience to guide them in the new set of conditions and the new opportunities for spending which the money economy brings.

[1] See p. 346, L. Baeck.

The impact of a money economy, the fact that the new African nations are now part of a world-wide economic structure, the slow shift from subsistence to cash-cropping and the great efforts at the diversification of the economy generally are all strongly felt in the urban areas. Most economics of the primarily agricultural producers, such as the East African territories, are 'one crop economies' and as such tied rather precariously to an uncertain world market. A drop in the world market price or failure to sell part of a crop not only exposes the producer to a 'slump and boom' cycle but also drastically interferes with the stability of urban employment. When agricultural commodities command a high price, urban employment, particularly in the building construction sector, is high and the effect of high and stable prices for cash crops will be felt throughout commerce and industry. Yet when the opposite conditions prevail the urban African worker is among the first to feel the consequences, as are those in the rural areas who to a certain degree have come to rely on remittances from kin and friends resident in the town. Leaving the town for the countryside will then merely throw an added burden on the rural family and kin. Certainly, there was a time when urban labour could readily be absorbed back into tribal life. Today this is less likely, as conditions in Nairobi, Kenya, indicate in consequence of very unsettled economic conditions over the last two years. In certain areas, notably the Copperbelt towns of Northern Rhodesia and in Katanga province in the Congo (Léopoldville), serious efforts have been made to create a stabilized labour force which is wholly dependent upon employment in the mines; this has led to the majority of the African workers permanently living away from their tribal homes. Under such conditions any reduction in productivity and employment has the most serious economic, social and political consequences with the result that disturbances might turn against traditional African and imposed non-African authority alike.

But the stabilization of the African labour force is by itself not the key to the reduction of economic pressures as the source of many urban problems. Indeed, there is little to support the underlying assumption that stabilization of labour results in more stable urban communities if for no other reason than that a permanently settled labour force makes demands on the limited amenities which are provided. Even more fundamentally, it has yet to be fully accepted that higher wages are the price to be paid for stabilization of African labour. But again, increased wages alone will be no substitute for the much needed social security arrangements and social welfare services. Few African territories can afford elaborate social security provisions and problems facing the social planner differ markedly from those of the rich countries. If it is the object of the various African governments to build-up 'integrated urban communities', an economically viable basis will have to be created which not merely supports the African urban resident but allows for the expression of individual aspirations. In recent years development policies in the British African territories have been geared to achieve this objective.

(iii) The Social Setting

It is evident that many current social problems have their origin, as suggested above, in the conditions of the physical environment and the consequences of economic development. But this alone cannot account for the etiology of the manifold problems which are the social concomitants of industrialization and urbanization. It would certainly be easier for the social planner if he accepted the simple fact that Africans, whether of rural or urban background, may not wish to be moulded in the image of the West, and further that many people prefer the unregimented conditions, the violence and excitement, confusion and constant diversions which is a feature of so much of the African urban milieu.

The complexity of this system,[1] which appears to be a composite of overlapping sub-systems, has been portrayed in a number of urban surveys and more recently in a more analytical and theoretical manner, indicating strongly that the urban areas of Africa have much in common with those anywhere else. Yet there are certain features to which special reference should be made if the force behind the urban milieu is to be understood. As it is impossible to enter into any detail in the course of a brief character-ization, it will have to suffice to restrict this analysis to three features: tribalism in African urban areas, family life, and new urban associations. The former will give an insight into the structural features of the urban social system, the second into a specific institution and the last is an example of a special feature of African urban life.

The analysis of tribalism in the new context of heterogeneous African urban areas has recently been dealt with most creatively by Gluckman, Mitchell, Epstein and Southall. Gluckman[2] tells us that traditionally tribalism meant membership in a political system and a shared domestic and economic life based on kinship. Particularly in its political aspects the British administrators have, in the past, lent their 'powerful support to the continued working of the African tribal political systems, as systems', whereas today tribalism in towns is an important system of classification and the 'basis for grouping people into categories' but 'not an organized set of political relations'. While it is true that the urban migrant moves along kinship channels in his attempt to establish himself, i.e. to find

---

[1] I.e. the African urban social system.   [2] See p. 346, M. Gluckman.

housing and initial means of support, yet as an urban worker in an industrial complex, and as a political being *vis-à-vis* non-Africans, tribalism is far less important than his role as a miner, an artisan or unskilled labourer, i.e. as a townsman. Gluckman strongly emphasizes this view and beckons us to realize that the 'starting-point of our analysis of tribalism in the towns is not that it is manifested by tribesmen, but that it is manifested by townsmen'. He presses for this view on the grounds that contemporary anthropological theory stresses the 'difference between persons and the roles they occupy in the social structure' and that 'our theories stress the extent to which the social structure exerts pressure which controls the behaviour of the occupants' roles'. Thus the urban milieu is influenced not by tribesmen but by townsmen, for 'an African townsman is a townsman, an African miner is a miner: he is only secondarily a tribesman'. Yet Gluckman acknowledges that 'the African is always tribalized, both in towns and rural areas; but he is tribalized in two quite different ways'. Of course, we must remember that Gluckman is writing about Central Africa where, as pointed out earlier, the percentage of the total population classified as urban ranges from 13 per cent. in Southern Rhodesia to 19 per cent. in Zambia. A larger and more established African urban population is therefore more likely to lead to such observations and theoretical insight.

However, the theoretical basis which helps us to understand tribalism in towns is only part of our documentation of its operation. A large number of more practical implications should be considered.

The most important of these is the fact that Governments and companies have changed their policies from encouraging and working with tribal-centred groups to lending support to functionally centred groups based on the new industrial, political and 'class' order evident in African urban areas. Yet in matters *between* Africans, such as the struggle for leadership power, and certain forms of mutual aid, tribalism still plays a part. Secondly, many of the new institutions at present work against the formation of more permanent corporate groupings which are needed if an integrated urban African society is to develop. This is so because, it is assumed, change only occurs when new norms gain general acceptance and the breach of traditional ones does not lead to serious sanctions detrimental to the individual and the group. Thirdly, as tribalism still does operate in the African urban area and strongly influences the social organization of daily life, many of the problems which do arise might be profitably analysed in terms of a number of propositions about in-group and out-group ethnocentrism.

Furthermore, tribalism is evident in the ecological pattern of many urban areas, particularly in those areas where movement and settlement are not regulated or restricted. Then, not infrequently, small tribal settlements grow up which, in the course of time, develop their own complex internal structures. But such development runs counter to sound urban administration, housing policy and town planning. In addition, tribal settlements not infrequently encourage tribal tensions and many a disturbance is rooted in tribal rivalries through which economic and social discontent is funnelled.

But even if and where tribalism is not an important consideration, the tremendous heterogeneity of the East African urban population and their racial diversity is very marked. It is not unusual to find from twenty to forty different tribes jostling one another in almost any urban area for housing, amenities, jobs and services. Thus many social problems inevitably arise through competition and close contact, through different living standards and varied cultural backgrounds. Petty disputes crop up almost constantly and the administration of justice becomes a particularly complex problem as the range of customary law is great.

Among all the problems which are alleged to have their etiology in urbanization and urbanism, frequent reference is made to the break-down of African kinship and family life in the towns. Perhaps nowhere have moralistic arguments so oversimplified the actual situation. While administrators have given encouragement to the modification of indigenous political and economic systems, the changing organization, purpose and function of the family has not been as readily understood, as most observers have seen the consequences of rapid change as a simple one-way cause and effect relationship.

It is no doubt correct that the African family is the 'most significant feature of African society' and its 'central institution', a fact which hardly makes it immune to change in a positive direction or proves that induced change is not desirable. Although many observers have recorded their observation that the African urban family is subject to unusual stress and that family life will before long approximate more closely to a Western pattern, others have noted the 'positive functions' and the 'diverse means to re-integrate themselves on lines other than those of kinship'. It is also often asserted that with the change to an urban environment the family unit generally embraces fewer functions and that we are witness to the 'extraction of the domestic family unit from the lineage', i.e. we see before us the emergence of the 'natural family'. Indeed, as some functions are and will be lost, new functions will develop sanctioned by a new normative system. We certainly cannot escape the observation that, where African urban life is highly restricted by official rules and regulations, family life fares no better than when movement into town is unrestricted and African enterprise is allowed to operate. There, Southall has pointed out, the 'situation is altogether more favourable to family life and even extended families and larger groups of kin may be found'. Nor can we escape the conclusion put forward by Hellman that 'no generalizations apply to all African urban families', a view also shared by Longmore.[1]

Not only is there a close interdependence between African urban family life and traditional family organization, but the urban situation, and particularly the problems of the urban labourer, are causally related to the special demographic characteristics of African urban areas and this, in turn, is a reflection of the pattern and rhythm of economic development. Thus virtually every urban study has indicated that those who come to live in the new African towns are young and unskilled males most of whom seek temporary employment after which they return to their homes, only to come back later for, perhaps, a more extended stay. Few of those with wives and children can afford to bring their families – at least not on their first visit. It is therefore not uncommon that a large number of single men outnumber the few women who live alone in town. Under such conditions young men form a variety of temporary unions which are usually fairly well adapted to suit their needs. Naturally, as such unions depend on the consent of both parties, their often great brittleness is the source of a good deal of conflict, although a considerable degree of stability also occurs. African family life is a reflection of the changing position of women and the degree to which women are being absorbed into new forms of association.

What, we might ask, is the future for African urban family life? Here there are two forces at work: the personal and the institutional. On the personal level the urban milieu provides a measure of freedom not enjoyed by rural women. The opportunities for earning a legitimate wage in the urban areas are considerable, a competitive position which is viewed with some alarm by many men, as also is the sexual freedom enjoyed by many women. More fundamentally, however, the future of African urban family life depends on the gradual emergence of a social system which allows for the more effective regulation and stabilization of marriage and family life. This in turn will depend to a large extent on the economic future of the various African territories whose economies are frequently so precariously poised that the slightest downturn sends a tidal wave throughout the economy, the consequences of which the African urban resident is among the first to feel. Whatever the economic future, the problems occasioned by sheer poverty must of course be tackled if conditions are to be created to induce stability. It is because of the fluidity of the conditions prevailing in the urban areas that Africans have created a large number of new associations which peculiarly meet their present needs.

[1] See p. 346, E. Hellman and L. Longmore.

The distinctive characteristics of the urban milieu are seen perhaps better than anywhere else in the voluntary associations which have developed over the years. Little, who has studied their history and organization in West Africa, views them as an important 'adaptive mechanism' assisting in the adjustment of migrants from the rural areas 'by substituting for the extended group of kinsmen a grouping based upon common interest which is capable of serving many of the same needs as the traditional family or lineage'. Furthermore, in terms of the urban milieu, the African voluntary associations 'provide an outlet for the energies and ambitions of the rising class of young men with a tribal background' and further 'encourages him [the migrant] to mix with persons outside his own lineage and, sometimes, tribe, the voluntary association helps him to adjust to the more cosmopolitan ethos of the city'. Thus, Little views as particularly important associations of what he terms the 'traditional-modernized' type, since 'their combination of modern and traditional traits constitutes a cultural bridge which conveys, metaphorically speaking, the tribal individual from one kind of sociological universe to another'. Towards this end important social control functions are exercised by many voluntary associations, such as the Luo Union in the British East African territories which has helped to return destitute Luo to their homes and to prevent excessive prostitution among Luo women, the *Kalela* tribal dance on the Copperbelt of Northern Rhodesia which mocks the activities of certain tribes resident in town and draws off inter-tribal tension and the *Awo Omama* Patriotic Union in Lagos which is attempting to reduce the amount of money asked for bride-wealth by the parents for an urban girl.

The activities of the voluntary associations are manifold, ranging from burial societies to recreation clubs and friendly societies, improvement societies, saving and contribution clubs and occupational and religious associations. Entry into membership is generally carefully controlled and rules and obligations imposed on the membership. Towards this end the associations define the duties of the officers managing the affairs of the association. As far as urban life is concerned, an important function of many associations is that they encourage their members to settle disputes among themselves in an amiable manner thus avoiding legal action against each other and in this manner contributing substantially to easing the burden of the urban courts. The real contribution of the African voluntary associations to urban life depends, Southall has suggested, on three phases:

the first phase in which the stake of most Africans in town is too fleeting for effective tribal associations to be formed, but in which both kinship and tribal bonds are seized upon situationally for mutual aid; the second phase in which tribal associations are formed for general welfare purposes, and the third phase in which Africans begin to move beyond a tribal basis to form associations for common interests and to express similar achieved status, cutting across tribal lines.

(iv) The Political Setting

Finally, in setting out some of the main characteristics of the new African urban areas and the urban milieu, mention must be made of the town as a focal point of political activity. Here two considerations are important: firstly, the problems of urban administration either by traditional or new local or central government authorities, and, secondly, the place of the urban area in national and political life generally.

The problems arising in imposing on an African urban area a traditional system of political administration have been reviewed by Southall and Gutkind whose conclusions point to the unsuitability of such traditional systems when faced with the problems of social control over more complex societies. In such societies highly specialized means of administration and enforcement are needed. In other situations, the African urban communities are under the administrative jurisdiction of an African Affairs Department incorporated in a local municipal government. At other times, as on the Copperbelt of Zambia, African urban communities live in company-owned estates and authority is exercised by both the municipalities and the companies, although until recently the latter viewed the estates as their sole preserve. In addition, governments have in the past encouraged the African Councils to assist in the administration of the urban areas and efforts have been made in the last few years to extend African Local Government authority over the smaller urban areas, a responsibility which, because it entails considerable cost and a low return, the African authorities have been reluctant to accept. In some ways this is hardly surprising, as in the past the claims of Africans resident in the urban areas were often totally ignored.

Of course the urban administrator faces some unusual political and social problems. Before a viable structure can operate effectively, better housing and sanitation and a greater control over private building must be exercised. As the new towns of East Africa have grown up in such a manner that first-class amenities are provided for the non-African areas and either none or few are found in the African parts, the cost of providing such services belatedly is likely to be enormous. Outside the urban areas land fragmentation has become a serious problem with the result that land acquisition will call for large sums in the way of compensation. Most serious, however, many a peri-urban area is seriously congested so that the re-settlement of large populations will soon have to be undertaken.

344

The African Urban Milieu: a Force in Rapid Change

Finally, since the end of the Second World War, the old and the new towns of Africa have contributed quite disproportionally to the national life of the new nations of Africa. It is in the towns that we witness the sharpest break with the past and see a major restructuring of African society taking place. It is also in the towns where African political movement is mainly taking place, where the parties have their headquarters, where the newspapers are printed and from where a vast amount of information radiates to the countryside. It is therefore no wonder that the European settler and the British administrator have often raised objections to the concentration of Africans in towns, a move which they held would 'corrupt' the 'tribal African' and make sedition and agitation the hallmark of the urban African. However, these fears have to a large extent proved groundless. Considering how severe the break with rural life has been, the African urban population has settled down remarkably well and shown unusual enterprise and flexibility in turning the strange to best advantage, giving the lie to much that has been predicted would happen. To many, indeed, the very uprootedness which Professor Frankel has characterized as being 'like cancer it is a silent disease: it kills when it is recognized too late', has meant new opportunity amid poverty and squalor. That better circumstances have not been achieved is hardly due to the fact, as Professor Frankel believes, that 'the social soil of Africa is shallow: the roots of modern civilization cannot penetrate deep to resist the storms of circumstance; the least disturbance, like the rain and the wind, create a dustbowl and a desert', but may more safely and logically be laid on the shoulders of the recent colonizers who until but yesterday did little to assist the African people to fortify themselves against the force of rapid change. Naturally, as in other parts of the world, the urban areas of Africa bring home to us in concentrated form the task before the African people. Yet they can rest secure in the knowledge that many generations of Africans have come and gone since the European powers first set foot in Africa, and that as a people Africans and their culture have shown remarkable resistance and adaptation. Indeed there is growing evidence that, while the Western world still reels in the human and social consequences of the industrial revolution, the new nations of Africa with a little imagination and skill could be that much wiser in shaping an urban milieu, the final product of which might not be megalopolis and strangulation. The best of urban life could thus find expression in the decline of cities and the rise of communities. The African background lends itself well to this great experiment.

FINAL OBSERVATIONS

In the comments made above an effort has been made to characterize just a few of the main features of the new African urban areas and African urban life. These characteristics have been viewed as an expression of rapid change, of a substantial break with tradition most clearly seen in the urban areas. Furthermore, because the urban areas have attracted a large number of people from the most varied backgrounds and traditions, the new towns are at one and the same time focal points in the formation of nationhood where stranger meets stranger, and also centres, where ethnic lines may often be more sharply drawn than elsewhere.

The characteristics of the urban milieu are an expression of the composition of the urban population, male-dominated, young and mobile, adaptable and full of initiative. Hence, the new African urban areas are not merely the focal point where the break with tradition may be seen most clearly, but also the centres in which a major restructuring of African society as a whole is taking place, a restructuring which is reaching deep into the countryside without losing any part of its force. As this process proceeds it is frequently discussed almost entirely in terms of disintegration and the towns are treated as the inevitable end-product.

But this is only one side of an altogether far more complex process as it is much too early to tell whether or not the new patterns of organization and the new collective associations which have emerged will contribute to a serious erosion of African life and culture or whether some important positive developments will emerge. It is too early to say much about the future and to read in present urban social structure a discernible pattern of future organization.

Additional References

G. Wilson, *An Essay in the Economics of Detribalisation*, Rhodes-Livingstone Papers 5 and 6 (Rhodes-Livingstone Institute, 1941 and 1942).

P. Marris, *Family and Social Change in an African City* (London, Kegan Paul, 1961).

L. Baeck, 'An Expenditure Study of the Congolese Evolués of Leopoldville, Belgian Congo', in *Social Change in Modern Africa*, A. W. Southall (ed.) (London, Oxford University Press, 1961), pp. 159–181.

M. Gluckman, 'Anthropological Problems Arising from the African Industrial Revolution', in A. W. Southall (ed.), op. cit., pp. 67–82.

E. Hellman, 'The Development of Social Groupings Among Urban Africans', in *Social Implications of Industrialisation and Urbanisation in Africa* (Paris, UNESCO, 1956), p. 736.

L. Longmore, *The Dispossessed* (London, Jonathan Cape, 1959), p. 112.

IIIe: Social Problems

When speaking in an African context it is useful to distinguish between two kinds of social problems: those that are universal, present in all societies throughout the world, though in differing degrees, and those which are directly related to rapid social change. Among the former may be listed problems of health and education, and the general contest waged by men everywhere against nature and ill-fortune to secure for themselves and their children a more contented, prosperous and satisfying life. Among the latter must be included at the personal level the psychological effects of the transition from the old to the new, of being torn from one's roots in a comprehended, stable way of life when, as it were, the pieces fit, to meet the challenge of a modern, impersonal, complex, unstable, industrial environment, with values, alignments and authorities all vastly different and where the fragmented segments of life grind and jar in chaos.

At the national level, these problems become crystallized along certain paths of deviant behaviour. There being more misfits in society, more people without the guidance and strength of any recognized ethos, there is a growing incidence of the kind of behaviour people in similar circumstances indulge in everywhere. Alcoholism, prostitution, gambling and violence are among the more common symptoms. Then again the *rate* of change leads to many problems, lack of housing, unemployment, and so forth. In short, there is the inability of a growing economy to meet the needs of an expanding list of social needs drawn up by a people made suddenly aware of their requirements and the political power that their collective strength provides.

In this section our attention turns to the basic social problems confronting the whole continent, the problems of health and education, and a review of some of the psychological pressures upon modern Africans.

347

32

Health Problems in sub-Saharan Africa[1]

George Kimble

In this and the following reading, Professor Kimble summarizes the principal problems of health and education.

Lacking a balanced diet and adequate protection against cold and damp, and living in ignorance of the elementary principles of sanitation and out of reach of hospitals, doctors and drugstores, the average tribal African lives in thraldom to sickness. For him sickness is the norm; it starts at birth, or even before, and continues until death. And he is a very lucky African who is not sick of more than one thing. The fact that this thraldom is seldom long makes it no easier to endure. Although reliable statistics are, in the nature of the case, unavailable, infant mortality rates have been put at anywhere between 100 and 800 per 1,000, with the mean 'in the region of from 300 to 500 in most of Africa'. Of the children surviving infancy, possibly no more than 50 per cent. on the average reach adulthood.[2]

We cannot hope to understand very much about the primitive African until we have succeeded in sensing something of the hopelessness, to say nothing of the pain, of living in a world of habitual sickness. . . .

The relative importance of these diseases varies from area to area with changes in the geographical and social environments, as does the resistance to disease and the degree of well-being and of physical fitness enjoyed by the tribal African. But almost everywhere he is exposed to three kinds of sickness. These Dr Jacques M. May categorizes as follows:

1. Sicknesses that affect him more or less permanently and make it difficult if not impossible for him to support himself for the better part of his life, which, depending on the disease, may mean a few months or many years.

[1] Reprinted from *Tropical Africa, II*, Twentieth Century Fund (New York, 1961).

[2] A. Macdonald, *The Development of Tropical and Subtropical Countries with particular reference to Africa* (ed. by A. L. Banks), p. 142 (Edward Arnold, Ltd., London, 1954).

2. Sicknesses that allow him to go on supporting himself, but with impaired vitality, and for less than the customary span of life.

3. Sicknesses that occur epidemically, whenever there is a favourable concurrence of organic and inorganic factors.

In the first group belong the following: malaria, trypanosomiasis (sleeping sickness), bilharziasis, leprosy, tuberculosis, ancylostomiasis (hookworm), filariasis, and a number of deficiency diseases.

In the second group come a number of other worm infections (such as ascariasis), yaws in its tertiary or late forms, various intestinal disorders, pneumonia, ulcers and venereal diseases. In their less serious manifestations some of the diseases belonging to the first group, such as ancylostomiasis and filariasis, should, strictly speaking, be included in this group.

In the third group belong plague, rickettsial diseases (typhus), yellow fever, relapsing fevers, smallpox, meningitis, influenza, and the epidemic 'explosions' of such endemic diseases as malaria and trypanosomiasis.

This is by no means the full list of major diseases, but it is long enough to serve our immediate purpose. Their distribution among the three groups would have been different a generation or so ago, before yellow fever, smallpox and other diseases had been effectively controlled.

Malaria has long been the chief threat to health and life in the whole of tropical Africa. It can be fatal, but its indirect effects in undermining health and thereby rendering its victims susceptible to other infections are even more serious. A debilitating disease, it is the begetter of much of the lethargy and sloth characteristic of so many Africans. . . .

In the African social drama sickness has a strong claim to being arch-villain. It is bad enough that a man should be ignorant, for this cuts him off from the commerce of other men's minds. It is perhaps worse that a man should be poor, for this condemns him to a life of stint and scheming, in which there is no time for dreams and no respite from weariness. But what surely is worst is that a man should be unwell, for this prevents his doing anything much about either his poverty or his ignorance.

In tropical Africa, most men, women and children are habitually unwell. Many are unwell from the day of their birth to the day of their death. Many are more than unwell; they are sick of diseases, such as sleeping sickness, that are incapacitating; or of diseases that are debilitating, such as malaria and bilharziasis; or of diseases, such as broncho-pneumonia and tuberculosis, that are distressing. Most of the sick are sick of more than one disease. It is nothing unusual for a person admitted to a leprosarium to be suffering from malaria, sleeping sickness, tertiary yaws, onchocerciasis and worm infections as well as leprosy. Left to their own devices, most of the sick have no prospect of ever being not sick.

The pharmacopoeia of the medicine man is an awesome assortment of herbs, entrails, charms and incantations. Its cures say more for the fortitude of the patient than for the skill of the practitioner.

Nor is it only a matter of the African suffering from diseases. It is also a matter of his living in a physical, social and psychological environment and on a diet that makes it hard for him to keep well even when he is not actually ill. The assault on sickness, therefore, calls not only for tactical warfare against specific diseases and localized foci of disease, but also for a strategy aimed at removing the predisposing causes of both disease and ill-health. It calls for prevention no less than cures. . . .

MEDICAL FACILITIES

Today, in the whole of tropical Africa, there are approximately 7,500 doctors and 125,000 hospital beds. By Western standards, these are still very modest figures – a doctor to about every 22,000 persons and a bed to about every 1,300.[1] Large parts of tropical Africa do not have a doctor to 100,000 persons or a bed to 10,000. In 1957 Ethiopia was reported as having one doctor for every 164,800 inhabitants,[2] the number of hospital beds was not known, but it was probably less than one for every 20,000. Some territories do much better, of course – better in a few instances than many 'older' countries. In 1956 the doctor-to-population ratio was approximately 1 : 3,600 in Southern Rhodesia and 1 : 8,800 in Kenya. In the same year the ratio of hospital beds to population in the Belgian Congo was approximately 1 : 400, or more than sixteen times higher than in India and more than four times higher than in Mexico.

In almost every African country, no matter where it stands in comparison with its neighbours, there is an acute awareness of the need for more doctors and more hospitals. In most, this awareness is being matched by action worthy of the need. Name almost any large city from Dakar to Addis Ababa or from Khartoum to Lourenço Marques, and you will find either that its largest, most up-to-date and often most handsome building is a hospital or that it has plans for such a building. Few American towns of comparable size can compete with Dakar, Kumasi, Ibadan, Luanda, Léopoldville or Brazzaville when it comes to hospitals. Or name any university or university college, and it is safe to say that no faculty has a higher priority with its treasury than the medical faculty, where it exists. . . .

But there is much more to the tactical assault on sickness than the provision of doctors and hospitals. If, to pursue our military analogy, the

[1] The corresponding figures for the United States are about 1 to 750 and 1 to 100.
[2] *New York Times*, 3 December 1957.

doctors are the officers and the hospitals the base repair and maintenance centres, the medical auxiliaries are the no less necessary 'other ranks', and the clinics, dispensaries and mobile units the indispensable field casualty stations.

In all of tropical Africa there are between 10,000 and 12,500 midwives and pharmacists and perhaps as many dispensers, and nurses, most of them African. While some of these are attached to base hospitals, more are field workers who carry the fight right into the enemy's camp, to places seldom if ever visited by doctors, and to people who have never seen a hospital. . . .

There is no territory in the whole of tropical Africa that cannot provide some evidence of medical gains, and there are next to no diseases that have not had their ascendancy challenged in the past generation. Few of the gains are general, however, and none is as yet secure. Losses, moreover, continue to be considerable. Indeed, it is impossible to read current medical literature without being gravely disconcerted. The enemy, it seems, gives ground in one place, or disease, only to gain ground in another.

Nor would it appear to be just a matter of giving and gaining, but rather of assault and counter-assault. . . .

CONTRIBUTORY FACTORS

How did this counter-assault manage to get under way? Of the many contributory factors, the following would seem to be especially notable:

1. The opening up of tropical Africa. Since about 1900, Europeans and Asians have become domiciled in almost every part of the region, and wherever they have gone, their diseases have gone with them. But whereas most of them enjoy some degree of resistance to the more disabling forms of these diseases, the Africans living round about them do not. There is little doubt that it was the newcomers who lit the fuse for the explosion of venereal and respiratory diseases reported from many areas in the past generation.

2. The growing mobility of the African. Thanks to roads, railways and airlines, and the increasing demand for migrant labour, the African has become a highly efficient carrier of diseases, both new and old. Syphilis and tuberculosis acquired by men working on the mines are often carried, when their term of service is over, to places 500 to 1,000 miles away, hitherto free of either disease. Much the same is true of leprosy. Bilharziasis acquired in an old Sudanese focus of the disease can be carried overnight to the Belgian Congo or east Africa by the itinerant seller of ivory and

metalware, unless his personal hygiene is as up to date as his mode of travel, as it sometimes is not. Sleeping sickness can be carried from one territory to the next by infected tsetse flies hiding in the nooks and crannies of a truck or car.

3. The inadequacy of the African's defences. These defences are inadequate on several counts. In some instances they are inadequate because – to all outward appearances at least – he does not care enough about good health. . . .

In most instances, however, the root of the trouble is neither unconcern nor poverty, but ignorance. Most Africans are so accustomed to being less than well that they frequently do not realize how unwell they are until it is too late to do much about it. Doctors almost everywhere lament that 'patients are generally not brought into hospital until the last stages have been reached and every other remedy has been tried without success'.[1] Most Africans still do not know enough to see the point of supplying themselves with pit latrines and a clean water supply, without which it is scarcely possible in most areas to avoid contracting bilharziasis, the dysenteries (bacillary and amoebic) and the typhoid fevers; or of sleeping in a well-ventilated atmosphere (instead of the customary fug), for want of which many are daily contracting tuberculosis and broncho-pneumonia. Increasing numbers of reasonably well-to-do Africans know too little about bought foods and beverages to be able to steer clear of nutritional diseases. Many of the most recently reported cases of kwashiorkor, pellagra and beriberi in Southern Rhodesia have been attributed to 'the inordinate consumption of white bread, buns, syrup and mineral waters'.[2]

Observations such as these, recurring like a refrain in medical reports, suggest that possibly another of the African's inadequacies, when it comes to defending himself against disease, is his lack of confidence in himself and the folkways of his people. In many areas, certainly, he has virtually discarded his traditional food staples and beverages, along with his traditional wardrobe, such as it was. In many areas, too, his womenfolk are now weaning children after the nine-month period favoured by most Europeans.

Although missionaries advocate teetotalism in the African convert with good reason, having all too often seen what happens to the man who acquires a liking for Western drinks, the fact remains that native beer, brewed from maize, sorghum, palm sap or sugar cane, contains protective

---

[1] *Colonial Office Report on the Nyasaland Protectorate for the Year 1953*, p. 93, H.M.S.O. (London, 1954).
[2] *Annual Report on Public Health, Federation of Rhodesia and Nyasaland, 1955*, p. 18.

elements that are not found in mineral waters and white bread. Traders, missionaries and government officials have equally good reasons for encouraging the African to wear Western-style clothes, but the fact is that over most of the African tropics there are no clothes like no clothes, or at least like the fewest possible clothes. . . .

It is clear, therefore, that the battle for the health of the African and, to a lesser extent, the non-African has still to be won, and that it is most unlikely to be won by nibbling tactics, no matter how efficient, or by an army of patched-up casualties, no matter how brave. . . .

The only hope of a durable victory lies in changing the cultural and physical environment to the point where disease cannot get away with aggression. . . .

What is possible, and what the preventionist is trying to do, is (1) to so alter the physical environment of the vectors and hosts that they can no longer reproduce their kind in it; (2) to kill the vectors and hosts with insecticides; (3) to give individuals their own 'built-in' protection or protective screen; and (4) to destroy in the patient the parasitic cause of his disease or diseases.[1]

---

[1] Dr Stanley G. Browne, a consultant to this study, reports that this 'prevention by cure' is especially effective for such diseases as trypanosomiasis, yaws and leprosy. 'It satisfies both the clinician, out to help the sick individual, and the epidemiologist, who is primarily concerned with the good of the community. Furthermore, it demonstrates the concern of the public health authority and the value of its activities.'

33

Educational Problems in sub-Saharan Africa[1]

George Kimble

Nobody can travel in tropical Africa without soon being made aware of the importance attached by the African to learning. Ask a hundred literate men what they consider to be the greatest need of their people, and ninety will unhesitatingly reply 'education'. Ask a hundred schoolboys what they want to be and at least one-fourth of them are likely to reply, 'Either an education officer or a schoolteacher.' In education the African politician sees the key to better government; the African businessman, the key to greater output and higher consumption; the African welfare worker, the key to happier, healthier living. . . .

SOME OF THE PROBLEMS

Educational advance is beset, always and everywhere, with difficulties. If anything, tropical Africa has rather more than its share of difficulties and a greater capacity for slowing down the rate of educational advance than most places. Indeed, there can be few parts of the world where small difficulties develop into large problems with such ease and resist solution so obstinately. The problems are of many kinds and show no particular preference for people or place. Most of them, however, fall into four categories: environmental, social, financial and philosophical.

Environmental

Tropical Africa does not suffer the intruder gladly, whether he comes armed with axe, bulldozer, blueprint or Bible. If he is not careful, and knowledgeable, he may find that he has misjudged the pleasure of the land and its inhabitants. The educator may find that the site of a bush school has to be selected with due regard not only for soil drainage, ease of access and availability of building material, but also for the wishes of the local headman and his favourite fetisher, and the habits of mosquitoes and larger

[1] Reprinted from *Tropical Africa, II,* Twentieth Century Fund (New York, 1961).

354

fauna.[1] He may find that one of the most stubborn entries in his school accounts is one he had never thought of before going to Africa: delapidation of fabric, building and supplies due to torrential rainstorm, mildew, moth and termite. If his planning of the school calendar does not accord with the calendar of the farmers around him, he will find that his pupils vanish when the first rains fall and the planting season begins. A washout on the road has prevented many a tutor from reaching his weekly adult education class.

More serious is the debilitating effect, aggravated by the intestinal diseases from which most Africans suffer, of the high humidities and monotonously high temperatures of the rainy season. . . .

Social

Educational problems having their origin in the African's way of life – in his attitudes toward land and kin, his valuation of leisure, comfort and commodities, and his regard for the world of spirits – are at once the most numerous and the most serious. The administrator finds them wherever he goes, and among all sorts of men. Rather than disappear when people have learned to read and write, they may become more acute.

The problem of educating an African girl is one that Rebecca Reyher discusses at length in her working paper.[2] In the first place, there is the problem of getting the girl inside a school. Outside the towns, most parents contend that all a girl needs to know of such matters as cleanliness, good manners, industry in the house and field, sex, morality and family living, they or the initiation schools are capable to teaching her. They are also likely to say that the things she might learn in a white man's school could bring them and her future husband no profit, if indeed they might not make her less docile and effective in the performance of her wifely duties. If the parents are willing to enrol the girl – as more and more are, especially in the towns – they will still need to be persuaded of the advantages of keeping her in school after she has reached the age of puberty. Since a marriageable daughter is quite likely to be one of their chief 'capital assets', it is asking much of them to deny themselves such advantage as an early marriage contract might confer. . . .

No less an educational problem is posed by the African's regard for taboo, juju and the like, and the Westerner's determination to eradicate it

[1] A recent issue of the *Northern Light*, the magazine of the Government Secondary School, Tamale, Ghana, contained the following lament: 'In the past one of the greatest problems of the school has been the constant visits . . . of snakes, with attacks amounting to invasions at the beginning and end of the rains.'

[2] This refers to a paper on African education prepared for Professor Kimble by Dr Reyher. – Eds.

along with all other evidences of ignorance and superstition. One can teach children, or adults, the food value of an egg, but it is hard to persuade people to eat eggs when they have been brought up to believe that they make a man impotent and a woman barren. . . .

Financial

Almost all countries have trouble raising money for education; those of tropical Africa certainly have. The needs of the place are so many and *per capita* incomes so low that governments have tended rather naturally to give priority to enterprises promising early returns. Casting bread upon the waters of ignorance is not usually numbered among such enterprises; the returns come only after many days – indeed, years. The cost of ignorance, however, is such that no territory concerned with the long-range good of its peoples can afford to bear it. For just as knowledge is power, ignorance is weakness; and weakness is poverty – poverty of ideas, skills and ambition, if not of resources. . . .

How to snap the crippling chain of ignorance-weakness-poverty-ignorance has long been one of the most disconcerting questions to confront African administrators. It is still not resolved; but at least all governments are agreed upon the necessity of resolving it. Almost without exception, they are now spending far more money on education than they were doing at the end of the war. In some countries expenditures on education have come to constitute the largest single item in the territorial budget. In Nigeria the three regions (Eastern, Western and Northern) each spent about one-third of their ordinary budgets on education in 1956–7; and they have spent approximately one-fifth of their capital budgets for the 1955–60 period on educational projects. In Liberia, long the most illiterate of African countries, between one-tenth and one-fifth of the budget is currently earmarked for 'public instruction'. This is not to say that any one government is spending enough to break the chain, let alone exorcize the evil spirits that dance upon it. The revenue of Tanganyika in 1957–8 amounted to some $65 million, or less than $8 *per capita*; of the eight dollars less than two were available for educational purposes. . . .

Philosophical

By now it will be apparent that there is hardly an educational problem in tropical Africa that does not force one to consider the question of ends. The environments and cultures of Africa are different from those of Europe and North America; they make radically different demands upon the people and elicit very different responses from them. No educator can possibly ignore these demands and responses. But what shall he do about them? Shall he adapt his curriculum to fit them? Or shall he endeavour to change them, Westernizing the African's land, life and livelihood alike? What shall he do about religion? Shall he try to winnow the good from the bad in African belief and practice, or shall he assume that nothing of either is worth the winnowing? What shall he do about the African's political aspirations? Shall he educate for self-government, for association or for servitude? If there is insufficient money to do all that he would like for the African, what kind of schools shall he run with the money he has? And so on, *ad infinitum....*

THE EDUCATION OF THE SCHOOL-AGED

French Territories

Educational Policy. The aim of French educational policy down to 1958 was very simple – namely, to make worthy French citizens of all the inhabitants of the French possessions south of the Sahara. To achieve this aim, the government argued that it must provide schooling in French, along the general lines of the metropolitan curriculum, and for everybody. To implement such an ambitious policy posed an enormous problem. The area administered – consisting of French West Africa, French Equatorial Africa, French Somaliland, Madagascar and the Trusteeship Territories of Togoland and French Cameroons – was more than fifteen times as large as metropolitan France. Its total population was approximately 33 million, or about 70 per cent. as large as that of the mother country. Now that almost all the component parts of these territories are either autonomous members of the French Community or independent, some changes in their educational systems may be expected, but what those changes will be it is too early to say.

The people within this vast domain are widely scattered, much given to wandering and, for the most part, have not been greatly interested in French citizenship. With few exceptions they are too poor to support a heavy tax load. The languages and dialects are many. In what was French West Africa there are approximately a hundred, none of which is spoken or understood by a sufficient number of people to justify an attempt to make it the *lingua franca*. All of them are poor in the kinds of words and concepts with which the modern educator is concerned. Large sectors, moreover, are unattractive climatically, unpromising economically and all but inaccessible. It takes an uncommonly dedicated teacher to stand the cultural and physical isolation of the more primitive areas. While there are such teachers, the supply has never been equal to the demand, for few

357

educated Africans, it seems, are willing to submit for long to such discipline.

Consequently, the French have found it impossible to provide in tropical Africa education on the scale on which it is available in France. Even today, there are still many disconcerting blanks on the primary school map, and with few exceptions only the bigger towns offer post-primary educational facilities. In 1957, in the whole of French *Afrique noire*, some 1·2 million children, out of approximately 5 million children of school age, were enrolled in European public or private schools. Of these, only about 5 per cent. were enrolled in post-primary schools. In French Equatorial Africa out of a total enrolment of approximately 176,000 in 1957, only some 8,000 students were attending secondary or technical schools. In French West Africa the corresponding figures were approximately 380,000 and 20,000; in Madagascar, 332,000 and 19,000. Down to 1958 the only institution in the whole area offering academic and technical training at the university level was the University of Dakar. But even these figures represent a remarkable advance on those of the early post-war period.

It is probable – indeed, certain – that the French could have had more schools and more children enrolled in them if they had cared less about quality. But they have consistently striven to maintain metropolitan standards, particularly at the post-primary levels. And not without success, for it is claimed that neither the African nor the European students attending high schools in the overseas territories find it difficult as a rule to 'make the grade' when they switch to similar schools, or go on to college work, in France. Certainly, few concessions are made to the colour of a man's skin or to his cultural background. To become a university student, a teacher or a doctor, an African must have all the paper qualifications a Parisian would have. He is also expected to have much the same grasp of the French language as the Parisian; and it is noteworthy that most educated Africans from, say, the Ivory Coast have a greater mastery of French than most educated Africans from, say, Ghana have of English. . . .

Portuguese Territories

Educational Policy. The educational policy of the Portuguese is more modest than that of the French and rather differently conceived. Unlike the French, the Portuguese are in no hurry to make citizens, though they leave the way open to those who wish to become citizens and can measure up to the set requirements. Consequently, they do not feel under the same obligation to duplicate in Africa all the educational facilities provided in the homeland; nor have they attempted to do so. They also differ from the French in regarding instruction in religion as forming an integral part of their teaching responsibility. . . .

In the matter of language medium, however, the Portuguese share the French government's preference for the mother tongue. Indeed, they go further than the French. Because of the great diversity of ethnic groups and languages, they contend that their goal of 'cultural assimilation' can be reached only when there is a common tongue, and that tongue Portuguese. It would seem that to the Portuguese administrator the native languages are part of the barbarism he is seeking to overcome.

In line with their narrower conception of African needs, the Portuguese have limited the scope of their elementary school offerings to Christian morals, reading, writing, arithmetic and vocational training in such fields as farming, carpentry and needlework. By so doing, they affirm that they will effect 'a preliminary penetration of Portuguese culture' without turning the Africans 'from their tribal life or from their traditional way of living.' . . .[1]

School System. Primary education is free to all Africans residing within three kilometres (roughly two miles) of a school, but it is still not available to more than a minority. In 1957, in the whole of Angola, out of an estimated school-age population of more than a million, only 80,000 children were enrolled in primary schools. In all of Mozambique, out of an estimated school-age population of 1·5 million, approximately 360,000 children were attending primary schools. In Portuguese Guinea, with a school-age population of not less than 150,000, the number of enrolled students was about 11,000. To get to these schools, many children were walking more than three kilometres. But more schools are being built, at a faster rate now than ever before, and it is hoped that in the course of the next decade the theoretical compulsion upon Africans to send children between the ages of seven and twelve to school, can be transformed into a practical possibility.

Wherever feasible, the Portuguese provide separate elementary schools for European children and the children of Europeanized or 'assimilated' Africans. The basis of segregation is cultural rather than racial. The curriculum calls for four years of instruction in the case of European children or children of Europeanized Africans. African children who have not learned Portuguese at home may begin the curriculum only after two years of preparatory work.

Post-primary education is even less developed, and is generally available only in the big towns. In the whole of Angola in 1957 fewer than 13,000 students were enrolled in secondary, technical and normal schools.

[1] Agencia General do Ultramar, p. 44 (Lisbon, 1951).

359

In Mozambique about 10,000 were enrolled; in Portuguese Guinea and São Tomé and Príncipe, about 600. Significantly, in the light of Portuguese policy, most of these students were attending technical schools. In Portuguese Africa as a whole some 15,000 students, or over 60 per cent. of the total number of post-primary students, were attending technical schools; not more than 8,500, or 35 per cent. were attending secondary schools; only 820, or less than 4 per cent., normal schools. Significantly, too, most of the technical schools were simple affairs, offering instruction in such artisan subjects as carpentry and shoemaking.

Commonwealth Territories

Educational Policy. The British are habitually shy of statements of policy, particularly those relating to the imponderables of mind and spirit. Inconvenient as this trait may be to their critics, it has the advantage of giving them greater freedom of action to do things they believe need doing in a given situation, and of making it less difficult for them to switch to other things when the situation alters. This is not to say that they are a people without an educational policy, but rather that they have no special fancy for educational policies which leave nothing to the imagination. The *raison d'être* of their educational endeavour is clear, at least. In the words of W. E. F. Ward, the main business of education, as they see it, is

> to take boys and girls and develop them as human beings to the highest possibility that they have: to train them to make the best use of their gifts. . . . It is not the job of education to teach people to know their proper stations and to stay in them. We have rejected that idea of education in [Britain], and it has no place in Africa. . . . Our job as educators, whether Europeans or Africans, is to get the schools and colleges and universities into good order: to provide more trained teachers, to develop institutes of education and professional associations of teachers, to develop African local education authorities, and, of course, to provide more education as well as better education. If self-government and partnership are to work in Africa, the educational problems have to be solved. Once you begin education, you cannot stop it; you must go all the way. . . . .[1]

Primary Education. All of this is more easily said than done, of course. The building of 'pyramids' in Africa has always been a slow and costly process. But progress has been substantial, at all three levels of the pyramid, in all the Commonwealth territories, especially since the war. Literacy may still be as low as 10 per cent. in many out-of-the-way places, but in most of the larger towns at least 50 per cent. of the African children now attend primary school, and in some (notably Lagos, Nairobi, Salisbury, Dar-es-Salaam) the percentage is as high as 75. Within the next ten years

[1] *The Listener*, p. 54 (9 July 1953).

or so several governments expect to be able to provide free primary education for their entire school-age populations. Among these are the governments of Nigeria and Ghana. The educational ten-year plan embarked on in Nigeria in 1946 had as its main objective the provision of junior primary education within a generation for all Nigerian children of school age. This plan was later superseded by the even more ambitious 1955-60 development plans of the federal and regional governments, which have devoted a large proportion of their development moneys to 'crash' programmes of educational expansion. As a result of these, school enrolments went up in the Western Region by two-thirds of a million between 1954 and 1956, and in the Eastern Region by three-quarters of a million to 1,330,000. In Ghana, the Minister of Education was able to report in 1957 that

> throughout the length and breadth of southern Ghana and Ashanti, primary school facilities are available for the great majority of children of school age. In 1951 there were just over 1,000 primary schools; in 1957 the number has risen to over 3,000, and the period of tremendous expansion in primary education is over.[1]

This in a country where the rate of expansion of educational facilities down to the mid-1930's was so slow that it would have taken six hundred years to achieve universal primary education!

Secondary Education. The development of secondary schools has been much slower. Such schools, to serve their function – which, in the eyes of the student, is to enable him to obtain on graduating a certificate from one of the senior British universities that will be his password to 'white-collar' service – must be well equipped, well staffed, commodious (most schools have to reckon on having boarders as well as day scholars and many are for boarders exclusively), and must maintain educational standards comparable to those found in British schools of the same kind. Then again, until the recent expansion of primary education, the number of primary school graduates who were either able or willing to attend secondary schools and complete the arduous five-to-six-year curriculum was small. Many of those who were willing did not pass the highly competitive entrance examinations, and many of those who did, found it difficult to pay the tuition and, where they applied, the boarding fees.

Consequently, it is not surprising that up to the early 1950's, the percentage of primary school graduates who went on to do secondary school work was nowhere higher than about two, and in some territories less than one. Such figures, it has long been recognized, are too low for the good

[1] *Ghana Today* (10 July 1957).

of any territory moving towards self-government, to say nothing of territories already self-governing. Accordingly, large sums of money have been spent in the past decade on the building of new schools and the training of new African teachers. Between 1951 and 1958 the number of secondary schools in Ghana increased from thirteen to approximately sixty, and the number of secondary school students from less than 3,000 to more than 12,000. Over the same period the number of teacher-training colleges increased from twenty to thirty-four, and the number of trainees from less than 2,000 to more than 4,000.

In Commonwealth tropical Africa as a whole the number of secondary schools more than doubled (to over 600) in the first post-war decade, and the number of students more than trebled (to over 75,000). By the end of 1960 the number of such schools is expected to exceed 1,000 and the number of students to be well over 150,000. By the mid-1960's, therefore, the number of secondary school graduates coming on to the labour market in such territories as Ghana, the Western Region of Nigeria and Uganda will bear comparison with the number in some comparably sized American states. There will still be many primary school graduates who are unable to get a secondary education, but there should be enough to ensure that the foreseeable needs of government, commerce and industry for white-collar African employees can be met in most territories. . . .

Spanish Territories

The fact that the Spanish government does not make a habit of publicizing its colonial administration has led many people to infer that there is little to tell that any government would wish to tell. But in the field of education such an inference would seem to be unwarranted. Thus, in Spanish Guinea[1] in 1957, out of an estimated school-age population of approximately 65,000, not less than 21,000 were in primary school, over 200 in technical school and nearly 200 in secondary school. Such figures compare well with those of several much larger non-self-governing territories, including Bechuanaland, British Somaliland and Somalia, and, on a proportional reckoning, they outrank those of most other tropical African territories, non-self-governing or otherwise.

The educational systems for the children of European stock and for those of African stock are, in the phrase once so familiar to Americans, separate and unequal. The objectives of African education are stated to be the improvement of the African's living conditions and the inculcation of

[1] Comprising Rio Muni, or continental Guinea, the nearby islands of Corisco, Great and Little Elobey, and the islands of Fernando Po and Annobón in the Bight of Benin.

Spanish virtues, patriotism, and culture to the degree that this is possible without making him a rootless person.

In line with these objectives, the African is offered training of three types. The first, or pre-primary, type is concerned, in the main, with practical, manual matters, and is conducted largely by African 'auxiliaries'. The second, or primary, type offers the student the alternatives of training for 'the activities of the country in general' or preparation for the 'higher school' (*escuela superior indígena*), where he will receive the third type of training, namely, for auxiliary service in such fields as public health, public works, business and teaching. In addition, there are schools which offer instruction in clerical, agricultural and domestic work.

DAILY NEWSPAPERS: NUMBERS, ESTIMATED CIRCULATION, AND
COPIES PER 1,000 POPULATION

Territory	Year	Number	Circulation Total (thousands)	per 1,000
Angola	1956	3	24	6
Belgian Congo	1957	8	40	3
Ethiopia (inc. Eritrea)	1956	5	10	b
French Cameroons	1957	1	10	3
French Equatorial Africa	1954	4	1	b
(French) Togo	1954	1	1	1
French West Africa	1957	7	32	2
Gambia	1955	1	1	5
Ghana	1957	5	101	21
Kenya	1955	4	31	5
Liberia	1957	1	1	1
Malagasy Republic (Madagascar)	1957	17	20	4
Mozambique	1956	4	21	3
Nigeria	1957	13	224	7
Northern Rhodesia (Zambia)	1956	1	18	8
Southern Rhodesia	1956	3	51	21
Sierra Leone	1953	4	7	3
Somalia (Italian Somaliland)	1957	1	1	1
Spanish Guinea	1956	1	2	10
Republic of Sudan	1956	11	30	3
Tanganyika	1956	2	18	2
Uganda	1957	1	8	1
Zanzibar (inc. Pemba)	1955	1	a	1

Source: United Nations, *Statistical Yearbook* (1957, 1959 editions) (New York, 1957, 1959).

a Less than 500.   b Less than 1.

RADIO BROADCASTING:
TRANSMITTING STATIONS AND RECEIVING SETS

Territory	Transmitting Stations		Receiving Sets	
	Year	*Number*	*Year*	*Number (thousands)*
Angola	1958	16	1957	33*
Bechuanaland	—	—	1957	1
Belgian Congo (inc. Ruanda-Burundi)	1958	14	1956	16*
British Somaliland	—	—	1957	2
Ethiopia (exc. Eritrea)	1958	1	1957	50
French Cameroons	1958	3	1957	11
French Equatorial Africa	1958	3	1953	10
French Somaliland	—	—	1955	2
(French) Togo	—	—	1957	3
French West Africa	1958	7	1953	50
Gambia	—	—	1957	1
Ghana (Gold Coast)	—	—	1958	101
Kenya	1958	7ª	1958	25*
Liberia	—	—	1957	10
Malagasy Republic (Madagascar)	—	—	1957	55
Mozambique	1958	5	1958	36*
Nigeria (inc. British Cameroons)	1958	8	1958	73
Portuguese Guinea	1956	1	1958	1*
Northern Rhodesia			1955	40
Nyasaland	1958	8	1955	4
Southern Rhodesia			1951	24*
São Tomé and Príncipe	—	—	1951	b*
Sierra Leone	1956	3	1957	8*
Somalia (Italian Somaliland)	—	—	1951	2
Spanish Guinea	—	—	1958	1
Republic of Sudan	—	—	1957	7*
Tanganyika	1958	7ª	1958	19
Uganda	1958	7ª	n.a.	n.a.
Zanzibar	1958	3	1958	5

Source: United Nations, *Statistical Yearbook (1958, 1959)* (New York, 1958, 1959).

ª Total for Kenya, Tanganyika and Uganda.   * Number of licenses issued.
b Less than 500.   n.a.: not available.

Educational Problems in sub-Saharan Africa

So far little thought appears to have been given to the subject of higher education, possibly because it would almost certainly lead to Europeanization, and so to rootlessness.

The education of the sizeable European population of Spanish Guinea follows in all essentials the metropolitan pattern. The responsibility of providing education for Africans and Europeans is shared by the government and the missions; but only Catholic missions are eligible for grants and subsidies. . . .

The African Press

The region with the most influential African press is Commonwealth West Africa (Gambia, Sierra Leone, Ghana and Nigeria). It was here – in Sierra Leone in the early nineteenth century – that the first tropical African newspaper was printed, and it is here that most tropical African newspapers run today for the benefit of Africans are published. Nor is Commonwealth West Africa's dominance in this respect accidental. It was here that the European cultural tradition first got a footing. It was here that the African intellectual, and his progeny the nationalist, first emerged; and for such, journalism provided one of very few professional opportunities. Then, too, it was here, in the land of the cocoa bean and the palm kernel, that Africans first came to have spare cash for the purchase of such things as newspapers. . . .

34

The Needs of African Education[1]

Conference Proceedings

One of the most important and realistic results to have issued from any major African conference was the Report on the Development of Education in Africa, of which this brief reading is an extract.

This sets out, in realistic and closely reasoned terms, the most important needs that contemporary educational policy should endeavour to meet.

From: Report on the Conference of African States on the Development of Education in Africa. UNESCO Document (mimeographed) 59 EX/4 Add., pp. 2–5 (Paris, 31 May).

NEEDS

The African States defined clearly their educational needs in relation to the economic and social development of the region as:

(i) *Finance* for school construction, paying non-African teachers and providing scholarships for Africans to study abroad:

(ii) *Equipment* and books for secondary, general, technical and agricultural schools;

(iii) *Teacher training institutions* to produce primary teachers, and expatriate teachers for these and for expanded second level programmes;

(iv) *Reform* of the nature of education and of the content of textbooks in terms of the changing structure of existing economies and of the social and cultural conditions of Africa;

(v) *Education of girls*;

(vi) *Higher education* to meet the urgent need for high level manpower;

(vii) *Adult education* to eradicate the estimated current 100 million illiterates;

(viii) *Planning* of educational expansion both in quantity and quality.

[1] Reprinted from UNESCO Document 59 EX/4 Add. (Paris, 31 May 1960).

366

SHORT- AND LONG-TERM PLANS

Against these priorities (1. Secondary education, 2. Reform of the curricula, and 3. Training of teachers), the conference established for the African States long-term and short-term educational plans reflecting the analysis and priorities referred to.

The targets for the long-term plan (1961–80) are:

(*a*) Primary education shall be universal, compulsory and free;

(*b*) Education at the second level shall be provided to 30 per cent. of primary school leavers;

(*c*) Higher education, mostly in African institutions, shall be provided to 20 per cent. of those who complete secondary education;

(*d*) The improvement of the quality of African schools and universities shall be a constant aim.

The targets for the short-term plan (1961–5) are:

(*a*) An annual increase at the primary level of an additional 5 per cent. of the beginning school age group which will increase enrolment from the present 40 per cent. to 51 per cent. by 1965;

(*b*) Second level education shall increase from the present 3 per cent. of the age group to 9 per cent. by 1965;

(*c*) Special attention will be paid to the training of teachers at all levels and to adult education programmes.

COST OF THE SHORT- AND LONG-TERM PLANS

To meet the cost of these short and long-term plans the African States decided to make every effort to increase their contribution to education of 3 per cent. of the national income to 4 per cent. by 1965 and on to 6 per cent. by 1980. Even so, to achieve their modest, essential and realistic targets they face a deficit which rises from $140 million in 1961 to $450 million in 1965, reaching a peak of $1 billion in 1970 at which time their secondary and higher education bottlenecks will be broken, falling to $400 million in 1980, after which, with Africanization of their educational system and effective social development of the region, African education can stand on its own.

367

35

The Demand for and Support of Education in African Tribal Society[1]

O. F. Raum

This article by Dr Raum has been chosen from among a large number written about educational problems in Africa, because it examines more carefully than is customary the factors in the old forms of society which help to make education so popular and upon which a realistic educational policy for the future must be built.

It is probably true to say that of all the social institutions which are having to become adjusted on this continent, it is in the sphere of learning that the African has the most favourable opportunity. Not only is education an integral part of the old social forms, but its advantages are perhaps magnified by many Africans who see it as the sesame that others find in independence.

Here lies a great challenge, for if modern knowledge and technical skills can be introduced on a vast scale – and it is only the scarcity of resources, financial and human, that makes it so difficult – who can say where the limit may lie in eradicating human misery and advancing the economic prosperity and dignity of man?

In the average African tribe of the Bantu-speaking area we can distinguish three types of education.

INFORMAL EDUCATION

The informal education of the home aims at training the child in the norms of conduct appropriate to family, and kinship groupings. The educators, represented by the parents, act under the demands of the tribal *ethos* in rearing their children. These demands are expressed in traditional folk-lore, its proverbs and tales, in the system of reverential restraints or taboos, in the current social comment on the actions of the children and the educational abilities of the parents. Every African father and mother tries to induce in his or her children a behaviour which corresponds to these demands. In doing so, they use a series of educational measures, such as rewards and punishments, and supplement these with linguistic tools, as for instance promises and threats and the story. The

[1] Reprinted from *Yearbook of Education* (Evans Bros. Ltd., 1956).

latter follows either a traditional fairy-tale pattern or is the elaboration of an historical topic or of a contemporary example. It stresses, *inter alia*, the advantages of diligence and heroism and the drawbacks of deceit and stubbornness. In the particular situation of the family these norms appear by no means as being imposed from the outside. They arise as essential demands within the social dialectic of the elementary family, so as to ensure its integration.

Our assumption is that education being a social value has a price placed on it. This price can be expressed only in the idiom of the culture to which it belongs. Since primitive culture does not express its values in monetary terms, it is necessary for us to describe in detail how concrete or ideological equivalents of money secure the benefits of education. One thing is certain even for such societies. Education is a value, for which the 'producers of education', the parents and political leaders, are prepared to pay a price, and so are the teachers, who might be called the distributors of the commodity of education, as well as its consumers, the children, the novices of an initiation camp, the educands of tribal life. But education is a complex value, inasmuch as it consists of many parts and many aspects, which may be either offered with or subtracted from the commodity as a whole. Hence the determination of the cultural value of education is a difficult undertaking, because even were it possible to obtain figures for educational services from the national budget, very little would be revealed as to the status accorded to education within the cultural context concerned.

The time and effort which parents devote to training their children are a measure of the value education has in their society or in a particular family. In addition, African parents provide occasions for the celebration of ceremonies which accentuate certain traditionally accepted stages in the child's development. The food prepared for these events, the livestock slaughtered, the fees paid in kind to the ritual experts, present part of the educational bill each primitive family has to face. On these occasions parents have to submit to ritual abstentions from normally enjoyed 'pleasures', such as certain types of food, sexual intercourse, or selected occupations. These deprivations are willingly accepted by the parents to secure the well-being of their children. They should be listed as important items in assessing the value of primitive informal education. Other values which might compete with the demand for family education hardly exist under conditions unaffected by Western contact. For since this type of education is a basic requirement for the existence of the family, and is an essential of social life, it receives 'top priority'.

The African parent expects certain satisfactions from the successful transmission of the norms of family conduct. For instance, a woman has

369

her efforts in training her daughter recognized in the widespread custom whereby her daughter's betrothed presents her with some small gift. Usually one of the cattle constituting the bride-price is earmarked for the mother, and its name indicates that it is meant to compensate her for her parental care. Of course, the bride-price in itself is a recognition of the value of the young woman, and as the transaction affects the families rather than the bride and the groom, it is a measure of her value to the two contracting families.[1]

Parents are also given ideal rewards for their educational efforts. Families with a good reputation in educational matters have a higher standing in their community than families in which the education of the children is neglected. Such standing helps to promote the interests and influence of a family and its members in various ways. Fathers and mothers may receive honorary names referring to their children or to the establishment through their offspring of a new branch of the lineage. In ritual praises the successful education of their children may be mentioned. As spirit guardians, the fathers remain in an intimate personal relationship to some of their children, and mothers are not excluded from this privilege, although normally they are prevented by the prevalent patrilineal system from being made much of after their death.

RITUAL ACCENTUATION

The second type of primitive education takes the form of the ritual accentuation of the life stages of a child, the celebration of his advance in knowledge and bodily strength as traditionally defined. Its aim is to secure the growing individual's association with the mystic forces of the physical environment and of his social universe. The essential feature of these ceremonies is the rhythmical repetition of rites which link the child with these forces. In many of these ceremonies indelible signs are marked on the educand's body, be it by means of circumcision, mutilations on lips, ears, or teeth, or scarifications. The function of such signs is to act as a badge, to make the owner enjoy the fellow-feeling of being a member of a powerful solidarity, to remind him of his obligations to society, and legitimize his claims for help.

[1] The function of the bride-price as an educational yard-stick is not its only function. In addition it compensates the woman's paternal family for the loss of the children which she will bear to her husband's lineage. It is also a kind of insurance against conduct which might break up the marriage. For if the husband misbehaves, his wife will leave him and the cattle are forfeited to his family. If the wife behaves badly, she will be sent back to her father and he has to return the cattle paid for her.

Parents are coerced by the tribal value system into the efforts and expenditure required for the organization of these ceremonies. Well-to-do parents may have 'private' celebrations for their child. But it is more convenient for a number of parents to club together and arrange communal ceremonies. Experts are engaged, and an isolated ritual site is prepared, food is accumulated and new clothes and ornaments obtained for the children against the time when they pass out as graduates. If competitive claims have to be met (e.g. for a hut-building, a wedding, or a funeral), the fees in kind, the food required, may not be available. It is then possible for the harried parent to borrow the wherewithal from kinsmen. Or the child's attendance at the ceremony is postponed even to the extent of his becoming over-age. Teasing and ridicule, the powerful motivating forces for conformity of conduct in primitive society, in the end make the demand for perfoming the ceremony overwhelming.

A great number of educators may be engaged in these ceremonies. Old men act as teachers of moral lessons. Priests perform sacred rites which appeal to and thank the ancestral deities. Operators with a knack of using the traditional tools carry out the incisions and scarifications. Mentors are hired to stay with the educands in the isolation huts and train them in the lore which is to be memorized. Supervisors are appointed to see that the novices submit to the taboo régime of the ceremony. All these experts are paid fees in kind and consider these fees a return on the expenses incurred when they trained for their job. In their professional training they stayed for an extended period with a recognized master of their craft. They collected goods to exchange them for the professional accoutrement and esoteric knowledge. They submit to the abstentions and abandon their normal economic pursuits for the period of the ceremony. It is understandable that the 'popular' demand for the performing of the ceremonies frequently emanates from these functionaries, who wish to recoup themselves for the expenses of their training.

The educands, normally boys or girls of the same age, jointly undergo these rites of passage. If there is delay in the ceremony, it is caused by the poor state of the crop or some tribal circumstance, e.g. the death of the chief, or the threat of an inter-tribal conflict. Such occurrences necessitate the concentration of the economic resources on these more urgent matters. But adolescents may not agree with their seniors' judgement as to the pressing nature of the alternative enterprises. They may gather together, sing provocative songs, commit outrages, occasionally inflict self-mutilations and destroy property. In this way, they provoke their parents to hasten the ceremony. The educands are as ready to pay the price for this type of ritual education as their educators. Not only are they frequently called upon to build the ritual camp or hut. They must also submit to the hardships of the austere camp life, suffer the excruciating pain of the operation, attend to their wounds and observe the taboos of the isolation period. The intensity with which they demand these formative ceremonies compares favourably with the attitude of the average Western child towards school. Of course, the primitive child receives in return genuine satisfactions: the ceremonies introduce him to a higher status; a carefully adjusted increase in privileges and obligations admits him to wider social circles.

PREPARATION FOR PARTICIPATION IN PUBLIC AFFAIRS

In the third type of education known in primitive society, the young men are trained for full participation in the public affairs of the tribe. The aim is to introduce the prospective tribesman to the legal procedures and principles of his people, and to acquaint him with the constitution and the power set-up of the tribe and with its relationship to political forces outside it. The promoters of this type of education are the chief and his councillors. As the jural and political organism under their control needs to adjust itself to emergent internal and external circumstances, the tribal guardians add new items to their public educational programme and thereby give the tribe vitality.

As in the case of the ceremonies, this type of public training has to be organized, and the efforts devoted to its successful achievement are a fair measure of the value ascribed to education. The sons of noblemen and commoners are called to attend the royal court for important law cases. They have to be entertained, are given lodging and food and drink at the chief's expense. No lectures are given to them, but the young men attend the court sittings, hear the comments of councillors and spectators, and gradually learn to form their own judgement.

Where military organizations existed, the training of the youths in the war-like practices was entrusted to the officers with experience. Having been enrolled, the young men were drafted to military camps. In their training they learned the movements of military formations in both attack and retreat, the handling of small and large contingents, the tactical and strategical considerations appropriate to the weapons, the terrain, the military organization and aims of their people. The commissariat was a complex affair and called on the highest organizational abilities of the leading tribesmen. The emoluments of the officers in charge and the cost of the commissariat may be considered educational expenditure. Further expenses were incurred at the commencement of a campaign, when the tribal magicians were called in to administer charms and distribute amulets.

The demands competing for recognition over and against education are difficult to define in primitive society, which lacks the convenient index of an annual budget with departmental votes, and scarcely knows the representation of sectional interests. Undoubtedly the meagre economic resources of a people are strained by the larger tribal ceremonies, such as initiation, which sometimes combines with the military course. An initiation may therefore be held only at intervals of several years, and in some tribes only once in a generation. At any rate the time for celebrating ceremonies is after the harvest, in times of plenty, or in the winter months, when no other occupations interfere with their performance. On the other hand, their value is considered so high that they cannot be altered or abbreviated. And since their curriculum deals with such vital topics as marriage, the control of human fortunes by the ancestral deities, and the relationship between kinship groups and tribal institutions, attendance is compulsory for everyone. A further indication of the high value placed on the formative ceremonies are the tests which are part of them. They are scarcely examinations of memorized knowledge, but methods of symbolically expressing the candidates' allegiance to the moral values of their society. The tests do not isolate the individual as do our examinations, but are, on the contrary, group or companionship tests binding those who undergo them together in insoluble and lifelong bonds of comradeship. A clash between the claims of ritual and public education is occasionally noticeable in tribal life. For instance, the Zulu king Shaka abolished circumcision because the long healing period interfered with the military preparedness of his troops. We have here, in incipient form, a conflict between different types of education, such as might occur in a modern society.

To sum up: it has been established that primitive education may be viewed as an 'economic' process in which we distinguish the producers of the commodity 'education', its distributors, and consumers. The producers of education, the parents and political leaders, the tribe itself, are interested in promoting education, they appraise its function, advertise its advantages, and create additional values to make it appeal to the consumers. The teachers and experts, as distributors and transmitters of education, really form part of the producing side, although they may be passive in the elaboration of the commodity. The children are the consumers. They acquire an education and have to pay a price for it which is defined in the value idiom of their culture. Education should not be viewed exclusively as consumer-goods, since those possessing education may use it for the creation of new values. It may therefore be classed with the cultural producer-goods.

THE COMPETING EDUCATION OF THE WHITE MAN

With the advent of the white man an entirely new situation was created in the sphere of education. He offered an alternative education to supplant the indigenous education given in the family, the ceremonial camp, and the tribal institution. To use an analogy: the new masters did their best to offer their type of education at competitive prices and to depreciate the indigenous educational currency. Yet right from the earliest contacts with primitive peoples, there were far-seeing Westerners who realized the intrinsic value of the indigenous order. A great educational theoretician, Jean-Jacques Rousseau, sensed that the simplicity of the social norms in primitive society made for easier recognition of the fundamental moral norms of human conduct. While, in his advocacy of the noble savage's way of life, he went too far and under-estimated the values of his own advanced culture, the white man on the spot fell into the opposite error. He rejected in vehement language certain striking features of native life and many of its educational practices. Doubts were, for instance, raised about the value of the tests of hardship during initiation and in the ethical significance of kinship conduct.

The creation of the demand for Western education was thus accompanied by attempts to show up the spuriousness of the claims of traditional education. It was comparatively easy to disprove the claim that ritual education established a mystical association with the forces of the universe, because the material and military superiority of the white man was achieved without it.

CONFLICTS BETWEEN VALUE SYSTEMS

A revolutionary situation has arisen. It is characterized by the conflict between Western and African value systems and the intensification of this conflict by the emergence of an intermediate area of 'floating' values unattached to any of the traditional systems. This conflict results from the juxtaposition of two fully integrated cultures and their transforming influence upon individuals caught up in the contact situation.

As to the educational programme devised for the African, there is conflict in the white camp as well as in the African camp. Among the whites the so-called 'integrationists' demand the extension to the Africans of an education modelled entirely on the Western metropolitan pattern. Their reason may be either a belief in the uniformity of human needs and ideals or a conviction regarding the unchallengeable superiority of Western civilization over primitive ways of life. The 'differentialists' among the

374

whites prefer an education trimmed to suit the African in his special circumstances. This may be considered desirable again for two contrasting reasons. They either wish to preserve and genuinely stimulate the creative genius of indigenous culture, or hope to underpin and justify the order of privileged segregation of the white from the native. The conflict in the African camp may be said to centre in the struggle between the conservatives and the reformers. Among the conservatives are found the die-hard traditionalists, who are still opposed to modern education as a symbol of the Western way of life which countenances the demoralization of the native proletariat in the urban centres. Other conservatives are genuinely interested in retaining the spirit of the culture which their forefathers have created and which shows such an amazing vitality under the stress of culture contact. Among the reformers some realize that there is an urgent need for social and cultural adjustments within the African community, so that Africa can compete in the modern world on equal terms with other nations. Others are imbued with a radical spirit and would like to jettison traditional social machinery and the tenuous cultural bonds which help it to function.

To put it briefly, the conflict situation results in an intensification of the demand for education. It also increases the awareness of alternative ideals of education. The uniformity of educational thought seems a matter of the past. Greatly differentiated values emerge. Such sectional strife is, one must hope, preparatory to a new synthesis on a higher level. This makes itself felt even in the only group which has not been affected by the century-old campaign for Western education. The die-hard traditionalists are driven to re-create the demand for tribal ceremonies and institutions of primitive education. They are often prepared to go to great lengths to pay for them. However, such revivals cannot now hope to be acceptable for large sections of native society unless they make concessions to Western education.

Western education as a commodity for native populations in colonial territories is subject to great fluctuations in value. It is appreciated in those sections which have learned to make a living by it. It is decried by people to whom the graduates of Western institutions appear to be undermining the values of the old order. An element bringing high appreciation is its apparent scarcity, for it is still in limited supply. Because of this scarcity, an unequal distribution is almost a thing of necessity. This obviously enables some people to profit by it who are not really qualified to have a first call on educational resources and leads to the phenomenon of the 'educated' snob in native society, i.e. of the person who vaunts an education which is of no use to him. The fact that, in conditions of scarcity, waste occurs is a danger sign, indicating that the available education does not yet answer the needs of the native peoples.

36

The Psychological Pressure upon Modern Africans[1]

Leonard W. Doob

One must not fall into the rather easy fallacy of supposing that most Africans are basically similar just because they are named after the same continent, have a similar skin-colour and often smile. There is no such thing as *an* African personality. This having been said, the basic cultural uniformities that were discussed earlier and the common problems of economic, political and social transition, nevertheless do give genuine meaning to the title of this paper.

Much of this volume has necessarily been about human groups – societies, States and tribes – but, when all is said and done, the basic unit in human affairs is always the individual. It is not only right, therefore, but also necessary that in addition to the sociologists and the economists and the political scientists, there should be added the word of a psychologist.

Here the key word is 'security'. Nothing takes the sense of security away from a man more quickly than the sudden deprivation of accustomed things. Nothing is more dangerous for continued mental health, nor is any symptom in mental illness more common than a feeling of insecurity. Add these statements together and it will be readily understood how much insecurity there is in contemporary Africa, and how dangerous is this floating fund to the well-being of its peoples, its States and the whole political world. It is long likely to remain one of the basic causes of unrest and distrust in Africa.

The most conspicuous psychological fact about Africa is the simultaneous and continuous exposure of Africans to traditional and Western forms of culture. Everywhere the traditional society meaningfully survives. The most urbanized African knows that usually not far away is a village of his tribe where many if not most of the old ways are cultivated and practised. His native language, like that of his children, is an African language, no matter how fluently both of them speak English, French, Portuguese, Spanish, Afrikaans, or a lingua franca. At the same time even the remotest area in the interior has experienced some contact with the West. Planes are visible overhead and roads are being built and improved. Someone – often

[1] Reprinted from *Journal of Human Relations*, 8, 3/4 (Spring and Summer, 1960), by permission of the publisher, Central State College, Wilberforce, Ohio, copyright 1960.

not an African but a family from the Orient or the Middle East – has a shop which sells the trinkets, the foods, the cloth, and the mechanical devices of civilization. The government from the capital and the missionaries from the West are trying conspicuously to induce or compel the mass of Africans to improve their health, to wear respectable clothes, to increase the cultivation of a particular crop, to pay taxes, to support more schools, to abandon many traditional beliefs, and in hundreds of other ways to crawl less slowly into the modern world.

Under these circumstances Africans, even if they wished to, could not accept one society and then pay little or no attention to the alternative; they simply must experience both societies. Many, perhaps all of them, feel somewhat dissatisfied with the blend of cultures that inevitably occurs within them. Whether they wish to accept only a few innovations which they believe they can add to the old without appreciably affecting their adherence to the traditional pattern, or whether they seek to become as European as possible – those are the extremes in motivation between which Africans can be placed – they either regret the loss of the older forms, or are reprimanded by their more conservative peers or elders for deviating. Simultaneously, they often believe they really have been able to obtain only little more than a token from the West. The tin roof on the hut may be judged better than thatch, but Europeans have glass windows and electric lights. Exceptional Africans who are in professions like medicine, law, education, and the church may have prestige and a high, European standard of living, but they know that in Africa they labour under handicaps which usually do not exist or can be circumvented on the European continent. This discrepancy between what is on the one hand and what was or what could be on the other hand must continue to persist during a period of rapid change.

It is a discrepancy, moreover, that becomes more disturbing when it is so often coupled with the value judgement that the European way is superior to the African. No African can doubt that European vehicles of transportation are more efficient than his own. Traditional methods of cultivating the land may seem sacred and desirable; yet many Africans can perceive the soil erosion now plaguing so many areas (without realizing that the causes are numerous and complex), and frequently they are told that the agricultural salvation can come only by following the scientific wisdom of the West. Not for a moment do Africans feel that the basic values of their culture are inferior to those of the Europeans, although some of the converted may whisper the suspicion to themselves. The press of the alien, however, makes them defensively assert confidence in themselves, whereas formerly no compelling alternative society was even conceivable.

For centuries on the East coast but for less than a century in most other areas, all Africans have been compelled to acknowledge the superior weapons, the superior military and political organization, and hence the superior strength of outsiders. Now the power in many countries no longer belongs to Arabs or Europeans but has been passed to a microscopically small and not necessarily democratically inclined African élite. Most Africans must feel, consequently, that only the source but not the fact of their impotence has changed.

These African leaders, not the traditional ones but the sophisticated men who are pushing their countries toward independence and then desperately groping to participate economically and politically in the community of nations, are spokesmen for change. For it is they who form political parties, who urge people to grow cash crops, and who struggle to reduce illiteracy and disease. Their activities may convince people that Africans can become Europeans or at least that they can act like Europeans. At the same time the pressure to change appears to come from Africans who are not quite African; again and again the gap between people and their new leaders appears fantastically large. Indeed many African societies have had a tradition of extreme stratification, but the distance between the supreme leader who may have been an hereditary sultan with absolute powers and the followers who may have been little more than serfs was diminished psychologically by the patent fact that bottom and top were encased in the same culture and hence were struggling to achieve common and appropriate ends.

The external changes which Africans must make when they yield to the pressures of Europeans or their own *élite* are too numerous to catalogue. The psychological underpinning for these changes, however, can be conceptualized under three headings. First, there must be an extension of knowledge and interests. Originally Africans, like other non-literate peoples, knew and knew well the details of their own community. Now news from the outside is reaching them through their children who are at school, through their own leaders, and through the mass media of communication. It is relatively rare to find an African village which is without such contacts. Someone who is literate and reads a newspaper, however irregularly, reports to others his version of what he grasps. One battery-powered radio set may be in operation; and local African stations broadcast not only in a European language, but usually also in several vernacular languages that are considered quantitatively or politically important. Posters and public announcements are displayed on walls. A government agency, like the one charged with 'community development', is likely to dispatch a so-called 'mobile cinema' van which displays educational and entertaining pictures accompanied by commentaries in the vernacular. In many parts of Africa the people themselves move about, for example, to markets, and thus widen their contacts. Likewise the introduction of a material change evokes some curiosity and leads at least a few artisans to learn something about a motor or a tool. Widening the base of information, though usually very slow, can also occur in marked spurts. Thus this writer has found in villages in Northern Nigeria a close relation between alertness and literacy that had been acquired in government-sponsored classes for adults: whether more alert people initially attended the classes, whether attendance at the classes made them subsequently more alert, or whether both sequences produced the relationship is not known or perhaps knowable, but the fact by itself suggests the repercussions which follow one another.

The second alteration required by European culture is difficult to specify without appearing to exaggerate, for it refers to an ability to postpone present rewards for the sake of future gratification or to endure trouble at the moment so that it may be avoided later on. No African, no human being has ever been able to live only in the moment; but here it is contended that the Western or modern ways which Africans now learn place an especially high premium upon renunciation. Most public-health measures, for example, demand that action to ward off disease be taken by healthy people; as medical officers have been saying for decades in Africa, it is easier to persuade a man with a pain to swallow a pill that brings quick relief than it is to get him to dig the latrine that may prevent the recurrence of the pain. Similarly, saving is generally necessary before most of the attractive novelties from the West can be purchased. It may very well be that the greater curbing of momentary impulses is effectively attainable only through the partial replacement of external by internal controls: conscience or super-ego may have to function more frequently, social sanctions less frequently.

The unproven hypothesis just mentioned relates also to the third psychological change discernible among modern Africans: the pressure to abandon some of the certainties provided by traditional society and to seek out or at least not to resist innovation. Traditional societies in Africa obviously were not elysian since they were troubled by natural catastrophes, plagues, wars, slavery, shortages, and other miseries; but people at least knew roughly what to expect. Each person also had some assurance that the kind of existence which he had followed as a child would last during his life time. Now many Africans have experienced gentle or violent changes in their traditional ways, and they are urged in effect to keep changing.

Faced with such pressures and forced mildly or markedly to learn such changes, modern Africans seem significantly uncertain. Without exaggeration, one hypothesis suggests, the greatest of their uncertainties involves brute survival. Non-literate peoples who live close to a subsistence level are always vulnerable to natural vagaries. A severe storm or a larger than usual invasion of plant pests can produce starvation and death. Many but certainly not all parts of Africa have an uncertain climate which can swing between the extremes of droughts and floods. Tropical diseases like malaria, dysentery, leprosy, and bilharziasis, though mitigated by European medical science, still confront people, to which newer horrors – like kwashiorkor, a debilitating disease which results from protein deficiency – are added. Africans who modify or abandon the traditional economy (usually subsistence farming), in order to raise a cash crop or work for modern industry find themselves dependent upon employers or upon the prices of the world market which they themselves can neither comprehend nor control. Intervention by government, especially by stabilization boards, reduces but does not control the fluctuations. Even the African who is still linked intimately to his tribe is not completely safe; unlike his 'detribalized' relative in the city, he is not deserted during an emergency, but his society cannot guarantee that the welfare of all will ever be adequately maintained.

Other uncertainty arises from the dethronement of leaders. Traditional chiefs are increasingly losing their power; the respect in which they are held varies with local conditions, but any change in status is almost certain to be downwards. Modern political leaders, no matter how great their power, must establish their claims to obedience and veneration, and it is usually known that they can lose as well as win the power which they now enjoy. Even the role of Europeans is no longer certain. Clearly, they are not blindly loved or respected as some of the early missionaries and explorers were; nor are they universally detested as imperialistic oppressors or exploiters. In the multiracial societies where settlers and Africans have not yet stabilized the kind of relation to be evolved in the future, the actual, the potential, and the frequently noble contributions of Europeans are likely to be appreciated; but the ensuing gratitude contains elements of eservation and suspicion, even when the need for European assistance is desperately recognized, as in the independent countries. The Fathers are adored and hated.

Africans are also uncertain because they cannot assess the outcome of their critical decisions. The corn may grow taller after an application of a new fertilizer, but in the past without the use of chemicals good years have succeeded bad ones. Some Africans may have a modern house in town or in a company compound, and they may enjoy the comfort which it brings; but who knows whether they might not have been happier if they had continued to live in the village of their extended family? The religion from the West appeals to their senses and to most of their convictions but not to all their beliefs: maybe there are still evil witches about, maybe ancestors intervene to bring help or trouble, maybe magic is important.

The pressures upon modern Africans to remain traditional and to become modern, in brief, are strong and unresolved. They are producing conflict without a foreseeable outcome. They have added to traditional insecurity a host of new insecurities. Here is a bleak state of affairs.

In truth, though, it is not as bleak as the analysis would suggest. For the consequences of the pressure upon modern Africans are not devastating. One has to see the entire picture, as it were, to be depressed by it. Only the African who has somehow achieved perspective is able to point to these difficulties. A person with such social insight is likely to be part of the *élite* for whom living undoubtedly is tremendously exciting. He has learned enough of the spirit of the West to be thrilled by this pioneering period of independence and growth. He is pleased by his new power, by the problems to be solved, and even by the toil which is demanded of him.

The vast majority of modern Africans, it is felt, are making day-by-day decisions, the ultimate consequences of which – perhaps happily – they cannot foresee. The pagan who wants a bicycle to travel more quickly to market or a radio to hear the drums does not know that he is probably opening the fateful box of civilization for himself. In a manner certainly not unique, relatively unacculturated Africans seem able to tolerate contradictions without being appreciably disturbed. The kind of situation which produces a conflict in the African *élite*, which might lead to neurosis in Europeans, or which may cause the reader of this article to sigh with dismay, is not even inhibiting. The best and worst of the traditional and the Western cultures, however badly and inadequately mixed, can be enjoyed; and wonderful joy is still felt and exhibited in Africa. Africans can be friendly and attractive and lovable because, although they clearly recoil from misery and although they like hunger and insecurity no more than anyone else, they have not yet come to comprehend the dense, complex web in which, sadly, they must live.

IIIf: The Role of Africa in World Affairs

All except four of the independent countries of Africa have gained their independence since 1950, all except seven since 1957. The period in which Africa has been an independent force in world affairs is, therefore, a very short one; it is difficult to make any firm predictions about how its role will evolve. Consequently in the Introduction to this section we shall content ourselves with a discussion of a few salient issues which have already emerged in the relations of African countries with each other, and with the rest of the world. These issues can be divided into three groups:

i) those which concern the relations of African countries with each other, including Pan-Africanism and regional associations;

ii) those which concern Africa's relations with the U.N., which at present include their attitude towards the remaining colonies and white-ruled territories of Africa;

iii) those which concern their relations with the United States and the former European colonial powers, which include the problem of neo-imperialism.

We shall conclude with a brief discussion of the attitudes and policies of Western countries in their relations with African states.

I. INTER-AFRICAN RELATIONS

Since the arguments and prospects for Pan-Africanism are presented quite fully in the two final readings of this section we shall here merely summarize some of the forces working for and against the achievement of Pan-Africanism.

A most powerful force sustaining Pan-African sentiments is the shared experience of European colonialism in the past eighty years; while administrations have differed considerably most Africans have become accustomed to alien political rule, to social discrimination and often to political and economic oppression. The clear racial difference between ruler and ruled reinforce these shared emotions. But common opposition to colonialism, however strong the emotions it produces, is probably not a viable basis for positive policies leading towards unity. A general belief, however, that colonialism has died only to be replaced by a no less calculated neo-colonialism may cause the general feeling to crystallize into action. It is one of the main planks of the neo-colonialist doctrine that it is in the interests of foreign powers (generally meaning the U.S. and Europe) to keep Africa 'balkanized' for only thus can she continue to be exploited. We shall consider later whether the threat of neo-colonialism is real or imagined and only then can we make conclusions about its power to induce African unity.

Colonialism itself left behind some features conducive towards at least regional unity. In colonial times some groups of African countries were administered in Federations with, for instance, a common currency, transportation system, and so on; the breaking up of these informal federations may damage the welfare of the countries involved. We have seen in section IIId that such considerations did not prevent the disintegration of the colonial federation of ex-French West Africa. It remains to be seen whether similar even more informal elements of unity in the administration of ex-British East Africa (Kenya, Tanganyika, Uganda and Zanzibar) will disintegrate or be strengthened by the coming of independence.

As already mentioned in the Introduction, the physical geography of Africa presents certain barriers to unity: the Sahara desert separates North Africa from West and Central Africa. A further geographical barrier, in the form of various ranges of mountains, separates West from East Africa. Yet the Rocky mountains did not prevent the unification of the United States of America, nor the Urals, that of Russia; nor do the vast deserts of Australia hinder its political unity.

One feature of the political geography of Africa which demands, if not unity, then at least close co-operation on a regional level is that fourteen of its countries (colonial and independent) are entirely landlocked. These countries will require arrangements with their neighbours both about outlets to the sea for travel, and for imports and exports, and about the collection and apportionment of customs revenues. In the short term this may in some cases inhibit unity and cooperation: it may be economically costly, for example, for the Malawi government to involve itself too closely with efforts to drive the Portuguese from Africa since her most convenient route to the outside world is through Mozambique via the port of Beira.

Language difficulties, while they may not be hard to eliminate, still present an obstacle to full co-operation. But a much more explosive problem is that of boundary disputes. At present there are such disputes between Morocco and Algeria, Morocco and Mauretania and between Somalia and both Ethiopia and Kenya. The wish of the Somali government to create a greater Somalia incorporating the Somalis of Ethiopia and Kenya led the governments of those two countries to form in December 1963 a military alliance against the possibility of Somali encroachment. This followed shortly after an agreement whereby Somalia was to receive military aid from the U.S.S.R. Towards the end of 1963 a dispute also arose between Cameroon and Nigeria about the referendum in 1961 which caused the former Northern Cameroons to join Nigeria. Inter-African disputes such as these may sorely harass the forces of unity.

Probably the major unifying force in Africa is the universal desire among Africans to rid the continent of the last and toughest remnants of alien rule: to secure an African government in Southern Rhodesia, to remove Portugal from her African colonies (of which Angola and Mozambique are by far the most important) and to end the oppressive and racialist rule of the government of the Republic of South Africa. These issues have formed the basis of much joint action by African countries at the United Nations and prompted the setting up of the African Liberation Committee at the Conference of African States in June 1963. This committee was charged with the task of organizing 'freedom fighters' to operate in conjunction with the Angola and Mozambique Liberation movements officially recognized by the Organization of African Unity (also a result of the Conference). Several African countries, notably Algeria, offered facilities for the training of these freedom fighters.

The 1963 Addis Ababa conference will probably be seen as a landmark if hopes for African unity come to be fulfilled. In spite of divisions between those who favoured only complete African unity and those who preferred to see regional unity as a stepping stone to this goal, the actions and tone of the Conference were remarkably unanimous. The Organization of African Unity (O.A.U.) was established with a permanent secretariat. Committees of the Organization were to deal with political, economic and cultural unity and to co-ordinate and train liberation movements. Only time will show how active and successful these will be. The Organization survived its first major test when hostilities broke out in the fall of 1963 between Algeria and Morocco over a border dispute. The Foreign Ministers of the African states appointed the Emperor of Ethiopia, Haile Selaisse, to mediate the dispute on behalf of the O.A.U.; a cease fire was negotiated and adhered to although the dispute is not yet finally settled.

Of all the independent states of Africa only Togo and South Africa were not invited to the Conference and Morocco refused to attend because of the presence of Mauritania to which it lays claim. The differences of Casablanca and Monrovia powers, as well as the other disruptive forces which we have mentioned, largely fell away in the sense of urgency aroused by the major issue of the conference – the liberation of Southern Africa. If there was a keynote speech at the conference it was that of President Ben Bella of Algeria who called upon his hearers to 'die a little' for Africa in the continuing struggle for complete freedom.

2. AFRICA AND THE UNITED NATIONS

The year of the formation of the O.A.U. saw also the intensification of African activity at the U.N. The first reading in this section describes African activity at the U.N. up to 1962. In 1963 greater efforts were made to put pressure on Portugal and South Africa by means of sanctions and other policies. Combined African pressure gathered sufficient support to ensure the removal of South Africa from the International Labour Organization. And an embargo on the export of arms to South Africa passed the U.N. with the support of Britain and the U.S. This vote, although only the minimum demand of the African states at the time, was a notable advance. Africa has always been somewhat sanguine about the possibility of British and U.S. support for these kinds of pressure. Both countries have in the past supplied arms to South Africa, which in turn supplies them with much needed supplies of gold of which South Africa accounts for 70 per cent. of the world's supply. In addition Britain has over £1,000 million ($2,800 million) of investments in South Africa and the U.S. has about $300 million invested. In view of this economic vulnerability it says much for the effectiveness of African pressure that the U.S. and Britain agreed to support even a limited embargo. There is less chance of similar success with Portugal as long as she remains a member of the N.A.T.O. alliance.

The African nations will probably continue to press for more severe measures of this kind, especially for an embargo on oil supplies to South Africa; 1965 will see the decision of the World Court on the position of South Africa in South-West Africa (a former German colony mandated to South Africa after the first world war); South Africa has continually refused to acknowledge the continuance of the mandate under the U.N. and has virtually absorbed South-West Africa. Should the World Court decision go against South Africa then there may be African demands for a U.N. occupation of South-West Africa and its subsequent independence; this might involve a war between South Africa and the U.N. which would

385

be unlikely to succeed without the support of Britain and the U.S. If this situation arises it will be a testing time for African relations with the U.N. and the western powers. A failure of the U.N. to act could lead to a rejection of the world body as a stage for major political action.

Already African countries have realized that the possibility of effective U.N. action in Southern Africa is limited. It is this realization which led to the formation of the African Liberation Committee. In addition, the rapid joint action under the auspices of the O.A.U. which brought a cease fire on the border dispute between Morocco and Algeria, may perhaps set a pattern for the settlement of inter-African disputes outside the framework of the U.N.

3. AFRICA AND THE WEST – NEO-COLONIALISM

'Colonialism' and 'imperialism' are words which began life as descriptive terms and only subsequently became in addition terms of abuse. In contrast, the vocabulary of neo-colonialism has from the beginning been value-loaded, and has been consequently shunned by academic writers on Africa. This, we believe, shows unnecessary restraint: while neo-colonialism is a term charged with emotive content there are several objective features of Africa's relations with her former imperialists which can be conveniently accommodated by the term.

The term 'neo-colonialism' has often been used by Africans to describe actions and policies of Americans and Europeans which, whether calculated or unwitting, tended to preserve the present comparatively weak position of Africa in world affairs – through the prevention either of economic development or of political integration. We shall summarize these arguments and comment briefly on each of them.

1. It is said that the Western countries, by their unwillingness to enter into stabilization agreements for African primary commodities, encourage the fluctuation of export earnings which tends to hinder African development. This is probably the weakest of all arguments. The real benefits of price stabilization are controversial; in periods of rising prices, for example, the gains to African countries are likely to lag behind those gains which would have accrued in a free market and in periods of falling prices; the fact that they are artificially held up may encourage buyers to search for substitutes. Besides, the failure of commodity stabilization agreements may be the result of a refusal to co-operate by other producing rather than consuming countries. The argument is sometimes expressed in an even weaker form and seems to become: high prices encourage continued and potentially damaging concentration upon primary production and low prices are

386

undesirable for more obvious reasons. At this level it is hardly an argument (even if both assertions were true) but rather a general view that all is for the worst in the worst of all possible worlds.

2. It is argued that Africa depends for a major part of its income upon Western nations while Western nations economically could do without Africa and not be greatly damaged. This fact leads to a systematic weakness of Africa in all its dealings with Europe and the U.S. While Africa is a major source of a few important primary products, it cannot be denied that this is basically true. Its truth, however, does not make it an argument for the existence of neo-colonialism as a political or economic policy. It is an unfortunate fact about the world, certainly, and may perhaps be regarded as a condition under which neo-colonialism can exist. The most persuasive arguments for its existence are the more specific ones which now follow.

3. The banking system of Africa is largely under the control of Europeans and therefore credit for investment is more easily available to foreigners than to Africans. There is much truth in this charge. Many African banks are still branches of overseas banks. The predilection of these banks for rather conservative policies with regard to security for a loan has meant that Africans were often unable to qualify for loans which they could have put to good use. Before 1959, for example, an African who lived in an urban area in Northern Rhodesia was not able by law to own his own house, which might have provided him with the type of security the banks would require. The result of this has been that the banks of Africa have been and to some extent still are more ready to provide short-term export trading credit than long-term investment loans, except in some cases to foreign businesses. Whether the answer to this problem is to encourage or force the banks to change their policies or to set up new, perhaps government-owned, banks to fill the gap can be decided only after careful analysis of specific cases. It is probably true that there are great economies of scale to be gained, especially in investment banking. In this case the most logical approach may be for African governments to support as fully as possible the proposed African Investment Bank of the Economic Commission for Africa.

4. The economic dominance which foreign firms exercise in some African countries is said to restrict the economic development of those countries. There are several ways in which this may happen though they must be balanced against the fact that such firms also create development by their own expansion. But these firms may repatriate an inordinate proportion of their profits and reinvest only a little in their country of operation. The firms are unwilling to extend their field of operation into

387

other parts of the economy where profitable opportunities which would create development have not been taken up. This is one of the most powerful props of the belief in neo-colonialism and African governments have three main ways of dealing with it. They may nationalize the firm, they may increase the taxation which it must pay, or they may encourage or oblige it to invest a certain proportion of its profits locally. Nationalization may be unsatisfactory because it will discourage further foreign investment in other fields; it may lead to a flight of foreign capital damaging to the economy, and the administration of nationalized firms may take scarce administrative talent from other work which would be in the long run more useful. There may still be cases, however, where these dangers are not great and where nationalization may be beneficial. Taxing the firms more heavily suffers from similar drawbacks – a possible flight of capital and discouragement of foreign investment. The government of Ghana has already tried to enforce a law demanding that foreign firms invest a certain proportion of their profits locally and this technique is likely to be used elsewhere.

A further argument of this kind used against foreign firms is that they show an unwarranted propensity for employing their own nationals (often at inflated rates of pay) to do jobs which could well be done by Africans at lower cost even if the Africans might first have to be trained. In some cases, however, this is not the fault of the firms themselves. In the Zambian copper industry, for instance, far more Africans would by now be employed in senior posts if it had not been for the strength of the white Mineworkers Union.

5. It is sometimes complained that African countries while nominally independent have less real independence economically than most other countries, both as a result of heavy dependence upon export income and because of the dominant role played in African economies by foreign corporations. There are two main ways in which this situation could circumscribe the economic independence of a government. First, the investment and other policies of the firms concerned may be influenced by the economic policy of the governments of countries in which the firms originated. Economies, therefore, a large proportion of whose capital is owned by foreigners, may have the speed and nature of their economic development influenced by the policies of foreign governments. Secondly, taxation of foreign firms may account for a large proportion of an African government's income with which it must finance current expenditures of various kinds (e.g. education and social services) whose curtailment would be disastrous. It may, therefore, be difficult for a government to resist pressures from these dominant enterprises simply because so much of

388

current revenue depends upon their continued operation. The same argument would apply, of course, if the dominant corporations were domestic. Nevertheless, in many African countries they are foreign, and where they do abuse their power this will rightly be regarded as neo-colonialism.

We know of no well-documented case of the sort of circumstances outlined above; the present pattern of African economies, however, certainly admits their possibility in several countries.

6. The accusation has been made that in order to maintain their political and economic power in Africa ex-colonial and other Western nations tend to use opportunities to maintain Africa's present state of 'balkanization' and to prevent African unity and consequently greater African strength. Two examples are principally quoted to support this view. First, the support by the Belgian and British governments of Mr Tshombe's efforts to remove Katanga province from the newly independent Congo between 1960 and 1962. This support, given in direct opposition to United Nations resolutions and causing harassment to the United Nations Congo force, is said to have resulted from a belief that Mr Tshombe's government would pursue policies more generous to British and Belgian interests in the Katangan copper-mining industry than would the central Congo government in Leopoldville. While some of the facts of British and Belgian policy remain obscure, this seems to be the most likely interpretation.

The second example quoted is the association of some African territories (mostly ex-French colonies) with the European Economic Community (E.E.C.). This arrangement allows tariff-free entry to the E.E.C. of all the exports of associated territories and qualifies those territories to economic aid from a fund set up by the E.E.C. Some Africans, especially outside the associated territories, have argued that this constitutes an effort by the countries of the E.E.C. to maintain the traditional patterns of African economies and prevent the unity of associated and non-associated countries. Economic aid from the E.E.C. is unlikely to be given for projects which compete with European industry in African markets. Meanwhile the European countries will continue to have their secure sources of certain raw materials. To counter these charges the E.E.C. would argue that much of its economic aid will go towards helping to diversify African economies; there are often cheaper sources of supply of the relevant raw materials outside the associated territories which are consequently having their exports protected; besides, under the new implementing convention of 1963, discrimination against suppliers in non-associated territories is reduced; and finally both the Treaty of Rome and the implementing convention of the association agreement expressly allow the African associated territories to protect their industries with tariffs and neither expressly forbids the economic union of associated with non-associated territories. Moreover, if the associated territories do not like the arrangement they may leave. This defence is a strong one although the antagonists of the arrangement may still reply that any attempts to make use of the clause of the Treaty of Rome which allows associated territories to protect their industries may be resisted by the E.E.C., and that economic pressure may be put on territories which withdraw from the agreement in the same way as it was on Guinea when she voted to leave the French Community in 1958. Not enough evidence yet exists finally to prove or disprove any of these arguments.

It is clear from what we have said above that there is, as may be expected, a systematic tendency for Africa (and indeed much of the economically under-developed world) to be weak in its economic relations with foreigners. But those who argue that neo-colonialism exists mean more than this – they mean that this weakness is exploited by foreign governments and individuals. Such evidence as now exists is insufficient to show how widespread or conscious such exploitation is; there is no doubt, however, that the potentiality for it exists.

4. WESTERN POLICY AND AFRICA

We have no space to present a detailed discussion of the policy of individual Western countries in Africa; in this section, therefore, we shall present a few general observations about Western policy.

The relations of African countries with the West is still dominated by the aftermath of colonialism. In spite of this it is remarkable how cordial these relations have been. Nearly all the former French territories retain strong links with France, even Guinea having re-established some of the links broken in 1958. All the former British territories (except ex-British Somaliland which is part of Somalia and the Southern Cameroons which are part of Cameroun) have remained in the British Commonwealth. All African countries receive some Western aid[1] although in some cases this has been less than generous. Many Europeans and Americans are working in Africa for their own or for African governments, or privately, in friendly circumstances.

Some bitterness remains, however, and there are signs that it may be intensifying. This is partly the result of Western policy in Southern Africa. Most Africans believe that Western countries have not been willing enough to oppose Portuguese and South African policies of racial oppression either in the U.N. or by means of employing their economic and strategic

[1] The details of foreign aid are given in Appendix II, pp. 426–7.

power over these two offending countries. This is partly why African countries have decided upon direct action by themselves through the African Liberation Committee. The bitterness was intensified over British and Belgian activity during the Congo crisis and will be again if Britain agrees to grant independence to the white minority government in Southern Rhodesia. Many Europeans have been shocked and disappointed that the end of formal colonialism has not always meant the end of recrimination; actions which were generously intentioned have been interpreted as neo-colonialism. Western countries have come to realize that Africa is a continent which is often quick to take offence; and the potentially explosive problem of race is not shrugged off merely by the granting of independence to colonies.

In view of the political sensitivity of Africa it will be a hard task for the West to neutralize all these suspicions; it is, however, in its own interest to try to do so. We have seen that the growing doctrine of neo-colonialism thrives on the inequality of power between Africa and the rich nations of the West. One way to start to eliminate this would be to expand Western economic aid to Africa; to avoid accusations that this too involves neo-colonialism it may be better to attach no strings to such aid and to channel it through international organizations. The proposed E.C.A. Investment Bank may provide a useful vehicle for this.

Many Africans are still suspicious of Western attitudes towards racial discrimination and oppression. Two things would immeasurably reduce these suspicions. The first is a willingness on the part of the West to sacrifice a N.A.T.O. ally, Portugal, and some economic interests in South Africa in order to strengthen its committment to the ending of white rule in Southern Africa. The second is to pursue a more energetic policy against racial discrimination within Western countries themselves. This applies especially to the United States. It is hard for Africans to take American professions of liberal intentions more seriously until the position of American negroes is improved.

The question remains – why should the West want to please Africa in this way? The first reason is that there are a large number of people in European countries who feel a sense of guilt for colonialism which becomes a feeling of obligation to ex-colonies to assist their development. Also there are distant prospects that the problem of race may become such an explosive issue in the world that all that can be done now by white-ruled nations to allay suspicions of prejudice may reap added returns in the future.

To many people in the West the best reason for pleasing Africa is to prevent its being won by the East in the cold war. Most Western governments have by now relinquished the dogma that neutralism is immoral and that part of the purpose of the cold war is to persuade neutralist countries to become committed to the West. The West has discovered that neutralism may be more beneficial than commitment. The fact that as powerful a country as India and some of its neighbours have remained neutral and refused to join the West has removed a large area of the world from what might have been an expensive, exhausting and unsuccessful struggle for allegiance between East and West which would have created further explosion points in which a world war might have begun. Africa's geographical position away from the main areas of struggle in the cold war suits it well to be a neutral area; there is no tradition of cold war commitment among African states and a good deal of powerful neutralist sentiment. The neutrality of a large area like Africa in the interests of world peace may have to be maintained by various international agreements. There is some hope that, France notwithstanding, Africa will be designated a nuclear-free zone, a proposal which Western countries would be wise to support. But neutralism may not be secure in a situation of economic weakness. This is a further argument for an increasing volume of Western economic aid, to be channeled through international agencies. Unfortunately the realization by both East and West that economic aid does not buy friends for the cold war has led to a reduction in such aid. Russia has made no new commitments for economic assistance to Africa since 1961; and the U.S. Congress becomes increasingly unwilling to vote aid appropriations. The figure of 1 per cent. of national income of the developed countries proposed by the United Nations for economic assistance to poorer countries would vastly expand current aid at a cost which the nations of the West can surely afford.

There is no space here to investigate what Western policy should be toward inter-African disputes. The West has very few military commitments in Africa and would probably prefer to have none. If efforts to mediate the Algeria-Morocco dispute of 1963 within the framework of a purely African organization, the O.A.U., set a pattern then the West may be relieved, to its benefit, of involvement in such inter-African disputes. The Congo crisis has already shown the dangers of involvement. But when the issues of South Africa and the Portuguese colonies come to a head, as they must, Western countries cannot then shirk their responsibility to adopt a consistent and constructive policy; they will be forced to choose their friends.

37

Africa at the United Nations: Some Observations[1]

John H. Spencer

Since its formation, the United Nations Organization has occupied an important place in the mind of Africa. Firstly it is the mouthpiece through which a newly independent state may immediately have a voice in world affairs. By the end of 1965 there will probably be thirty-six African members of the U.N. – about one-third of its membership. Secondly, the issues in world politics which up to the present have most concerned Africans are colonialism and racial discrimination, to both of which the U.N. is comparatively sensitive. African members have used the machinery of the U.N. to put pressure on colonial powers to give independence to their remaining colonies. Most African states, however, now doubt that the U.N. will be strong enough by itself to solve the problems of the Portuguese colonies and South Africa; but the U.N. will certainly be one of the means used by Africans to reach a solution of these crucial issues.

This reading describes the relationship between African countries and the U.N. as it developed up to 1962; more recent trends have been discussed in the introduction to this section.

Within the space of less than six years, the African membership in the United Nations has increased from three to twenty-eight Members constituting the largest geographical group in the Organization.[2] Furthermore, as many as seven other territories may become independent and seek membership before the end of 1965.

I. THE RISE OF THE AFRICAN PRESENCE – FORMATION OF THE CAUCUS

This sudden and massive incursion of African states into the World Organization has naturally aroused curiosity concerning the role of these states within the United Nations and speculation with respect to their effect upon its functioning.

[1] Reprinted from *International Organization*, Vol. XVI, No. 2 (Spring 1962).
[2] South Africa, which is not in the African caucus, is excluded for the purposes of this study.

The African states can today amass, when they are fully united, some 26 per cent. of the votes in the General Assembly. Although this is not equivalent to the 39 per cent. position which the Latin American states had in the early years of the United Nations, it is nevertheless a major bloc of votes capable of exercising a pervasive effect upon Assembly proceedings. Over and beyond the mere votes alone, which thus far have often been widely divided save on clear-cut anti-colonialist questions and certain broad matters in the realm of peace and security, the operation of the African caucus functioning in collaboration with the larger Afro-Asian caucus has become one of the principal factors in General Assembly politics.

The African caucus may be said to date from the establishment of an 'informal working machinery' at the U.N. initiated by the First Conference of Independent African States meeting at Accra in 1958. It was only after the admission of the large number of new African states in 1960, however, and the eruption of the Congo crisis, that the caucus became a major force in U.N. politics. As the Congo situation developed the African Members became both increasingly vocal and dexterous in political manoeuvring. One measure of their influence was seen in their insistence upon the Secretary-General's accepting an Afro-Asian consultation committee on Congo affairs. Another was the vote taken at their demand on 11 October 1961, to censure the South African delegate for remarks in the General Assembly. On this occasion the African position resulted in a favourable vote of 67 to 1, with thirty-nine states abstaining or 'not participating'. This was a vast change from a decade earlier when the General Assembly had at one point selected the Union of South Africa, over objections of the African states, as the representative of that continent to help achieve a solution of the Eritrea situation.

By combining their forces with the Asian states in the Afro-Asian caucus, which when united commands 47 per cent. of the Assembly vote, the African states have been able to increase even further their leverage in the proceedings of the General Assembly.

2. AFRICAN STANDS ON SOME ISSUES BEFORE THE GENERAL ASSEMBLY

Space does not permit a detailed review of the positions which the African states have taken in the multiplicity of votes before the General Assembly. Their stands have varied from time to time, depending upon circumstances, upon the type of question before the Assembly, and upon political influences of many kinds operating both within the group and upon its members from other sources. The record shows that most of the African states voted more or less closely with the Western powers on a wide range of issues when they first became independent. As time has passed group pressures, anti-colonialist sentiments, desires to demonstrate complete independence, and an 'African view', as well as persuasion by external arguments and blandishments, have led many of the states to part company with the Western delegations and to vote differently.

In glancing back over the record one can discern certain broad patterns of voting on colonial issues, as distinguished from questions involving the East-West struggle and from what might be termed 'other questions' where neither colonial nor Cold War elements were at work.

Questions of 'colonialism' are quite understandably capable of evoking heated, emphatic, and vigorous shows of strength against what is identified as the colonialist policy or action. This has been particularly evident where the action has related directly to African territory, as in the case of Portuguese Angola, or French evacuation from the Bizerta base in Tunisia. On the resolution at the fifteenth session calling for early termination of colonial rule generally, the African states spoke with a common voice. On the Algerian situation, on the other hand, the African states found it impossible to speak with a single voice or purpose. At the fifteenth session some of them, notably the members of the leftist and politically aggressive Casablanca grouping of states, including Ghana, Guinea, Mali, Morocco, and the United Arab Republic, bitterly condemned French policy and pressed hard for a resolution demanding a U.N.-supervised plebiscite in Algeria. Other states, especially those in the Brazzaville grouping of former French dependencies, were disposed, because of their associations with France, to resist such moves in opposition to the Casablanca grouping, while still others, identified with neither grouping, abstained, were absent, or voted on opposite sides.

The same transpired at the sixteenth session on the resolution calling for the neutralization of Africa with respect to nuclear testing. Most of the Brazzaville grouping abstained with France in the balloting.

On issues closely related to the Cold War, divisions have occurred among the African Members. Some have inclined to move progressively in the direction of an Eastward orientation, lining up their votes time and again with the Soviet bloc. This has been particularly characteristic of the Casablanca grouping. However, in such questions as disarmament, Tibet, Hungary, Cuba, and indeed, even on the Congo, the Casablanca group has not presented a united front. And one can even see tendencies on the part of such states as Liberia, Libya, the Sudan, and Ethiopia, which had previously been generally friendly toward the West, to cast their votes for

Soviet-favoured proposals, as in certain resolutions on summit talks, the Congo, and Cuba. On the other hand, members of both the Brazzaville and the Monrovia groupings have on many occasions voted in substantial numbers in the same way as the Western powers, or at least abstained and refused to vote against the West, as in the fifteenth session on the question of the admission of Communist China.

On the Congo question, a sharp cleavage developed among the African delegations. The members of the Casablanca grouping, in particular Guinea and Mali, on the one hand, pressed for strong, forceful measures by the U.N. to compel President Tshombe of Katanga Province to desist from demands for independence and to remain a part of a unified Congolese state. The members of the territorially closer Brazzaville grouping, on the other hand, were outspoken in opposition to the military operations of the UNOC (U.N. Operations in the Congo) forces and were often critical of U.N. activities in the area. For their part they were sympathetic to and supported the stand of Mr Tshombe in favour of a loose confederation.

One could see in these postures, on the one hand, the fears of such leaders as Nkrumah and Touré that success on the part of Tshombe in rebelling against a central régime might give encouragement to resistance to their own totalitarian-like régimes and create a precedent for U.N. sanction of separatism. Members of the Brazzaville grouping, on the other hand, wished to forestall the rise of a potentially powerful, highly centralized régime in the heart of black Africa. They viewed Tshombe as a bulwark against a possible communist threat and as a stable element in the chaotic Congo political situation. Moreover, they disliked the spectacle of the U.N. intervening in what they considered to be a domestic situation. For what was done here could easily become a precedent for U.N. intervention in other internal disruptions or situations irrespective of the injunction in Article 2, paragraph 7, of the Charter against intervention by the World Body in 'matters which are essentially within the domestic jurisdiction of any state'. There was far more than a legal technicality at stake in the contrary positions taken by various African states on the Congo affair.[1] Nevertheless, despite this common attitude, the Brazzaville grouping, like the others, has failed to maintain a unified front on this problem during the fifteenth and sixteenth sessions.

On what might be generalized as 'other questions', and even on matters that slip into the East-West struggle but are of distinct and direct vital

[1] For an incisive discussion of this problem, see R. C. Good, 'Four Tendencies at the United Nations', *Africa Report*, June 1961 (Vol. 6, No. 6); and 'Congo Crisis: The Role of the New States', in *Neutralism*, published by the Washington Centre of Foreign Policy Research, 1961.

concern to the African states *per se*, these countries have lined up with the West when they have found its position compatible with what they conceive to be their particular interests. Thus, in 1961, the African states were generally opposed to the Soviet Union's 'troika' proposal for the Secretary-Generalship. Where their emotional desires for a peaceful world are brought into play they may find themselves in agreement with the Soviet bloc against the West, as happened at the sixteenth session on the draft resolution calling for an immediate nuclear test moratorium without international inspection pending conclusion of a general arms control agreement. On economic aid and development proposals looking toward larger expenditures or more liberal loan arrangements, the African states generally can be expected, out of what they conceive to be their own self-interests, to vote for larger, more costly programmes than the Western powers are willing to accept. And many of them, faced as they are with the most difficult economic and financial outlooks, can be expected to cast their votes against heavier assessments or to resist making contributions for carrying out these programmes.

3. ASSOCIATIONS WITH ASIAN STATES – INFLUENCE OF MEMBERSHIP IN AFRO-ASIAN CAUCUS

An important element in the activities of the African states at the United Nations is their participation in the larger Afro-Asian caucus. Although the Asian members are numerically fewer than the African, and although the principle of alphabetical rotation is followed each month in the choice of president, the pervasive influence within this caucus is unquestionably Asian. This development reflects several influences among which are the cumulative effects of the Bandung, the Afro-Asian, and the All-African Peoples Conferences and the decisive support supplied by the Asian U.N. Members over the past decade to the emerging African group in their campaign for the admission of new Members from their continent. This has resulted in a generally close co-ordination between a substantial number of the African states, especially those forming the Casablanca grouping, and the Asian 'neutralists', who often appear to be more pro-Soviet in their stance than genuinely neutral in the full sense of the term.

In view of all the subtle differences in the outlooks and policies of the various African and Asian states, it is difficult to affix any hard and fast number to the Afro-Asian caucus members that are 'pro-East', 'pro-West', or 'neutralist'. During the fifteenth and sixteenth sessions of the General Assembly, voting alignments of Asian and African states on a number of highly political issues seemed to imply that a majority of these states were 'pro-Eastern'. But this interpretation can be deceptive. For not every time African states and the communist powers voted alike were the Africans voting *for* the Soviets; quite often it was the Moscow-controlled bloc trying to identify itself with Africans and Asians in order to insinuate the notion that Moscow is their true friend and supporter.

The voting margins have been too tenuous to permit the projection of any assured conclusions. On some of the most important contests at the fifteenth and sixteenth sessions substantial numbers, including some at least of the largest and potentially most effective leaders in the African scene, voted with the Western powers. Again, on some items the voting result was as much an identification of certain Western powers, especially the United States, with African positions and interests as vice versa. Thus, one must be careful in applying a 'pro-West' label simply because of surface appearances of the voting tallies.

No hard and fast pattern is discernible as yet among the list of abstainers on General Assembly votes. These vary with the issues presented and the diplomacy that goes on behind the scenes and within the U.N. walls. Somalia, Togo, and the Congo (Brazzaville) abstained on a high percentage of votes at the fifteenth and sixteenth sessions. About all one can say is that African states, like some others, are quick to take advantage of the protective camouflage which the international conference machinery can offer.

4. THE ISSUE OF SELF-DETERMINATION

On no question have Africans felt more strongly than on self-determination. From the time that a sense of national consciousness began to stir among the African peoples, and leaders began to call for an ending of colonial ties, the concept of self-determination became the principal touchstone of African politics. Although this was not always spelled out in precise terms, the meaning was clear: sever the colonial rule, give the lands independence, let the African peoples decide for themselves what policies should be applied within their lands, within Africa as a whole, and what role their country should occupy in international relations. Along with this went, in many cases, resentments born of the sense of class consciousness, racial discrimination, and inequalities of social and educational opportunity which Africans so often experienced.

There is little question that the struggle for self-determination, and the need for friends and supporters within the United Nations on matters affecting the destinies of Africa, contributed to the coalescing of the African and the Asian states during the 1950's. For Asians too were preoccupied with similar issues in their own part of the world.

In the settlement of the problems of the former Italian colonies after World War II, including especially the assignment of Somalia to Italian trusteeship, Africans felt that African self-determination was at stake and they saw non-Africans making the decisions. Likewise, within the Trustee-ship Council and in the General Assembly non-African combinations determined what should be done with respect to the trusteeship and the non-self-governing territories in Africa. All of these incidents, plus the struggles of Tunisia and Morocco for independence, together with hatred of the *apartheid* policies being pursued in South Africa against the black man, fired emotions and fed the urge to obtain the right of self-determina-tion.

Viewed in the large, the long struggle for self-determination in Africa, both north and south of the Sahara, came to eventual fruition outside rather than within the United Nations. In a very real sense the U.N. was instrumental in advancing the independence of Somalia, Togoland, the Cameroons, and Tanganyika by means of the stimulus, pressures, and assistance brought to bear through the trusteeship system. The U.N. certainly aided Libya in achieving its independence and establishing its statehood. It would be foolhardy to say that the debates and resolutions in the General Assembly on the Tunisian and Moroccan questions in 1950–1 did not play some part in hastening ultimate French agreement to their independence. And at the time of Suez, the actions of the special emergency session of the General Assembly in calling by an overwhelming vote for a cease-fire and the withdrawal of British, French, and Israeli forces from Egyptian soil, together with the establishment of the U.N. Emergency Force to take over at Suez and then to police the Gaza Strip, certainly were not an insignificant factor in preserving the independence and the integrity of Egypt.

For the vast majority of the newly-independent states, nevertheless, actions taken by Britain, France, and Belgium outside the Organization through collaboration or at least agreement with the nationalist leaders of the various lands were the decisive factor in their attainment of inde-pendence. It is understandable, therefore, that while the African states have been eager to become Members of the World Organization for the prestige, sense of equality, and economic and technical assistance which they may gain from it or through it, their leaders and people adhere to the view that their independence has been achieved largely through their own efforts rather than through the United Nations.

5. CURRENT CONCERN FOR STATUS QUO AND TERRITORIAL
INTEGRITY

With the attainment of independence, the African states have now 'crossed the divide' from the dynamics of 'self-determination' into the area of status – that is, the maintenance of independence and of frontiers – and the protection of territorial integrity. Positions are now reversed. The concept of territorial integrity is a meeting place of the old quest for self-determination and the new concern for *status quo*. With this reversal comes a fear lest the United Nations should serve as a means or instrumentality to re-establish, in one form or another, the *'status quo ante'*. And with this one sees the anomaly of certain Western states pressing for self-determination in Algeria, the Congo, and New Guinea over Afro-Asian opposition.

For many of the African states the problem has become transformed from the political issue of urging self-determination to the legal and political one of insisting on territorial integrity. Such a concept has no meaning in itself without the territorial definition supplied by the adoption of the existing boundaries drawn in the past by the colonial powers, however artificial they may be in terms of ethnic, economic, or geographic factors.

The magnitude of the dangers which may be involved in the further application of the principle of 'self-determination' to peoples within the emerged states can be sensed in the facts that the Lunda, Chokwe, Bakongo, and Azande tribes extend far beyond the borders of the Congo into Zambia, Angola, the Congo (Brazzaville), the Central African Republic, and the Sudan, respectively; that the Somalis lay claim to one-third of Ethiopia as well as to a substantial portion of Kenya; and that the Ewe cut across the frontiers of Ghana, Togo, and Dahomey. It is not without moment that President Sylvanus Olympio of Togo, who launched his career by serving as spokesman at the General Assembly for a Ewe national state, should now look with favour on the retention of the present non-ethnical boundaries of Togo.[1]

It is not surprising that African and Asian states supported and frequently invoke the provisions of resolution 1514, passed at the fifteenth session of the General Assembly, calling for respect for territorial integrity. Nor is it unusual that they should resist efforts to make Ruanda-Burundi into two separate states in accordance with the alleged desires of the populations rather than a unified state. It was in keeping with the same

[1] S. Olympio, 'African Problems in the Cold War', *Foreign Affairs*, Vol. 40, No. 1, pp. 50–57 (October 1961).

attitude that the majority of the Afro-Asian states opposed draft resolution A/L.368 presented at the sixteenth session by the Brazzaville group, and supported by the Netherlands, calling for the application of self-determination to the settlement of the problem of New Guinea. Speaking in opposition to this proposal the Indian delegate declared:

> You cannot split up the peoples of any country. If you do that then what is there left? . . . Are we going to push this principle of self-determination, however good it might be, to destroy the integrity of States and to affect the sovereignty of countries?

And the Indonesian delegate affirmed that 'the recent history of the Congo offers ample proof that full self-determination based upon regional or ethnical considerations only creates confusion and suffering for the people concerned.'[1]

Thus, the United Nations is faced with the seemingly paradoxical situation in which some African and Asian states that had formerly long and strenuously pressed for 'self-determination' in North Africa now align themselves to block a proposal to that end offered by other African states. The piquancy and measure of the reversal are further revealed by the fact to which the representative of the Central African Republic made acidulous reference,[2] that the opposition to self-determination for New Guinea rested essentially on espousal of the Dutch colonial definition of the territories.[3] The position of the Brazzaville group has been almost equally clear; in 1961 it opposed a U.N. plebiscite in Algeria,[4] and through its leader, the representative of the Ivory Coast, it expressed support for the recognition of pre-existing colonial frontiers in Africa.[5]

[1] A/PV.1065, 27 November 1961.

[2] 'One of the principal arguments advanced in support of that thesis by Mr Subandrio . . . is that when a colonial territory accedes to independence, its sovereignty should be exercised within the limits of the former colonial sovereignty. This is a principle which is doubtless quite just in most cases, but certain qualifications must be introduced when it is a question of territories whose peoples are not united by racial or cultural links or by common beliefs.' (A/PV.1065).

[3] 'The right of self-determination applies, of course, to the entire population *of a colony as a unit and to the entire territory of a colony as a unit* [italics added]. . . . The right of self-determination is not something to be applied to racial, cultural, or ethnic groups *within a colony*.' A/PV.1065, 27 November 1961, Subandrio, representative of Indonesia.

[4] 'In our opinion, the problem of self-determination raises several awkward problems. . . . We consider that we could never agree to the right of self-determination being exercised otherwise than for the whole body of the Algerian people and for the whole of the Algerian territory.' A/PV.956. 19 December 1960, D'Arboussier, representative of Senegal.

[5] 'At the moment of accession towards independence, in order to avoid internecine wars which might jeopardize the independence just acquired with such difficulty it was agreed to accept the territorial limits obtaining at that time.' A/PV.1043,

Sensitive to press criticism of the ambivalent stand taken by some on the Congo situation, the Foreign Minister of Nigeria at one point observed:

> Where, they said, is the principle of self-determination as regards Katanga ? I said the following: how would you as an American like it if the State of New York or the State of California were to be cut off from the United States because the people wanted self-determination ?[1]

Thus, following the example of the Latin American states in the nineteenth century, the African states, having won the struggle against colonialism, are now insisting upon respect of pre-existing colonial boundaries.[2] Ethiopia has long contended for the validity of the boundary line drawn between itself and the territory of Somalia by the treaty with Italy in 1908. Recently the representative of Liberia, the frontiers of which had been determined by agreements with colonial powers, cautioned others with these words:

> We know that brothers and sisters were separated mutually by boundaries imposed to meet the requirements of the colonial powers. Much as we deplore those arbitrary acts, those boundaries have become fixed after a period of time and form all boundaries of the independent African States. What chaos, what confusion, what hatred could be engendered by each of the new African countries against each other were those boundaries to be changed or readjusted. . . . My advice to my fellow African States, especially those that live in African States, is to let sleeping dogs lie.[3]

And in similar vein the Foreign Minister of Nigeria remarked at the sixteenth session:

> I am not happy to listen in this Assembly and find one African State raising a question of a boundary dispute with another State here when in fact we can treat this as a domestic affair and deal with the matter at home. I am appealing to all concerned: African States, do not make speeches at this rostrum about boundary questions. That is why my country, in its foreign policy says, 'Leave these territories as they are.'[4]

27 October 1961. The political relations between the Congo (Brazzaville) and the Congo (Leopoldville), in general, and with respect to the provinces of Katanga and Leopoldville, in particular, cannot be ignored in this connection.

[1] A/PV.1031, 10 October 1961. See also opposition of the Sudan, itself a former beneficiary of self-determination. A/PV.1065, 27 November 1961, Ambassador Adeel on West Irian question.

[2] See Rupert Emerson, *From Empire to Nation*, Chapters VI and XVI (Cambridge: Harvard University Press, 1960).

[3] It would seem that the basic issue involved in the recent admission of Mauritania was less the threat to the territorial integrity of Morocco, as exploited by it in the discussions, than the threat to African boundary treaties generally if the colonial arrangements establishing the frontiers of Mauritania were to be drawn into question by the General Assembly through refusal to admit Mauritania to membership.

[4] A/PV.1031, 10 October 1961.

Thus it appears that the General Assembly is not likely to become the forum in which decisions will be taken on controversies relating to boundaries in Africa if the African states can prevent it.

The same deep-seated concern for preserving their territorial integrity and independence can be said to underlie the suspicion with which some African states have viewed the activities of the Secretariat in the Congo and elsewhere. These actions have stirred fears lest the United Nations should intrude upon their independence or integrity, or should in effect re-establish a form of trusteeship in lands which have but recently emerged from this status. Thus, even before the Congo crisis, the proposal of the Secretary-General to establish a U.N. 'presence' in Africa in the form of personal ambassadors, as previously attempted in the Middle East and south-east Asia, evoked serious misgivings in African quarters.

The sudden interposition of the Secretary-General in the final phase of the boundary discussions between Ethiopia and Somalia in 1958 for the announced purpose of resolving the issues by his personal intervention was felt to be a factor contributing to the breakdown of negotiations and the failure to obtain a solution of this issue. Similarly, truce talks with the government of Katanga have produced periods of sudden opposition and obstructionism. There is a pervasive fear among African states lest the Secretariat be inspired to action along the lines of the late Secretary-General's political testament contained in the introduction to his last annual report.[1] If it is true that to a degree the General Assembly has assumed parliamentary powers, then the assertion of political and executive functions by the Secretary-General would exacerbate the fears already entertained with regard to the Assembly. Yet, such a course claimed the support of the late Secretary-General.[2]

The African states were, consequently, in the main laconic in their defence of the Secretary-General when at the fifteenth session he came under attack from the Soviet bloc for allegedly over-reaching his powers. This did not preclude, however, their standing firm against Soviet machinations to replace the Secretary-General with a triumvirate that could be blocked at any moment by a veto from within the office by the Soviets or

[1] See *International Organization*, Vol. 15, No. 4, pp. 549–63 (Autumn 1961).

[2] In his view, the Secretary-General was 'one in whom there would be combined both the political and executive functions of a President with the internal administrative functions that were previously accorded to a Secretary-General. Obviously, this is a reflection, in some measure, of the American political system, which places authority in a chief executive officer who is not simply subordinated to the legislative organs but who is constitutionally responsible alone for the execution of legislation and in some respects for carrying out the authority derived from the constitutional instrument directly.' Dag Hammarskjöld, *The International Civil Servant in Law and in Fact*, p. 11 (Oxford: Oxford University Press, 1961).

the West or a 'neutralist'. On the contrary, they used their persuasion and influence to elect an acting Secretary-General who albeit was from an Asian neutralist country. Although U Thant was known for active diplomacy on behalf of his country, he had not prior to his election publicly espoused the late Secretary-General's theory of executive-political leadership.

6. CONCLUSION

The present attitude of many African states is scarcely one of unbounded confidence in United Nations operations. There is some hope, however, that the U.N. can be beneficial to these states, in helping them preserve their territorial integrity and in extending to them increased economic and technical assistance. The fact that the African states are able to work together with the Asian states on many questions has given them a measure of assurance that in the General Assembly at least their views can be registered with effect and that proposals which they deem inimical to their interests can be blocked. Conceivably, the transformation of some political questions into juridical ones, or at least their acquisition of a more highly juridical colouration than before, may well lead to disposition to refer some legal disputes relating to such matters as boundary lines to adjudication by the International Court of Justice. To the extent that this should occur in place of public debate and bloc voting in the General Assembly it would amount to a departure from reliance upon the Afro-Asian caucus with its numerous cross-currents and uncertainties.

For many problems regional institutions and solutions may serve a useful purpose in the African scene. The convening of no less than twenty-five regional conferences since 1957, and the recent organizational proposals of Casablanca, Monrovia, Dakar, and Lagos lend support to this hypothesis. A comment by President Youlou of the Congo (Brazzaville) exemplifies a feeling that is widely prevalent: 'We cannot allow the fate of our brothers on the other side of the Congo to be decided quite arbitrarily by those who do not know their country and their spirit. . . . Africa is our affair, our problems cannot, I repeat, be solved by any but ourselves, the great African family.'

It is quite conceivable that African states which resent the discussion of African problems at the U.N. could accept to do so *en famille*, by 'palaver' as it were, in regional meetings removed from the U.N. Although the movement toward regionalism has already produced rival systems, the desire to find accord through regional channels cannot be gainsaid.

The success of the moderate elements at the Monrovia and Dakar gatherings in May and June of 1961, and the results achieved at Lagos in January 1962, give solid reason for encouragement. Fortunately the Lagos grouping constitutes the largest, and at the moment, the most active, regional organization.[1] For the near future regionalism can perhaps afford a theatre in which relations between the West and African states might be explored without the handicaps of protective colouration or parliamentary compromise that must almost inevitably appear when matters are being debated or voted upon within the United Nations. At the same time the United Nations can continue as a forum in which the African personality can be brought to bear upon world problems, whether in a unified or divided voice. It can provide an instrumentality for helping to keep or to restore peace, for mobilizing political pressures to speed the process of independence for the remaining colonial lands. And, of course, it is in the eyes of all Africans an indispensable channel for the funneling of economic, financial, and technical assistance for the realization of their aspirations of economic growth and cultural advancement.

[1] See Rupert Emerson, 'Pan-Africanism', *International Organisation*, Vol. xvi, No. 2 (Spring 1962) pp. 275–90; and Erasmus H. Kloman, Jr., 'African Unification Movements', ibid., pp. 387–404.

38

The Prospects for Pan-Africanism[1]

W. E. Abraham

The most powerful effective force for Pan-Africanism is likely to be, not a half-mystical sense of unity, which undoubtedly exists among many people, but rather a realization that through African union the strength of Africa may increase relative to other countries: this argument is presented in this reading. The author's belief that regional unities are a step towards continental unity is shared by most Pan-Africanists. A few governments, however, most notably Ghana, have now rejected this in favour of an 'all or nothing' approach. Uganda's partial support for this line at the Addis Ababa conference in 1963 may merely be part of an effort to secure a more favoured position if it agrees to enter the proposed East African Federation. The Ghanaian government's disenchantment with its earlier view (upon which the short lived Ghana-Guinea-Mali Union was based) results from a belief that regional units will serve only to entrench local interests at a slightly wider level than now and thus block the path to continental unity. At present the evidence suggests that in practice the majority view, as expressed in this reading, will prevail; but the Ghanaian government's fears may yet prove to be well founded in the long run.

Objections to Pan-Africanism have usually been founded on economic or political matters. It is clear that Africa is united in its interest in economic development. Politicians and statesmen of Africa have said that without economic strength and resilience, political independence is precarious. It might therefore appear to be natural to ask here why one does not seek the integration of Africa through political bonds. Why does one appeal instead to cultural links? The reason is that no area of 'Sudan' Africa is sufficiently developed economically for this to be done significantly. In Europe, most countries are highly developed economically, hence it is possible to integrate Europe without undue hazards for the individual regions of Europe. Indeed the strength of the European economies creates a certain inter-dependence, a certain inescapable economic contact in trade. Hence there already is an economic bond founded on the acknowledged necessity of rationalizing this economic contact. Indeed, the fullness

[1] Reprinted from *The Mind of Africa* (Weidenfeld and Nicolson, London, 1962).

of Africa's cultures is the strength of the cultural argument for Pan-Africanism, just as the fullness of Europe's economies is the strength of the economic argument for Pan-Europe.

The economies of Africa are not full, strong or resilient. They therefore do not yield the bond which the European economies do.

This does not, however, imply that Pan-Africanism is devoid of economic boon for Africa. It is at this point that the objection to it from economic considerations wobbles. Africa is the richest continent in the world. But most of its riches lie stupefied in potentiality and dormancy. Of natural resources, it suffers from an *embarras de richesse*. They are duplicated and re-duplicated all over the continent. Though its geological survey is not yet complete, it is already known to contain in scandalous profusion cobalt, copper, radium, uranium, diamonds, vanadium, manganese, chrome ore, bauxite, iron, coal, oil, gold, tin, etc. A complete geological survey will no doubt reveal further incidences of some of these deposits. Even at the level of raw-material economy, these mineral substances can assist greatly in the formation of capital and the acquisition of wealth in Africa. But need Africa tie itself down to a raw-material economy? What Africa needs to do about its mineral deposits is first to promote an intensive and exhaustive geological survey after the fashion of the Soviet Union. The proof of diverse and plentiful mineral deposits was essential in the confirmation of the Revolution's success. Indeed, no single state of Africa has the full complement of capital and skill to exploit its resources in the most advantageous way. Capital they might be able to attract externally through loans or investment. Skill they might be able to entice. But if there are large numbers of countries nibbling at the foreign aid which America, Russia, and Europe are disposed to offer, then it is clear that not much will come the way of any individual country. On the other hand, with the example of Great Britain and her £7 million World Bank loan to look to, a united Africa with a composite surplus could ask for and obtain far larger loans than any single African country today can persuade world bodies and other agencies to part with. The larger loans which could become available could more confidently than now be employed in effective exploitation of some of our resources. A united Africa will be able to treat some of its repetitious resources as reserves, and concentrate and streamline effort in the exploitation of them in selected areas. The capital amassed as surplus from such a venture could then be deployed in other areas. Because investment would be rationalized on a continental basis, the rate of growth of the economy of the continent would be far in excess of what it would be otherwise.

Skilled personnel whom industrialized countries can spare are of course limited also, and a united Africa can make better use of them through concentrating them on selected projects than a divided Africa can through dissipating them on competing projects atrophied of care and staff. If Africa unites, of course, there will be problems of currency. Indeed, in the earlier stages it would be unwise to abolish the present currency patterns in favour of an African currency; for one thing, the industrial capacity of Africa to back its own currency will not have been established; for another, a united Africa stands to benefit from the links it will inherit with foreign currencies, thus placing it in a naturally favourable position for purposes of exchange. And the fact that its economy will then be linked with a number of currencies will make it better able to cope with fluctuations in these currencies. Nor need internal trafficking be hampered by this polyvalence in currency. The situation need not be worse than it is today, and the currencies would be interconvertible.

Though Africa is under-developed, its economy is none the less heterogeneous. Its economy is uneven. It is pointed out by critics of Pan-Africanism that the difference between rich states and poor states, even such as these are in Africa, would be an obstacle not easily to be surmounted. It is said that these discrepancies will account for a certain spontaneous reluctance on the part of richer African regions to throw in their lot too much with that of the poorer regions. Of the British colonies, Ghana is undoubtedly the richest in natural resources, even anticipating Zambia. Of the ex-French territories, the Gabon is similarly the richest in natural resources, being most weighted with manganese, uranium and iron around Franceville, Mounana and Nyanga-Chibanga. The ex-Belgian Congo, it is now common knowledge, is also fraught with uranium, copper, and bauxite. Compared to these, many areas of Africa stand denuded both of the favours of God and those of man. But if the indications of the economic benefits of Pan-Africanism are correct, then the best course for the richer African states is indeed to throw in their lot with the poorer ones. The sense of brotherhood engendered in the unity of African cultures should make this kind of temporary and enlightened immolation possible and acceptable. The identity of the African cultures, impregnated by a common experience of extra-continental domination and common aspirations, creates a magnetic bond which can be used to bind all regions into a Pan-Africa. In a Pan-Africa, the African regions can in unison compose their colonial Jeremiad, and also together triumph over it. Already the pattern of inter-African aid is being set. By far the most spectacular example of it is Ghana's placing of £10 million at the disposal of Guinea. Nigerians are already talking of aid for Sierra Leone, though in terms of thousands of pounds.

Pan-Africa will be a sort of mutual insurance, economically speaking, for the different regions of Africa. They would practically be guaranteed against total collapse. This kind of insurance would enable them also to rationalize their agriculture. Cocoa is exported in large quantities by Ghana, Nigeria, the Ivory Coast and the Cameroons. A surfeit of it on the world market, thanks to Brazil's unabated contribution, is practically guaranteed. Brazil, with its alternative of coffee, was quite prepared recently, when cocoa prices plunged to tragic depths, to control its marketable volume of cocoa. But African countries, dependent as they were on the revenue from its produce, were quite unable to join Brazil in its proposed adventure. Pan-Africa can diversify and plan its agricultural effort, thus regulating the amount of produce in world markets in order at once to prevent surfeits and obtain the maximum reward for its export effort. Some of the labour so freed can be suitably (and incidentally, quite adequately) employed in the production of food for Pan-African consumption. In the same way, palm oil production in Nigeria, the ex-Belgian Congo and Dahomey can be regulated. Thus, the competitive economies of Africa seem themselves to point at Pan-Africanism as a device of optimum leverage.

The under-population of Africa is dragged not infrequently like a very dead red herring across the path of African unity. It is only in comparison with other continents that Africa is under-populated. In terms of its own economic advance, the continent is most clearly not under-populated. Indeed, its limited population is both an economic and a social benefit. The economic problems which an over-populated but economically feeble polity has to face are in this way avoided in Africa. The fact that there is only a small number of mouths to feed, compared with India or China, say, means that Africa can quite quickly amass agricultural surpluses, and retain some of its agricultural effort in export activities. The under-population of Africa will also hasten the modernization in technical terms of the continent, for it will create a natural need for mechanization and automation. In this way, Africans will be enabled to become very rapidly acquainted with technology and be freed in adequate numbers for all types of human and social endeavour consonant with the humanism of their communalism. Here the African's demonstrated speed of learning will tell in his favour. He has already demonstrated his speed of learning in his mastery of European metropolitan languages and sciences. Rule of thumb and sleight of hand are not likely to present grave difficulties. In two generations, the African has mastered European learning. The pace to which he has thus accustomed himself will carry him over his technological age.

Pan-Africanism finally promises to neutralize the effects of the uneven distribution of population over Africa.

Though Pan-Africanism might seem an internal concern of Africa, in its economic and political posture it excites the interest and concern of other continents, especially Europe, with which Africa has up to now been most closely associated. Both Africa and the European Common Market pose problems for each other. The European Common Market depends on the raw materials of Africa and Africa depends on its trade with Europe. But it is most unlikely that the picture which Africa has of its own future is one of a perpetual producer of raw materials for the industries of others. Africa certainly has to sell the raw materials which it cannot use itself. But it has to industrialize, to use more of its own raw materials. A raw-material-producing country which re-imports its materials as finished products inevitably loses because there is absolutely no comparison between the prices which Africa is offered by Europe for its raw materials, and the price which Europe asks of Africa for the finished goods. On balance, therefore, Africa loses considerably. But the Common Market countries would wish to guarantee the sources of their raw materials. It would, therefore, suggest itself to them to retard the industrialization of Africa as much as they dare. It is essential to Africa that it should not be split by the Common Market. Though the Common Market has little to offer Africa really, it could entrench divisions in that continent through its proposed tariff walls. If the Common Market should stay associated with some but not all African countries which have competing economies, then this is going to prove an added difficulty in the unity of Africa.

It is also sometimes said that the multiplicity of languages in Africa is an effective barrier to Pan-Africanism. The Africanist Delafosse distinguished four main language groups in the continent which he identified as the Sudanese, the Nilotic, the semi-Bantu, and the Bantu. Unfortunately his categories have been effectively assailed by the critical acumen of experts like Greenberg who argued that calling any African language semi-Bantu was of the same order of absurdity as calling English semi-German. Westermann, another pundit of African linguistics, invented the piquant expression 'remnant' language for the non-Ewe languages of Togoland. Rather sadly, however, he vouchsafed no clue as to what they were supposed to be remnants of. It is hard on oneself to yield to the guidance of the traditional African linguists. They do not seem to have been sufficiently sensitive to the distinctions between race and economic, occupational, and technological characteristics. George Murdock, for instance, says rightly of the traditionalists that many of them 'appeared to regard the herding and milking of cattle as a linguistic trait and an overriding one at that'.

The Prospects for Pan-Africanism

At this point, African linguistics are thrown into an ecstasy. Delafosse, who is often quoted by critics of Pan-Africanism who take their standpoint from a putative irreducible lingual babel, is one of those who greatly mixed up categories. He hopelessly substitutes typological for genealogical criteria, surprisingly even at times when he purports to establish genealogical groups. When general and undoubted connections have already been established between typological and genealogical criteria, then it may be methodologically correct to base a conclusion of one type on evidence of the other type. But it is apparently only in Delafosse's mind that doubt about such connections has been sweetly stifled.

When the 'babel' theorists come to avow general similarities among African languages, they tendentiously designate these points of resemblance as connections. It is pointed out that these languages generally employ suffixes, prefixes, and infixes. But so does Greek, for example, in the infixing of *m* in *lambano* from the root *lab*. There is an alleged shortage of vocabulary for abstract terms and a corresponding richness in concrete designations, and in the importance of position to syntax. There are non-African languages of which all these are true. And as to the importance of word order to syntax, this is natural in uninflected languages of which English is an excellent example. Sometimes even where English inflects, but not sufficiently to avoid confusion, word order is still significant to syntax. Consider, for example, the sentences 'Give him her' and 'Give her him'. The explanation of these similarities in Africa through the dynamic expansionism of Islam and commercial relations is not strong enough. A language can only be either inflected in the main or not. Given these two alternatives, and the paucity of other devices to which a language can resort for syntactic purposes (e.g. word order, tone, etc.), it is naïve to see in the mere fact that two languages have similar devices a mystery that calls for theory-spinning.

Whatever one makes of the linguistic palavers, it is clear that the diversity of languages in Africa has not yet made inter-regional contact impossible. Official languages continue to be French and English, Spanish and Portuguese. With these blessings, there is no reason why the pentecostal tongues in Africa should constitute an impediment to unity. The diversity of languages can, so far from being an impediment, indeed be an instrument of unity in the natural interest and effort it creates in the literatures of these languages and so in the qualitative and effective understanding to which such natural interest and effort lead.

Though Pan-Africanism is positively recommended, the means of its attainment is one which obviously ought to be discussed and examined. Nothing could be more disastrous for Africa than that a false general

These minor divisions, however, are more a reflection of the problems involved in their own relationships, rather than of any essential disagreement over the total extinction of alien rule and white domination in Africa. For the African leaders and peoples still under alien rule, there is a general feeling of fraternity and a strong identification with their situation and aspirations.

In turning to the character of the emerging relationships among Africa's independent states, it is clear that the attainment of sovereign statehood leads suddenly to the formalization of relations. The transformation that occurs can best be illustrated by the different styles of conduct and themes expressed at conferences dealing with Pan-African affairs since 1958. The Cairo conference of January 1958, was a reflection of the wide anti-colonialist affiliations of Pan-Africanism developed among the 'exiles' abroad during the inter-war period. At the time of its origin, Pan-Africanism was only one aspect of a larger anti-colonial phenomenon. Solidarity among coloured, colonial, and proletarian peoples everywhere was an important theme. But the effort at the Cairo Conference to translate anti-colonial unity into positive action was not successful. Latent differences between the participants became apparent. The conference demonstrated the difficulties of making anti-colonialism a meaningful unified force.

Only a few months after the Cairo conference in April 1958, the first Conference of Independent African States was held in Accra. Delegates arrived in the pomp and ceremony that protocol demanded. Formal statements were made. The eight participating states proclaimed 15 April as African Freedom Day, reaffirmed the principles of Bandung, had their delegates photographed in somewhat stiff but fraternal poses, and departed as officially as they had arrived. Although the conference emphasized the need for unity and the freedom of Africa, the presence of so many representatives from the Middle East tended to weaken its Pan-Africanist importance. Implicit in the behaviour of the official delegates was a recognition that heads of state needed to act differently on the diplomatic stage than off it. International politics came to Africa with that conference.

Far different was the All African Peoples Conference held in Accra in December 1958. There was no mistaking the spirit of Pan-Africanism. Party officials from all parts of Africa arrived and bitterly attacked the colonial boundaries as hang-overs from imperialism; called for the ending of the colonial system, the abolition of passports for African tourists, visitors, and students to facilitate their free movement through Africa, and the formation of an African Legion composed of volunteer fighters for freedom; and attacked the policies of specific countries such as Portugal and South Africa.

414

These three conferences illuminated some of the major tendencies that play their part on the contemporary scene. At the Cairo conference some of the ugly realities of world politics introduced a note of caution. Africa and Asia no longer seemed quite so close together. At the Conference of Independent African States there was a note of cautious jubilation, but already international protocol had introduced a reserve and formality in relations. Only at the Accra conference of December 1958, was the older fraternal spirit and the more characteristic ebullience of both the nationalist movements and the Pan-Africanist traditions very much in evidence.

The realization of the goals of political Pan-Africanism are more and more a matter of external bargaining and negotiation. Pan-Africanist activity has become heavily affected by African power politics. Pan-African allegiances that cut across state lines have become increasingly suspect. They not only threaten the control of a political leader over his own party and state; they also weaken his ability to mobilize the people of his state for national development. Charges of interference or imperialism are the result. Thus, Pan-Africanism can easily become involved in both the internal politics and the external relations of African states in such a way as to confound both. And precisely because their relations are so close, the situation is dangerous. Thus, Ghana's Pan-Africanist impulse regarding the unification of Ghana and Togoland appears to many as an excuse for Ghana's national ambitions. Somewhat similar overtones can be discerned in the relations between Guinea and her neighbours. A union of the French Sudan and Guinea (despite Mali) remains a possibility. In Dakar this appears as the territorial ambition of Guinea to act as the centre of a new French-speaking bloc, not as a co-operative partner in the furtherance of Pan-Africanism.

If Pan-Africanism is not to be part of the pattern of interstate relations within Africa, must it develop through Congress-type political groupings which cut across territorial boundaries? For the time being it is useful to use political parties and movements as advance forces of Pan-Africanism because of the uneven development of independence. This makes it possible for political leaders of independent African states, in their capacities as party leaders, to meet the party leaders of countries still under colonialism, as occurred at the Accra conference. Yet when colonialism is finally extinguished throughout Africa, what will prevent such party-to-party activities from being branded as subversive if, in their consequences, they do not happen to suit the purposes of political leaders in power?

Among the many factors affecting the relations between Africa's new states and the prospects for political Pan-Africanism, at least three might be briefly noted. The first concerns the position held by certain territories which leads them to make special claims to leadership in political Pan-Africanism. Here we are concerned with that array of new states in the vast stretch of Africa previously known as British and French West Africa. Elsewhere the situation is still so fluid that it is virtually impossible to isolate key trends and determinants for discussion. In West Africa there are five centres of rival leadership, each with a distinctive claim: (1) Senegal, which has historically occupied the dominant position in French-speaking West Africa and which has always felt a conscious mission of leadership in relation to the rest of that area; (2) Ivory Coast, the richest of the ex-A.O.F. territories and the main base of the R.D.A.; (3) Guinea, the maverick territory representing the militant left-wing tradition of ex-A.O.F. and still the centre of attraction for such groups throughout West Africa; (4) Ghana, which through its prime minister has assumed the initiative and presented itself as the vanguard in the liberation of Africa and as the main carrier of the true spirit of Pan-Africanism; and (5) Nigeria, the awakened giant that is not prepared, in the words of the Sardauna of Sokoto, 'to sacrifice the leadership which she is bound to play on the continent and in the world as a whole'. Each of these five core areas can rightfully claim a special role whether the criterion be historical or militant leadership, wealth, the first on the ground, or size. To date, all other territories of West Africa are in effect appendages to these five or, like Togo, they quietly go their own way. But the main point here is that there is more than one core area around which unity can be developed. This suggests that there will either be competition for leadership, or at least a reluctance on the part of anyone to accept the leadership of one of the other four.

A second relevant factor concerns the variant approaches to political Pan-Africanism which each of these represents. The present Mali leaders, if we interpret Senghor correctly, desire to recreate the 'grand design' of the Emperors of Mali and Songhai, with the initial focus on French-speaking areas, and only ultimately to include the former British areas. Both Guinea and Ghana, in their own ways and orbits, are carriers of the original universalism of Pan-Africanism, an orientation that has been tempered by the influence of President Tubman of Liberia. The Ivory Coast has sought to draw within its orbit those territories attracted neither to Mali or Guinea, nor to suprastate political unification, who are willing to maintain close links with her and with France. Nigeria remains cautious and aloof. The diversities of these approaches or attitudes to political unity are understandable, but the fact that there is more than one approach, each backed by the power and influence of different states, aggravates, if indeed it does not engender, competition among those states.

A third, and for the immediate future perhaps the most important, factor is the widely different types of relationships between African states and non-African states. We have already noted the effect this differential external orientation and involvement has had upon competing parties in Africa's states. As the external relations of the new states become more clearly defined and stabilized, we will have a stronger basis for making generalizations. For the present, the union of Mali and Guinea seems most improbable in the light of the new Franco-Malian agreement; the union of Ghana and Guinea will in all probability not move beyond a symbolic link in view of the rather heavy involvement of Guinea with the Eastern bloc and, what in Guinea's eyes must be the equally heavy involvement of Ghana with the Western bloc. The union of Nigeria and Ghana, for reasons known to all, is perhaps the least probable of all. Indeed, even within Nigeria there are considerable differences of view among the regional leaders regarding Nigeria's orientation in world affairs.

In defining its political relationship with former metropolitan countries, the general trend now is for each state to attain full independence and then negotiate, on the basis of complete equality, the character of the post-colonial ties. Armed with the badge of sovereign equality and with membership in the United Nations, together with a public affirmation of a 'non-alignment' policy, the overseas political involvements of the new states do not pose an insuperable obstacle to closer political union in Africa. It is more in the realm of economic and military links – which admittedly have political implications – that problems are bound to arise.

In the economic sphere the differential affiliations of Africa's new states with monetary zones and trading areas, as well as the marked variation in their national directions of trade, are considerations of no little consequence in obstructing the development of closer inter-African relationships, not only economically but politically. An emerging trend, which could possibly become dominant, is for the new African states to avoid single commitments and to diversify their foreign economic involvements.

In view of Africa's profound military weakness and the need to create national armies of varying size and strength, the different overseas defence links of the new states are bound to continue for an indefinite future. Presumably the officer corps will be trained in the military academies of the former metropolitan powers until national military academies can be established in Africa. Similarly, there will be different sources of arms and equipment for Africa's national armies. As national military establishments are developed, there is no immediate reason to believe that Africa's new states will escape what appears to be a universal phenomenon, namely, a contagious arms build-up among states closely contiguous who evaluate their power and security in relationship to their neighbour. There is a strong probability that there will be competition among the new states for military aid.[1]

All of the foregoing factors tend to perpetuate and, in some instances, to intensify differentiation. Indeed, it can be stated as a general proposition that any policy or set of circumstances that tends to differentiate one national society from another tends to strengthen a distinctive feeling of national identity, that is, nationalism. This differentiation is the product not only of the colonial period, and of the differences in tempo and manner of attainment of their national independence, but also of the separate and distinctive paths each has selected in the course of post-independence development. The more these paths diverge, either in direction or in the tempo of development, the more complicated will be the process of unification.

To complete our catalogue of problems of political Pan-Africanism, two other points should be made. One concerns the different levels of economic development and wealth of African states. The most obvious consideration here is the disinclination of more developed and wealthier states to unite with less developed and poorer states for the very understandable reason that this would mean a dilution of their wealth and a lowering of the standard of living of their people. Five examples illustrate this point: the territorial separatism of Liberia, the Ivory Coast, and the Gabon; and the regional separatism of the western region of Nigeria and the Katanga province of the Congo. This is not an African phenomenon; Europe, which has pursued unity for centuries, has struggled with the same problem.

The second point is the existence of a variety of ethnic loyalties, both latent and manifest, which if politicized could lead to greater fragmentation of existing states as well as to an aggravation of tensions between states. This potentiality has no doubt been greatly exaggerated by external observers; nevertheless, it would be unrealistic to deny its potential effect upon the realization of Pan-African unification.[2]

[1] Arnold Rivkin has commented: 'The situation is ripe for a dozen India-Pakistan situations where military aid to one party in a local dispute will inevitably cause a grievance in a rival country. If, as is likely, the competing country turns elsewhere for military assistance, then an armaments race is set in motion between African states and indirectly between the U.S. and the Communist bloc – or perhaps the United Arab Republic.' *West Africa* (16 January 1960).

[2] There are many well-known situations in which the activation of ethnic loyalties of groups within African states could lead to greater fragmentation. Here we are primarily concerned with those that could and probably will aggravate the relations between states. The list would be very long were we to enumerate all such potential situations. Those that have already become politically relevant include the Sanwi (Ivory Coast) and the Somali (Ethiopia-Somalia).

Finally, in reflecting on the future prospects of political Pan-Africanism from the standpoint of international politics, it is important that we relate the African situation to similar situations elsewhere in the world or in history. Here we are concerned with two points: the question of coercive unification, and the fate of other pan-movements in history.

In his provocative little book *From Many, One* [Harvard, 1948], Clarence Crane Brinton has analysed the various efforts made throughout history to create larger political unions and concludes that all instances of successful unification have been a mixture of consent and coercion, with coercion predominating and decisive. The ironical situation confronted by political Pan-Africanists is that at this moment in history when they most passionately desire a larger political unity, and are possessed of what may be a fleeting opportunity to achieve it, they are inhibited by a new international ethic of which they have been the foremost proponents. Their struggle for freedom and entry into the world community has been a crucial contribution to the emergence of a new concept of international morality in which colonialism, imperialism, and the use of force or the threat of force are no longer tolerable. The continent of Africa is saturated with a hypersensitivity about a forceful alien domination. The strong reaction to Ghana's suggestion for unification with Togoland is very much evidence in point.

Also, it is most unlikely that any power external to Africa would attempt in the foreseeable future, any form of forceful domination of Africa. Other forms of penetration and influence may be attempted, but not force. The new international ethic, the alertness of the United Nations, the fact that the Western colonial powers have been chastened, coupled with the extreme competitive deference to African sensitivity on the part of the two superpowers – the United States and Russia – suggests that African states will not be confronted with a threat of forceful external domination that could galvanize them into a defensive union. Perhaps the white supremacists of the Rhodesias and the Union of South Africa can constitute the unifying enemy. Only time will tell. The main point we want to suggest is that if it is to occur in Africa, suprastate political unification must be largely the product of voluntary consent. Will this be forthcoming and adequate for the purpose?

Although Pan-Africanism is in certain respects unique, there are important ways in which it resembles other pan-movements that have emerged during the past century. It does not fit neatly into any single category of pan-movement.[1] It is partly pan-national and partly pan-

[1] In this penetrating analysis of pan-movements, written some twenty-seven years ago, Professor Hans Kohn observed that 'Pan-Africanism is somewhat difficult to classify.' He added, prophetically, that it, 'bids fair to become a growing

continental in character. To the extent that it is directed toward the political unification of a distinctive racial group (i.e. Negro African peoples) it falls in the pan-national category. It differs from so-called pure pan-national movements – Pan-Germanism and Pan-Arabism, for example – in that the peoples being united do not have an identical language or nationality. Here it resembles more closely such supra-national movements as Pan-Slavism and Pan-Turanism (Turkish unification). To the extent that it is directed toward the political emancipation and unification of all of Africa, irrespective of nationality, language, race, or religion, it falls into the category of pan-continentalism. Here it can be related to two types of continental solidarity movements distinguished by principles of unity and motive. Where the basic principle of unity is geographical contiguity and the motivating force is the desire to transcend parochialism and to achieve the power, security, and economic benefits of large-scale political organization, it resembles Pan-Europeanism and Pan-Americanism. Where the principle of unity is common status (i.e. colonialism) and the motivating force is the desire to remove alien rule and all the indignities and disabilities connected therewith, it resembles Pan-Asianism and Latin-Americanism.

The political development of these other pan-movements are here very much in point. Most of them at one stage or another embraced political objectives. Several had a common political origin. Pan-Slavism derived considerable support from non-Russian Slavs desiring freedom from Turkish and Austrian rule, although it was also used intermittently by Russia as an instrument for expansion. Pan-Germanism was initially supported by liberal and reforming elements, but it later became a tool in German expansion, both under Bismarck and under Hitler. Pan-Turanism, Pan-Arabism, Pan-Asianism, and Latin-Americanism originated among reforming groups seeking national or racial emancipation. With certain exceptions, none of the historical pan-movements have achieved their political objectives without a strong measure of coercion. Most of the Slavs are now embraced within what is in effect one sovereign state (U.S.S.R.), although the fiction of sovereignty of the satellite states is preserved; but, in any event, unification was achieved not through Pan-Slavism – which the Soviet government repudiated – but through Russian military power. Pan-Germanism did help Bismarck and Hitler to unite the German peoples, but Austria remains out and Germany is now indefinitely divided.

force and to constitute one of the major problems of the twentieth century.' See 'Pan-Movements', *Encyclopaedia of the Social Sciences*, ed. E. R. A. Seligman, Vol. II, pp. 544–53 (New York: Macmillan, 1937).

In his survey of all pan-movements, Professor Kohn reached the following conclusion:

> . . . when an independent and established state participates in a pan-national movement for the ostensible purpose of assisting weaker co-ethnic groups in the improvement of their position, the intentions of the former are likely to be diverted to imperialistic aggrandizement at the expense of the latter. . . . From the point of view of realistic politics the smaller nations involved in such a movement are likely to waver between distrust of their more powerful neighbours and a desire to participate in the benefits of inter-continental solidarity; while the larger nations, even if innocent of actual expansionist ambitions, are at least tempted to demand the position and perquisites of leadership.[1]

In the contemporary world, the only recent concrete example of a pan-movement being linked with actual political unification and transfer of sovereignty by consent is that of the United Arab Republic and Pan-Arabism. When we turn to sub-Saharan Africa the Mali Federation suggests itself as the second such example. This union (of Senegal and the French Sudan), however, occurred prior to independence; the real test is whether full sovereignty, once won, will be voluntarily surrendered to a higher government. Again, this is not just an African problem; it is a world problem.

CONCLUSIONS

In the foregoing analysis we have endeavoured to state as boldly as possible what we believe are the key issues and problems raised by the political aspects of Pan-Africanism. In making our points we may have overstressed certain features, overlooked others, and in general painted a dismal and depressing picture.

Certain concluding observations are appropriate. One is that it is both imprudent and unrealistic to make generalizations and to suggest probabilities regarding African political developments at this stage when systems and boundaries are still in the process of definition by revolutionary and dynamic forces. Comparisons we have made to experiences elsewhere have involved long-established and relatively stabilized states, which may be totally irrelevant to the unfolding African scene. Who would have predicted, for example, the formation of a Mali Federation by a free act of will of the diverse peoples forming the union? Again, it was not so long ago that several usually well-informed persons predicted the break-up of Nigeria into three or more separate states as an illustration of

[1] Ibid., p. 551-2.

African 'Balkanization'. Before Africa finally stabilizes, many unexpected developments are bound to occur.

A second point concerns the implications of the arrival on the political scene of an entire new generation of African youth, more educated in many instances than the practical politicians, and themselves imbued with a passionate belief in the necessity and the realization of political Pan-Africanism. This new generation is extremely impatient with parochialism and is hypercritical regarding their present leadership. One generation, of course, seldom understands the contribution of the previous one. Just as the older politicians and Pan-Africanists of the inter-war generation often feel bypassed by the inheritance that the younger groups of nationalists obtained for themselves, so these leaders, now no longer so young, may find themselves less highly regarded by those pushing to become their successors. Only recently, members of the All-African Students' Association of North America discussed the need to rid the new African states of their present leadership, which having served the cause of independence, was less suitable for the cause of African unity.

The emergence of this new and more militantly Pan-Africanist generation could be the decisive factor in the success of political Pan-Africanism. In their penetrating historical study of the process of successful voluntary political integration in a number of European countries, Karl W. Deutsch and his associates introduced the concept of 'take-off'. Here they refer to a period in which

> . . . small, scattered, and powerless movements (directed toward integration) change into larger and more co-ordinated ones with some significant power behind them. Before take-off, political integration may be a matter for theorists, for writers, for a few statesmen, or a few small pressure groups. After take-off, integration is a matter of broad political movements, of governments . . . often an affair . . . of the organized persuasion of large parts of the political elites or the politically relevant strata of the time. . . . We may consider take-off to have occurred as soon as at least one major social or political group, or political institution, has become committed to the cause of integration. In most of our cases, the period of take-off was followed, within a period of one to two generations, either by the attainment of integration or by the abandonment of the attempt.[1]

They found, among other things, that the 'take-off' was facilitated by 'the arrival of a new generation in politics; the younger men were usually more committed to new ways of doing things and more willing to accept the new size of political units than their predecessors had been'.

One final point is the special advantage and opportunity possessed by

[1] Karl W. Deutsch, et al., *Political Community and the North Atlantic Area* (Princeton: Princeton University Press, 1957).

the present African leaders to make crucial decisions regarding unification at this malleable stage in their history. Although democratization tends toward the development of restraints against freedom of action in foreign policy, this has not yet occurred. The idea of unity commands wide acceptance. John Marcum has stated the point most succinctly: 'The fluid period of decolonization and common struggle for independence provides a fleeting moment in history during which federalists might overcome the opposition of local political, administrative and economic interests before the latter rigidify within the narrower limits of smaller and separate states'.[1] Political Pan-Africanists in the Congo, Equatorial Africa, and East Africa might ponder the wisdom of revising George Padmore's dictum, appropriate at the time but now out of date, and adopt the slogan 'Unity first, then independence.' It will take perseverance and patience if the stage of nationalism in Africa is in fact to serve as the pre-condition of a wider United States of Africa, and not grind to a halt in unions that have more shadow than substance. Today's leaders not only have a fleeting opportunity; they carry a heavy responsibility for the well-being of African posterity.

---

[1] John Marcum, 'The Challenge of Africa', *The New Leader*, p. 17 (8 February 1960).

Appendix I—Some African statistics and data

Country	Population (millions) 1961	Area (1000 sq. miles)	Capital City	Former colonial power and date of independence	Population (millions) 1961	Value of exports 1960 ($ mill.)	Percentage of exports going to ex-colonial power	G.N.P. per head 1961 ($ per year)
Morocco	12·0	167	Rabat	Fr. (2.3.56)	12·0	353·8	40	150
Algeria	11·3	851	Algiers	Fr. (17.62)	11·3	394·3	86	281
Tunisia	4·3	48	Tunis	Fr. (20.3.56)	4·3	119·7	47	161
Libya	1·2	680	Benghazi and Tripoli[a]	It. (24.12.51)	1·2	11·2	—	204
U.A.R. (Egypt)	26·6	363	Cairo	U.K. (1922)	26·6	550·2	2	120
Sudan	12·1	967	Khartoum	U.K. (1.1.56)	12·1	124·7	26	94
Mauritania	0·79	418	Nouakchott	Fr. (28.11.60)		—		—
Mali	4·2	463	Bamako	Fr. (20.6.60)	4·2	113·0 }	67 }	58
Senegal	3·0	76	Dakar					175
Niger	3·2	494	Niamey	Fr. (3.8.60)	3·2	12·6		40
Chad	2·9	514	Fort Lamy	Fr. (11.8.60)	2·9	—		40
Ivory Coast	3·4	127	Abidjan	Fr. (7.8.60)	3·4	151·3		184
Upper Volta	4·4	106	Ougadougou	Fr. (5.8.60)	4·4	4·3		40
Togo	1·5	22	Lome	Fr. (27.4.60)	1·5	14·5		70
Dahomey	2·1	45	Porto Novo	Fr. (1.8.60)	2·1	18·3		40
Guinea	3·1	97	Conakry	Fr. (2.10.58)	3·1	55·1		60
Ghana	6·9	92	Accra	U.K. (6.3.57)	6·9	294·2	31	199
Sierra Leone	2·5	28	Freetown	U.K. (27.4.61)	2·5	76·9	74	70
Gambia	0·28	4	Bathurst	U.K. (18.2.65)[b]		7·8		—
Liberia	1·0	43	Monrovia	(26.7.1847)[b]	1·0	82·6	48	159
Nigeria	40·2	357	Lagos	U.K. (1.8.60)	40·2	462·0	57	82
Cameroun[c]	4·1	183	Yaounde	Fr. (1.1.60)	4·1	97·0		86[d]
Gabon	0·4	102	Libreville	Fr. (17.8.60)		—		200
Congo (Brazzaville)	0·8	139	Brazzaville	Fr. (15.8.60)	0·8	92·3	52	40
Central African Republic	1·2	238	Bangui	Fr. (13.8.60)	1·2	—		40
Ethiopia	19·1	457	Addis Ababa	—[e]	19·1	78·0		44
French Somaliland	0·07	8	Djibouti	Fr.[f]	0·07	0·9		—
Somalia	2·0	246	Mogadiscio	U.K. & It. (1.7.60)	2·0	20·4[h]	16	40[f]
Uganda	6·8	93	Kampala	U.K. (9.10.62)	6·8	120·1	24	6·8
Kenya	8·4	225	Nairobi	U.K. (10.12.63)	8·4	112·6		80
Tanzania: Tanganyika	9·4	363	Dar es Salaam	U.K. (9.12.61)	9·4	158·5	31	59
Zanzibar	0·3	1	Zanzibar	U.K. (9.12.63)	0·3	15·7		—

	Population	Capital	Former power (date)			
Rwanda	2·8	Kigali	B. (1.7.62)	2·8	—	40
Burundi	2·3	Kitega	B. (1.7.62)	2·3	—	60
Congo (Leopoldville)	14·5	Leopoldville	B. (30.6.60)	14·5	—	88
Zambia	2·5[l]	Lusaka	U.K. (24.10.64)	} 489·0[k]	} 44	} 163
Malawi	2·9	Zomba	U.K. (6.7.64)			
Southern Rhodesia	3·2[m]	Salisbury	U.K.[n]	576·8		
Bechuanaland	0·3	Gaberones	U.K.		—	[0]
Basutoland	0·7	Maseru	U.K.		—	[0]
Swaziland	0·6	Mbabane	U.K.	—	—	70[p]
Angola	4·8	Luanda	Portugal	124	—	70[p]
Mozambique	6·6	Lourenço Marques	Portugal	73·0		
Malagasy (Madagascar)	5·6	Tananarive	Fr. (26.6.60)	5·6	56	75
South-West Africa	0·5	Windhoek	South Africa	74·9	27	[0]
South Africa	18·0	Pretoria	U.K. (1910)	18·09	1224·4	427[0]

— = does not apply or is not available.

Sources: Population figures and estimates of Gross National Product (G.N.P.) are from *Estimates of Gross National Product.* Statistics and Reports Division of the United States Agency for International Development.

Figures for the value of exports and the proportion going to the former colonial countries are from *African Statistics,* Annex to the *Economic Bulletin for Africa* of the United Nations Economic Commission for Africa, Vol. II, No. 1 (January 1962).

a. A new capital Barqu Jebel is being constructed.
b. Founded by freed slaves from the United States.
c. Consists of that part of the German colony, Kamerun, mandated to France after the First World War and the Southern Cameroons (mandated to Britain).
d. This figure refers to the southern (formerly French) region only.
e. An ancient kingdom independent for centuries. Occupied by Italy in 1935.
f. Voted to remain a French colony in the 1958 referendum.
g. The former Italian and British Somalilands united at independence.
h. This figure is for 1959.
i. This figure refers only to the eastern (formerly Italian) section.
j. Including about 50,000 whites. There is also an important Asian minority as there is in Uganda, Tanganyika, Northern and Southern Rhodesia.
k. This figure refers to 1959.
l. Including about 70,000 whites.
m. Including about 200,000 whites.
n. Southern Rhodesia was granted internal self-government under a white government in 1923.
o. The figure of gross national product for South Africa is calculated to include South-West Africa, Bechuanaland, Swaziland and Basutoland.
p. This figure refers to 1957. *Source:* Norton Ginsburg, *Atlas of Economic Development* (University of Chicago Press, 1961).
q. Including about 3,000,000 whites and about 1,500,000 Asians and 'coloured' people of mixed descent.

Appendix II
Economic Assistance to African Countries

Table 1

MAJOR SOURCES OF ECONOMIC AID – OFFICIAL GRANTS AND LOANS, 1961

Source of Aid	Aid to Africa, north of the Sahara ($ mill.)	Aid to Africa, south of the Sahara ($ mill.)
Bilateral:		
All countries of the O.E.C.D.[a]	788·33	741·16
of which:		
Belgium	0·0	70·50
France	464·20	306·70
United Kingdom	9·13	222·66
United States	316·00	75·00
Multilateral:		
European Economic Community[b]	0·0	14·94
United Nations Technical Assistance and Relief Agencies	2·59	39·86
International Bank for Reconstruction and Development	3·70	51·70

(All figures exclude military aid.)

Source: O.E.C.D., *The Flow of Financial Resources to Developing Countries in 1961.*

a. The countries of the Organization for Economic Co-operation and Development are Austria, Belgium, Canada, Denmark, France, the Federal Republic of Germany, Greece, Iceland, Ireland, Italy, Luxembourg, the Netherlands, Norway, Portugal, Spain, Sweden, Switzerland, Turkey, the United Kingdom and the United States. The figures in the table also include aid from Japan.

b. The Nations of the European Economic Community are Belgium, France, the Federal Republic of Germany, Italy, Luxembourg and the Netherlands.

[REFERENCES AND NOTES TO TABLE 2 OPPOSITE]

— =not available, does not apply or nil; unfortunately in many cases it is impossible to tell from the sources which is meant.

Sources: Figures for O.E.C.D. and Sino-Soviet Aid are from O.E.C.D., *The Flow of Financial Resources to Developing Countries in 1961.*

Figures for United States Aid are as given by the United States Agency for International Development.

a. This includes Cameroun, Central African Republic, Chad, Congo (Brazzaville), Dahomey, Gabon, Ivory Coast, Malagasy, Mali, Niger, Senegal, Togo and Upper Volta, which are not listed separately in the O.E.C.D. data.

b. This is mainly aid to regional organizations.

Appendix II

Table 2

RECIPIENTS AND SOURCES OF ECONOMIC AID IN AFRICA

Recipient Country	Net official bilateral grants and loans from O.E.C.D. countries, 1961. ($ mill.)	United States' grants and loans, 1962. ($ mill.)	Sino-Soviet Bloc, grants and loans (commitments from 1954–62). ($ mill.)
Algeria	437·9	—	—
Cameroun	—	12·5	—
Central African Rep.	—	0·2	—
Chad	—	0·3	—
Congo (Brazzaville)	—	1·2	—
Congo (Leopoldville)	74·92	66·9	—
Dahomey	—	0·7	—
Ethiopia	20·10	6·3	114
Gabon	—	0·4	—
Ghana	2·62	63·8	200
Guinea	2·31	6·1	125
Ivory Coast	—	2·1	—
Kenya	77·79	3·2	—
Liberia	26·63	10·8	—
Libya	36·52	—	—
Malagasy	—	0·7	—
Mali	—	2·6	100
Morocco	126·37	—	5
Niger	—	1·2	—
Nigeria	30·18	21·0	—
Rhodesia and Nyasaland	37·87	2·8	—
Senegal	—	3·0	—
Sierra Leone	14·60	1·5	—
Somalia	20·59	11·5	63
Sudan	15·07	9·8	25
Tanganyika	24·74	2·4	—
Togo	—	1·2	—
Tunisia	77·07	—	46
Uganda	14·27	3·6	—
U.A.R. (Egypt)	110·47	—	671
Upper Volta	—	0·9	—
Zanzibar	0·57	0·1	—
Other U.K. Colonies	29·13	—	—
Franc area not separately specified[a]	319·47	—	—
Portuguese colonies	31·60	—	—
Other	13·40	8·1[b]	0
Total Africa	1530·51	244·9	1349

Bibliography

There is a large and rapidly expanding volume of literature about the continent of Africa. In addition to the books from which extracts in the present volume have been taken, the following is a short list of books which may be regarded as necessary reading for a balanced view of contemporary African problems in their widest context.

Part II

Balandier, G., *Sociologie des Brazzavilles Noires*, Paris, Armand Colin, 1955.
Banton, M., *West African City: a study of tribal life in Freetown*, London, O.U.P. for International African Institute, 1957.
Colonial Office, *Survey of Problems in the Mechanisation of Native Agriculture in Tropical African Countries*, London, H.M.S.O., 1950.
Colson, E. and Gluckman, M., *Seven Tribes of British Central Africa*, London, O.U.P., 1957.
Fearn, H., *An African Economy*, O.U.P. for East African Institute, 1961.
Fortes, M. and Dieterlen, G., *African Systems of Thought*, London, O.U.P., 1965.
Fortes, M. and Evans-Pritchard, E. E., *African Political Systems*, London, O.U.P., 1958.
Middleton, J., *Tribes Without Rulers*, London, Routledge, 1958.
Radcliffe-Brown, A. R. and Forde, D., *African Systems of Kinship and Marriage*, London, O.U.P. for International African Institute, 1950.
Richards, I. A., *East African Chiefs*, Faber and Faber, for East African Institute, London, 1960.

Part III

Almond, G. and Coleman, J. (eds.), *The Politics of Developing Countries*, Princeton, Princeton U.P., 1960.
American Assembly, *The United States and Africa*, revised ed., New York, Praeger, 1963.
American Society for African Culture, *Pan-Africanism Reconsidered*, California U.P., 1962.
Carter, G., *The Politics of Inequality*, 2nd ed., New York, Praeger, 1959.
Duffy, J., *Portugal in Africa*, London, Penguin Books, 1962.
Hailey, Lord, *African Survey*, revised ed., London, O.U.P., 1957.
Hodgkin, T., *Nationalism in Colonial Africa*, London, Muller, 1956.
Legum, C. (ed.), *Africa, a handbook to the continent*, London, Blond, 1961.
Nkrumah, N., *Africa Must Unite*, New York, Praeger, 1963.
Rivkin, A., *Africa and the West*, New York, Praeger, 1962.
Segal, R. (ed.), *Political Africa, a who's who of personalities and parties*, New York, Praeger, 1961.
Senghor, L., *On African Socialism*, New York, Praeger, 1964.
Southall, A. (ed.), *Social Change in Modern Africa*, London, O.U.P. for East African Institute, 1963.

Bibliography

Thompson, V. and Adloff, R., *The Emerging States of French Equatorial Africa*, Stanford U.P., 1960.

In addition, the following periodicals specialize in African affairs.

Africa, International African Institute, 10 Fetter Lane, London, E.C.4.

Africa Digest, Africa Bureau, 65 Denison House, Vauxhall Bridge Road, London, S.W.1.

Africa Report, African-American Institute, Dupont Circle Building, Washington 6, D.C., U.S.A.

Africa South, Abford House, Wilton Rd., London, S.E.1.

Africa Today, American Committee on Africa, 801 Second Avenue, New York, N.Y., U.S.A.

African Abstracts, International African Institute, 10 Fetter Lane, London, E.C.4.

Afrique Action, 198, Avenue de Paris, Tunis, Tunisia.

Journal of African Administration, Colonial Office, London, S.W.1.

Journal of African History, Cambridge U.P., 220 Euston Rd, London, N.W.1.

Présence Africaine, 16 Rue H. Barbusse, Paris 5e, France.

Race Relations Journal, S.A. Institute of Race Relations, P.O. Box 97, Johannesburg, S. Africa.

Uganda Journal, Uganda Society, Kampala, Uganda.

West Africa, 7–9 Breems Buildings, Fetter Lane, London, E.C.4.

West African Worker, Accra Trade Union Congress, Accra, Ghana.

Notes on Contributors

George Kimble

   Chairman of the Department of Geography, Indiana University, and formerly Director of the American Geographical Society. He is the author of many magazine articles and several books.

Melville J. Herskovits

   Late Director of Programme of African Studies and Professor of Anthropology at Northwestern University, Professor Herskovits, who died in 1963, had taught at the Universities of Columbia, Illinois and Harvard. A past President of the American Folklore Society and former editor of the *American Anthropologist*, he wrote extensively about African cultures, primitive economics and general anthropology.

Simon Ottenberg

   Has taught at the Universities of Chicago, Washington State and at the University of Washington, where he is now Associate Professor of Anthropology. He has conducted extensive field work in Nigeria, and has published numerous articles in many anthropological journals.

Phoebe Ottenberg

   Has taught at the University of Washington. As an Area Research Fellow for the Social Science Research Council, she made a study (1951–3) of marriage and co-wife relations in the Nigerian polygynous family.

Max Marwick

   Formerly Professor of Anthropology at the University of Witwatersrand, Dr Marwick now holds the Chair of Sociology at Monash University, Australia. Has published many articles on Bantu culture.

Meyer Fortes

   William Wyse Professor of Social Anthropology in the University of Cambridge. He was trained as a psychologist but later studied under Malinowski and Seligman. Dr Fortes has taught at the London School of Economics, and the Universities of Chicago and Oxford. Author of several books about African societies and two major works on the Tallensi.

E. Evans-Pritchard

   Head of the Oxford Institute of Social Anthropology, he has taught at the Universities of London, Cairo, Cambridge and Chicago. Apart from a general interest in anthropology, he has specialized on the peoples of the Sudan and Cyrenaica. Author of many books and articles.

Daryll Forde

   Director, International African Institute and Head of the Department of Anthropology, University of London. Has taught at the Universities of Wales and California. Editor of *Africa*, *African Abstracts* and the *Ethnographic Survey of Africa*. Author of several books and numerous papers on broad aspects of African culture and on social anthropology.

Notes on Contributors

E. W. Smith
Formerly a member of the Methodist Mission in South Africa and Northern Rhodesia, and editor of *Africa*. He has written many books on Africa.

Max Gluckman
Professor of Anthropology at the University of Manchester, Dr Gluckman was formerly Director of the Rhodes-Livingstone Institute for Social Research. He is the author of several books specializing in the cultures of southern Africa.

T. O. Elias
First Attorney-General and Minister of Justice for the Federation of Nigeria. Formerly visiting Professor of African Studies at the University of Delhi. Since 1956 he has been an Examiner for the Universities of Oxford and London.

Isaac Schapera
He has taught at the Universities of Witwatersrand, Cape Town and Chicago, and is at present a member of the Department of Social Anthropology at the London School of Economics. He is an expert on the Bantu peoples of Southern Africa, about whom he has written extensively.

Lucy Mair
Lecturer in Social Anthropology at the London School of Economics and prolific writer on African affairs. Particularly interested in tribal structures and political development.

W. St. Clair Drake
Formerly at the University of Ghana, he is now Professor of Sociology at the University of Indiana.

Pierre Gourou
Professor at the University of Paris and Director of the Geographical Institute of the free University of Brussels.

Jomo Kenyatta
President of Kenya. A former student at the London School of Economics, Mr Kenyatta studied anthropology under Professor Malinowski.

James Coleman
Professor of Political Science at University of California (Los Angeles) and Director of African Studies Centre.

R. I. Rotberg
Assistant Professor of History (African) at Harvard. Prolific writer on African history, especially British Central Africa.

Thomas Hodgkin
Fellow of Balliol (1945–52), he has held visiting lectureships at North-western University, McGill and at the University of Ghana. Director, Institute of African Studies, Ghana. Published works on nationalism in Africa and on political developments.

431

Notes on Contributors

Gwendolen Carter
Professor of Government at Northwestern University and Director of their African Studies Programme. Author of books on political aspects of African development.

Martin L. Kilson
Assistant Professor of Government at Harvard.

Immanuel Wallerstein
Assistant Professor of Sociology at Columbia University and a member of the Programme of Studies on Africa.

Judge O. D. Schreiner
Past President of the South African Institute for Race Relations.

Colin Legum
Commonwealth correspondent of *The Observer*. Author of several books on African affairs.

Guy Benveniste
Special Assistant to the United States Assistant Secretary of State for Educational and Cultural Affairs.

W. E. Moran, Jr.
Dean of the School of Foreign Service at Georgetown University, Washington, D.C.

Walter Elkan
Lecturer in Economics at Durham University. Has published books and articles on African economic problems, particularly those of Uganda. Formerly on staff of Makerere College, Uganda.

Mark Karp
Associate Professor of Economics at Boston University and Research Associate of the Boston University African Studies Programme.

Elliot Berg
Taught at Harvard. Now Head of the Harvard Development Advisory Service Mission to Liberia. Author of articles and books on African economics and the impact of trade unions on Africa.

H. J. Symons
Associate Professor of African Government at the University of Cape Town. Restricted by South African Government, December 1964.

Guy Hunter
Formerly Co-ordinator of Studies to the Duke of Edinburgh's Conference. Was attached to Institute of Race Relations, London, 1959–61 as Director of Project which resulted in the publication, *The New Societies of Tropical Africa*.

Peter S. C. Gutkind
Associate Professor of Sociology, Institute of Social Studies, The Hague. Formerly Consultant on Social Problems in British Central Africa.

Notes on Contributors

O. F. Raum
Professor of Education, University College, Fort Hare, South Africa.

L. W. Doob
Professor of Psychology, University of Columbia. Author of books and articles on psychological topics.

J. H. Spencer
Professor of International Law and Diplomacy at the Fletcher School of Law and Diplomacy, Massachusetts. Formerly (1943–61) Senior Adviser in foreign affairs to the Ethiopian Government.

W. E. Abraham
Associate Professor of Philosophy at the University of Ghana. Governor of the London School of Oriental and African Studies, Fellow of All Souls College, Oxford.

David Apter
Professor of Government at the University of California, Berkeley. Author of books and articles on the recent history and politics of African countries.

Peter J. M. McEwan
Research Associate and Director of Family Research Unit, Harvard. Formerly Visiting Professor of Sociology and African Studies, State University of New York, and one time Research Fellow, Rhodes-Livingstone Institute for Social Research in Central Africa. Author of numerous articles on social problems of Africa.

Robert B. Sutcliffe
Assistant Research Officer, University of Oxford Institute of Economics and Statistics. Formerly attached to research staff of Rhodes-Livingstone Institute for Social Research. Author of articles on economic aspects of under-developed nations.

Index

435

DATE DUE